Beyond Structural Adjustment

Beyond Structural Adjustment
The Institutional Context of
African Development

Edited by Nicolas van de Walle,
Nicole Ball,

and Vijaya Ramachandran

BEYOND STRUCTURAL ADJUSTMENT

First published in 2003 by PALGRAVE MACMILLAN™
175 Fifth Avenue, New York, N.Y. 10010 and
Houndmills, Basingstoke, Hampshire, England RG21 6XS.
Companies and representatives throughout the world.

PALGRAVE MACMILLAN is the global academic imprint of the Palgrave Macmillan division of St. Martin's Press, LLC and of Palgrave Macmillan Ltd. Macmillan® is a registered trademark in the United States, United Kingdom and other countries. Palgrave is a registered trademark in the European Union and other countries.

ISBN 1-4039-6316-9 hardback 1-4039-6317-7 paperback

Library of Congress Cataloging-in-Publication Data

A catalogue record for this book is available from the British Library.

First Palgrave Macmillan edition: November 2004

10 9 8 7 6 5 4 3 2 1

Printed in the United States of America.

CONTENTS

ACKNOWLEDGEMENTS

This collection of essays has its origins in a project undertaken by the three editors for the Overseas Development Council (ODC) from 1999 to 2001. We wish to thank John Sewell, the ODC's last president, for his support through out the life of the project. We are grateful to the Ford Foundation for the generous financial support it provided to the project, and to Manuel Montes for his steadfast support throughout. In addition, Nicole Ball thanks the Swiss Development Corporation, which provided additional support for the security component of the project. Following the untimely closing of ODC, the project was housed at Georgetown University. We wish to thank Lola Brown and Mary Schmiedel for their excellent administrative support, and Paloma Bauer for research assistance.

Finally, an early version of Chapter 6 by Jesse Ribot appeared in the journal *Public Administration and Development* (Vol. 23, No. 1, 2003) under the title "Democratic Decentralization of Natural Resources: Institutional Choice and Discretionary Power Transfers in Sub Saharan Africa." We thank the editors of that journal for permission to reprint this material.

CHAPTER 1

INTRODUCTION: THE STATE AND AFRICAN DEVELOPMENT

NICOLAS VAN DE WALLE

M ost observers recognize that strong and effective governance is a key to Africa's recovery. As the World Bank famously put it back in 1989, "underlying the litany of Africa's development problems is a crisis of governance" (1989, p. 60). The region's burst of political liberalization and democratization in the early 1990s significantly increased popular participation in political life, even if not all countries have made a smooth transition to multi-party electoral politics (Smillie, 1993; Bratton and van de Walle, 1997; Joseph, 1998). The emergence of independent media, opposition parties, and an increasingly rich and varied civil society have all been striking innovations. On the economic front, the mid-1990s witnessed a burst of growth, bringing many countries of the region their best economic results in two decades.

Yet few observers would argue that this wave of good news has strengthened states or their ability to promote development. On the contrary, many of the states in the region continue to be in crisis. In the worst cases, central states are threatened by the kind of complete collapse that has already been witnessed in Somalia or Congo. Even in the most stable countries, states do not appear capable of spearheading structural transformation of the economy, given myriad problems of low capacity, fiscal crisis, and corruption.

The weakness of central state institutions exacts a cost. In some countries, there has been a clear deterioration of infrastructure, as an increasingly bankrupt state is unable to maintain the achievements of the past. Even more seriously, many observers have noted rising crime and lawlessness, particularly in the countryside, far away from the capital, where the reach of the state is weakest and law and order often not enforceable.

At the same time, the vacuum left by state retrenchment is being filled by new institutions, in innovative ways which suggest bright new possibilities (Fowler, 1991; Bratton, 1994). All over the region, there has been a veritable explosion of non-governmental organizations (NGOs), village associations, and civic groups of various persuasions and aims. In addition, virtually every country in the region has begun ambitious decentralization reforms to shift various policy responsibilities from the central state apparatus down to the provincial, district and local level. This combination of a continuing crisis of African state structures and the emergence of a significant voluntary sector and of local governments could have important economic and political implications for the region. As I will argue below, the donor community has advanced a fairly idealized version of the current evolution that suggests that a distinctly African model of development is slowly emerging in which a retrenched state provides a small number of public goods, but then takes a back seat to actors in civil society for most development activities. Yet, little is known about the evolving relationships between central states and these emerging institutions.

This book focuses on the implications of this evolving institutional landscape for the development of the Sub Saharan Africa region. It examines the empirical record, in other words what is currently happening across the region; but also it ponders the normative implications of this evolution, in other words, what should be happening. The different contributions following this first chapter examine the impact of the growing institutional pluralism on aid and economic policy making. Focusing on the evolving nexus between the state and these other developmental institutions, the authors analyze how the emergence of new institutional actors is altering the developmental role of the state. How are they affecting state capacities and the ability of the state to finance its developmental responsibilities? Does the role of foreign aid change as these new actors gain in importance? How much are NGOs and local governments changing the process and outcomes of development policies? To what extent are development responsibilities being devolved away from the central government? What are the implications of the current evolution for donors and policy makers?

These are the questions addressed by the authors in the chapters that follow. First, Elbadawi and Gelb examine the general financial context in which development will take place in the region. They argue that debt relief, greater aid effectiveness and a sustained increase in the flow of external resources to the region will be necessary to revitalize local economies. The necessary role of external aid is an implication of the chapter by Rakner and Gloppen, which examines the ability of African governments to finance their development through own-revenues. The authors argue that tax reform has not progressed far in the 1990s, and they suggest that more systematic democratization of public life is necessary before African political systems exhibit the kind of public accountability that is the hallmark of modern government.

A second set of chapters examines the institutional reform record in the 1990s. Olowu analyzes the evolution of civil service reforms in the region. Ribot looks at decentralization efforts and the emergence of local government. Nicole Ball and her colleagues examine the efforts to reform the important security sector, a critical factor for economic growth, since both domestic and international investors express concern about insecurity in various investor surveys. Goldsmith's contribution focuses on the efforts of the donors to promote state capacity and argues that the record is more positive than many observers have argued.

A third set of chapters examines the developmental role of non-governmental actors. The contributions vary in their approach and concerns but all share the view that private actors should be complementary with the central state, rather than in competition with it. All agree that a stronger central state ultimately helps private actors and vice versa. In her contribution, Tripp focuses on the NGO sector and civil society and their evolving relationship with the states of the region. Cotton and Ramachandran examine the private sector's potential contribution to development. They argue that governance reforms by the central state are necessary before the private sector can help promote development. A similar message is provided by Emery's chapter, which examines the many continuing obstacles to private investment created by the policies of state institutions.

The rest of this introductory essay sets the stage for these different contributions. In the next section, I review the intellectual climate in which institutional reform was first conceived and initially implemented. A normative theory of state reform emerged from the debates within the scholarly and policy communities in the 1980s and early 1990s. I then ask whether the actual institutional evolution during the 1990s followed this idealized vision. Even as new actors have emerged and considerable institutional innovation has taken place, the developmental focus of the state has changed little. Governments have employed a political logic rather than a developmental one to shape their focus, in a context of aid dependency and resource scarcity. A final section then asks what impact the emerging institutional dispensation can have on development outcomes. As long as the central state is so weak, I argue that state elites will view other developmental actors as competitors rather than complements. Strengthening the central state is thus a paradoxical prerequisite for a stronger private sector. In the best-case scenario, I argue that slow incremental change is most likely and that the donors need to become more aware of these institutional issues, which are likely to hold the key to future development.

THE DYNAMICS OF STATE RETRENCHMENT

The last three decades have witnessed sharp changes in how the development community understands the role of the state. In the first period, running roughly from the 1960s to the early 1980s, a significant, interventionist role for the central state was considered essential to overcome the widespread *market failures* that were believed to characterize developing country economies. By the 1980s, the pendulum had swung back: the excesses of state intervention had lead the development community to view *government failure*, the negative, unintended effects of state intervention, as often worse than the market-induced ills it was designed to overcome.

Today, we have entered a third, somewhat more nuanced doctrinal phase. On the one hand, there is a growing realization that markets left alone can result in unacceptable inequities. Evidence from East Asia has brought the state back into favor insofar as the success stories in that region clearly relied on particularly effective governments to promote poverty alleviation and growth (Wade, 1990). On the other hand, mounting evidence suggests that states are most likely to be effective agents of development when they are "embedded" within a network of links to societal institutions and organizations. (See Evans, 1995, in particular.) A well-organized and representative civil society can enforce accountability on the state, preventing its *predatory* tendencies from emerging, and push it to act more systematically in the public interest. A strong and diverse civil society is also increasingly viewed as a prerequisite of private sector–driven development, perhaps because it will constitute a first line of defense against the rent-seeking proclivities of the state. In sum, states will ensure the supply of good sectoral policies and developmental prerequisites, such as the rule of law and stable property rights, only if these are demanded by strong societal actors. Whereas, in an earlier era, the development community had agreed that there was a "cruel choice" between development in and pluralistic political institutions, the new consensus in the 1990s is that, on the contrary, economic growth and poverty alleviation benefit from a dynamic and strong civil society (e.g., the World Bank, 1997a).

Regarding the low-income countries of Sub-Saharan Africa, these doctrinal debates have often taken a different outlook, perhaps because the central state's weaknesses there have been so patent. The dominant view, first expounded in the World Bank's "Berg Report" in 1981, has been that the state should adopt a developmental role commensurate with its internal capabilities (the World Bank, 1981). Every World Bank report since the Berg Report has reiterated the pragmatic argument that even if the central state in Africa should be strengthened in the medium term, in the meantime its developmental role should be circumscribed to fit what it was actually capable of doing and what the private sector was not doing.[1] In sum, to quote a formula that made the rounds in Francophone Africa in the mid 1980s, Africa needed "*moins d'Etat, mieux d'Etat*" (less state but better state).

For the donors, intellectual debates about long-term development strategy have been largely pushed aside by the practical dilemmas of how to overcome the legacy of weak indigenous institutions in a climate of economic crisis and fiscal stringencies. Donors have always sought viable organizational vehicles with which to deliver services and overcome endemic deficiencies in skilled-staff availability, communications, and infrastructure. The need to move relatively large volumes of aid has led most donors to favor expedient and short-term solutions to institutional issues. Not finding these vehicles within the state, donors have long turned their attention to other implementation mechanisms available in the short term, from stand-alone project units, to parastatals, and, in the more recent past, to NGOs (see van de Walle and Johnston, 1996; Meyer, 1992).

The emergence of the NGO sector and, more generally, of civil society, in the 1980s and 1990s should be understood in this context. On the one hand, the turn away from statist solutions to development problems within the donor community created a demand for new institutions and considerable resources to fuel their development. On the other hand, a number of political factors, including the wave of political liberalization that swept the continent after 1989, was also fueling the growth of various non-state actors. This evolution was soon reinforced by the donors, who came to view the growing institutional pluralism in Africa as contributing to their efforts to create a smaller but more effective state. Thus, as argued by Robinson (1993), the rise of the NGO sector during the last decade was driven by the "twin poles" of neo-liberal economic thought and liberal democratic politics. NGOs have benefitted from the belief that the private sector is preferable to the public sector, and by the view that they are vehicles for democratization.

The growing attention to *decentralization* emanates largely from the same logic. Local governments were theorized to be both potentially more effective than central governments at promoting development, and more democratic because more accountable and responsive to the citizenry. Local governments that are accountable and pluralistic will be able to assist, harness and coordinate the rich resources posited to exist at the local level. As a result, most donors have enthusiastically promoted national policies of decentralization and administrative devolution.

In the idealized interpretation of this evolution, particularly the version endorsed by the donors, the central state will shed many of its current activities, at which it was never good at anyway and that it can no longer afford, and these will be appropriately devolved to local governments and to the voluntary and private sector. Shed of its peripheral functions, a leaner and more effective state will be able to excel at a small number of essential functions. Following standard economics doctrine, for instance, the World Bank's *1997 World Development Report* argues that low-income states should focus on the following "core public goods and services": "a oundation of lawfulness, a stable macro-economy, the rudiments of public health, universal primary education, adequate transport infrastructure, and a minimal safety net" (World Bank, 1997a; see also Stiglitz, 1986).

THE EVOLUTION OF DEVELOPMENT INSTITUTIONS IN AFRICA

How wide has the gap been between this ideal and reality? In this section, I characterize the institutional situation in Africa in the early 2000s. I focus first on the proliferation of new institutions, then on what has happened within the state itself, before turning my attention to the emerging relationships between institutions.

THE EMERGENCE OF THE NGO SECTOR

I adopt a fairly broad definition of NGOs, defined as as any private organization involved in development activities in which generating profit is not the only or primary purpose. I distinguish between "southern," or national (SNGO), and "northern," or international NGOs (NNGO). Most of this chapter is about the SNGOs. In recent years, the strengths and weaknesses of the NNGOs have attracted much debate in the West. In the African context, however, the big NNGOs are typically lumped into the same category as the official donors by governments and local actors by virtue of the fact that they bring their own money to the table.

A second useful distinction is between NGOs and smaller, village level, "self-help" organizations, variously called "village associations," "grassroots organizations," or "people's organizations" (POs). NGOs are organizations with a paid staff that have been formed to benefit not only their members but also to provide some kind of service to non-members. Village associations, on the other hand are more informal groups, based on kinship, locality, gender or workplace, and so on, designed primarily to benefit their own members (Semboja and Therkildsen, 1995, p. 1).

A small number of church-based charity groups have been engaged in the development activities in Africa for the entire post-colonial period (e.g., Otayek and Dialo, 1998). Village level associations have also long existed, due to longstanding mission efforts and to traditional forms of self-help organization. But most states frowned upon independent organizations and extremely few of these early indigenous organizations prospered beyond the individual village, unless they were integrated into cooperative structures controlled by the state. This began to change in the 1970s. In the Sahel region, for instance, the drought in the mid-1970s brought about the first influx of secular foreign NGOs (Gabas, et al., 1996). The continuing development difficulties of the region in the 1980s led to the steady influx of new NGOs, notably the first SNGOs, many of which emerged as offshoots of NNGOs or were created by local staff who had gained their first development experiences in the NNGO world. In the last ten years, democratization and growing external support have together provided the impetus for further growth.

There remains enormous variations across the region, due to a mixture of historical and political reasons. By way of example, Senegal and Niger can be compared.

Senegal has one of the best-structured and oldest NGO sectors in Africa. Appreciated for its relatively open political system, Senegal has long been a regional hub for northern NGO activities. The Conseil des Organizations Non-Gouvernementales d'Appui au Développement (CONGAD), an association of NNGOS and SNGOs, was established in 1982. In its 1995 report, it claimed to have 78 member organizations, including 41 Senegalese NGOs. One prominent member was the Federation des Organizations Non-Gouvernementales au Senegal (FONGS) itself a federation of some 24 peasant organizations claiming to represent well over 2,000 village level associations. CONGAD almost certainly includes a large proportion of the most professional and institutionalized NGOs in the country.

The leading Senegalese NGOs in the country are well institutionalized, with experienced managers who often have previous experience in both the civil service and the international NGO community. The Senegalese NGO USE (Union, Solidarité, Entraide) has a staff of well over 100 and annual development expenditures of billion of

Communauté Financièze Africaine Franc (CFAF), financed by over half-a-dozen western donors. USE now enjoys a relatively high profile in the regions of the country in which it is active with various village level projects. Indeed, it has been successful enough that its president entered politics in 1997 and was elected to Parliament in one of the very region in which USE had been particularly active.

CONGAD's relationship with the government underwent something of a crisis in the early 1990s. Probably precipitated by the growing importance of the NGO community, the crisis was set off when NGOs were accused of abusing the import tax exoneration privileges extended to NGOs. The government threatened to change the basic framework of its understanding with the NGO community. In the end, the government withdrew these threats and, in 1996, appointed a prominent CONGAD member as Minister of Women's Affairs, the ministry in charge of relations with CONGAD. The government also agreed to a longstanding CONGAD demand to attribute it a seat on the Conseil Economique et Social, an advisory council which meets with the government on a regular basis to discuss policy issues.

Niger stands on the other extreme from Senegal, with a considerably less developed and more recent NGO sector. A handful of foreign NGOs have been in the country for a long time: the earliest foreign NGOs in the country were the French volunteer organization, Association Française des Voluntaires du PROGIES (AFVP) (established in Niamey in 1963), the Rotary Club (1967), Caritas Niger (1969), Africare (1971), and Care International (1973) (see Berbedette and Ouedrago, 1993). But given the outright hostility of previous authoritarian governments to the non-governmental sector, foreign NGOs have been noticeably weaker than in more inviting neighboring countries like Senegal. This has impacted negatively on the local NGOs, both at the national level, but also at the level of village associations, which have not suffered from the less auspicious context. As recently as 1990, there were only six registered Nigerien NGOs. In early 1998, following a spurt of activity in the context of the country's democratization, some 159 local NGOs were officially registered with the Ministry of Plan. An evaluation by the Dutch government (Naino, 1997) estimated that only 26 of these local NGOs fulfilled even minimal criteria of being operational. Only nine were viewed as actually capable of carrying out the simplest development tasks without external financial and technical assistance.

Registration with the Nigerien government is typically considered desirable, as the legal status of NGO confers on the organizations significant benefits such as customs exemptions. It seems likely that at least some NGOs may have been registered to gain access to these benefits a single time, or in the hope that they could find profitable project activities. The Ministry of Plan has never deregistered an NGO.

Nigerien NGOs appear to be almost entirely dependent on donor support for their financial resources. Moreover, few, if any, appear capable of independently designing and implementing a development project. Even the most professional local NGOs get the major proportion of their revenues by serving donors (including western NGOs) as subcontractors, delivering services in the context of a specific donor project. Typically, they have not contributed to the design of the project and require technical assistance and institutional support from the donor to carry out the services they have agreed to undertake.

Other countries in Africa exhibit the similar range of patterns as those in Senegal and Niger. In most cases, the 1990s witnessed a sharp rise in the number of NGOs, thanks to a mixture of donor support and indigenous demand, in the context of some form of political liberalization. In each country, the best available numbers are typically collected by the national Ministry of the Interior, which is charged with registering them. These official totals, invariably at least in the hundreds, are almost certainly substantial exaggerations of the real presence of NGOs, and as few as a quarter of all registered NGOs may be able to claim even minimal ongoing developmental activities in the country.

One of the earliest arguments for the growth of the voluntary sector was that it represented another mechanism for resource mobilization. Thus, it was argued that organizations that were more legitimate than the central state would find their activities supported by resources otherwise not available for development. This has been strikingly evidenced in the west, most notably in the United States by the real success of a small number of NGOs to raise development finance for their activities. Organizations like Care, Oxfam or Save the Children have long managed to raise tens of millions of dollars a year through private fund raising campaigns. Overall et al. (1997, p. 6) estimate that only some 30 percent of total income of Northern development NGOs comes from official donors—although these numbers vary significantly across donor countries.

The rates of dependency of African NGOs are considerably higher. No systematic data exists for the African region, but it is instructive that Hulme and Edwards (1997, p. 7) speak of dependency ratios of 80–95 percent for SNGOs in other regions of the world with historically stronger civil societies, and that Therkildsen and Semboja (1995, p. 12) argue that non-church African NGOs involved in social services in East Africa are not able to raise more than a tenth of their funds locally.[2] In general, there is little evidence that SNGOs constitute a significant source of additional resources for developmental public goods in the Africa.

Nonetheless, NGOs are an increasing presence in social service provision: although cross-national variation is significant, between a fifth and half of all health and education services in the region may today be provided by NGOs. (Robinson, 1997; Semboja and Therkildsen, 1995). Note that there is also significant private for-profit health care and education provision in the region. It is probably the case that NGO provision is typically more accessible to the poor than for-profit provision, but there is extremely little empirical evidence to confirm this. In any event, the combination of the two suggest that the state's role in the provision of these social services is limited and getting smaller.

DECENTRALIZATION

The 1990s has also witnessed a strenuous effort by donors and governments in the region to promote administrative decentralization. The donors have argued that they view decentralization as a key component of their efforts to promote democratization of African political life, and to improve the efficiency of public services. Virtually every country in the region has an ongoing decentralization program financed by external donors. Invariably, a process of institutional reform seeks to shift resources and responsibilities to local government structures.

In Mali, for example, laws passed in 1995 created 701 rural and urban "communes" to replace the old system of 270 *arrondissements*, which are eventually to have responsibilities for primary education, health care, local road construction and maintenance, public transportation, water distribution, sports, and cultural events (In addition to the 701 communes, the reform creates 52 Cercles or counties and eight Regions; see Lewis 1997). In Burkina Faso, the government created the Commission Nationale de Decentralization (CND) in 1993 in order to promote decentralization. An ambitious program was defined that eventually created 33 municipalities in the country's principal towns, and will eventually result in up to 500 municipal councils. In Senegal, In February 1996, the state created regional Councils (Conseils regionaux) and in the big cities, *maire d'arrondissements*. They also granted new prerogatives to the municipalities, notably in taxation and land management.

Decentralization has proceeded perhaps the furthest in Uganda, where it has been a cornerstone of the Museveni regime. The Constitution of 1995 and the Local Governments Act of 1997 set forth the current institutional structure of local governance, with 45 District councils and 903 sub-county level councils, and officially transferred an array of responsibilities from central to local government. The structure of local government is complex, with five levels going from the district level, to the County, Sub-County, Parish Council, and Village Council levels (van de Walle et al., 2001).

What are the prospects for these new local governments? In most of the countries in the region, decentralization has foreseen the transfer of certain responsibilities to the local level, and communities have been given new fiscal prerogatives. There is very little systematic evidence available on how much has already been achieved. There is evidence of significant fiscal devolution to primary cities like Dakar or Kampala. In Mali, Hal Lippman and Barbara lewis (1998; 6–13) also suggest that the process has proceeded furthest for large towns, but notes that even in the biggest cities, how much fiscal devolution is implied by the creation of these new local administrations is unclear. Despite the impetus officially given to the process by the government, in practice the Ministry of Territorial Administration has often resisted giving up its longstanding prerogatives.

The situation is somewhat different in the countryside, where it is usually quite premature to speak of significant devolution at this point. There is anecdotal evidence of new elected officials in rural communities undertaking relatively bold initiatives on their own, usually in the realm of small village level infrastructure or health and education services.

The critical role of the donors in empowering local authorities is underlined by the absence of local revenues available to them. The International Monetary Fund (IMF) unfortunately does not provide any recent data for the Africa on revenues disaggregated by level of government. Several other countries in Africa nonetheless suggest how small a proportion of overall funding is likely to come from locally. Thus, in 1991, Kenya's central government collected 98.3 percent of national taxes and local governments only 1.7 percent, despite long-established traditions of local administration and stronger municipal government than in most African countries. Similarly, Uganda's district councils manage to raise well under a fifth of the revenues needed for their activities (van de Walle et al. 2001). In time, perhaps local authorities will be able to generate revenues to finance their activities; for now, they are entirely reliant on donors.

THE EVOLUTION OF THE CENTRAL STATE

Turning to the evolution of central state structures, I look for evidence that states have, first, become smaller, and second, more focused on core developmental tasks.

THE SIZE OF CENTRAL STATES

It would be remarkable if twenty years of more or less constant fiscal crisis had not resulted in a smaller state. The broad averages reported of government revenue and expenditure data reported in Table 1.1 suggest that relative to the economy (which itself has often shrunk) there has been a slight "slimming down". The difference between tax and overall revenues, including external grants, suggests that foreign aid has, to a large extent, compensated for any decline in tax revenues.[3] In addition, we can point to minor progress on certain elements of the state reform package, which presumably has resulted in a smaller economic role for the state. This is notably the case for privatization, which picked up considerably in the 1990s after a slow start (Bennell, 1997). Price liberalization, and various types of deregulation have also been achieved (van de Walle, 2001).

Most observers suggest that progress on civil service reform has been slow and inconsistent (Olowu, in this volume; Goldsmith, 2000; Nunberg, 1997). For reasons that are well explained in Olowu's chapter in this volume, the numbers suggest that the popular image of mass retrenchments imposed on African civil services by the IMF and World Bank is at least a simplification. Table 1.2 provides some regional averages and individual country data. Some countries have undergone significant retrenchment, but others continued to hire new civil servants throughout the 1990s. Indeed, Lienert and Modi's (1997) data indicates growth in the number of civil servants between 1986 and 1996 in 11 of the 18 cases for which they have data. If one uses the share of government revenue as an indication, the data suggest a slight decline in the proportion of spending going to the wage bill. Since many of these countries have undergone a sharp increase in debt servicing obligations, however, the proportion of the wage bill relative to other recurrent expenditures probably has not decreased. The wage bill still constitutes

Table 1.1 The Evolution of the Size of Government in Africa, 1980–1998 (as a Percentage of GDP)

	1980	1990	1998
Government Consumption	18.1	16.5	15.1
Total Tax revenues	14.0	16.2	16.4
Government Revenues (including Grants)	16.2	23.8	23.1

Notes: Numbers based on unweighted average of national country data. Each indicator included a large number of missing values.
Source: the World Bank, *African Development Indicators*, 2000 (CD Rom)

Table 1.2 Civil Service Reform in Africa

	1986	1996
Average Government wage Bill (as a % of GDP)	7.0	5.8
Benin	9.9	5.3
Kenya	9.2	9.4
Mali	7.3	3.7
Zimbabwe	10.5	11.7
Central Government Employment		
Burkina Faso	28,700	32,000
Congo	73,300	70,000
Ghana	301,000	330,000
Kenya	423,700	485,000
Madagascar	107,600	93,500
Senegal	68,100	67,0000
Uganda	239,500[*]	159,000

Notes: data adapted from Lienert and Modi (1997).
[*] data from 1987

overwhelmingly the largest single item in the recurrent budget, but individual wages continue to be eroded by inflation and are probably not competitive to attract the best graduates.

A Refocus of Central State Activities?

First, and most generally, has the state shifted its own expenditures away from consumption towards investment? Public investment data are not always reliable in Africa, as the boundaries between the capital and recurrent budgets have long been porous; nonetheless, World Bank data (1997b, p. 25) suggests that the proportion of GDP devoted to public investment was not different in the 1990s than in the 1980s. This confirms the strong consensus that African governments continue to devote inadequate resources to investment (e.g., Sahn, 1992; Fischer et al., 1998).

More specifically, have African states refocused their attention onto their core public functions? First are what are called the pure public goods: macro-economic stability, law, and order. This is not the place to review the course of macro-economic stabilization in Africa. Clearly, there has been significant progress in the 1990s in reducing fiscal and balance of payments deficits, establishing reasonable exchange rates and low inflation, and promoting liberalization (Fischer et al., 1998); just as clearly, progress has been uneven and vulnerable to reversal.

Over the last decade, there has been significant liberalization and deregulation, although in most countries less than suggested by both the International Financial Institutions (IFI) donors and their critics, and much of it reversible. Governments often continue to ignore the spirit of liberalization by continuing to interfere in markets that are officially now liberalized. The case of Senegal provides a good example. Elliot Berg (1997) argues that much of the reform progress there has little impact on private sector investment that continues to be undermined by "skepticism about the government of Senegal's commitment to liberalization; the lack of transparency in decision making and implementation coupled with a generalized suspicion that the playing field is uneven; and the persistence of administrative delays, weaknesses and harassment" (p. 17).

Law and order, on the other hand, is clearly getting worse all over Africa. Although crime statistics are unreliable, there is a widespread consensus that the state's ability to police the territory has worsened during the 1990s (Perouse de Monclos, 1997; Anangwe, 1995; *Jeune Afrique*, 1997). Stick up, highway robbery, car theft, physical assaults, and other criminal events are said to have undergone rapid increases; almost invariably, African populations have disparaged the ability of police services and the judicial system to deal with what is widely perceived to be a dramatic crime wave. The ills that effect these services are well known: corruption, lack of professional standards, inadequate training, and so on. Somewhat ironically and belying its nature as a pure public good, African citizens are increasingly resorting to private provision of security and safety services to palliate for these public deficiencies. All over Africa, there are reports of neighborhood watch groups forming to ensure the security of areas inadequately policed by the state.[4] Donors have been extremely reticent to provide support for law and order, despite arguing that it is a critical public function.

Next to be examined is basic infrastructure. A particularly scarce resource in Africa, water, provides an axiomatic area for public management, both for water supply and sanitation. There is no systematic data for government effort in their provision, but a recent World Bank report (Sharma et al., 1996) estimates that the overall per capita availability of water and the proportion of the population with access to sanitation is declining. It is not clear how much of the current effort is provided by the state, as opposed to other actors, but the report argues that 84 percent of public efforts in this area were financed by the donors in 1990–94, up from 66 percent in 1975–79 (p. xv). The report notes the central role of governments in this area but argues that African governments "lack the institutional capacity necessary for comprehensive and sustainable water resources management" (p. 27).

I would add two items to the Bank's list of pure public goods. First, the timely production of reliable national statistics is a non-excludable public good, with significant positive externalities, since they benefit a wide variety of agents, from government officials who need good data to make intelligent public policy, to businesses and economic agents that use data for their investment decisions. The patent deterioration of national statistics in the region is thus a serious deficiency, and one that is a staple feature of the public policy literature on the region (e.g., Yeats, 1990). Preparing this chapter provided an ironic confirmation of the dramatic failure of states in the region to collect basic data and/or make it available. Little time series data existed to confirm assertions about the evolution of the role of the state. The donors have invested resources in improving African economic data—although it is often not made available to Africans, but there is no evidence that African governments have recommitted themselves to this task.

A second public good omitted from the Bank list is national defense. It does appear that military budgets have increased over the last decade in a majority of countries in the region, although defense statistics are notoriously inaccurate and should be taken with a grain of salt (they are usually said to be understated, however). Data is presented in Table 1.3. Certainly, the number of soldiers in the national armed forces appears to

Table 1.3 Growth in the Armed Forces in Africa, 1985–2000 (selected countries)

	# of Soldiers, 2000	Defense Budget % of GDP	
	(1985 = 100)	1985	2000
Average, Africa	160	..	..
Of which:			
Botswana	225	1.1	3.7
Burkina Faso	170	1.1	1.6
Cameroon	179	1.4	1.3
Chad	247	2.9	1.0
Gabon	196	1.8	0.3
Ghana	46	4.6	1.0
Mozambique	39	8.5	2.5
Mauritania	185	6.5	2.9
Nigeria	81	1.7	0.9
Senegal	93	1.1	1.4
Uganda	250	1.8	1.8

Source: UNDP, The Human Development Report, various years.

have grown substantially in the sub-region, again with some important exceptions. States in the region have legitimate security concerns that could justify these increases; however, increasing military expenditures is probably not what the development community has in mind when it calls for a refocus of state activities to core functions.

What has been the evolution in other public goods, in particular the evolution of the state's role in social services? Somewhere between a third to half of health and education services appear to be provided by NGOs and the private sector in what is a rapidly growing non-governmental role. What has happened to the state during this time? The evidence is scanty and difficult to interpret. Table 1.4 provides some evidence on expenditures on health. The data provides evidence of a sharp rise in public spending on health since independence, but one primarily accounted for by rising foreign aid to the sector, which by the latter period amounts to between a sixth to half of the overall public effort. In addition, the data suggests a substantial amount of private expenditures in health, usually well over one percent of Gross Domestic Product (GDP). This is confirmed by a more recent study of the Health sector in Mali (World Bank, 1998a) that estimates at 29.2 and 3.3 billion Communauté Financièze Africaine CFA the amount private households and NGOs respectively spend on health annually, compared to 24.2 billion CFA spent by the donors and state together.[5] I could find no data regarding the evolution of private expenditures over time, however.

Table 1.4 Health Expenditures, Selected African countries 1960–1998 (As % of GDP)

	Public Expenditures			External Resources as % of Public Exp.
	1960	*1990*	*1998*	*1998*
Burkina Faso	0.6	1.0	1.5	31.9
Chad	0.5	..	2.3	34.3
Gambia	..	2.2	2.3	17.1
Ghana		1.3	1.7	22.7
Mali	1.0	1.6	2.1	24.4
Niger	0.2	..	1.2	36.2
Senegal	1.5	0.7	2.6	13.1
Tanzania		1.6	1.3	..
Zambia		2.6	3.6	43.0
Sub Saharan Africa	..	2.5		

Source: Calculated from World Bank, (1994, Table A-13), WHO (2002).

What about changes within the health sector: have governments dramatically changed their focus within the sector? Individual country case studies provide some clues. The World Bank's study on the health sector in Mali (1998b), for example, suggests that the government is undertaking a reform effort to emphasize community and preventive health care more than in the past, in keeping with longstanding donor prescriptions (e.g., The World Bank, 1994). That this effort has begun to bear fruits is suggested by the doubling of vaccination rates since 1987, and by the 50 percent increase in contraceptive prevalence. This is not, however, the result of a significant reallocation of resources by the government, as much of the reform effort is driven by aid money, which finances over a quarter of the health sector (World Bank, 1998b, p. 30). Indeed, the report notes that in 1997, the government did not allocate any budgetary resources for primary health care and health education programs, which were entirely funded by donors (p. 31). That year over 80 percent of government health expenditures went to, in order of importance, central administration, logistics, secondary care, and training.

Table 1.5 presents UNESCO data on the evolution of education. No breakdown of public and private spending for education is available.[6] The data, with a majority of missing values, is probably not good enough to claim a clear trend in either direction. What about intra-sectoral

Table 1.5 Education Expenditures, 1985–1995

	Public Expenditures (As % of GNP)		As % of total Government expenditures	
	1985–7	1995–7	1985	1993–95
Botswana	7.3	8.6	22	24
Burkina Faso	2.3	3.6	21.0	11.1
Cote d'Ivoire	..	5.0		
Chad	..	2.2	..	..
Gambia	3.2	4.9	12.3[i]	12[*]
Ghana	3.4	4.2	..	..
Kenya	7.1	6.5	21	18.5
Mali	3.7	2.2	30.8[i]	13.2
Niger	3.1[i]	2.3	22.9[i]	10.8
Senegal	..	3.7	23.0[i]	33.1
Zambia	3.1	2.2		
Sub Saharan Africa	..	5.3	..	..

Source: UNDP (1998, p. 163); UNESCO (1996); World Bank (1997, p. 348)
[i] for 1980. [*] for 1990.

shifts? It should be noted that the one area of education in which the state has a local monopoly in the countries of the region, namely tertiary education, is an area in which governments have been under severe pressures from the donors to reduce their investments. The donors have long argued that African governments spent a disproportionate part of their education budgets on university level training and research, at the expense of primary education. This is resulting in a significant intra-budgetary shift of resources within education, away from universities and towards primary education (Blair and Jordan, 1994), precisely the area in which non-state actors are also increasing their role.

The education sector in Mali may serve as a nice illustration. In 1995, the World Bank estimated at 32 percent, the gross enrollment rate. Roughly a third of total enrollments are accounted for by private Coranic schools and other private schools, in rapid expansion. According to a 1992 article by Gérard (p. 69), privately run primary schools increased from two in 1985 to 105 in early 1992. Enrollment rates vary significantly between town and rural areas. Thus, the enrollment rate varies from 90 percent in Bamako, the capital, to 11 percent in North region. This low rate of enrollment results mostly from an insufficient number of schools and teachers, despite the fact that the government has regularly allocated some 20 percent of its national budget to education and benefited from substantial support from the donors. France has traditionally been a significant source of money and educational policy ideas. In 1995, the World Bank began a 50 million dollars Education Investment Program, the fifth of a series of loans to the sector that had contributed 51 million dollars to the sector since 1962.

Although government funding declined slightly during the 1990s, the government has pushed through a series of ambitious reforms, the main objective of which appears to decentralize primary responsibility for education to the local level (Gérard, 1992). The government appears to want to reduce its budgetary commitment, but retain a critical regulative role. One initiative consists of providing partial funding to parent associations to allow them to build schools for private instruction. To qualify for funding, the association has to provide 25 percent of the total cost, a figure Gérard viewed as prohibitively high for most villages (p. 66). How will the government maintain its regulatory function as it withdraws from direct provision? Though a major architect of this policy, the World Bank itself admits that the Ministry of Primary Education is poorly equipped to play such a role, as it suffers from "weak capacity for policy analysis and planning, overly centralized decision-making, poor personnel and financial management" (1998b, p. 2).

IMPLICATIONS FOR DEVELOPMENTAL GOVERNANCE

Judging from this brief review of the situation, it is hard to avoid the conclusion that the recent retrenchment of the state has largely been haphazard, disorganized and often counterproductive. The discourse of *"moins d'etat, mieux d'etat"* has been mostly rhetorical. States have gotten a little bit smaller, but mostly through fiscal pressure rather than because they have become more focused. Although there has been some limited intra-sectoral budgetary shifts in health and education, they appear to have been driven almost entirely by donor spending. There is, moreover, little evidence of an attempt by either donors or African governments to prioritize the activities of the state, or to plan for a division of labor with local governments or civil society actors. Paradoxically, donor inattention to the central state's myriad problems has accompanied a push of support for new institutions that will require significant human and financial resources for the foreseeable future to be effective.

In this confusion, significant new modes of developmental governance are nonetheless emerging in the region that should be assessed realistically. In this section, I discuss patterns in three areas: the *emerging division of labor* between central states and other actors, the nature of *decision making processes*, and *decision making outcomes*. In each case, it is difficult to share the official optimism, but real opportunities for improved governance are possible and are probably being taken advantage of in many villages and towns all over the region.

AN EMERGING DIVISION OF LABOR?

As stated above, the normative theory of state retrenchment advanced by the donors advocates that the states focus on fewer activities. In fact, there is little evidence that the central states of the region have refocused their energies onto a narrower, more "public" set of activities, except for the limited amount of privatization and deregulation that has occurred. Instead, what is emerging is often an effectively privatized delivery system that exists side by side with a hollowed out public system that continues to receive public resources (albeit inadequate ones) whether or not it actually provides services.

Where the voluntary sector is in clear expansion, it is rarely completely replacing the state sector. Either communities are organizing to ensure the provision of goods or services they have never received from the central government (e.g., Leclerc-Olive, 1997), or the voluntary sector is expanding in a specific area because of foreign aid support that would probably have once gone to a government or parastatal organization. Given the importance of aid resources in the region, aid agency decisions have a powerful impact on the evolution of this division of labor between state and non-state actors. In overall volume, donor support has in fact remained focused on central governments, even if a larger share than ever before is making its way towards voluntary and local government organizations.

Rather strikingly, the areas of fastest growth in the voluntary sector are also areas in which aid is officially committed to increasing its support to governments. This is notably true of education and health, in which major sector wide programs of aid are being devised that include support to all three sets of actors. The reverse side of this coin is that donor resources are not focusing on at least some areas that the current orthodoxy views as pure public goods, such as law and order.

The evidence suggests that local states do not necessarily become stronger as they get smaller. Too often, the current evolution is motivated by and in turn reinforces dynamics that are potentially quite destructive for states. Given the current emphasis of seeking alternatives to the state, relatively little attention is being paid to strengthening the state in the long run. As a result, states are in fact likely to be ineffective in the key areas on which they focus their attention if and when they become smaller.

At least some in the donor community seem to believe that benign neglect of the state is a viable strategy in the long run. Rather than undertake politically difficult and expensive frontal public sector reform, why not allow the state to slowly die on its own? Without support, the logic dictates, the sturdiest branches of the central state tree will survive and become tougher, while the rest will slowly wither away into irrelevance. The best civil servants will leave on their own and join NGOs and local governments, where their skills will be put to better use. In a decade or so, it will be possible to formalize a de facto division of labor between the central state, local government, and civil society.

While this approach is recognized as inefficient and time-consuming, it is viewed as a practical approach, given the impossibility of reforming the state. Unfortunately, the evidence from the region suggests the approach is likely to prove unsuccessful, for several reasons. First, it offers no answer for the current fiscal crisis in most of these countries. Even if local government can be entirely self-financing, which is far from obvious, the central state's "fixed costs" have to be financed in some way. We know from experience that fiscally strapped governments in the region have tended to maintain the recurrent budget and sacrifice the investment budget, which includes many of the core public good functions of the state, such as infrastructure development and maintenance. These cannot be devolved effectively to local governments and NGOs.

Second, benign neglect of the state is incompatible with another current donor strategy to support and strengthen an insulated "core" administration that is capable of maintaining macro-economic stability and provide minimal regulatory functions. Again, the evidence from the last decade is that it is very difficult to shield this technocratic core from the decay of the rest of the state, without in effect taking it over and turning it into an appendage of the donor organizations. To maintain professional standards in the context of advanced decay, donors provide generous project assistance, offer salary supplements, hire outside of the civil service, and staff key positions with foreign experts. Invariably, this leads to micro-management by the donors, resentment from the rest of the civil service, and a loss of ownership, which in time undermines institutional effectiveness. Even then, there is much evidence that the growth of the NGO sector has resulted in a brain drain from the higher levels of the civil service, as ambitious public sector managers are attracted by the higher salaries and more flexible working conditions available in the NGO sector. Civil servants have long been attracted to the private sector, where salaries are typically 5 to 10 times higher, certainly high enough to pick and choose the best-trained civil servants (Cohen, 1992). Donor funding can typically provide financial inducements to only a small number of senior civil servants to remain in their positions, and even then only temporarily. In Senegal, for instance, Berg (1998, p. 13) reports on a World Bank project to provide assistance to two key divisions in the Ministry of Plan and Cooperation. All but four of the 15 staff members involved were paid directly by the project in the early 1990s, with substantially better salaries and benefits than those prevailing in the civil service. Within a couple years, however, most of these staff were gone and the reform program was in the hands of a "thin group of inexperienced, badly paid *fonctionnaires*" (in italics in the text).

Third, and most preoccupying, neglecting the central state almost certainly insures that state agents do not cooperate with the new institutions the donors empower. For one thing, state agents compete for external resources with these institutions. They are likely to undermine activities they are excluded from and induce inclusion by various threats and "taxes". Interviews with ministry staff in the region suggested relations characterized as often by envy, resentment and cynicism, as by collaboration. In this context, it must be recognized that central states cannot effectively regulate the institutions they are in effect competing with for donor resources. Far from wanting to improve the performance of these competitors, state agents face incentives to limit their effectiveness and alter program objectives. The financially strapped administration does not regulate or monitor in defense of the public good—it appropriates and extorts to ensure its own survival.

Even when the relations between the civil service and the voluntary sector are not hostile, they may not be entirely healthy either. In Niger, virtually every NGO I met in the summer of 1998 was staffed by moonlighting or ex–civil servants. Some had indeed completely left the civil service out of ambition and dissatisfaction with the public sector. These were often quite savvy policy entrepreneurs, using skills and knowledge of the aid business they had learned in the civil service. More, however, appeared to involved in "straddling" strategies, in which they retained one foot in the civil service even as they tried to sustain an NGO. Often their civil service position helped them gain access to donors, whom they could approach for support in two capacities. In such cases, the creation of new NGOs appears to be primarily motivated by the search for donor funding, viewed as increasingly uncertain in the ministry. In other instances, indeed, the impulse to leave the civil service comes from the donors themselves, who let the civil servant know they would reward a flexible, non-bureaucratic subcontractor with project funding. Even when such straddling avoids troubling conflicts of interest, it typically results in a blurring of the boundaries between public and private functions.

The current institutional evolution, conditioned as it is by resource scarcities and pro-active donors, suggests a great deal of confusion about the appropriate role of public institutions. In at least some cases, NGOs appear to compete with private sector companies for clients; if so, the NGO may well derive an unfair advantage from subsidies it gets from donors. This is probably true of NGOs, that are often little more than consulting firms, and it may well be true of NGOs that offer goods and services which are excludable in consumption, and thus could be provided by market forces. Berg (1997, p. 10) gives an example of a private firm in Senegal, specializing in rural water supply and management, which has to compete with official and NGO aid to the sector. Similarly, as noted above, the World Bank has encouraged local health authorities in Mali to run profitable pharmacies in order to finance other activities. While these health centers may be in areas not currently served by private sector pharmacies, they effectively serve to deter pharmacies from investing in those areas in the future. Under the guise of encouraging local authority to raise its own finance, in such cases, it is hard to avoid the conclusion that the donors are helping to reintroduce the kinds of pseudo-public firms at the local level to that which they have only recently painfully eliminated at the national level.

Complex links between the state and the voluntary sector are not to be avoided per se. Studies of the role of the state in the development of

East Asia emphasize the multiple, overlapping, and organic nature of links between the state and civil society (Evans, 1995; Wade, 1990). Similarly, Tendler (1997) has recently shown that developmental success in Brazil is not systematically linked to either the national, state, and NGO level of institutions, but rather certain institutional characteristics that can be found at each of three levels, when they are abetted by flexible partnerships between them. In sum, in what has been called a process of *embeddedness*, state structures derive both their internal legitimacy and their external accountability from these ties. In Africa it has been argued that, as the state retreats, it can forge extensive links with the organizations and actors that have taken its place, allowing it to continue to act effectively in its core functions.

Semboja and Therkildsen's (1995) analysis of social service provision in East Africa is highly instructive in this regard. They do note examples of collaboration between state, donor, and societal actors to ensure provision of much needed social services. Some communities are seeking for and finding innovative new private-public partnerships to come up with cost-effective solutions to old problems. At the same time, they find little evidence to suggest these partnerships help strengthen the states. They find much more evidence that relations between the state and the new actors can be also competitive rather than collaborative, particularly when both sets of actors are competing for donor resources. On the one hand, fiscally strapped states are unlikely to see the diversion of these funds away from them with equanimity. On the other hand, NGOs may well view talk of partnership with the state as the first step towards regulation and cooptation, and resist it steadfastly (Hulme and Edwards, 1997).

Given this diagnostic, donors should seek to multiply the linkages between the state and non-state actors, in a way that supports both state legitimacy and institutional pluralism. In a word, what is needed are state-society linkages that "embed" the state. By often viewing the voluntary and local government sector as alternative to the central state, rather than as complementary to it, the donors have often served to heighten the sense of rivalry between them. Instead, donors should use the leverage of aid to forge cooperative behavior between these different agencies, by multiplying both formal links and creating incentives to collaborate. Various corporatist structures serve to link state decision makers with various NGO umbrella organizations, apex groups, production associations, and unions. They help improve the regulatory framework NGOs operate in and the procedures that are being set up to link NGOs with ministerial and other territorial administrations. The important lesson of this discussion, nonetheless, is that successful public-private partnerships require effective state structures rather than weak ones that are being starved of resources.

NEW DECISION-MAKING PROCESSES?

As Tripp argues in this volume (see also Bratton, 1990), the actual impact of NGOs on policy making varies significantly. In Africa, some NGOs and decentralized actors are genuinely influential. In Senegal, as described above, CONGAD is a respected policy voice, whose advice is solicited by the government, and the leading NGOs in the country are development players in their own right. Tripp (2000) finds evidence in East Africa that the voice of women has been enhanced in the policy making process, thanks to the empowerment of the NGO sector. In Niger, on the other hand, it is hard to avoid the conclusion that most NGOs are creations of the donors and have no independent voice.

When you leave the capital and head to the African countryside, the picture is even less auspicious.[7] Long standing membership organizations such as the ones in eastern and southern Africa discussed by Bratton are most likely to have an impact. They have often been involved in sector-wide discussions with the government, as when a farmer organization is consulted about the setting of producer prices. The case of (Syndicat des Producteurs de Coton et de Vivriers (SYCOV),[8] the cotton producer's association in Mali, is exemplary in this respect (Josserand and Bingen, 1994; Bingen, 1998). It emerged from long standing village associations as a full fledged producer's union during Mali's democratization period in the early 1990s. Since then, SYCOV has become an influential player in that country's cotton zone. It is both an almost official interlocutor for the national cotton parastatal, the Compagnie Malienne pour le Dévelopment des Textiles (CMDT), and the Ministry of Rural Development for a number of policy issues relating to rural development; and an organization increasingly involved in village-level development activities, for which it has received donor support in addition to its members' dues.

Organizations like SYCOV are rare, however. Most associations are very small and localized. In a phenomenon that Antoine Sawadogo has neatly called the "bureaucratization of the village" (cited in Naudet, 1998), a multitude of village associations have formed. The number of these associations is impressive, estimated well into the thousands for each country in the region. They are built on longstanding traditions of community solidarity, but also increasingly on the possibility of external support (Gueneau and Lecomte, 1998). Donors want to reach these associations directly with aid, rather than go through state agents.

Indeed, the most successful NGOs are the ones who can credibly claim to know the field well enough to be effective intermediaries to these associations on behalf of the donors. Individuals who used to play this role as state agents find themselves ideally placed to undertake the same tasks, but now as fledgling NGOs. Gueneau and Lecomte's (1998) analysis of NGO-village association relations suggests they often reproduce the problems of the relationships between the villagers and the extension agents of the past: villager preferences are often ignored in favor of the preferences of the outsider, local politics are misunderstood, and the NGOs are suspicious of village organizations that are too strong or too well informed.

The simple equation of institutional pluralism with more participatory and accountable public decision making seems naive. First, apart from a small number of producer groups like SYCOV, most local non-governmental[8] and decentralized actors do not have a seat at the table when significant policy decisions are made, by either donors, external NGOs, or governments. They may continue to be viewed as little more than service providers and implementors once key issues have been decided. Since they typically rely almost entirely on external donors not only for their operating funds, but also for their operational capacity, they are almost entirely absent from the decision making phase of the projects.

The current donor rhetoric has actually been rarely translated in new development modalities. Many observers note that the donors continue to treat NGOs as secondary actors (e.g., Bossuyt, 1997, p. 409, for the EU; see also Hulme and Edwards 1997), and even large amounts of aid resources do not necessarily empower the NGO community. This may be a particular issue if the local NGOs that emerge are predominantly staffed with ex–civil servants who had already received donor support in their previous positions. Indeed, it may be the case that the growth of donor-supported NGOs may have some negative effects on the development of healthy indigenous civil societies engaged in productive relationships with the local state (Bebbington and Riddell, 1997).

Second, the voluntary sector appears to be riddled with many of the same governance problems that plague the state. They tend to be dominated by a single leader, often the founder, who is rarely accountable to a professional board, and manages the NGO with little transparency (Bratton, 1994). Budgeting and accounting procedures are primitive. Many such leaders are dedicated and honest, but at such low levels of institutionalization, and given the rapid expansion of the sector, it has attracted many opportunists.

Can NGOs improve service delivery and serve as effective lobbies for better governance? Sure—if and when projects are well-designed and improve the capacity and leadership of these NGOs—but probably not much more than previous project dependent structures from project units to authorities, parastatals, and cooperatives, that were also at times effective. If the straddling strategies described in the previous section are accurate, the evolution is not the involvement of a wider set of interests in decision making, but rather new institutional labels for the same interests. Greater institutionalization, accountability, and transparency are unlikely to result when the civil society is made up of moonlighting civil servants.

This assessment appears to be true of most decentralized actors as well, although a firmer judgment has to be deferred until the availability of more information. With the notable exception of a handful of large towns in each country, municipal and regional services appear to have little existence apart from aid. Although a rural associational life can be very rich in parts of Africa, the penetration of NGOs is actually quite limited, as they remain very focused on the capital and large towns. Even more than NGOs, moreover, local government agencies are both an instrument of aid and a recipient; that is to say they get aid to undertake some service, but the aid is also designed to help them become operational. There is an anecdotal evidence of village–level structures lobbying government and donor organizations for support for projects. This lobbying may have increased in intensity as a result of rural democratization, but much less than its advocates suggest. Moreover, for every situation in which local structures promote social capital and a more responsive government there is one in which they are divisive. From his research in South Eastern Niger, Olivier de Sardan (1997) reports mostly village-level struggles over external resources, in which institutional affiliations interact with ethnic and clan dynamics to turn what donors view as public goods into privately appropriated resources. Administrative decentralization does not end these struggles, it only gives them new arenas and resources.

Often, civil servants and professionals originally from the village, serve as intermediaries between national and village-level associations. So for example, Tidjani's fascinating study (1998b) of the Timidria Association in Niger[9] emphasizes the critical role of school teachers and other low level civil servants in broadening the movement's appeal and linking its work to a rhetorical discourse that could be marketed to the donors in Niamey. But there is little evidence that these relations go beyond lobbying for excludable goods and services and move to the realm of sector-wide policy making and pure public goods. Non-state actors lobby for a school in region X, but they do not participate in budgetary discussions about education, or the setting of national education policy, which remains as narrow a process as in the past.

NEW DECISION-MAKING OUTCOMES?

Finally, we need to ask whether the evolution of development institutions in Africa has the capacity to alter the actual outcomes of policy. First, are institutions additive in some positive sense? That is, are the growing importance of NGOs and local governments resulting in more children educated, or more wells dug? The previous section showed that NGOs have not brought extra resources to the region, just displaced governments as recipients of existing external resources. Advocates of NGOs suggest nonetheless that non-state actors use resources more efficiently. Establishing a counterfactual to the present evolution is difficult. Certainly, the social statistics do not suggest a sharp improvement or deterioration in recent years. Literacy and health indicators seem relatively stable. Some observers would like to credit the emergent civil society for at least some of the positive spurt of economic growth in the region in the 1990s. I think it is much more likely that this growth has resulted from improvements in national macro-economic policy, notably following the 1994 devaluation, as well as exogenous factors such as an upswing in commodity prices and good weather.

Second, what are the distributional effects of these new development actors? Are they likely to empower segments of the population previously neglected by policy makers? In a common past critique of African political economy, policy has unduly benefited urban, male, and upper income groups (e.g., Bates, 1981). In some parts of the development community, it is held as axiomatic that the spread of NGOs is part and parcel of a process by which civil society promotes grassroots democracy that empowers new social actors. In the donor community in particular, NGO activity is often treated as synonymous with civil society promotion, and it is generally assumed that NGOs empower relatively disadvantaged segments of the population.

The evidence is nonetheless mixed that these new civic actors are representative of new constituencies that were previously neglected by policy makers. Associational life in the villages has definitely strengthened the capacity for empowerment of previously neglected groups. The large number of women's associations that have mushroomed up all over Africa at the village–level over the last two decades have probably empowered a traditionally ignored group, resulting in a bit more policy emphasis on issues of importance to women (Tripp, 2001). The evidence from the first generation of NGO projects suggest that they are better able to target the poor than traditional aid modalities, albeit not the poorest segments (Riddell and Robinson, 1997).

Overwhelmingly, however, these new institutions reflect and reproduce existing patterns of social power. The more the dominant factor in the development of NGOs is donor funding, the less NGOs are likely to be representative of the values and aspirations of local populations, particularly of traditionally excluded social categories. NGO staff, even when they do not emerge from the civil service, are typically from the same educational and social background. Overwhelmingly, NGOs staff are urban professionals, who may not have much professional experience in the countryside. In his review of NGOs in Niger, Naino (1997, p. 7) notes that 69 Nigerien NGOs were represented at that country's National Conference in 1991, of which only 5.3 percent of the 1204 participants could claim to be from the countryside. In fact, it would have probably been harder for NGOs to emerge so quickly, had they not been able to speak the language of governments and donors. As argued to me by one interviewee in Senegal in July 1998 a prominent NGO leader, one of the reasons he was effective in getting things done was that he had gone to school with many of the high level officials in the state that now oversaw areas in which he was active.

Similarly, as Ribot argues persuasively in his contribution to this book, decentralization rarely empowers new social groups. Rather, it is much more likely to benefit the existing rural power elite. In Senegal, governmental attitudes about decentralization are conditioned by the perception that the new positions and offices created will help revitalize the ex-single party, the Parti Socialiste, with access to new forms of patronage and resources (Interviews, Dakar, July 1998).

CONCLUDING REMARKS

A clear implication of the preceding analysis is that the impact of new non-governmental institutions has been circumscribed by the continuing crisis within the states of the region. If we conceptualize public and private actors as essentially complementary rather than alternatives, NGOs and local governments should be seen as needing effective states, which supply adequate public goods. In most African countries, without better roads and communication, with notable deficiencies in law and order, and without macro-economic stability or policy predictability, the impact of these new development agents will necessarily be limited. At present, the fact that state decay is in effect the primary force behind their growth and new prominence should alert us to the limits of these recent trends.

In fact, the promotion of new development institutions by the donors has tended to weaken Africa's central states, not strengthen them. They appear as increasingly empty vessels, continuing to command significant resources, but progressively abandoning key components of their developmental mission. Much external assistance has unwittingly abetted this process.

Balancing the construction of stronger state with the need to nurture a vulnerable fledgling civil society nonetheless poses special dilemmas for donors, torn between distinct developmental imperatives. On the one hand, a vibrant political system and market economy are clearly strengthened by diversity and institutional pluralism. No one is particularly nostalgic for the days in which an incompetent and venal state dominated African societies and squashed all independent initiatives in its misguided attempt to promote socialist development. On the other hand, it is also generally recognized today that sustained development requires an interventionist and effective central state to spearhead the development process. Particularly in an environment characterized by both extreme resource scarcities and widespread market failures, state institutions must play a critical role. Moreover, it is generally agreed that the plethora of development organizations that exist in most African countries need some coordination to be fully effective, and the state is the obvious vehicle for that coordination. The need for a strong state with the ability and willingness to coordinate and regulate the development process has to be reconciled with the advantages of pluralism and market capitalism. It will not be easy for donors to strike the appropriate balance between these two imperatives.

Notes

1 This was again the central message of the Bank's 1997 World Development Report (World Bank, 1997a), which focused on the state.

2 This is compatible with my own anecdotal evidence based on interviewing in West Africa in the summer of 1998. It might be noted that these numbers can also be deceiving. Some NGOs distinguish funds they receive from donors to perform specific services, usually as sub-contractors in aid funded projects; from grants they receive from donors to undertake projects they have themselves designed. At least some NGOs appear to tabulate the latter as self-funded activities. While they do suggest a greater degree of project-level autonomy, such grants do not lessen overall financial dependence on official donors.

3 Interpreting these differences requires caution, however, as there is large inter-country variation and the estimates for each indicator are based on a different set of countries

4 See *Jeune Afrique* (1997) for multiple examples. In an interesting paper, Amukowa Anangwe (1995) argues that in Rural Kenya, at least, "the main-

    tenance of law and order depends on the effectiveness of the voluntary sector, whiles the role of the state is more complementary than critical". See also Mwaikusa (1995) for similar analysis of Tanzania.

5   Interestingly, the report estimates that 84.9 percent of private household expenditures for health go to the purchase of modern medicine (31).

6   On the questionable quality of education statistics, see Samoff (1991).

7   In this study I focus on decision making processes within the recipient countries of Africa. Of course, many western NGOs represent a significant aid constituency in their country of origin and their political influence in the legislature makes it difficult for donor agencies to ignore them. I will, however, ignore those issues.

8   Again I distinguish local from international NGOs in this paragraph. The latter often sit at the policy making table as donors, particularly when they bring significant funding to the discussion.

9   The Timidria Association is a network of village associations and like-minded individuals, created in 1991, originally with the objective of lessening ethnic tensions in the country. In the mid-1990s, it claimed to have 80,000 members. In addition to Tidjani's analysis, see Berbedette and Ouedrago (1993).

References

Anangwe, Amukowa. "Maintenance of Law and Order in Western Kenya," in Semboja, Joseph and Ole Therkildsen (eds.) *Service Provision Under Stress in East Africa* (London: James Currey, 1995), pp. 105–120.

Bates, Robert H. *Markets and States in Tropical Africa; The Political Basis of Agricultural Policies.* (Berkeley: University of California Press, 1981).

Bebbington, Anthony and Roger Riddell, "Heavy Hands, Hidden hands, Holding Hands? Donors, Intermediary NGOs and Civil Society Organizations," in Hulme and Edwards, pp. 107–127.

Bennell, Paul. "Privatization in Sub-Saharan Africa: Progress and Prospects during the 1990s," in *World Development*, vol. 25, no. 11 (1997), pp. 1785–1803.

Berbedette, Loic and Josephine Ouedrago. *Place des Organizations du Monde Rural dans l'Eclosion Associative au Niger.* Swiss Aid and the International Six Association (Niamey: October 1993).

Berg, Elliot. "Aid and Public Sector Reform." Paper prepared for the University of Copenhagen Conference on Aid. October 9–10, 1998.

Berg, Elliot. "Sustaining Private Sector Development in Senegal: Strategic Considerations". Processed (DAI: Bethesda, MD, June 1997).

Bingen, R. James. "Cotton, Democracy and Development in Mali," in *Journal of Modern African Studies*, vol. 36, no. 2, (1998), pp. 265–285.

Blair, Robert and Josephine Jordan. *Staff Loss and Retention at Selected African Universities: A Synthesis Report.* AFTHR Technical Note no. 18. Technical Department, Africa Region (Washington: The World Bank, 1994).

Bossuyt, Jean. "La Participation des Acteurs Décentralisés et non Gouvernementaux," in GEMDEV, *La Convention de Lome en Questions* (Paris: Karthala, 1997), pp. 407–424.

Bratton, Michael. 1994. "Civil Society and Political Transition in Africa," in John W. Harbeson, Donald Rothchild, and Naomi Chazan (eds.) *Civil Society and the State in Africa* (Boulder, Co: Lynne Rienner Press, 1994).

Bratton, Michael, "NGOs in Africa: Can they Influence Public Policy?," in *Development and Change*, vol. 21 (1) (1990), pp. 87–118.

Bratton, Michael and van de Walle, Nicolas, *Democratic Experiments in Africa: Regime Transitions in Comparative Perspective* (New York: Cambridge University Press, 1997).

Cohen, John, "Foreign Advisors and Capacity Building: the Case of Kenya," in *Public Administration and Development*, vol. 12 (1992).

Evans, Peter. B. *Embedded Autonomy: States and Industrial Transformation* (Princeton N.J.: Princeton University Press, 1995).

Fischer, Stanley, Ernesto Hernandez-Cata, and Mohsin S. Khan *Africa: Is This the Turning Point?* IMF Papers on Policy Analysis and Assessment. (Washington D.C.: the International Monetary Fund, May 1998).

Fowler, Alan. "The Role of NGOs in Changing State-Society Relations: Perspectives from Eastern and Southern Africa," in *Development Policy Review*, vol. 9, no. 1 (1991), pp. 53–84.

Gabas, Jean Jacques, et al. *L'Efficacité de l'Aide Francaise au Burkina Faso* (Paris et Ouagadougou: COBEA/ORSTOM/FASEG, 1996).

Gérard, Etienne. "Entre Etat et Populations: L'Ecole et l'Education en Devenir," in *Politique Africaine*, no. 47 (October, 1992), pp. 59–69.

Goldsmith, Arthur A. "Sizing Up the African State," in *Journal of Modern African Studies*, vol. 38, no. 1 (2000), pp. 1–20.

Gueneau, Marie-Christine and Bernard J. Lecomte. *Sahel: Les Paysans dans les Marigots de l'Aide* (Paris: l'Harmattan, 1998).

Hulme, David and Michael Edwards (eds.). *NGOs, States and Donors: Too Close for Comfort?* (New York: St. Martin's Press, 1997).

Jeune Afrique. "Le Boom de l'Insecurité." Paris. (March 12, 1997).

Joseph, Richard. 1998.[11] frica, 1990-1997: From *Abertura* to Closure," *Journal of Democracy* vol. 9, no. 2, 3–17.

Josserand, Henri and R. James Bingen. *Economic Management in the Sahel: A Study of Policy Advocacy in Mali.* Decentralization, Finance and Management Project. (Washington, D.C.: Associates in Rural Development, February, 1995).

Leclerc-Olive, Michèle. "Espaces 'Metisses' et legitimité de l'Etat: l'experience Malienne," in GEMDEV *Les Avatars de l'Etat en Afrique* (Paris: Karthala, 1997).

Lienert, Ian and Jitendra Modi, "A Decade of Civil Service Reform in Sub-Saharan Africa," IMF Working Paper WP/97/179. (International Monetary Fund, Fiscal Affairs Department, December 1997).

Meyer, C. "A Step Back as Donors Shift Institution Building from the Public to the Private Sector," in *World Development*, vol. 20 no. 8 (1992), pp. 1115–1126.

Mwaikusa, Jwani T. "Maintaining Law and Order in Tanzania: The Role of Sungusungu Defense Groups," in Semboja, Joseph and Ole Therkildsen (eds.) *Service Provision Under Stress in East Africa* (London: James Currey, 1995), pp. 166–178.

Naino, Abdoul-Kader Amadou. "L'Environment des ONGs Nigeriennes." Report for the SNV, Netherlands Aid Agency (Niamey, April 1997).

Naudet, David. "Chapitre sur L'Aide Décentralisée: Premiers Eléments." Unpublished paper, Paris, 1998.

Nunberg, Barbara. "Rethinking Civil Service Reform: An Agenda for Smart Government." Working Paper, Poverty and Social Policy Department, The World Bank, (Washington, D.C., June 30, 1997).

Psacharopoulous, George and Nguyen Xuan Nguyen, *The Role of Government and the Private Sector in Fighting Poverty.* World Bank Technical Paper, no. 346 (Washington D.C.: The World Bank, 1997).

Olivier de Sardan, J. P. "Chefs et Projets au Village." Unpublished paper (Bureau de Coordination de la Cooperation Suisse au Niger, July 1997).

Otayek, René and Daouda Dialo, "Dynamisme Protestant, Développement Participatif et Démocratie Locale," in *Afrique Contemporaine,* no. 185 (first trimester, 1998), pp. 1933.

Perouse de Montclos, Marc-Antoine, "Faut-il Supprimer les Polices en Afrique?," in *Le Monde Diplomatique* (August, 1997), p. 2.

Robinson, Mark, "Governance, Democracy and Conditionality: NGOs and the New Policy Agenda," in A. Clayton, *Governance, Democracy and Conditionality: What Role for NGOs?* (Oxford: INTRAC, 1993).

Robinson, Mark, "Privatizing the Voluntary Sector: NGOs as Public Service Contracters?," in Hulme and Edwards, pp. 59–78.

Riddell, Roger C. and Mark Robinson. *Non-Governmental Organizations and Rural Poverty Alleviation.* (Oxford: Clarendon Press, 1995).

Sahn, David E. "Public Expenditures in Sub Saharan Africa During a Period of Economic Reform," in *World Development*, vol. 20, no. 5 (May 1992), pp. 673–693.

Samoff, Joel. "The Facade of Precision in Education Data and Statistics: A Troubling Example from Tanzania," in *Journal of Modern African Studies,* vol. 29, no. 4 (1991), pp. 669–689.

Semboja, Joseph and Ole Therkildsen (eds.). *Service Provision Under Stress in East Africa* (London: James Currey, 1995).

Sharma, Narendra P. *African Water Resources: Challenges and Opportunities for Sustainable Development.* World Bank Technical Paper, no. 331. (Washington, D.C.: The World Bank, 1996).

Smillie, Ian and H. Helmich, (eds.). *Non-Governmental Organizations and Governments: Stakeholders in Development.* (Paris: OECD, 1993).

Stiglitz, Joseph E. *Economics of the Public Sector.* (New York: W.W. Norton & Company, 1986).

Tendler, Judith. *Good Government in the Tropics* (Baltimore M.D.: Johns Hopkins University Press, 1997).

Therkildsen, Ole and Joseph Semboja, "A New Look at Service Provision in East Africa," in Therkildsen and Semboja, pp. 1–34.

Therkildsen, Ole and Joseph Semboja, "Short-Term Resource Mobilization for Recurrent Financing of Rural Local Goverrents in Tanzania," *World Development*, vol. 20, no. 8, pp. 1101–1113.

Tidjani Alou, Mahaman S. "La Decentralisation au Niger: Essai d'Approche." Unpublished Paper, Niamey, 1998a.

Tidjani Alou, Mahaman S. "Courtiers Malgré Eux: Trajectoires de Reconversion". Unpublished Paper, University of Niamey, Niger 1998b.

Tripp, Aili Mari, *Women & Politics in Uganda* (Madison: University of Wisconsin Press, 2000).

United Nations Development Program. *Human Development Report, 1998.* (New York: Oxford University Press, 1998).

van de Walle, Nicolas. *African Economies and the Politics of Permanent Crisis, 1979–1999* (New York: Cambridge University Press, 2001).

van de Walle, Nicolas, team leader. "Democracy, Governance and Conflict Strategic Assessment for Uganda." Report presented to United States Agency for International Development, Democracy and Governance Center (Washington, D.C.: Management Systems International, January 25, 2001).

van de Walle, Nicolas and Timothy Johnston, *Improving Aid to Africa* (Baltimore M.D.: Johns Hopkins University Press, for the Overseas Development Council, 1996).

Wade, Robert. *Governing the Market: Economic Theory and the Role of Government in East Asian Industrialization* (Princeton N.J.: Princeton University Press, 1990).

World Bank. *The World Bank and the Health Sector in Mali: An OED Country Sector Review* Report, no. 18112 (Washington, D.C.: The World Bank, June 30, 1998a).

The World Bank. "Fact Sheet, Mali-Education Sector Investment Program (EDSIP)" at the World Bank website www.worldbank.org/pics/pid/ml40650. (1998b).

The World Bank. *The World Development Report, 1997* (Washington, D.C.: The World Bank, 1997a).

The World Bank, *African Development Indicators, 1997* (Washington, D.C.: The World Bank, 1997b).

The World Bank, *Better Health for Africa* (Washington, D.C.: The World Bank, 1994).

The World Bank, *Sub-Saharan Africa: From Crisis to Sustainable Growth, A Long Term Perspective Study.* (Washington, D.C.: The World Bank, 1989).

The World Bank. *Accelerated Development in Sub Saharan Africa* (Washington, D.C.: The World Bank, 1981).

Yeats, Alexander J. "On the Accuracy of Africa Observations: Do Sub-Saharan Trade Statistics Mean Anything?," in *World Bank Economic Review*, vol. no. 4, 2 (May 1990), pp. 135–56.

CHAPTER 2

FINANCING AFRICA'S DEVELOPMENT TOWARD A BUSINESS PLAN?

IBRAHIM ELBADAWI AND ALAN GELB[1]

INTRODUCTION

Almost two years ago at the United Nations, more than 150 heads of state and government endorsed the Millennium Declaration in an effort to ensure that globalization brought opportunities and benefits to all countries. They emphasized the importance of making poverty eradication the central focus of development efforts, and gave new impetus to the goal of halving poverty by 2015, as well as attaining number of other economic, social, and environmental objectives. The UN Financing for Development process, which included a major conference in Monterrey, Mexico in March 2002, revolves around the means to reach these goals. It includes consideration of how to mobilize private and public capital flows, as well as the important roles of international trade, sound domestic policies, and other dimensions of a supportive environment to promote such flows and to ensure development effectiveness.

Nevertheless, this discussion on the levels of financing needed to attain development goals takes place against a contentious background relating to both the *quantity* and the *quality* of assistance. Aid levels have been declining since the early 1990s. Aid fatigue prevails in many donor capitals, underpinned by a feeling that aid systems, shaped by three decades of cold war competition, have not been effective in developmental terms, particularly as measured against the criteria of the Millennium Declaration. There is also a recognition that to some degree limited aid effectiveness has been partly due to the mechanisms of aid delivery themselves, so that debate on the appropriate policy frameworks for recipient countries (on which there has been increasing convergence over the 1990s) has been complemented by debate on how to reform systems of foreign assistance. Several questions form part of this debate. *Amounts and allocation*: what criteria should guide the allocation of assistance across countries, and how much assistance can countries absorb productively? *Donorship and ownership*: if conditionality is of limited effectiveness, how can it be replaced by accountability and ownership on the recipient side? Does aid encourage or hamper the emergence of the underlying institutional and political foundations needed for sustained development? *Transactions costs and debt overhang*: how can the new paradigms be shaped for development partnerships between Africa and the industrial countries—and perhaps also between African countries themselves—and reduce the high transactions costs of assistance? What is the role of debt relief in the restructuring of aid? *Needs versus dependence*: does assistance crowd in or crowd out private capital and strong institutions? Does it enable or inhibit export diversification and growth? Is more aid now needed to escape a development trap or is there a danger that high aid levels will lead to extended periods of aid dependence? Should there be a "New Marshall Plan for Africa"?

This chapter surveys recent research on these topics and outlines features of the rapidly changing picture as assistance to Africa moves toward a new paradigm. While much thinking and research points in the same broad direction, different studies emphasize different aspects of a complex problem and some are still in process. Not enough time has elapsed to fully evaluate the impact of the changes, which have accelerated since 1999. Recognizing that all are involved in a learning process, the chapter is therefore preliminary; it aims to sketch a picture and encourage debate.

Much of the literature on aid effectiveness argues that creating the incentives needed for Africa to develop and break free of poverty requires a re-balancing of power and accountability.[2] Civil society (and in particular, excluded groups) need to be economically empowered through increased transparency, better monitoring of public spending, and wider discussion and sharing of development policies and objectives. Governments also need to become more accountable to firms, providing a better business environment for producers so that they are better able to compete in the global economy. At the same time, African governments—especially the increasing number of representative governments—should both be held more accountable for development outcomes and empowered relative to donors, and this requires increased government capacity. Development partners, in turn, need to re-shape the aid regime to facilitate these changes, to sustain assistance or increase it in the face of new threats such as HIV/AIDS, and to reduce the high transactions costs of the current fragmented system. It is also increasingly clear that industrial countries need to open markets and curb agricultural subsidies.

This chapter picks up some of these topics. It first reviews African economic performance and aggregate financing considering four types—domestic savings, private flows, official development assistance (ODA), and debt relief,—against estimates of the financing needs for poverty-reducing growth. It then reviews some of the growing body of research on development effectiveness, relating this to both the quantity and allocation of aid and the quality of assistance, and relates this to observed features of aid flows. It concludes by noting the role of three important initiatives in changing aid mechanisms: debt relief through the Highly Indebted Poor Countries (HIPC) program, the Poverty Reduction Strategy Paper (PRSP) process, and the New Partnership for African Development (NEPAD). These three initiatives were developed sequentially and individually rather than as an integrated program, and there may be some tradeoffs and tensions among their objectives. But the chapter concludes that they can build on each other to fit into a consistent process of restructuring aid.

Restructuring will, however, take time. The system of foreign assistance that has been built up over decades of cold war competition will not be changed overnight. On the recipient side, the quality of governance, especially in the areas of conflict resolution, public budget, and financial management, and the monitoring of development effectiveness, has emerged as the key barrier to both higher aid and new aid modalities. On the donor side, the problem is how to accommodate the rhetoric of increasing "ownership" and how to place recipients in charge of development programs. Most donors are constrained by long-standing processes and established systems of accountability to their own domestic constituencies, and progress has been quite slow in terms of adopting new modalities of support and harmonizing requirements. Some promising cases have emerged, and these need to be monitored carefully with a view to learning from successes and failures.

BACKGROUND: GROWTH, FINANCING TRENDS, AND MILLENNIUM GOALS

GROWTH TRENDS

Africa's economic performance improved considerably in the second half of the 1990s. On a population-weighted basis, growth peaked at almost 6 percent in 1996 as well-managed countries were able to take advantage of a generally favorable world environment to boost growth and raise income per head. Performance has diverged among countries, with a number continuing to show negative growth (figure 2.1), but well-managed, poor countries are still averaging 4 percent, considerably better than before 1995. Growth has somewhat declined in the last two years and currently averages about 3 percent, far less than what is needed to meet the . . . Declaration poverty reduction goal. To simply prevent the number of poor from rising, growth needs to average about 5 percent. To meet the Millennium Declaration goal of halving poverty by 2015, 7 percent growth is needed, together with generally favorable distribution.

Several factors have underpinned the growth trends shown in Figure 2.1. On the positive side, the growth trends shown in figure 2.1 economic management has improved in many countries. Africa entered the new century with growing consensus on the basic requirements for development—good governance, peace and security, a healthy, literate population, sound macroeconomic management, and a growing and competitive private sector. The need to maintain macroeconomic stability is now generally accepted, as is the need to allow market forces to play a central economic role and to encourage private sector activity. Globalization is increasingly recognized as a process that needed to be confronted, not by withdrawal but by engagement, and in a way that reversed the long process of marginalization that had endured since the late 1960s.

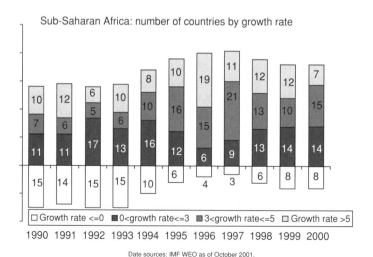

Date sources: IMF WEO as of October 2001.

Figure 2.1   Growth in Africa = 1990–2000

On the negative side is the political fragility of many states, and increasingly the rising prevalence of HIV/AIDS, which threatens to cut growth by 1 to 2 percent in heavily affected countries. Virtually all of the countries experiencing negative growth in recent years have been affected by conflict or have experienced severe problems of political governance. Ending conflicts would boost Africa's overall growth by 1 to 2 percent, even taking into account only the direct effects on the countries concerned. Also on the negative side has been a severe deterioration in the terms of trade, especially for agricultural and non-oil primary exporters. Since 1980 these products have seen a decline of almost 40 percent in world purchasing power and the trend has accelerated with the slowdown in world markets in 2001. A third adverse factor, the decline in financing flows, is discussed below.

FOREIGN DIRECT INVESTMENT (FDI)

Private flows to Africa have been rising in recent years (FDI has averaged about $9 billion) and have reached over three times the levels of the early 1990s. But they are still highly concentrated on extractive industries and are mainly to oil exporters, North Africa, and South Africa. Overall, FDI to Africa is perhaps one third of its potential level, as judged by experience in other developing regions, and net private resource transfers are reduced relative to net flows by substantial remittances of profits and dividends. (See Table 2.1.)

OFFICIAL DEVELOPMENT ASSISTANCE (ODA) TRENDS AND ALLOCATIONS

Compared with other parts of the world, and even to other poor regions, Africa is far more dependent on development assistance relative to either domestic savings or private inflows. Official flows have fallen by one third over the decade of the 1990s (Table 2.1), or about 40 percent on a per capita basis. Especially for the poor countries that are not oil exporters, net resource inflows are overwhelmingly made up of ODA. For this group, only about one fifth of net resource inflows or ten percent of net resource transfers come from private sources.[3] About one fifth of ODA flows have been in the form of non–project funding supporting adjustment programs, and estimates suggest that up to one quarter of ODA supports technical assistance.

Development assistance has been fairly concentrated, rather like FDI but to a different set of countries. Table 2.2 shows levels of net ODA flows and net International Development Association (IDA) flows to four groups of countries: those with income levels above the IDA cutoff,

Table 2.1 Resource Flows & Transfers

						Sub Saharan Africa					
	1970	1980	1990	1993	1994	1995	1996	1997	1998	1999	2000
Net Resource Flows	1271	10630	15860	14985	18455	22073	15261	18522	14096	19374	15717
Net flow of long-term debt	852	7733	5073	4952	4410	3974	750	2090	-286	-167	639
Foreign direct investment (net)	93	53	894	1864	3327	4482	5083	8226	6198	7722	6763
Portfolio equity flows	0	0	0	17	861	4869	2013	1507	681	3899	893
Grants (ex. technical coop.)	328	2844	9893	8151	9857	8748	7415	6699	7503	7920	7422
Memo: official net											
resource flows	821	6416	14516	12462	13514	11611	9368	8665	8713	8452	8520
Private net resource flows	451	4214	1344	2523	4941	10461	5893	9857	5383	10923	7196
Net Transfers	342	5325	9843	10647	9757	13745	6321	10950	6175	11373	7789
Interest on long-term debt	193	2375	4361	2699	3971	3996	4814	3721	3818	3598	3117
Profit remittances on FDI	737	2930	1656	1638	4727	4332	4126	3851	4103	4403	4811
Memo: official net transfers	707	5726	11805	10511	11486	9598	6714	6585	6681	6478	6963
Private net transfers	-366	-402	-1963	136	-1728	4147	-393	4366	-506	4895	825

and IDA countries broken into three groups according to the World Bank's Country Policy and Institutional Assesment (CPIA) ratings averaged the period for 1998 to 2000.[4] IDA allocations are determined by CPIA ratings, and would therefore be expected to be quite selective according to this classification—indeed, the highest-rated group of countries received eight times as much IDA per head as the lowest-rated group. Despite the fact that other donors do not use the same rating system as IDA (some do not use a formal rating system at all), overall ODA allocation has still followed the general rating pattern, albeit with lower selectivity. High-rated countries have received about five times as much ODA per head as the lowest-rated group.

As seen in Table 2.2, ODA flows have been constrained by two sets of factors. First, aid fatigue has resulted in a 15 percent decline in flows to even the best-rated group of countries over the 1990s rather than the increase that might have been expected from greater selectivity in allocating assistance.[5] In addition to fiscal constraints, ODA flows are subject to increasing scrutiny for development effectiveness. There is a great thirst in donor capitals for success stories—for evidence that assistance is being used productively to deliver services and to improve development outcomes, especially in the areas indicated by the millennium goals. Progress in this area is essential if resource flows are to be increased or even sustained.

Second, ODA for the lowest CPIA group of countries is far smaller and has declined even more sharply. This group includes many conflict-affected countries with low capacity for absorbing assistance productively. Poor countries in SubSaharan Africa that suffer from these difficulties now absorb about $7 per head in net ODA flows, relative to the $37 per head utilized by poor, yet well-managed, countries. If all poor countries were to receive the same level of ODA per head as the countries in the highest CPIA group, total ODA would need to be twice as high as current levels.

Domestic savings

Rates of domestic savings in Africa average around 13 percent of GDP. In some countries gross domestic savings are barely 5 percent or less of GDP, far too low to underpin a sustainable growth process at rates sufficient to cut poverty. In contrast, domestic savings rates may be 20 percent or more in even poor Asian countries. Domestic savings rates are influenced by many factors, including income levels and the rate of income growth. Also important are the opportunities and the security provided to domestic savers, including sound financial systems, effective legal frameworks, and good governance in general, as well as other factors that reduce the incentives for capital flight. There is an urgent need to

Table 2.2   ODA & IDA Flows by Country Groups

	Average 1990–1992	Average 1998–2000	Percent change
SSA			
Total net ODA, million current $US*	16000	11620	−27.4
ODA per head, current $US	33.0	19.0	−42.5
Total net IDA, million current $US	1878	2094	11.5
IDA per head, current $US	3.9	3.5	−10.7
IBRD countries			
Total net ODA, million current $US	488	905	85.3
ODA per head, current $US	12	8	−34.3
Total net IDA, million current $US	1.5	−1.3	−185.9
IDA per head, current $US	0.04	−0.03	−173.1
IDA country CPIA <3			
Total net ODA, million current $US	2799	1549	−44.7
ODA per head, current $US	15.8	6.9	−56.0
Total net IDA, million current $US	258	214	−17.1
IDA per head, current $US	1.5	1.0	−34.0
IDA country 3< = CPIA <3.5			
Total net ODA, million current $US	8294	5399	−34.9
ODA per head, current $US	45.1	24.1	−46.7
Total net IDA, million current $US	831	1060	27.5
IDA per head, current $US	4.5	4.7	4.5
IDA country CPIA > = 3.5			
Total net ODA, million current $US	4419	3767	−14.7
ODA per head, current $US	53.8	36.7	−31.8
Total net IDA, million current $US	787	821	4.3
IDA per head, current $US	9.6	8.0	−16.5

stem both human and financial capital flight and increase domestic savings rates in Africa, although rates cannot be expected to increase too sharply in poor countries because of the need to increase consumption levels at the same time.

Poor trade performance has probably depressed domestic savings. For Sub Saharan Africa, the loss of world export share since 1970 is equivalent to a flow of $70 billion per year in foreign currency—five times as large as annual net ODA flows to the region in the 1990s. Relative to other regions, this has reduced income growth, considerably depressed the propensity to save, and probably encouraged capital flight through requiring domestic assets to depreciate in value relative to those abroad. The weakness in export revenue has been partly due to terms of trade declines for traditional commodity exports. But, in addition, Africa has lost market share in many traditional exports and the region has also failed to diversify towards a wider range of products, including processed and manufactured goods and services, whose share in world trade has been rapidly increasing. In recent years this has begun to change, with a slow but steady trend toward producing and exporting a wider range of products. It is vital for Africa's development that this trend continue and intensify.

A more immediate concern is the question of whether ODA crowds in or crowds out domestic savings and investment. Cross-country patterns (see below) suggest that the crowding-out effect has dominated in the last decade. Adjusting for income levels, two thirds of foreign savings has been associated with increased consumption, while net ODA flows show little association with higher investment levels.

RESOURCES AND THE MILLENNIUM DECLARATION GOALS

How much would be required, in terms of investment, to reach the millennium goal of halving poverty by 2015? While the world was projected to cut the proportion of people living in poverty from 22 percent in 2000 to 11 percent in 2015, continuing past trends for Africa would leave severe poverty levels at around 37 percent in 2015, little better than at the turn of the century.

First, to reach high growth rates, it is vital to improve resource use and the business environment to increase efficiency, which has been only half of Asian levels in terms of growth per unit of investment. Without such an improvement, the investment levels required to attain high growth rates are unrealistically high as a share of GDP.

Second, if the efficiency of investment were increased to Asian levels, Africa would still need investment rates on the order of almost 30 percent of GDP for an extended period. Currently, investment averages about 20 percent of GDP. Of this, only two-thirds is funded out of domestic savings, while the remaining one third is funded by foreign savings. The investment requirements of rapid growth therefore indicate a resource gap on the order of 10 percent of GDP, which is larger than current ODA flows.

Third, to this figure would need to be added the incremental costs of addressing other development goals, including in the areas of infectious diseases (in particular, HIV/AIDS) and other health goals, as well as those in the areas of education, gender equality and environment. Few countries are on track to reach such goals, particularly in the health area.[6] The ECA has estimated Africa's financing requirements at $40–50 billion per year, relative to current inflows of around $20 billion.[7] Other estimates also suggest comparable increases, and also indicate that poor yet well-managed countries are able to absorb additional resources productively.

All of these estimates need to be taken with caution, because of weaknesses in the costing of programs and the linkage between inputs and development outcomes in many countries. Nevertheless, they suggest at least an order of magnitude for financing requirements, and the extent to which current resource flows, whether from domestic savings, private inflows or development assistance, will need to grow in order for Africa to catch up with world trends. On the other side of the growing gap between estimates of resource needs and actual levels is the insistence of donors for evidence of success stories—for assurance that aid will be used effectively, as well as the need to raise private savings and attract investment.

RESEARCH FINDINGS ON AID EFFECTIVENESS AND EMERGING ISSUES
RESEARCH FINDINGS

Recent cross-country econometric research on aid effectiveness (e.g., Burnside and Dollar, 2000; Collier and Dollar, 2001; World Bank, 1998) produced two fundamental results:

1 Aid is only effective in "good" policy environments, as measured by a broad index of policy and institutional quality (CPIA) or a narrowly defined set of macroeconomic indicators.
2 Regardless of the policy environment, aid is subject to diminishing returns. Related work produced two more conclusions:
3 Conditionality has limited effectiveness. Econometric research fails to finds systematic correlation, much less causation, between aid/conditionality and policy (Dollar and Svensson, 2000; Knack, 2001). However, country-specific research based on ten African countries

(Devarajan et al., 2001) offers a more nuanced, and somewhat more positive, finding. Aid and conditionality can have a positive role in anchoring good policy in countries in which the strategic decision to undertake reforms has been initiated from within, and they may provide a signaling or a commitment technology for broad macro-institutional reforms. However, these studies also suggest that there are limits to conditionality as instruments for promoting "good" policy environments and that it has little, if not perverse, effects once the reform process move into more complex phases.

4 Aid contributes to better policy environments if it promotes knowledge and accountability, and both require appropriate aid modalities. For example, the mobilization of domestic pressure for change requires knowledge, which raises the question about what forms of aid delivery are more effective as instrument of knowledge transfer (Collier, 2000). Moreover, research on aid fungibility provides evidence that narrowly focussed project-based and donor-driven accountability is illusionary and that recipient accountability could be better promoted by broad programmatic lending in a context of a transparent and locally supported reform agenda (Devarajan, Rajkumar, and Swaroop, 1999).

These and associated studies have produced guidelines for the allocation of aid to address specific poverty reduction targets (Collier and Dollar, 2002a, 2002b; Collier, 2001):

- Donors should primarily allocate aid to those countries where money is most effective (i.e. where there is good policy environment in place or strong commitment and stakeholders' consensus); moreover, such countries can absorb larger amount of aid than they are presently receiving.
- Though economic reform is a homegrown political process, not just a technocratic process, aid delivery mechanisms should be designed with the objective of promoting reforms through enhancing knowledge and accountability.
- Poor countries with poor policy environments should still receive assistance because the efficient allocation criteria is also partially based on poverty. However, the balance between knowledge transfer and dialogue and financial transfers will be more toward the former in these countries.

As Ndulu (2001) observes, aid practice in Africa has been evolving in tandem with the research advances, and this has helped reduce the cost of the development learning curve. Indeed, the emerging consensus in the aid and development policy (e.g., as articulated by the Comprehensive Development Framework [CDF]) is now fully anchored in sweeping new modalities such as the PRSP process. However, there are several under-researched issues that center around the concept of aid dependence and essentially define the unfinished agenda for research.

Unpacking Aid Dependence

Early studies of aid dependence focussed on macroeconomic, "Dutch Disease"-type effects: They examined whether high and unsustainable aid flows crowd out export competitiveness by appreciating the real exchange rate and whether aid crowds out domestic savings. We return to these issues below, but now focus on another potential impact of high levels of assistance: its potential to crowd out domestic institutions.

Aid dependence as institutional dependence?

As aid has expanded over the years far beyond its "gap filling" role into a "multi-faceted business" involving both sides of the aid community, it is increasingly recognized that it exacts very substantial costs on aid-receiving countries.[8] Azam and others (1999) posit a vicious cycle: where institutional capacity is initially weak, the attraction of gap-filling aid to donors and recipients will be strong enough to displace the recipient's institutional capacity, locking donors and recipients into a permanent situation of high aid and low institutional capacity. Negative institutional effects escalate as aid becomes more important for a country. Berg (1987) argues that for countries where aid flows are relatively large—say 5 percent of GDP—these effects are unsettling; at higher aid levels, they become devastating. Therefore, according to Berg, a 5 percent aid GDP ratio (about 2 percent in Purchasing Power Parity (PPP) terms) is the approximate threshold, beyond which institutional deterioration accelerates as aid ratios increases.

This concern over the impact of aid dependency on institutions and governance motivates some to argue that measures aimed at enhancing aid effectiveness should be linked to *lower* aid, even in the short-to-medium run (Kanbur, 1998). This micro-institutional argument is far more radical than the "revisionist" macroeconomic "gap-filling" approach, which recognizes the need for ultimate and substantial reductions of aid for Africa, but reasons that even *higher* aid may be needed in the short run in support of poverty-reducing growth policies before ultimate elimination of development aid can be achieved (Amoako and Ali, 1998).[10]

The tension between large needs and possible adverse side effects only serves to increase the focus on how to improve aid mechanisms in order to soften the tradeoffs. In addition to

1 *quantitative level* of assistance, we focus on two dimensions:
2 *Aid delivery mechanisms.* Delivery mechanisms influence the quality of aid through their impact on the underlying institutional environment. High percentages of tied or project aid reduce the options of aid-receiving countries and their capacity to own and develop their own development strategies, as well as to respond flexibly to emerging contingencies. The heavy use of expatriate technical assistance for implementation of donor projects has probably weakened local capacity in aid-receiving countries, with perverse institutional consequences: "Technical assistance has displaced local expertise and drawn away civil servants to administer aid-funded programs—precisely the opposite of the capacity-building intentions of donors and recipients. In some countries technical assistance accounts for 40 percent of aid, and much of the remaining aid is tied. But with large number of technical experts from donor countries—estimated by some at 100,000—a lot of technical assistance is also effectively tied, flowing back to donor countries with less long-run impact on the development of recipient countries' economies" (World Bank, 2000, 244). Local officials often find it easier to leave management to the donors and technical assistance is written into projects without much review. This is because the key public-sector civil servants of recipients countries are few and many expatriates are brought in to service donor financial management and reporting requirements.

Aid delivery mechanisms are also influenced by numbers of non-coordinated donors. Multiple donor requirements lead to management burdens arising from varied and complex donor administrative accounting and monitoring requirements.[11] In addition, recipients can play donors against each other, reducing incentives for donor coordination. Without coordination, donors can also "free ride" on each other in the sense that they may tend to leave the "difficult" tasks to the other donors.

3 *Debt overhang.* Debt overhang is likely to have directly adverse effects on growth and investment (Elbadawi, Ndulu and Ndung'u, 1997). High debt creates expectations of future taxes and policy reversals, which reduce the incentives for current investment. High fixed-debt service obligations increase leverage and raise uncertainty, especially if donor funding is decided on a short-term basis. In such circumstances, investors will exercise their option to wait until returns are great enough to compensate them for risk. High ratios of debt service to government revenue also imply a potential internal transfer problem. In addition, high indebtedness can also weaken the effectiveness of aid in enhancing growth through increasing the weight of

externally driven project-based financing relative to budget resources
to support the core functions of the state.

Assessing the quality of aid: Africa Is clearly different

Elbadawi and Randa (2003) construct three sub-indexes for debt overhang, aid dependency, and aid delivery using principal components. The
three indexes are in turn used to construct an overall quality of aid index,
again via principal components.[12] In the first sub-index, the stock of
external debt ratio has been the highest in SSA compared to all other
aid-recipient regions throughout the period. However, debt service
ratios (relative to exports and to government revenues) for SSA were
comparable to the median ratios of the aid-recipient sample. (See table
2.4.) In the second sub-index, thresholds suggested by the above study
indicate that throughout 1979–98, the number of highly aid-dependent
countries in SSA has exceeded those in other regions by a wide margin,
rising from 13 in 1981–84 to 25 in 1993–96, and even when declining
to 20 in 1997–2000 they still account for the more than 80 percent of
the total number of highly aid-dependent countries in the sample. On
the other hand, the number of highly aid-dependent countries in other
regions reached a maximum of only 3 in 1989–92 and 1993–96 for the
Latin American and the Caribbean region (LAC). (See table 2.5.)[13] In
the third sub-index, a concentration index on the number of donors
providing 75 or more of development aid to any given country suggests
that SSA and South Asia have had many more large donors (and hence

Table 2.3 Africa: Current Trends versus International Goals

	Number of Countries:		
Development Goal	*On Track*	*Off Track*	*Seriously Off Track*
Universal primary education			
by 2015	21	9	13
80% primary completion by 2005	12	2	18
Halve adult illiteracy by 2005	16	19	5
Gender equity in primary and			
secondary enrolment by 2005	9	13	13
Reduce (a) infant and (b) child			
mortality to one third of			
1990 level by 2015	(a) 1,(b) 1	(a) 15,(b)10	(a) 31,(b) 35
Halve malnutrition by 2015	6	1	33

Source: World Bank, 1991.

Table 2.4 External Debt Ratios (%) by Region: 1981–2000

	1981–84	1985–88	1989–92	1993–96	1997–00
Overall Sample					
External Debt to GDP	49	67	67	63	62
Total Debt Service to Exports	19	26	19	16	15
Total Debt service to					
Govt. Revenue	26	32	27	26	26
Sub Sahara Africa					
External Debt to GDP	55	98	85	111	97
Total Debt Service to Exports	19	26	21	17	15
Total Debt service to					
Govt. Revenue	24	33	28	25	22
Middle East and North Africa					
External Debt to GDP	42	42	51	54	66
Total Debt Service to Exports	20	25	11	9	9
Total Debt service to					
Govt. Revenue	38	50	29	23	31
Latin America and the					
Caribbean					
External Debt to GDP	48	67	52	42	38
Total Debt Service to Exports	28	30	21	21	20
Total Debt service to					
Govt. Revenue	38	42	36	31	32
East Asia					
External Debt to GDP	54	80	90	71	59
Total Debt Service to Exports	19	24	21	18	17
Total Debt service to					
Govt. Revenue	26	31	36	30	27
South Asia					
External Debt to GDP	28	38	45	51	52
Total Debt Service to Exports	15	25	21	13	9
Total Debt service to					
Govt. Revenue	13	24	22	18	18
Eastern Europe					
External Debt to GDP	30	21	13	34	41
Total Debt Service to Exports	17	23	7	13	17
Total Debt service to					
Govt. Revenue	18	10	5	10	20

Source: Elbadawi and Randa (2002), using data from World Bank SIMA database

Table 2.5 Aid Dependency by Region: 1981–2000

	1981– 84	1985– 88	1989– 92	1993– 96	1997– 2000
Overall Sample					
Low Aid Dependent	24	20	25	32	36
Moderately Aid Dependent	30	28	27	20	22
Highly Aid Dependent	15	23	30	30	24
Sub Sahara Africa					
Low Aid Dependent	1	1	1	2	2
Moderately Aid Dependent	15	11	8	5	10
Highly Aid Dependent	13	18	23	25	20
Middle East and North Africa					
Low Aid Dependent	2	2	2	3	4
Moderately Aid Dependent	3	3	3	4	3
Highly Aid Dependent	1	1	2	0	0
Latin America and the Caribbean					
Low Aid Dependent	14	10	10	15	16
Moderately Aid Dependent	7	9	8	3	3
Highly Aid Dependent	0	2	3	3	2
East Asia					
Low Aid Dependent	6	6	5	5	6
Moderately Aid Dependent	1	2	4	4	3
Highly Aid Dependent	1	1	1	1	1
South Asia					
Low Aid Dependent	1	1	1	1	2
Moderately Aid Dependent	4	3	3	3	3
Highly Aid Dependent	0	1	1	1	0
Eastern Europe					
Low Aid Dependent	–	–	6	6	6
Moderately Aid Dependent	–	–	1	1	1
Highly Aid Dependent	–	–	0	0	0

Notes:

1. *Source*: Elbadawi and Randa (2003), using data from World Bank SIMA database

2. Low Aid Dependent is where $0 < \dfrac{Aid}{GNP}\% < 2$

3. Moderately Aid Dependent is where $2 \leq \dfrac{Aid}{GNP}\% < 10$

4. High Aid Dependent is where $\dfrac{Aid}{GNP}\% > 10$

Table 2.6 Characteristics of Aid by Region: 1981–2000

	1981–84	1985–88	1989–92	1993–96	1997–00
Overall Sample					
Index of donor concentration	0.25	0.24	0.25	0.23	0.22
Optimum Tech Assistance	6.62	6.52	6.07	4.17	4.14
# of Countries experiencing					
Excessive tech Assistance	2	5	6	10	2
Sub Sahara Africa					
Index of donor concentration	0.22	0.19	0.21	0.19	0.18
Optimum Tech Assistance	7.70	6.52	6.75	5.31	5.15
# of Countries experiencing					
Excessive tech Assistance	2	5	5	9	2
Middle East and North Africa					
Index of donor concentration	0.30	0.33	0.28	0.33	0.36
Optimum Tech Assistance	6.62	6.52	6.07	4.17	4.14
# of Countries experiencing					
Excessive tech Assistance	0	0	0	0	0
Latin America and the Caribbean					
Index of donor concentration	0.31	0.33	0.26	0.22	0.21
Optimum Tech Assistance	6.62	6.52	6.07	4.17	4.14
# of Countries experiencing					
Excessive tech Assistance	0	0	1	1	0
East Asia					
Index of donor concentration	0.30	0.31	0.27	0.29	0.31
Optimum Tech Assistance	6.62	6.52	6.07	4.17	4.14
# of Countries experiencing					
Excessive tech Assistance	0	0	0	0	0
South Asia					
Index of donor concentration	0.16	0.15	0.15	0.17	0.17
Optimum Tech Assistance	7.70	6.52	6.75	5.31	5.15
# of Countries experiencing					
Excessive tech Assistance	0	0	0	0	0

Table 2.6   Characteristics of Aid by Region: 1981–2000—cont'd

	1981– 84	1985– 88	1989– 92	1993– 96	1997– 00
Eastern Europe					
Index of donor concentration	–	–	0.27	0.23	0.23
Optimum Tech Assistance	6.62	6.52	6.07	4.17	4.14
# of Countries experiencing Excessive tech Assistance	0	0	0	0	0

Notes:
1. Source: Elbadawi and Randa (2003), using data from World Bank SIMA database
2. Optimal technical assistance is calculated as

$$T^* = \frac{0.5960}{2 \times 0.256 \times \overline{I}}$$ where &$$$;$\overline{I}_t$ is the average level of the quality of

institutions in countries in the same income group according to the World Bank classifications. The optimal technical assistance index is derived from the following parsimonious equation:

$$I_t = -7.8247 + 0.5960 T_{t-1} - 0.0256 T^2_{t-1} \times I_{t-2} + 1.4107 \ln y_0$$
$$\quad\quad\quad\quad (4.37) \quad\quad\quad\quad (-3.71) \quad\quad\quad\quad (3.88)$$

$N = 231$, # *of countries* = 84, $F(3.144) = 10.39[0.0000]$, $R^2 = 17.79$
Breush Pagan = 3.49 [0.0000]
t-values in parenthesis

3. The donor concentration index is given by the Herfindal-Hirschman Index, based on the share of aid that each donor provide as percentage of total aid received by a country (a low index means donor fragmentation).

more aid fragmentation) than East Asia and Middle East and North Africa (MENA) and Eastern Europe regions (with a low concentration index). However, very high levels of technical assistance (as defined relative to an "optimizing" ratio related to measures of institutional and governance capacity) appear to be a particular African problem: the countries receiving "excessive" technical assistance were all African, except for one LAC country in 1989–92 and 1993–96. (See table 2.6.)[14] This corroborates the strong critique of technical assistance "Can Africa Claim the 21st Century" of The World Bank (2000), which argues for alternative approaches to capacity building in Africa, including subsidizing repatriation of African professionals abroad (see also Ndulu, 2002).

Figure 2.2 shows indicators of the quality of aid (QA) by region, using the composite index, while figures 2.3a and 2.3b show changes over time, for all countries and for SSA respectively, distinguishing the four components separately. Compared to other regions, QA in SSA has been low and continued to decline for most of the period prior to 1996 and has clearly differs from other regions. For the overall sample, the quality of aid hits its lowest level in period two (1989–92), which witnessed

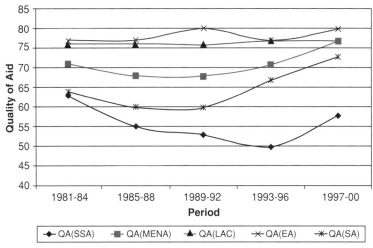

Figure 2.2   Quality of Aid by Region (1981–2000)

Notes to Figure 2:

1. The Debt Overhang index (DO) is given as a weighted average, where the weights are given by principal components: $DO = 0.4078 EXTDEBT + 0.3151 TDSEXP + 0.2771 TDSGR$

2. Donor Fragmentation (DF) is given by $(1+(1-HHI))^{1+\alpha}$. Where HHI – is the Herfindal-Hirschman index of donor concentration. Where α is the aid dependency

3. Excessive Technical Assistance (ET) is given by $(1+\frac{T}{T^*})^{1+\alpha}$ where T^* is derived in Notes to table 2.6.

4. The three sub indices are transformed into a positive index:
   - Partnership Index = $I(DF)$
   - Aid Delivery Index = $I(ET)$
   - Debt Index = $I(DO)$

   Where $I(X) = \dfrac{X_{max} - X_i}{X_{max} - X_{min}}$ Xmax is the maximum value, Xmin is the minimum value

5. The quality of Aid and debt overhang variable are calculated using the principle component analysis covariance approach to give us the weights as:
   $QA = 0.5351 I(DF) + 0.2737 I(ET) + 0.1912 I(DO)$

high lending activities associated with the early wave of economic reforms (Figure 2.3a, 2.3b), but improved considerably between periods two and three (1997–2000), with aid quality in the latter period even surpassing that of period one (1981–84). In SSA, however, although QA has improved in the latter period it was still lower than the first period. Clearly, according to these comparisons, SSA entered the twenty-first century with much to be done in terms of reducing both the quantitative and institutional dimensions of aid dependence.

Elbadawi and Randa assess the relative roles of aid and policy in enhancing aid effectiveness. Their simulation results shown in figure 2.4 suggest that improved aid quality can lead to a significant improvement

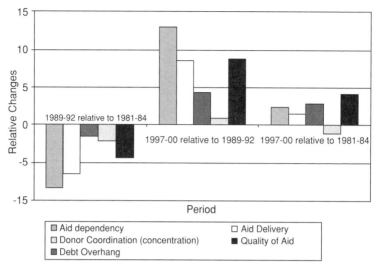

Figure 2.3a　Quality of Aid over time (overall sample)

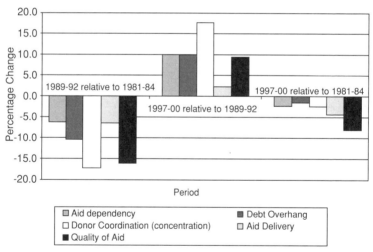

Figure 2.3b　Quality of Aid over time (Sub Sahara Africa sample)

in aid effectiveness in addition to that gained from a better policy environment. They simulate that if the quality of aid in SSA rose by 24 percent (to reach the median of the aid-recipient countries in the sample), per capita GDP growth in SSA would rise by about 1.8 percent per annum.

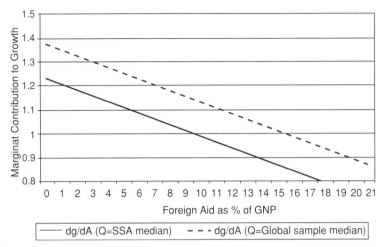

Figure 2.4 Marginal Contribution of Aid to growth, if Sub Sahara–Africa Quality of aid increases to the median of aid-receiving countries

Note: based on the estimated equation of Elbadawi and Randa (2003)
Notes to Figure 4

1. The simulation is based on Econometric results in Elbadawi and Randa (2003)
$$g = 24.64 - 2.90 \ln y_{t-1} + 4.98 \ln sch_{t-1} + 3.17P + 29.60Q - 0.01A^2 + 0.22P \times A + 1.03Q \times A$$
$$(0.98)^* \quad (3.74) \quad (0.89)^* \; (15.5)^{***} \; (0.00)^* \quad (0.10)^* \quad (0.41)^*$$

g – growth of GDP per capita, y is GDP per capita, sch is the number of primary school years. P-policy (as measured as World Bank's CPIA), Q-quality of Aid, A-foreign aid as ratio of GDP. The sample median for P, Q, and A is 6.79, 3.10, 0.68 respectively. The respective values for SSA median are 13.03, 2.89, 0.57
2. *, **, ** significant at 1%, 5%, and 10% respectively.
3. Standard errors in parenthesis.
4. The estimated equation based on Fixed Effects GMM IV estimation technique.
5. The bold line uses sub Sahara Africa median values. The dotted line uses SSA values except for quality of aid that uses the sample average. That is SSA median country could improve the quality of aid to sample median values.

AID, SAVINGS AND INVESTMENT

Even though capital accumulation may follow rather than lead the growth process, international evidence, including that of the high performing East Asian economies, suggests that sustaining high rates of growth requires substantial levels of physical capital accumulation. To the extent that SSA faces binding lending constraints in the international capital markets or external balance conditionality imposed by bilateral and external donors, national savings will drive aggregate investment (Summers, 1988), and hence national savings will influence the prospects for sustainability of growth. The recent experiences of Mexico and Chile, for example, have shown that high national savings is a prerequisite for avoiding financial crises and subsequent collapse of growth in the medium- to long term (Williamson, 1994).[16]

Foreign aid has traditionally been regarded as complementary to national savings. This suggests that, for given levels of domestic savings, more foreign aid (or foreign savings[17]) should contribute to higher investment. The complementarity between domestic and foreign savings can be derived from "poverty trap" models of development (in which foreign savings inflow helps to avoid the traps) or models in which countries converge to common steady state income levels (Boone 1994).[18] However, recent literature on the macroeconomic effects of foreign aid has found that higher aid is mostly translated into consumption rather than investment (Boone 1994, Obstfeld 1995). This means that, on average, foreign savings substitutes for domestic savings by easing liquidity constraints or by induces "Dutch Disease" effects.

For Africa, data suggests strong and robust negative association between the two variables. Moreover, Granger causality analysis suggests that the observed correlation between the two variables has causal interpretation—from foreign aid to domestic savings (Elbadawi and Mwega, 2000). Figures 2.5a and 2.5b illustrate the negative correlation between gross domestic savings and foreign savings for all SSA countries; these patterns are similar for all of SSA, excluding oil exporters and South Africa. These patterns are quite similar to those in other regions as well, but given the high average aid dependency of SSA and its low average domestic savings, the negative correlation translates into a larger crowd-

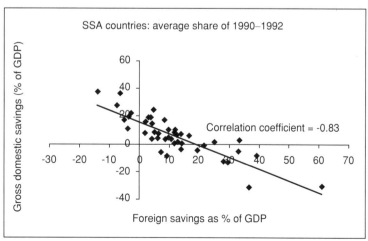

Data sources: Africa LDB as of December 4, 2000. Lesotho is excluded.

Figure 2.5a   Foreign and Domestic Savings in SSA: average 1990–1992

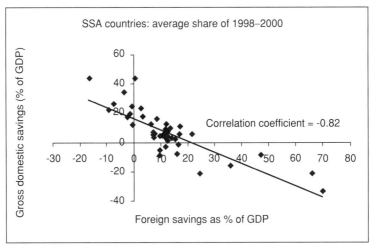

Data sources: Africa LDB as of December 4, 2000.
Data are for last three years available.

Figure 2.5b   Foreign and Domestic Savings in SSA: average 1998–2000

ing out effect in Africa. Correspondingly, ODA in Africa has only a modest relationship with levels of domestic investment.

These patterns are consistent with Elbadawi and Mwega,[19] who estimate a crowding-out elasticity close to one.[20] Simulations based on Elbadawi and Mwega's model suggest that aid dependency accounts for a large share of the savings shortfall in Africa relative to the high performing Asian economies. They estimate that aid dependency in moderate and high-saving African countries have caused savings rates in these countries to lag behind those in the East Asian economies by 3.7 and 1.7 percent age points of disposable income, respectively, from 1970 to 1995. Finally, lower aid dependence also provides an appreciable contribution to the higher private savings rate in moderate-saving African countries (13–15% of GDP) compared to their low-saving counterparts (around 5% of GDP).

Given the relatively low savings ratios in SSA, even for the high savers, the possibility of an adverse impact through aid dependency is a serious one. More needs to be understood about the channels through which such an effect might occur and how the mechanisms of assistance might be recast in order to soften the tradeoffs.

Aid, Export Competitiveness and Market Access

Especially for countries with small internal markets and lagging export performance, as is the case for most African countries, assessment of the impact of aid on export competitiveness should be given high priority in development policy. The concern appears justified despite the argument that aid has spurred growth when delivered in "good" policy environment, even when such environments happen to be affected by "Dutch Disease" (Collier, 2001). For example, van Wijnbergen (1986) shows that excessive resource or other flows could be have an adverse long-run impact when export production is characterized by positive (learning-by-doing) externalities and capital market imperfections—as in the cases of non-traditional, and especially manufacturing, exports from SSA. However, the effect of aid on competitiveness could be positive if it finances key infrastructure or eases bottlenecks that raise production costs of exporters. In theory, exporters could counter the resource squeeze due to transitional aid boom by borrowing and investing in the export sector to ensure that the sector productivity is quickly recovered once the real exchange rate equilibrium is restored following a decline of aid to more sustainable levels—but this requires good capital markets, which cannot be assumed in Africa.

The impact of assistance on export competitiveness and economic diversification should also be a critical issue for Africa because of the impact that declining competitiveness itself has had in reducing the growth of incomes and the level of savings. As noted previously, relative to the end of the 1960s, Africa's loss of world trade share—because of terms of trade losses, loss of market shares in traditional exports, and failure to diversify into fast-growing global product lines—is equivalent to some $70 billion or one fifth of GDP.

Real exchange rates in SSA have, in fact, depreciated sharply since the second half of the 1980s.[22] By and large the depreciation of the 1980s and early 1990s were necessary corrections for unsustainable macroeconomic policies and sharp appreciations during the 1970s. Deprecations also accompanied shifts in key economic policies associated with trade and current account liberalization and fiscal reforms, as well as a sustained deterioration of the terms of trade for many African exports. As most economies in the region complete "first generation" macro and trade reforms, real exchange rates will be driven by three factors: long-term trends in the terms of trade; the productivity of Africa economies relative to their main trading partners (the Balassa-Samuelson effect); and aid and other capital flows (Elbadawi, 1998). Preliminary estimates using this framework suggest that terms of trade and productivity deteriorations have, respectively, caused the real exchange rate to depreciate by 26 percent and 36 percent over 1985–94, whereas aid flows have operated in the opposite direction, supporting real appreciation of more than 40 percent. This contrasts with the limited effect due to changes in policy fundamentals (trade and fiscal policy), which account for less than 2 percent of real exchange rate depreciation.[23]

For poor countries in which productivity is low, maintaining a depreciated currency may be necessary for the competitiveness of exports, which are likely to be dominated by primary products. As economies becomes more complex and gain comparative advantage in manufacturing and other transaction-intensive exports, improved productivity would allow for more appreciated currencies (Williamson, 1997; Elbadawi and Helleiner, 1998). Therefore, in this export-orientation model, the observed real currency depreciation in SSA could apparently be justified as part of an appropriate development strategy. However, this model assumes that real depreciation will be associated with growth and export diversification, which would eventually lead to a re-appreciation of the real exchange rate as productivity growth takes root. Unfortunately, while a few countries have made progress in diversifying trade, in most cases depreciations in Africa appear to have taken place in a vacuum in which economies have failed to achieve adequate economic diversification or begun to close the productivity gap with the rest of the world.

Might aid dependence have limited export diversification? Elbadawi (1999) estimates a model for the determination of non-traditional exports for a panel of African and other developing countries. The results suggest a threshold, beyond which more ODA usually hindered rather than helped export expansion. The optimum aid/GDP ratio consistent with export diversification is estimated at 5 percent of GDP, equal to the threshold suggested by Berg (1987), beyond which aid dependency starts to adversely affect institutions in recipient countries. These estimates are speculative, but they strengthen the case for complementary measures to encourage trade growth and export performance, including the opening of industrial-country markets to African exports, especially agriculture, nontraditional exports, processed products and labor-intensive manufactures. At the same time, African countries need to do more to open their markets to each other, including by addressing a wide range of procedural and regulatory obstacles that keep markets small and fragmented.

DEBT RELIEF AND THE RESTRUCTURING OF AID

Although debt relief attained a high international profile after the mid-1990s, HIPC is only the latest in a set of arrangements for alleviating the burden of debt service payments for poor countries. In 1967 United Nations Conference on Trade and Development (UNCTAD) had argued that debt service payments in many poor countries had reached a critical situation. After 1987, successive G-7 summits offered progressively more lenient terms on bilateral credits owed by poor countries. In the late 1980s and 1990s, as a number of poor countries slipped from International Bank for Reconstruction and Development (IBRD) to IDA status, the World Bank and the International Monetary Fund (IMF) began offering a form of debt relief to low-income countries by enabling them to repay high-cost loans with low-interest credits.

These initiatives, even when coupled with increasing volumes of official financing, did not represent a simple addition to the resources available to poor countries. For many they were largely offset by a continuous deterioration in the terms of trade. Excluding South Africa and the oil exporters, over the period 1970–97, terms of trade losses offset approximately 95 percent of the increased net transfers to African countries.[24]. Meanwhile, the level of their external debt increased to 106 percent of GDP or to 83 percent of GDP in net present value (NPV) terms. Further debt relief was needed, and political support mounted for a "final" resolution of the problem.

The Highly indebted poor Countries Initiative (HIPC) took previous debt reduction programs further in a number of ways. It developed a comprehensive approach based on equitable debt reduction by all donors, and it extended relief to multilateral debt. It also estimated the relief needed to bring countries to a "sustainable" and uniform NPV debt level, either 150 percent of exports or 250 percent of government revenues, lower than typical levels for non-HIPC countries. The HIPC relief was announced as additional to ongoing aid flows—against the backdrop of a steady decline in ODA flows in the 1990s. To help prevent the recurrence of debt problems in the future, relief was to be provided in two phases, interim and final, which would be determined by success in meeting criteria for good economic management at the decision and completion points, respectively.

By early 2002, debt sustainability analyses had identified 42 countries as potential HIPCs, of which all but five were in Africa. Twenty four of these countries have passed their decision points and are receiving debt service relief; all but four are in Africa. Progress of many of the remaining countries towards decision-point criteria has been slowed by conflict-related factors.

Relief from HIPC, including associated traditional debt relief mechanisms and additional announced bilateral relief linked with HIPC, is substantial. In NPV terms, the debt of the post–decision-point countries will fall by $35 billion, a decrease of almost two thirds, and 60 percent of the total relief is provided by HIPC itself. On average, countries are estimated to receive over 90 percent of their projected final flow of relief from debt service during the interim period before reaching the completion point. Relative to previous payments, the debt service of the post–decision-point countries is roughly halved relative to GDP, falling from 4.0 percent in 1998 to 2.2 percent in 2001. Debt service due after HIPC is lower by over $1 billion, of which over $800 million represents lower debt service from African countries.

The strong "moral" arguments that had promoted HIPC in the international political arena led to the view that fiscal resources freed up from debt service by HIPC should be used to increase essential poverty-reducing expenditures, including basic health, education, and rural infrastructure. According to budget trends, it appears that about 80 percent of the relief received by African countries is being allocated to poverty-related spending. On average, social expenditures are estimated to have increased from 5.5 percent of GDP in 1999 to 6.7 percent in 2001, rising to three times the level of debt service.

The HIPC program is not over, nor is it a complete response. Looking forward, there are several challenges.

1 Extend decisions under the HIPC framework to more countries that are eligible. This is a major challenge as many of the countries that have not qualified have been in conflict or have had serious governance problems. Flexible approaches will be needed for the special circumstances of countries emerging from conflict, which face in some cases accumulated arrears and ruined performance records.

2 Recognize that the financing needs of low-income countries extend well beyond debt relief. During the 1990s the countries that qualified for debt relief were receiving external support—net of all debt service—equivalent to about 10 percent of their GDP. A reduction of only 10 percent in ODA flows would offset all that has been mobilized through debt relief, while a 20 percent cut would offset even a total cancellation of all debt service.

3 Avoid the recurrence of a serious debt overhang. Debt sustainability requires a combination of several things: faster growth underpinned by increased efficiency of resource use as well as higher investment, a financing package including rising domestic savings and FDI, as well as ODA provided on a more *concessional* basis than in the past. Sustainability will be less likely if primary commodity prices continue their steep secular decline, causing dollar-denominated obligations to grow relative to depreciating domestic aggregates. Finally, since debt service savings are equivalent to financial support to the budgets of HIPC countries, the effectiveness with which they are seen to be used—meaning the effectiveness and transparency with which all

budgetary resources are used—will be an important criterion for future levels of assistance. Especially for land-locked or conflict-affected countries with small export bases and little prospects for major breakthroughs in the areas of productivity growth or economic diversification, a higher grant element in overall ODA may be called for, even in the longer term. The inclusion of grants in IDA's thirteenth Replenishment is part of the solution.

Despite the rhetoric surrounding debt relief—and the very real contribution of HIPC and traditional mechanisms towards reducing the burden of debt and debt service for the poorest countries, relief is therefore not an end in itself. It offers a breathing space to enable the restructuring of the external assistance strategies and mechanisms created and sustained through the decades of Cold-War competition. The financial side of HIPC is only one element of its overall role in the restructuring of aid relationships. There are at least three other aspects:

Reducing defensive financing

Birdsall, Claessens and Diwan (2001) argue that net aid transfers have evolved differently according to the debt status of recipient countries. In low-debt countries, transfers as a share of GDP respond positively to the quality of economic management. In high-debt countries however, and particularly in high multilateral-debt countries, policy selectivity is weakened—with the possible exception of IDA, none of the donors exercised policy selectivity in these countries. High debt has therefore weakened the ability to select recipients according to their income levels and policies. HIPC therefore opens a window for the more effective allocation of foreign assistance and better incentives for both donors and recipients.

Shifting toward budget support

As Africa shifted from trade dependence to aid dependence, African countries became "cash poor and project rich." As debt relief is the equivalent of indefinite cash support to the budget, it makes it easier for countries to finance their "own" programs and weakens the institutional "crowding out" associated with multiple donor-driven projects.

Focussing on public financial management and economic governance

Prior to HIPC, donors interpreted accountability in narrow terms. Project audits stressed the use of specific project resources, ignoring fungibility. Program assistance was based on estimates of foreign exchange gaps, was conditional on policy reform, and was usually disbursed against imports subject to a limited negative list. But programs generally did not specify the use of the counterpart funds generated for the budget.[25] Consequently, neither project nor program aid offered substantial encouragement toward sound overall budget management, the effective use of locally mobilized fiscal resources, and domestic accountability within recipient countries. Indeed, both weakened incentives by placing higher priority on other areas in the face of limited administrative capacity.

The HIPC confronted the donors with a new problem: how to account to their own constituencies for the use of HIPC resources, when these were part of the general budget rather than channeled through specific programs. Assessments of public budget and financial management showed that HIPCs required substantial upgrading of budget formulation and reporting, and especially of execution and audit to track how the resources liberated through HIPC would actually be used.

In the short term, the problem has been approached in some countries through the creation of a "virtual poverty fund," in which certain budget lines, distinguished according to their relevance to poverty alleviation, would be tracked more intensively to give comfort to donors. But at the same time there is a recognition that the only way to improve the impact of HIPC would be to substantially upgrade public budget and financial management, with a view to improving general transparency and accountability. By the end of 2001 action programs had been developed to strengthen this area for all HIPC countries.

Perhaps unexpectedly, HIPC has therefore triggered a critical shift in the reform of aid processes toward emphasizing economic governance. For the first time, pressure for accountability has moved away from exclusive accountability to donors for their individual resources and toward broader accountability to both donors and domestic constituencies in aid-receiving countries for the use of all budget resources. In this way, debt relief has spurred the restructuring of aid relationships toward greater domestic ownership.

PRSPs and NEPAD

The PRSP process and The New Partnership for African Development (NEPAD) represent the latest stages in the process of restructuring Africa's aid relationships. In December 1999 the boards of the IMF and the World Bank approved the PRSP process, a new approach toward poverty reduction. The objectives of the process were multiple: to ensure country ownership of poverty reduction strategies, to develop strategies that take a long-term and comprehensive perspective, to focus on results that matter for the poor, and to build stronger partnerships between low-income countries and the international donor community. These goals reflect the principles of the Comprehensive Development Framework (CDF). For HIPC countries, the PRSP process also aimed to ensure that debt relief was provided in the context of a poverty-focused strategy.

The implementation of the PRSP is in its early stages: 39 countries have completed interim PRSPs but only eight countries have completed full PRSPs. Little evidence is yet available on how well the strategies embodied in the PRSPs will be implemented and how effective they will be in their impact on the poor. Any conclusions are therefore tentative: however, some findings from an international conference held in January 2002 to review implementation over the first two years provide useful indications of achievements and remaining challenges.[26]

The first conclusion is that PRSPs are already making a difference by mainstreaming and broadening national poverty reduction efforts. There has been substantial, often enthusiastic, buy-in to the process, by donors, within recipient countries, and by a wide variety of civic groups and non-governmental organizations (NGOs). PRSPs have led to an upgrading of the dialogue on poverty, away from a focus only on the social sectors and with stronger links to budgetary processes and the medium-term allocation of resources.

Processes do not of course change instantaneously. Particularly during the interim phase there has been a trade-off between getting PRSPs moving (including through the link to debt relief via HIPC) and waiting for the development of fully consultative processes and for the formulation of full strategies by countries with limited capacity. There is a danger of expecting too much too quickly—countries that had previously been evolving and implementing a consultative program directed toward poverty reduction have been able to move faster toward the PRSP mechanism than those which had not. Some participants, including some bilaterals and NGOs, still see the process as overly dominated by the International Financial Institutions (IFIs). In some countries a narrow view of consultation has prevailed, with producer organizations and private sector groups having limited input into strategy. Parliaments, in particular, have sometimes not been adequately involved, despite their key functions of budgetary approval and oversight.[27]

The PRSPs are focusing attention on a range of complementary reforms, particularly in the area of public-sector governance. An analysis of budget trends for 32 low-income countries suggested that full PRSPs were associated with a 25 percent increase in pro-poor spending, rising from 6.5 percent of GDP between 1999 and 2001. These budget increases are encouraging, but will require improvements in budget execution, service delivery, and access for the poor to make a significant impact. Programs to upgrade public sector management, including financial management and service delivery, have been ongoing in many countries but progress has often been slow. The PRSP process provides a new impetus to these programs and to the development of medium-term outcome-oriented budgeting. At the same time it is shedding light on major knowledge gaps, whether in terms of costing programs of service delivery or in the underpinnings and requirements for poverty-alleviating growth. This has resulted in a tendency for some PRSPs to present "shopping lists" rather than prioritized and costed programs.

On the donor side, PRSPs have also drawn attention to the need for complementary changes. One need is for assistance to be more predictable, to match the longer-term budgeting process recommended for PRSP countries, usually through a Medium Term Expenditure Framework. Another need is for a greater proportion of donor assistance to shift toward programmatic modalities, and for donors and governments to agree on necessary conditions for moving toward budget support coordinated around the annual budgeting cycle of the recipient country. A wide variety of experience now exists regarding funding mechanisms, including the pooling of donor funds to support sector-wide approaches (SWAPs). These experiments need to be carefully monitored and used as inputs into an enhanced process of benchmarking donor performance in the support of the PRSP approach.

The PRSP process has also drawn attention to the need for better monitoring of development programs themselves, including their outputs and outcomes. The core of the PRSP approach is to reduce the number of uncoordinated requirements made by multiple donors. There has been little or no progress in this area, and movement will not be possible without improvements in country-led processes of benchmarking and performance assessment, whether in the areas of budget and financial management, the delivery of core social services—such as education and health—or the creation of a competitive business environment via efficient infrastructure and functional legal and judicial systems. The PRSPs are therefore increasing the need for information and analysis. If approached creatively, the need to improve the monitoring of development effectiveness and plug knowledge gaps opens up substantial possibilities of demand-led capacity building for African statistical and research organizations, which are now underutilized in many countries.

A good example of this is offered by the health sector in Ghana. Dissatisfied with the results of an overly centralized approach and the "mushrooming" of traditional projects, each with their own procedures and reporting cycles, in 1995 the Ministry of Health (MOH) decided on a sector-wide approach. Following a long participatory process, a medium-term health strategy was adopted and translated into a five-year program and resource envelope. The strategic directions and expenditure envelope are revised annually according to the conclusions of two major meetings (the so-called health summits) held by the MOH, its cooperating partners, and other stakeholders, including the private sector. In 1997, the MOH and a core group of partners—the World Bank, The aid agencies of the United Kingdon, Denmark and the Netherlands, the European Union, and the Nordic Development Fund—signed a "memorandum of understanding" outlining the operational implications of the movement toward single government systems and common implementation, including the pooling of a part of their funds. The Ministry of Health and donors are monitoring the program against a list of 20 indicators covering the fiscal effort of government and donors, implementation of key policy initiatives, the degree of implementation of work programs, and the performance of centers, including but not limited to measuring efficiency factors and comparisons between public and private providers. Reports on these indicators are provided semi-annually. Performance is also monitored through national assessments of health status, health services outcomes and outputs The New Partnership for African Development (NEPAD), the latest African development initiative and the development program of the African Union, represents a further step toward anchoring development in the collective vision and commitment of African leaders.[28] While first and foremost a compact between African governments and their people, it calls for a new relationship between Africa and the international community to reduce poverty and overcome the development gap that has widened over centuries. The NEPAD is still young. Its framework document was only finalized in October 2001, and it is currently in the process of developing its operational program of action. Many of its themes and goals—in the areas of governance, democratic consolidation and conflict management, health and infectious diseases, education, infrastructure (including ICT), private sector development, agriculture and market access, among others—parallel the directions in country-level development plans. However, NEPAD seeks to lend a new impetus towards these directions through a number of mechanisms.

The first innovation of NEPAD is the use of an African Peer Review Mechanism to encourage collective action to promote standards, whether of governance, accountability, or sound economic management. Participating countries (or "policy clubs") are to enter into a series of commitments to create or consolidate basic governance processes and practices, while a forum operating at the level of heads of state will serve as a mechanism through which the leadership will monitor and assess progress.

A second feature of NEPAD is its emphasis on facilitating, at the political level, regional and sub-regional approaches toward the provision of essential regional public goods as well as the promotion of intra-African trade and investments. The NEPAD recognizes that African countries are small and interdependent, and that collective action is needed to address impediments to full economic cooperation. The investment potential in such areas is considerable. An assessment of seven multi-country projects in the areas of energy, transport, water management, and telecommunications/ICT identified capital projects totaling some $20 billion, a considerable part of which could come from private sources. Other regulatory changes to open up Africa's markets also have potential to encourage private investment—for example, adopting common certification for new seed varieties would encourage private investment in research and bio-technology which is almost absent in Africa today, in part because of the costs and delays in obtaining approvals in numerous small markets.

As a new initiative, NEPAD still faces many challenges. These include the need for more discussion and internalization within Africa; so far, formulating and developing the initiative has been a largely top-down process. To build credibility, NEPAD will need to focus on a few areas where quick gains can be demonstrated. Especially because most development programs will need to be implemented at the country level, NEPAD will also need to work in tandem with the PRSP process, which has emerged as the core mechanism for country-donor interaction. These are challenges but not insuperable ones. The adoption of the PRSP process itself, for example, offers an example of how a top-down initiative can serve as a focal point for a wide range of stakeholders and a spur to consultative processes, given commitment and political will.

CONCLUSION

During the 1990s, Africa had seen an increasing divergence between the estimates of financing needs for accelerated development, on the one hand, and the actual resource envelope, on the other. This chapter provides a selective review of research related to these issues and assesses recent initiatives to change the relationship among Africa and its development partners. These initiatives are important because without an increase in aid effectiveness, as seen by donors, assistance is unlikely to rise and may indeed continue to fall. The question goes well beyond volumes of assistance to encompass several dimensions of quality, and the way in which aid depends on—and also shapes—the quality of economic management and governance.

Recent research suggests that aid is only effective in good policy environments, that aid is largely fungible, and that traditional conditionality may not be helpful once reforms move into more complex "second-generation" phases. It is encouraging that the recent changes in aid systems, mechanisms, and allocation processes appear to be evolving in line with these directions. Research may have helped to cut the cost of the development "learning curve." Indeed, the most recent comprehensive study on Africa's development[29] builds on these research lessons to argue that wining the fight against poverty and violence requires comprehensive, owned, widely shared, and sustained development processes. This, the reports emphasizes, would require a major rebalancing of power and accountability—from governments to civil society, especially excluded groups; also from governments to producers, and from donors to governments, especially the emerging group of representative governments in the region.

Since "Can Africa Claim the 21st Century" was written, several existing and new initiatives have started to make a difference in the directions called for by the study. The new aid processes and delivery mechanisms aim to shift accountability processes, away from those directed narrowly towards multiple donor constituencies and towards broader constituencies, including those in recipient countries. Highly indebted poor countries (HIPC) has contributed to this realignment, and the PRSP process is already beginning to make an impact, while NEPAD has the potential for reinforcing similar principles at the continent-wide level. However, to understand the impact of these new initiatives a process for continuous evaluation and response—in terms of design and implementation—needs to be put in place. There is now even more scope for research to assist the change by highlighting cases of good practice and thus to encourage replication and adaptation.

This chapter identifies three areas for future research. First, several issues remain under-researched in areas relating to aid dependency, growth, competitiveness, and debt sustainability. The second and third set of issues relate to the challenges of promoting change, respectively in donors' behavior and in African countries, to ensure the success of the new aid modalities and to allow the concepts and practice of new (CDF-like) development to take root in Africa.

SUSTAINABILITY

This chapter reviews a range of issues that argue for placing the question of sustainability of economic reforms, assistance programs, development strategies, and of course, development outcomes at the top of the research and policy agenda in Africa. By and large, the tragedy of development in Africa has been more an outcome of failure to sustain the implementation of new initiatives and reforms than of failing to try them. In Africa today, the combination of slow growth (itself due to causes such as bad governance and conflict, poor health and HIV/AIDS), declining productivity, and secularly weakening terms of trade for already highly aid-dependent economies constitute the main factors militating against sustainability. Under "business as usual," African countries will not break out of aid dependency and will continue to face its multiple consequences, including the crowding out of institutions, savings, investment, and exports. With growing populations, this would likely lead to a downward spiral, including greater difficulty in reaching a social consensus on development policy and increased violence and conflict. In such a scenario, it is not clear whether the already aid-cynical donor community would be willing to go back to the drawing board to produce another approach.

DONOR PRACTICES

Programs such as HIPC, PRSPs, sector-wide approaches, and budget support will not be successful in promoting aid effectiveness without major changes on the part of donors. This is an area where much remains to be done. Donors will need to re-focus some assistance on complementing private sector initiatives to boost efficiency and growth, as well as to improve market access. The available evidence suggests that little has changed so far. Despite the rhetoric, donors have been slow to cut the high transactions costs of ODA and are only beginning to operationalize a harmonized approach based on the PRSP process. Practice has also been slow to change in the area of technical assistance. Despite good intentions, such change in donors' practices are not likely to be easy, as they are subject to politically driven processes of accountability in donor countries. Changing donors' behavior, therefore, requires more directly engaging with stakeholders in these countries.[30] More research on the political economy of aid in donor countries could improve our understanding about the prospects for changing donors' behavior.

Changes in Africa

"Can Africa Claim the 21st Century" called for African countries to develop a "business plan" to shape a process of change toward greater development effectiveness, both at country and regional levels. Many countries started to develop such plans in the context of the PRSP. A few already have them in place and were able to mobilize local and donor support around them. At the regional level, NEPAD has the potential to reinforce many of the principles identified in the report through encouraging collective action on the part of African leaders as they resolve to take control of Africa's development, and can complement country-level PRSPs by bringing in the regional dimension. As a new initiative, NEPAD faces many challenges, including those of transforming itself from a largely top-down initiative into one driven by bottom-up informed, empowered, and concerned citizens.

Why did Asian countries seek accelerated development and growth so strongly? Will a similar urgency and determination mark the future of Africa? The success of NEPAD and country-level national programs requires that Africa prioritize certain processes and institutions—to address particular threats such as HIV/AIDS and conflict, to improve budget and financial management and make public service delivery more equitable and efficient, and to encourage private investment and trade and to monitor development outcomes. However, there is still a huge knowledge gap on what factors influence the decision by societies to adopt certain development strategies and processes and their likely impact on different social, political and global environments. All of these issues suggests improved opportunities for synergies between Africa's researchers and policy makers in the future.

Notes

1　This paper represents the views of the authors and not necessarily those of the World Bank.

2　See chapter 8 of "Can Africa Claim the 21st Century?," a collaborative study issued in 2000 by the African Economic Research Consortium (AERC), the Economic Commission for Africa (ECA), the African Development Bank (ADB), the Global Coalition for Africa (GCA), and The World Bank.

3　For comparison, at about 1 percent of GDP public inflows to South Asia—a comparably poor region—have been only about one fifth of their level to this group of African countries. And in the 1990s private inflows to South Asia have exceeded public inflows by a substantial margin.

4　Performance assessment is according to the World Bank's Country Policy and Institutional Assessment (CPIA) ratings which are used to allocate IDA.

The CPIA covers a broad range of areas, including macroeconomic and structural policies, public sector management and service delivery, and policies for equity and social inclusion. Net IDA flows to these countries have increased over the 1990s by 4 percent. The African Development Bank carries out a similar annual assessment exercise, using related criteria.

5   Because the country groupings are based on ratings from 1998 to 2000, countries in the top group are more likely to have risen in the ratings since 1990–92 than to have fallen. This implies that, all else being equal, increasing ODA flows would have been expected to this group.

6   For a recent assessment of progress toward the millennium goals, see *Global Poverty Report 2002*, prepared for G8 Summit, African Development Bank with The World Bank.

7   The Report of the Commission on Macroeconomics and Health (December 2001) argued that a global program requiring $27–38 billion per year between 2007 and 2015 could result in a direct economic benefit, in terms of reduced levels of disability, of around $186 billion per year.

8   Brautigam and Botchwey (1998), identify five types of institutional and governance costs due to aid dependency: institutional overload and capacity weakening; loss of sovereignty and weakened ownership of policies and plans; further instability, repetitive budgeting and budget fragmentation; reinforcement of patronage; and undermining of accountability and democratic decision-making.

9   An upcoming multi-donor study on evaluation of CDF finds that very limited change in donors' behavior has been noted in the area of harmonization of policies and procedures according to the systems and practices of the aid-recipient countries (CDF Evaluation Synthesis Report, November 2002).

10 To the extent that the new orientation of the aid regime is about changed behavior on both sides of the aid equation, the literature is yet to seriously evaluate the extent of change in donors' behavior at the operational level (Helleiner, 2000).

11 This involves issues of aid management—receiving aid missions, negotiating agreements, coordinating aid programs with domestic programs and policies, meeting the diverse and burdensome reporting and accounting requirements of the different donor agencies, and ironing out the numerous little bumps that are typical in implementation of these programs. An informal survey suggested that managing the aid system can absorb half the time of key officials in poor countries with weak administrative systems.

12 As used here, the overall quality of aid index (QA) is a weighted average of three components—including the two sub-components of "Aid Delivery Mechanisms," "Donor Fragmentation" and "Excessive Technical Assistance"—and the aggregate index of debt overhang. The latter is constructed as a principal component-weighted average of three debt ratios (stock of debt to GDP, debt service to exports, and debt service to government revenues), while the average (time-invariant) indexes of the extent of aid dependency was used as exponent in the construction of the two indexes of "aid delivery." Hence QA is directly influenced by the nature of the aid

delivery mechanism and debt overhang, with the degree of aid dependency providing the magnification effect. See notes to figure 2.2 for an explicit algebraic definitions.

13 See notes to table 2.5 for the criteria of classification of countries according to the degree of aid-dependency.

14 See notes to table 2.6 for the criteria for assessing "excessive" technical assistance.

15 On the direction of causation between savings and growth, Schmidt-Hebbel and others (1996) review several theories ranging from the classical permanent income and life-cycle hypotheses to the more recent and less conventional models (e.g., Carrol, Overland, and Weil, 1994; Carrol and Weil, 1993; Cole, Mailath, and Postlewaite, 1992; Fershtman and Weiss, 1993; Zou, 1993). They find that these models broadly suggest that growth drives savings. Moreover, it is argued that even when savings is assumed to automatically translate into capital accumulation and hence growth, failure to account for the reverse causation from growth to savings is likely to overstate the contribution of savings to growth (Carrol and Weil, 1993).

16 However, the recent East Asian experience suggests that avoiding financial crises requires more than just attaining high national savings.

17 In SSA, and except for the case of a few oil-exporting countries, foreign savings (defined as imports of goods and nonfactor services net of exports) are largely a result of foreign aid.

18 If incomes converge, then poor countries will save a part of the transfers, as these are temporary. LDCs also may have a higher marginal productivity of capital, which induces them to postpone consumption to the future. Foreign aid may also be utilized to construct infrastructure, leading to a reduction in distortionary taxes and hence promoting economic growth. The above assumes that aid was given in the context of a "good" policy environment, as (Burnside and Dollar, 2000). When, however, incomes across countries do not converge, the flow of foreign aid is likely to be perceived as permanent and therefore is largely spent on consumption.

19 Elbadawi and Mwega's model accounts for five types of variables, characterizing the life cycle, fiscal policy, the financial sector, macroeconomic, and external environment and foreign aid.

20 However, the scale variable by Elbadawi and Mwega is gross disposable income rather than GDP.

21 The exceptions are the large countries of the CFA prior to the 1994 devaluation.

22 The exceptions are the countries of the CFA Zone where real exchange rates appreciated up to the 1994 devaluation.

23 Calculations by Gelb and Ye (2001) suggest that the Balassa effect for Africa could be quite powerful. At income levels of $350 the ratio of PPP GDP to market GDP is typically around 3, and at $26,000 the ratio is 1. Assume a linear relationship between the log of the level of PPP income/head and the ratio of GDP in dollars relative to PPP dollars. Then, if real income rises by 10 percent, the ratio of dollar income to real income will increase by 6 per-

cent so that income will appear to increase by 16 percent in dollar terms. Over the past 30 years, real income per head has been constant (or falling) in Africa, whereas in much of the rest of the world it has increased by at least 50 percent. This would imply an overall real appreciation of the currencies of the rest of the world relative to those of Africa of about 25 percent, or almost 1 percent per year.

24 For calculations, see chapter one of "Can Africa Claim the 21st Century."

25 An exception is structural support from the European Union where counterpart funds have been provided to support specified expenditures.

26 In particular, many useful points are made by the study commissioned by DFID: "Institutionalization of PRSPs in Eight African Countries."

27 See, for example, The World Bank's CDF Secretariat report "Comprehensive Development Framework: Meeting the Promise? Early Experience and Emerging Issues," (August 2001).

28 For information on NEPAD see *www.nepad.org.*

29 See the collaborative report. "Can Africa Claim the 21st Century".

30 These issues are addressed at length in a forthcoming multi-agency evaluation report on the implementation of the Comprehensive Development Framework.

References

African Development Bank and The World Bank (2002), "The Global Poverty Report 2002: Achieving the Millennium Development Goals in Africa: Progress, Prospects, and Policy Implications." Downloadable from http://www.afdb.org/knowledge/publications/pdf/global_poverty_report_jun2002.pdf.

Amoako, K. Y. and Ali, A. A. G. (1998), "Financing Development in Africa: Some Exploratory Results." African Economic Research Consortium Collaborative Project on the Transition from Aid Dependency. Economic Commission For Africa, Addis Ababa, Ethiopia.

Azam, J-P, S. Devarajan, and S. O'Connell (1999), "Aid Dependence Reconsidered," Centre for the Study of African Economies, University of Oxford, Working Paper Series 99–5.

Berg E. (1997), "Dilemmas in Donor Aid Strategies," in Gwin C. and J. Nelson, "Perspectives on Aid and Development". Overseas Development Council, Washington D.C., pp. 79–94.

Birdsall, N., S. Claessens, and Ishac Diwan (2001), "Will HIPC Matter? The Debt Game and Donor Behavior in Africa." Carnegie Endowment for International Peace, Economic Reform Project, Discussion Paper no. 3, March.

Boone P. (1994), "The Impact of Foreign Aid on Savings and Growth." Mimeo London School of Economics, June.

Brautigam, Deborah and Kwesi Botchwey (1998), "The Institutional Impact of Aid Dependence on Recipients in Africa." Unpublished manuscript, American University School of International Service.

Burnside and Dollar (2000), "Aid, Policy and Growth," *American Economic Review* 90, p. 847–868.

Carroll C. and D. Weil (1993), "Savings and Growth: A Reinterpretation". Cambridge, MA: National Bureau for Economic Research. Working Paper, no. 4470, September.

Carroll C., J. Overland and D. Weil (2000), Savings and Growth with Habit Formation. *American Economic Review.* Vol. 90, 3, 341–355.

Cole H. L., G. J. Mailath, and A. Postlewaite (1992), "Social Norms, Savings Behavior and Growth." *Journal of Political Economy*, vol. 100, no. 6.

Collier, P. (2000), "Consensus-Building, Knowledge and Conditionality," *World Bank Economic Review.* Proceedings of the Annual Bank Conference on Development Economics, Washington D.C.: The World Bank.

Collier, P. (2001), "Principles of Aid Effectiveness," in *African Development Aid in the New Millennium: Conference Issues and Papers*, Dar es Salaam, Tanzania, April. African Economic Research Consortium, P. O. Box 62882, Nairobi, Kenya.

Collier, P., D. Dollar (2000a), "Aid Allocation and Poverty Reduction," *European Economic Review*, 46, p. 1475–1500.

Collier, P., D. Dollar (2000b), "Can the World Cut Poverty in Half?," *World Development*, 29, p. 1787–802.

Collier, P., D. Dollar (2001), "Development Effectiveness: What Have We Learnt?" Mimeo, Development Economic Research Group, World Bank, Washington, D.C.

Devarajan S., Rajkumar, A. S., and Swaroop V. (1999), "What Does Aid to Africa Finance?" World Bank Policy Research Working Paper, series no. 2092. Washington D.C.: The World Bank.

Devarajan, S., D. Dollar, and T. Holmgren, eds., (2001), *Aid and Reform in Africa: Lessons from Ten Case Studies.* Washington D.C.: The World Bank.

Dollar, D. and J. Svensson (2000), "What Explains the Success or Failure of Structural Adjustment Programs?," *Economic Journal*, vol. 110 no. 466: 894–917.

Elbadawi I. A. (1998), "Real Exchange Rate Policy and Non-Traditional Exports in Developing Countries." Research for Action Series, no. 46, World Institute for Development Economic Research: Helsinki.

Elbadawi, I. (1999), "External Aid: Help or Hindrance to Export Orientation in Africa?" *Journal of African Economies*, vol. 8, no. 4: 578–616.

Elbadawi, I. A. and Helleiner G. (2000), "Africa Development in the Context of New World Trade and Financial Regimes: The Role of the WTO and Its Relationship to the World Bank and the IMF," in T. A. Ademola (ed.), *Africa and the New World Trading System*, Routledge (forthcoming).

Elbadawi, I. and Francis M. Mwega (2000), "Can Africa's Saving Collapse Be Reversed?," *The World Bank Economic Review*, vol. 14, no. 3: 415–43.

Elbadawi, I. and J. Randa (2003), "Beyond Good Policy: Quality of Aid and Growth," series no. 20433. Development Economic Research Group, Washington, D.C.: The World Bank.

Elbadawi, I., B. Ndulu, and N. Ndungu (1997), "Dealing with the Debt Burden of the Highly Indebted Poor African Countries," in Zubair Iqbal and Ravi

Kanbur (eds.) *External Finance for Low Income Countries*, Washington D.C.: International Monetary Fund.

Fershtman C. and Y. Weiss (1993), "Social Status, Culture and Economic Performance." *The Economic Journal*, vol. 103, July.

Gelb, A. and X. Ye (2001), "Debt Sustainability for Africa's Non-Oil HIPCs: A Note," Africa Region. Washington D.C.: The World Bank.

Helleiner, G. (2000), "Towards Balance in Aid Relationships: Donor Performance Monitoring in Low-Income Developing Countries," Mimeo, Munk Centre for International Studies, University of Toronto.

Kanbur, S. M. Ravi and Todd Sandler, (1999), "The Future of Development Assistance: Common Pools and International Public goods." Policy essay no. 25. Washington, D.C.: Overseas Development Council.

Knack, S. (2001), "Aid Dependence and the Quality of Governance: Cross-Country Empirical Tests," *Southern Economic Journal*. Vol. 68, 2, 310–330.

Ndulu, B. (2001), "Putting the Principles of Aid Effectiveness into Practice in Africa," in *African Development Aid in the New Millennium: Conference Issues and Papers*, Dar es Salaam, Tanzania, April. African Economic Research Consortium, P. O. Box 62882, Nairobi, Kenya.

Ndulu, B. (2002), "Human Capital Flight: Stratification, Globalization and the Challenges to Tertiary Education in Africa." Mimeo, Washington, D.C.: The World Bank.

Obstfeld M. (1995), "Effects of Foreign Resource Inflows on Savings: A Methodological Overview." Mimeo. Washington, D.C.: The World Bank.

Schmidt-Hebbel K., L. Serven, and A. Solimano (1996), "Savings and Investment: Paradigms, Puzzles, Policies." *World Bank Research Observer*, vol. 11, no. 1.

Summers, L. (1988), "Tax Policy and International Competitiveness," in Jeffrey Frankel (ed.) *International Aspects of Fiscal Policies*. Chicago: University of Chicago Press.

van Wijnbergen, S. (1986), "Aid, Export Promotion and the Real Exchange Rate: An African Dilemma." Mimeo, Washington, D.C.: The World Bank. October.

Williamson, J. (1994), "The Washington Consensus Revisited," in Louis Emmerij (ed.) *Economic and Social Development in the Twenty-First Century*, Baltimore, MD.: Johns Hopkins University Press.

Williamson, J. (1997), "Exchange Rate Policy and Development Strategy," in Elbadawi and Soto (eds.) *Foreign Exchange Markets and Exchange Rate Policies in Sub-Saharan Africa, Journal of African Economies*. Supplement to vol. 6, no. 3: 17–36.

World Bank (2000), "Can Africa Claim the 21st Century?", Washington D.C.: The World Bank.

World Bank. (1998). *Assessing Aid: What Works, What Doesn't, and Why*. Washington, D.C.: Oxford University Press.

Zou H. (1993), "The Spirit of Capitalism, Savings and Growth." Mimeo, Washington, D.C.: The World Bank.

CHAPTER 3

TAX REFORM AND DEMOCRATIC ACCOUNTABILITY IN SUB-SAHARAN AFRICA

LISE RAKNER AND SIRI GLOPPEN

"The spirit of the people, its cultural level, its social structure, the deeds its policy may prepare—all this and more is written in its fiscal history . . . The public finances are one of the best starting points for an investigation of society, especially, though not exclusively of its political life"
—Schumpeter [1981] 1954: 7.

INTRODUCTION

Can improved revenue collection and tax policies provide for more democratically accountable government? The theoretical literature, mainly derived from a Western political setting, has concluded that political considerations are important in shaping tax policies and their implementation. In the context of Africa, however, little is known about the actors involved in determining tax policies, the institutional channels applied, the conflicts arising, and the outcomes arrived upon (Fjeldstad et al., 2000). In Sub Saharan Africa this question has gained a new urgency as many countries in the region are currently facing two interrelated challenges: Under pressure from the international finance institutions many countries are currently reforming their tax systems to extract more revenue from their citizens as aid transfers are in rapid decline. In addition, a great majority of Africa's nations have in the early 1990s moved towards pluralist systems of rule. If Western experiences hold true, democratization will have profound implications for taxation. In democratizing environments it will be necessary to build institutional capacity and political legitimacy in order to generate revenues from citizens; confiscatory or coercive forms of revenue extraction are considered incompatible with the long-term process of democratic consolidation.

In this chapter we discuss the relationship between taxation and accountability in the context of tax reforms currently undertaken in a number of Sub Saharan African countries as part of larger structural adjustment programs. In order to assess whether the tax reforms have provided a "governance bonus" in terms of greater responsiveness in state-society relations, we focus on three interrelated issues affecting the relationship between taxation and accountability. First, we consider the *internal accountability* of the tax system and ask whether the tax reforms have resulted in a system of taxation with greater reach, higher level of efficiency and transparency. Second, we ask whether the tax reforms have created closer links between African governments and their citizens and thereby increased *democratic accountability*. Third, we discuss to what extent and in what ways *external accountability* relations between African governments and international donors affect domestic accountability relations. The empirical discussion is illustrated by the tax reforms currently undertaken in Uganda, Tanzania and Zambia. Like many other countries in Sub Saharan Africa in the early 1980s these three countries faced fiscal crises as the main revenue base—export taxes—declined or collapsed. Tax reforms were introduced as part of the economic restructuring agreements with the international donor community. The creation of semi-autonomous revenue authorities, elimination of export taxes, simplification of import tax brackets, and implementation of Value Added Tax (VAT) as a replacement of sales taxes were central components of the reform processes. In all three countries, these reforms resulted—at least initially—in increases in the ratios of tax revenue to GDP, administrative improvements, and a marginal widening of the tax base. However, the tax reforms have only to a limited degree resulted in closer links between government and citizens and so far, the reforms have not provided the basis for more democratically accountable governments. One reason is that the tax reforms have not focussed on the forms of taxation most profoundly affecting the relationship between governments and citizens—direct taxes.[1] Large sectors of the economy, most notably agriculture and the informal sector, remain outside the tax system. The literature linking taxation to demands for accountability implicitly presupposes a form of "tax culture"—a system of taxation that reaches the majority of income earners—were it to be assumed that most people pay their taxes. Clearly, the tax reforms in Uganda, Tanzania and Zambia have not reached this stage. Nevertheless, with respect to formal sector business our analysis does suggest that, in the longer term, there may be a connection between tax reforms and accountability in a Sub Saharan African setting, as commercial businesses are beginning to use their associations to inter-

act with government and revenue authorities over tax collection procedures. In the post-colonial era, economic elites have generally not been
included in the fiscal net, and as a result, taxation has not stimulated
effective demands for power sharing. Our analysis suggests that this may
be changing.

The chapter is structured as follows: the second section discusses the
relationship between taxation (and tax reforms) and democratic
accountability. As this discussion reveals, the implied link between taxation and democracy is based on historical developments in the Rich
countries of the Organization for Economic Cooperation and
Development (OECD). In section three, we assess the relationship
between revenue generation and accountability in Sub Saharan Africa. In
section four we analyze the relationship between tax reforms and
accountability on the basis of the experiences in three Sub Saharan
African countries: Tanzania, Uganda, and Zambia. A final section concludes the chapter.

The Links Between Taxation and Accountability

Generally, *accountability relations* seek to assure that a person/institution
entrusted with a particular task (a) carries out the given mandate, and (b)
does so in a way that is in accordance with the norms and rules applica-
ble to this activity. It involves at least two parties—the one who has been
entrusted with something that gives rise to the accountability obligation,
and the principal who gave the mandate in the first place, or an agent
delegated this authority. *Democratic accountability* is a special case where
the principal is "the people" and the parties owing accountability are
those entrusted with political power. A situation characterized by democratic accountability can be defined as a situation where:

1 Political power-holders carry out their mandate and exercise their
   powers in a way that is *transparent*, in the sense that it enables other
   institutions—and the public—to see what is actually done, and assess
   whether it is in accordance with the mandate and the relevant norms
   and rules;
2 Power-holders are *answerable* in the sense of being obliged to provide
   reasons for their decisions in public (which also implies an element of
   responsiveness);
3 There are *institutional checks or control mechanisms* in place to prevent
   abuse of power and to ensure that corrective measures are taken in
   cases where the mandate is contravened or rules are violated.[2]

Democratic accountability requires in addition institutional mechanisms through which "the people" can punish (remove) officials who do not meet the standards, and influence laws and policy decisions.

Taxation is believed to promote these qualities in public officials and institutions because this is necessary in order to make the population accept their tax obligations. If governments are perceived as accountable, more people will pay their taxes "voluntarily", which lowers the need for coercion and generally reduces the costs of tax collection. Conversely, if people do not see their governments as accountable, there is an increased likelihood that state demands for (new or higher) taxes will be met with protest and violence that is costly and might even jeopardize the position of those in power.

The starting point for an emerging new literature on the interconnections between taxation and democracy in the developing world is the acknowledgement that bargaining over tax policies and the budget is the primary way in which different state and societal goals can be reconciled in a democracy (Moore, 1998). This finding is based on a common interpretation of early modern European history where—over the past two centuries—taxation and disputes over the use of revenues stimulated the development of greater citizen rights with democratic institutions enforcing greater transparency in expenditures. History provides numerous examples of democratic concessions granted in order to broaden the tax base, and of tax payment being used as an explicit condition for citizens to qualify as a voter or candidate for office. This illustrates both a demand from taxpayers that if they are to contribute they should also have a say in how the money is used, and an acknowledgement from governments of the validity of this claim—whether for pragmatic reasons or on grounds of reasonableness (Tilly, 1992; Brautigam, 1991). The link between taxation and accountability is typically illustrated by the battle cry from the American colonies' fight for independence from "Britain—no taxation without representation" (Bailyn et al., 1967). Because taxpayers were consulted about the revenue raising system compliance in tax collection became quasi-voluntary (Levi, 1988) thus, reducing collection costs. Furthermore, the fact that rulers and the more wealthy and influential sections of society bargained over the sources and uses of revenue it helped to generate a consensus over national policy issues. Finally, taxpayer status became a valid basis for claiming political influence. Thus, the notion that politics determine the formulation and implementation of tax policies is firmly established in European and, more generally, Western scholarship (Brennan and Buchanan, 1980; Levi, 1988; Steinmo, 1993). We find that this—admittedly rather sketchy—history of western Europe provides a framework for analyzing state society relations in the developing world with relation to fiscal issues.[3]

TAXATION AND DEMOCRACY IN SUB SAHARAN AFRICA

Why should it be expected that a greater fiscal dependence of African governments on tax revenues could lead to greater accountability of states to their citizens-taxpayers? In most developed countries, issues of taxation rank high on the agendas of political parties, parliaments, and governments; however, they are far less prominent public issues in developing countries. Unlike in some OECD countries, taxpayers in developing countries rarely mobilize politically. The main reason is that only a minority of citizens form part of the tax-net through payment of direct taxes to the state. In the post-colonial period, direct forms of taxation have been limited in Sub Saharan Africa due to problems of information, taxable incomes, infrastructure, and political sensitivity. By the time of independence, direct taxation was perceived as illegitimate, and often the first thing a new independent government did was to eliminate direct taxes (hut taxes) imposed by the colonial governments. Constrained by political concerns, nationalist leaders relied instead on revenues paid by enclave mining interests or "easy taxes" such as commodity exports and excise duties. Apart from the civil service and farmers producing for export, according to Guyer "neither the poor nor the rich in much of present day Africa [. . .] are taxed anything remotely close to the proportions of their income and wealth that their counterparts in peasant and capitalist history have often been forced to pay (Guyer, 1992: 45). Based on World Bank data showing that in low income countries tax revenue as percentage of GDP has declined by almost 3 percent between the 1970s to the 1990s, Brautigam (2002) argues that the failure of revenue-raising seems most acute in countries that receive large amounts of aid.

Seconding the claim that aid and aid dependency has thwarted the development of tax accountability relations, Moore (1998) challenges the linkage between democracy and revenue mobilization in what he refers to as the "fourth world," or developing countries. According to Moore, the more states depend on unearned income the less accountable they will be towards their citizens. Moore argues that the more a state earns its income through the operation of a bureaucratic apparatus for tax collection, the more the state needs to enter into reciprocal arrangements with citizens about provisions of services and representation in exchange for tax contributions. Thus, when state incomes are derived from aid and economic rent, minimal attempts will be made to raise revenue from direct forms of taxation and, as a result, effective democratic governance will be undermined. The argument raised by Moore is important because it points to the exceedingly important role played by external forces in post-colonial Africa. With significant unearned incomes, arguably, African states may in the last decade have faced more organized and effective pressures for accountability and transparency from the international donor community than from their own citizens and parliaments (Brautigam, 1999).

TAX REFORM AND ACCOUNTABILITY AS A CONDITION FOR AID

In the late 1980s, after a series of external shocks, most African countries faced deep fiscal crises due to, among other factors, adverse terms of trade. The cases of Uganda and Zambia are illustrative. In Uganda, the main revenue source basically collapsed with the demise of the International Coffee Agreement in the 1980s and the subsequent fall in coffee prices. In Zambia, the dramatic decline in world market prices on copper reduced government revenue by half between 1975 and 1980. Since the late 1980s, a great number of Sub Saharan Africa's countries have received substantial amounts of aid aimed at stimulating economic policy reform. Increasingly, however, it was realized that the fiscal crisis was also a crisis of *governance* as the central state apparatuses in most countries of the region were plagued by political and institutional weaknesses that undermined their abilities to promote economic development, and collect revenue to sustain state activities. From the early 1990s onward, both the multilateral and bilateral aid agencies began to emphasize "good governance" in their aid programs. Aid has come with a series of "dual conditionalities," and a relatively united body of multi- and bilateral donors have come to see political and economic governance as interconnected (World Bank, 1998, van de Walle, 2001).

Initially, the international donor community's concern with taxation was linked to reforming the tax systems to support the market-based reforms. In the 1990s, the belief that higher taxes could produce more accountable government—and that aid would reduce the pressure on governments to democratize—became influential among some of the main donor agencies (DFID, 2000; Brautigam and Knack, 2002). The emphasis on reforms of the tax system as part of the larger structural adjustment programs is a reflection of this "dual conditionality agenda"—From a donor perspective, where good (accountable) government is high on the agenda, an improvement of the domestic tax base is considered to weaken the dependence on foreign aid and to make governments more accountable. Arguably, by stressing transparency and autonomy of the tax administration, and the need to widen the tax net, major aid donors have in the 1990s founded their aid policies on an implicit connection between taxation and accountability—based on West European history.

Taxation and Accountability in Uganda, Zambia, and Tanzania

To rephrase, our main concern in this chapter is whether tax reforms have yielded an unintended "governance bonus," or democratic accountability in the form of greater responsiveness of states to citizen-taxpayer demands. We emphasize that the expected relationship between taxation and accountability is mainly relevant for certain forms of taxation, the revenue sources that are highly "visible" or "felt" and thus directly link citizens to the state. These are primarily direct taxes (corporate and personal taxes). Where indirect taxes are relatively visible and felt by large sections of the populations, such taxes may give rise to demands for something in return and a say in how the money is spent. Value Added Tax (VAT) illustrates this: while referred to as an indirect tax, it is intended to be broad in reach and is often highly political, because it is felt by a great number of citizens.

In order to establish whether the implied relationship between taxation and accountability holds with regard to tax reforms currently carried out on the African continent, we need to establish whether tax reforms have lead to greater reach, higher levels of efficiency and transparency. In other words, we need to assess whether *internal accountability mechanisms* have been strengthened. Strengthening internal accountability is important in order to achieve the broader goal of increasing *democratic accountability* between the government and the taxpaying voters. Lastly, *external accountability mechanisms* between governments and donors (multilateral and bilateral) play a crucial role in initiating and driving the reforms by creating incentives structures and placing conditions on the recipient governments. External accountability relations between the governments and international donors may therefore affect domestic accountability relations. The relationship between these three forms of accountability and the structure of the empirical analysis is illustrated in figure 3.1.

1 With regard to the *internal accountability* of the tax system, we ask to what extent the reforms have succeeded in creating more efficient

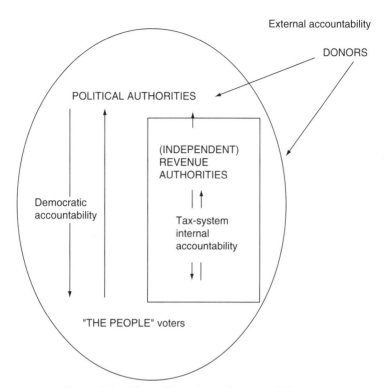

Figure 3.1   Three dimensions of accountability

and trustworthy tax systems-transparent systems capable of ensuring that tax money is not embezzled, and that those who should pay tax do in fact pay.

2 We also ask whether the conditions are in place for taxation to have a positive effect on *democratic accountability*. Have reforms changed the nature of the tax system to the extent that taxes are being felt by a majority of the population? And, if so, has this triggered a response in the form of demands for greater accountability by the citizens? Do we find evidence of governments more willing to justify their decisions in public, and be constrained by institutions representing the public will?

3 Has *external accountability* aimed at strengthening domestic accountability structures through tax reforms succeeded, or has external accountability relations, in fact, hampered the development of domestic structures for democratic accountability?

The internal accountability dimension of tax reforms

If the tax collection apparatus is inefficient, incompetent, and corrupt, this is a strong disincentive for potential taxpayers. As part of the economic restructuring process, the international donor community has emphasized administrative reforms through the establishment of independent revenue authorities. Inspired by the executive agency model, currently eight countries, mainly in east and southern Africa, have established semi-autonomous revenue authorities.[4] The new revenue authorities were perceived to have a positive effect on accountability relations: by placing the responsibility for revenue collection outside the civil service, the aim was to "bypass" deficiencies in existing state institutions through higher salaries and more flexible procedures for hiring and firing employees. In addition, the executive agency model was regarded as an effective mechanism to limit direct political intervention in day to day operations. The new executive revenue agencies established in Uganda (1991), Zambia (1994), and Tanzania (1996) should be regarded as semi-autonomous, as the employees are still public servants. The challenge facing the revenue authorities in all three cases was to increase the contribution of locally raised revenue to the domestic budget from the very low levels prevailing in the 1980s and 1990s. It was also necessary to restructure taxes away from export taxes to a tax system that could facilitate private sector/export promoted growth. In all countries export taxes acted as a major disincentive for the agricultural sector and they were abolished in the early stages of reform.

Enhanced efficiency through the executive agency model?

In terms of increased levels of efficiency in revenue collection, evaluations of the tax reforms in the three countries are generally positive, pointing to increased levels of administrative efficiency and greater compliance from formal sector taxpayers.[5] However, measured by the amount of revenue collected in relation to total GDP, the tax reforms in all three countries present a mixed picture (Table 3.1). Uganda initially provided a striking success case. Total revenue rose from 7 percent of GDP in the early 1990s to 12 percent by 1999, a success coinciding with the establishment of Uganda Revenue Authority (URA) in 1991. However, the ratio has remained stagnant since 1995, suggesting that overall revenue performance has reached a plateau below the level needed to achieve fiscal sustainability. According to Therkildsen (2002), since 1996 the URA

Table 3.1 Tax revenues (ex. grants) in percent of GDP: Tanzania, Uganda, and Zambia

	1991	1992	1993	1994	1995	1996	1997	1998	1999	2000
Uganda	6.97	7.79	9.53	10.63	11.34	12.34	11.56	12.18	11.94	11.8
Tanzania		12.5*	9.5*	11.0	11.3	11.4	12.1	10.9	10.1	10.0
Zambia	18.7	17.5	15.8	20.1	18.4	na	18.5	18.1	17.6	19.8

Sources: URA, TRA, and ZRA Annual Reports (various years); Fjeldstad (2002); Obwona and Muwonge (2001); Gray, Shera, and Condy (2001). *In 1995 the Tanzania Ministry of Finance revised their statistical analyses, changing base line year, updating the revenue-base for various sectors etc. The figures prior to 1994 are therefore somewhat (more) uncertain and may not be comparable (Fjeldstad, 2002).

has become increasingly vulnerable to political interference and the public criticism of the revenue agency by high-level political figures has undermined the credibility of tax administration. In Zambia the ratio of tax to GDP improved from 17.5 percent to 18.5 after the creation of Zambia Revenue Authority (ZRA).[6] In Tanzania tax income increased from 11 percent of GDP in 1995–1996 to 12 percent the year after, but the ratio has later dropped to ten percent, suggesting perhaps that the effects of the "agency model" may be short-lived (Fjeldstad, 2002).[7]

Improved reach through a widening of the tax net?

The tax base was narrow in all three countries prior to the reforms. Success in widening it would be an important indicator of their success from an accountability perspective. The record in all three countries is strikingly similar: the reforms so far have focused on increasing collection through improving the compliance of existing and known taxpayers. According to a recent evaluation study by the British Department of International Development (DFID) of tax reforms in a number of Sub Saharan African countries, the failure to tax the informal sector and agriculture, and the continued tendency of granting tax exemptions to powerful businesses/individuals with close political connections provide the main reasons why collection appears to have stagnated at a relatively low level (DFID, 2001).[8] Echoing the DIFD finding, tax reforms in Uganda, Tanzania, and Zambia appear to have worked within a largely static tax policy framework. In all three countries, increases in revenue are largely due to enhanced collection compliance. In the case of Uganda, the growth in the number of taxpayers does not reflect the rather broad and rapid economic growth recorded in recent years. To illustrate: since 1998 the Uganda Revenue Authority (URA) has been instructed to implement a Presumptive Income Tax on informal sector enterprises with low turnover under International Monetary Fund (IMF) conditionality. However, the process has been met with little enthusiasm in the URA, as the collection is not regarded as cost-effective.[9] Taxing the informal sector is also regarded as politically sensitive and the reform has been met with little enthusiasm in political circles and in the press (Gray et al., 2001; Anene and Garyio, 2000; Therkildsen, 2002). Similarly, the accounts from Tanzania Revenue Authority (TRA) indicate that more than 70 percent of taxes collected are consumption taxes. The regional distribution also points to a relatively limited tax net: close to 80 percent of revenues come from the region of Dar es Salaam (Temu and Due, 2000; Luoga, 2001).[10] In Zambia both the agricultural sector and the non-agricultural informal sector, which account for almost the entire labor force, remain outside the tax net. Recent tax reforms have sought to bring Zambian street vendors and Asian traders into the tax net. However, as the Minister of Finance has continued to grant significant exemptions to corporations and individual businessmen, most people perceive the attempts to tax parts of the informal economy as unfair. These concerns were illustrated in the 2001 election campaign, as a number of party programs raised unfair tax policies as a major concern (Gray et al., 2001; Rakner and Svåsand, 2002).

The transparency and autonomy of tax reforms

The executive agency model was intended to ensure autonomy of the revenue authorities from political interference. However, evaluation reports have noted an unwillingness of the government budgetary authorities to allow the revenue authorities direct access to their administrative and operational budgets by retaining a portion of the revenue collected (DFID, 2001; Therkildsen, 2002; Fjeldstad, 2002). Thus, the new revenue authorities have been given internal autonomy, in terms of hiring and firing practices, but the revenue authorities still lack autonomy from political interference from central government. Perhaps as a result, evidence from Uganda, Zambia, and Tanzania suggests that corruption remains a major problem and that the initial commitment to eradicate corruption may erode over time within the revenue authorities (DFID, 2001). The close connection between the political elites and the executive directorship of the revenue authority is believed to be a major problem in Zambia (Gray et al., 2001). Tax exemptions are granted at the discretion of the Minister of Finance, and at its peak (1998) 500 large corporations were tax exempted in Zambia (ibid.). In both Uganda and Tanzania, studies suggest a tendency of the fight against corruption to be undermined over time (Fjeldstad 2002; Gray et al., 2001; Obwona and Muwonse, 2001). Based on survey data from their membership, the Uganda Manufacturing Association (UMA) claims that smuggling is increasing in Uganda and that up to ten percent of revenue is lost to smuggling (Obwona and Muwonge, 2001).

To sum up, based on available evidence we conclude that the internal accountability dimension, but only to a limited extent, has been strengthened by the tax reforms in Uganda, Tanzania and Zambia. While compliance from known taxpayers has been increased, the tax base remains narrow. Furthermore, studies and reports from all three countries suggest that the level of transparency and independence from the central government remains low. Can it then be argued that the tax reforms have affected democratic accountability to the extent that the tax reforms have been felt by any major groups in society?

Assessing the democratic accountability effect

As argued above, in the case of *democratic accountability* the principal is "the people" and the parties owing accountability are those entrusted with political power, in the case of taxation primarily the executive government, the legislative, and the revenue authorities. For taxation to have a positive effect on democratic accountability, we need to assess whether the reforms have changed the nature of the tax system to the extent that taxes are being felt by a majority of the population. If so, has this triggered a response in the form of demands for greater accountability by the citizens? Do we find evidence of governments more willing to justify their decisions in public, and be constrained by institutions representing the public will?

The discussion above revealed that so far the authorities in Uganda, Tanzania, and Zambia have not succeeded in widening the tax base to any great extent. The attempts to do so—as part of the conditions set by the international donors—indicate that these reforms are administratively complex and politically sensitive. In all three countries it has proven difficult, or even undesirable, to apply the tax law with full force to informal operators. The way value tax added (VAT) has been introduced illustrates the failure of the reforms to widen the tax net: a uniform VAT (with major exemptions) has replaced business turnover taxes and sales taxes in all three countries. However, as food commodities are zero-rated and most agricultural inputs are exempted, VAT has not included many new groups into the tax net. The experiences with VAT in Zambia may serve as an illustration: with 11 registered VAT suppliers, of which 5 are active, a large part of the economy—and the bulk of the rural economy—largely falls outside the VAT net.[11] Initially, the implementation of VAT was met with strong resistance. Organized through Uganda Imports and Exports and Traders Association (UGIETA), the Ugandan traders launched a one-week strike in July 1996 to protest its an implementation (Garyio, 2000; Ssewakiryanga, 2000). The immediate response of the authorities was to arrest traders, but eventually the matter was solved through a decrease in the number of firms eligible for VAT. The 1996 Ugandan traders strike was not repeated in Tanzania and Zambia. However, the high thresholds for inclusion in the VAT net and the large number of zero-rated products illustrate the political sensitivity of the VAT issue.

TAXATION IS FELT BY BUSINESS

The only group visibly affected by the central government tax reforms is the formal business corporations. In all three cases the revenue authorities have tended to target more effectively large taxpayers already in the net, rather than widening the tax base. There is a widespread perception in the business community in these countries that the revenue authorities have concentrated unduly on known corporate taxpayers.

The effectiveness of the new institutions like Tanzania Revenue Authority with regard to this group is illustrated by studies conducted on the Tanzanian manufacturing sector. Until 1995, the manufacturers rarely raised the issue of taxation in member meetings or in member surveys carried out by their association, the Confederation of Tanzanian Industries (CTI). Since 1996 it has become the main issue of concern.[12] Formal sector business is also the group most affected by the overlapping central and local government taxes in Tanzania (Luoga, 2001). Similar studies conducted in Uganda and Zambia indicate that taxation is the primary complaint by the business community. The private sector in Zambia perceives Zambia Revenue Authority as focusing its efforts on a small segment of the economy, which may have serious implications for sustainable revenue collection.[13] Surveys of Ugandan firms reveal that high taxes, excessive levels of tax bureaucracy, ad hoc assessments, and audits are their major complaints (Obwona, and Muwonge 2001, 74).

Corporate taxes in Tanzania, Uganda, and Zambia are not high by international standards. The complaints raised may stem from the fact that, as in most of Sub Saharan Africa, a tax-paying culture is lacking. As argued by the former director of the board of Tanzania Revenue Authority, "The problem is the transition of mindsets of people, who are not used to paying taxes, because 100 percent profit is considered normal profit."[14] Nevertheless, the *perception* by corporate business of the tax system as unfair is a major hindrance to the development of voluntary compliance and a level of trust between the tax authorities and the taxed. The frequent audits conducted by the Ugandan tax administration illustrate the lack of voluntary compliance and low level of mutual trust (Obwona, and Muwonge 2001, 62). In extreme cases, as suggested by the Zambian example, differences in the actual treatment of formal and informal sector enterprises by tax authorities may create incentives for businesses to deregister to avoid taxation.

While the tax reforms so far have drawn few new groups and individuals into the tax net, a voice and an organized response to the new revenue policies appear to be developing within the business community. In Tanzania, the tax grievances of large taxpayers are increasingly being taken to the legal system (Luoga, 2001). Organizations like the Tanzania Chamber of Commerce, Industry and Agriculture (TCCIA) and the CTI have also on a few occasions employed economic consultants and presented their grievances to the authorities. On a number of occasions the demands from the business community have resulted in changes of the existing tax laws (Rakner, 2001). The Tanzania Taxpayers Association (TATA) was recently established as a result of the growing awareness of the impact of taxation on business. In Uganda, the Uganda Manufacturing Association (UMA) is increasingly handling taxpayers' problems. The complaints from, among others, the business sector resulted in the creation of a Tax Appeals Tribunal within the Uganda Revenue Authority in 1998. A task force on taxation has been in operation in Zambia since 1997.[15] Similarly, in Tanzania the business sector has been invited as members of the Task Force on Taxation and it is increasingly acknowledged that business is now acting as a voice. According to observers, a very constructive dialogue has developed with an increased understanding on both parts on the needs of government and business and a culture of reaching compromises appears to be developing.[16] This is important in a country where the private sector was something completely shunned two decades back. It may be argued that the task force, which is an oral forum, has contributed to this cultural change more than in the case in Uganda, where the Tax Tribunal only opens for written complaints and policy questions from business.[17] There can be no doubt that this mobilization is motivated by businesses' desire to reduce tax payments. However, the fact that these issues are being treated through formal, public organizations, rather than through bribery and public deals, may indicate the beginning of a link between economic elites and government in issues of revenue generation.

Formal business constitutes a small segment of society in these countries. These developments, nevertheless, indicate that the tax reforms have resulted in some new demands on these governments, potentially creating new accountability structures. But how are the governments responding? In all three countries business complains that, so far, the consultations taking place are neither transparent nor effective. Furthermore, studies from Tanzania (Luoga, 2001) Uganda (Anene and Gariyo, 2001), and Zambia (Gray et al., 2001) point to the limited trust between the tax administration and the public, to the excessive imbalance in the taxpayer tax authority relations, and to the lack of efficient safeguards against misuse and abuse of power. Despite efforts to increase customer care and services, the tax systems in all three countries still appear adversely affected by lack of trust that again manifests itself in low levels of voluntary compliance. In part, this is due to the external accountability dimension of tax reforms in Sub Saharan Africa. So far, the need to satisfy donor conditionality for increased tax/GDP ratios appears to have weighed more heavily on the Ugandan, Tanzanian, and Zambian authorities than any concern with building a (semi) voluntary tax relationship with its own citizens.

External accountability

With aid increasingly being conditional and with tax reform part of the conditionality agenda, aid and taxation *may* be positively related. But is this so? Has *external accountability* aimed at strengthening domestic accountability structures through tax reforms succeeded, or has external accountability relations in fact hampered the development of domestic structures for democratic accountability? There are—as we have seen—indications that it may not be so easy to introduce democratic accountability through externally imposed tax reforms. The tax reforms carried out in Tanzania, Uganda, and Zambia have, to a large extent, been formulated and imposed by the international donor community. In all three countries, the IMF has maintained a lead role in advising governments on major issues of design of tax policies. To meet the targets set by the IMF and the Ministry of Finance, the revenue authorities have focussed on increasing collection and compliance from existing taxpayers rather than attempting the more complicated task of widening the tax base. The long-term process of building wide tax nets and cultures of voluntary compliance requires different and more time-consuming practices. According to the evaluation by DFID in 2001, some countries have concentrated exclusively on increased compliance by known (existing) tax payers—at the expense of widening the tax net—in order to meet IMF demands (DFID 2001, 52). These processes are also politically more sensitive, as the resistance to taxing agriculture in Uganda and Zambia indicates. In the case of Uganda, Therkildsen (2002, 28) argues that donors and the Ugandan Ministry of Finance, by pushing for high revenue targets, have undermined the Uganda Revenue Authority's credibility in the eyes of the public, as the targets have been unrealistically high.

There are also incidences where attempts to meet externally set tax GDP targets may undermine democratic accountability, as legal processes and tax payers' rights are set side in order to comply with external accountability demands. The semi-military operations to prevent smuggling and tax evasion in Uganda are illustrative. During the 1990s a succession of more or less militarized units have been established to curb smuggling and tax evasion, such as the Anti-Smuggling Unit (ASU), followed by the Revenue Protection Service (RPS) and the

Table 3.2 Reform of tax administration in the 1990s

Reform of tax administration	Expected effect on accountability	Tanzania	Uganda	Zambia
New Revenue Authority	Positive—Depending on internal accountability	TRA 1995	URA 1991	ZRA 1994
Answerability/Autonomy	Positive	More, but not financial independence	Reduced since 1996, no financial independence	No financial independence, MOF grants exemptions
Controllability/Corruption	Negative	Less, but increasing	Remains major concern	Reduced
Transparency/Responsiveness	Positive	Positive-emerging Task Force on Taxation	Positive Tax Appeals Tribunal (1997), Taxpayers Charter (2002)	Emerging Task Force on Taxation

Special Revenue Protection Service (Kjær, 2000; Therkildsen, 2002). As these operations have been staffed by military personnel, the practice should be characterized as a militarization of the revenue collection. The Ugandan press has carried numerous articles reporting on the public complaints about the misbehavior of these units.[18] The anti-smuggling units employed by the Ugandan government represents one of the most blatant examples of how the long-term process of building a tax culture based on quasi-voluntary compliance is undermined by the short-term goal of meeting tax demands set by the international finance institutions.

CONCLUDING REMARKS

In this chapter we have discussed whether recent tax reforms have contributed to the goal of increasing state accountability to citizens-taxpayers in Sub Saharan Africa. The view that taxation produces more representative government is based on a common interpretation of political development in early modern Europe and colonial America. Theoretical literature concludes that domestically derived revenues will spark demands for citizens' participation and contribute to democratic accountability in state-society relations. In the context of Africa, so far little is actually known about the relationship between taxation and democracy. There are, however, a number of reasons why we may expect the taxation-accountability link to become more prevalent in Sub Saharan Africa. As part of the economic restructuring processes, many African countries have embarked on the process of replacing the import and export taxes that used to be a major source of income with levies that bear more directly on individual citizens and enterprises. In a situation of decreasing aid transfers, many countries are currently reforming their tax systems in order to derive more revenue from their citizens. At the same time, a great majority of Africa's nations have in the early 1990s moved toward pluralist systems of rule. However, for taxation to create the unintended consequence of a "governance bonus" to the extent that states become more responsive to citizens' demands, taxes must, first of all, be broad-based. At a minimum, the economic and political elites must be covered by the tax net. Taxation-accountability linkages are products of consistent long-term political, institutional, and cultural processes. As a result, it may not be surprising that the tax reforms in Tanzania, Uganda, and Zambia so far only to a limited degree have contributed to increasing state accountability to citizens/tax payers. It is, however, worrying that donors' insistence that states meet short and medium targets for increasing revenue collections appear to mitigate against accountability to citizens. In some instances, arbitrary,

Table 3.3 Nature of tax reform in the 1990s

Form of taxation	Expected accountability effect	Tanzania	Uganda	Zambia
Direct taxes (Personal income tax, Corporation tax)	Visible, "felt" taxes—positive Accountability Effect	Little change. Collection targeted on business corporations	New Income Tax act; increased compliance; but little emphasis on informal sector; business targeted	Little change. Limited to formal sector; major exemptions granted large corporations
Indirect taxes	Less visible, narrow reach—less clear accountability effect	57% total revenue*	82.5 total revenue**	61% total revenue***
Export taxes Import taxes Excise duties		Eliminated Replaced export taxes Little change	Eliminated Replaced export taxes Increases	Eliminated Replaced export taxes Little change
VAT	Visible, "felt" taxes with broad reach—positive Accountability Effect	VAT introduced in 1998, but most basic goods exempted; narrow reach	VAT introduced in 1996 at 17%. Initial strikes and riots by business. Agriculture and basic goods exempted	VAT introduced in 1995 at 17.5%. Agriculture and basic goods exempted; narrow reach

*1997/98 Financial year, source: TRA Annual Report
**1998/99 Financial year, Annual Background to Budget. Republic of Uganda
***1997/98 Financial year, Ministry of Finance, Republic of Zambia

coercive treatment of taxpayers by revenue officials has been motivated by the need to meet donor-imposed revenue targets. Nevertheless, our analysis does find evidence that there may be a more positive connection, in the longer term, between these donor-imposed targets and accountability. Commercial businesses are beginning to use their associations to interact with government and revenue authorities over tax collection procedures. While there can be no doubt that this mobilization is motivated by businesses' desire to reduce tax payments, the fact is that these issues are being treated through formal public organizations, rather than through bribery and public deals. This may have positive consequences for legality, legitimacy, and accountability in environments where taxpayers currently have few or no legal rights.

Acknowledgements

Lise Rakner is a Senior Researcher at the Michelsen Institute in Bergen, Norway. Siri Gloppen is a Postdoctoral Fellow, Department of Political Science, University of Bergen. This paper was written in connection with the research program Taxation, aid and democracy funded by the Norwegian Research Council and Danida. A shorter version has been published as "Accountability through Tax Reforms? Reflections from Sub-Saharan Africa", in M. Moore and L. Rakner (eds.), *The New Politics of Taxation and Accountability*. IDS Bulletin 33 (3) July 2002. We thank Odd Helge Fjeldstad, Bertil Tungodden, Mick Moore, Deborah Brautigam, and Nicolas van de Walle for their constructive comments.

Notes

1   Arguably, there may be a number of reasons for governments to emphasize so-called easy taxes, or indirect taxes that do not affect the individual taxpayer directly. In poor African countries, these taxes are often the most important taxes and effective taxation demands a focus on these taxes. However, a tax-system that primarily is based on indirect taxes cannot be expected to yield a so called governance bonus or a democratic accountability effect, which is the focus of this chapter.

2   The discussion here parallels Schedler's distinction between two dimensions of accountability; "enforcement" and "answerability," in which the latter consists of two parts—monitoring and justification. (Schedler 1999, pp. 13–29). See also G. O'Donnell (1999, pp. 29–71) with comments by R. L Sklar, P. Schmitter, and M. F. Plattner.

3   Part of this discussion is based on Mick Moore and Lise Rakner (2002): "Introduction: The New Politics of Taxation and Accountability." *IDS Bulletin* 33 (3).

4 Ghana (1985), Uganda (1991), Zambia (1994), Kenya (1995), South Africa (1996), Tanzania (1996), Rwanda (2000), and Malawi (2000).

5 For Zambia, see Harvey et al. (1996); Gray, Shera, and Condy (2001). For Tanzania, see Fjeldstad (2002); Rakner (2001); Temu and Due (2000). For Uganda, see Obwona (2001); Gray, Karuga, and Ssemegere (2001); Therkildsen 2002.

6 However, due to a 2 percent contraction of the Zambian economy between 1997 and 1999, the GDP/tax ratio is probably not an adequate reflection of the efficiency of the Zambian Revenue Authority (Gray, Shera and Condy 2001).

7 The pattern of initial increases in revenue collection followed by subsequent stagnation or decline is also found in the case of Ghana (Devas et al. 2001) and Kenya (Glenday 1997).

8 The countries included in the evaluation are Ghana, Pakistan, Uganda, and Zambia.

9 Interview, Justin Zake, Uganda Revenue Authorities, Kampala April 4, 2001.

10 Partly, this is explained by the fact that Dar es Salaam is the major import harbor, from which both consumer and capital goods are transported across the country.

11 As agricultural products and inputs are zero-rated, in effect the greatest benefits are accruing to large commercial farmers who purchase inputs.

12 Personal communications, Hajih Semboja, member of Taxation Task Force, Dar es Salaam, March 22, 2001.

13 Business confidence surveys carried out in Lusaka and on the Copperbelt confirm these perspectives. See M. Taylor and D. Aarnes (2002).

14 Interview, Benno Ndulu March 28, 2001, World Bank, Dar es Salaam, first chairman of the board of the Tanzanian Revenue Authority.

15 In the case of Zambia, the relationship between business and the Chiluba administration has been poor/non-existent since 1996. However, the new MMD administration taking office after the 2001 elections has opened for more active consultations with business. Among other things, the Mwanawasa government has reconstituted a dormant tax policy review committee. According to the ministry of finance, as a way of reinforcing the consultative process, the committee will now open for written submissions from the private sector, non-governmental organizations, and the public regarding tax and non-tax revenue proposals (*Post* June 11, 2002).

16 Personal communications, Hajih Semboja, member of Taxation Task Force, Dar es Salaam, 22/3 2001.

17 We are grateful to Odd Helge Fjeldstad for bringing this difference between Uganda and Tanzania to our attention.

18 To illustrate: "Traders Accuse URA" (of using a militarized approach), *New Vision* November 11, 1993; "Stop Using Guns, URA told," *New Vision* September 3, 1994; "Col. Lutaya's ASU Won't Draw Any tears," *Monitor*, November 13, 1995.

References

Adam. M. and C. Caiphas (2002): "Subterranean sector and tax evasion in Uganda's small firms" Institute of Economics, Makerere University. Paper presented at the Taxation, Aid and Democracy Workshop, Windhoek, Namibia 4–5 April.

Anene, C. and Z. Gariyo (2001): "The rights of tax payers vis-à-vis tax authorities in Uganda". Paper prepared for the Taxation, Aid, and Democracy Research Programme. Chr. Michelsen Institute, Bergen, Norway.

Bailyn, Bernard (1967): *The Ideological Origins of the American Revolution.* Boston, MA: Harvard University Press.

Bratton, M. and N. van de Walle (1997): *Democratic Experiments in Africa Regime Transitions in Comparative Perspective.* New York: Cambridge University Press.

Brautigam, D. (2002): "Building leviathan: Revenue, state capacity and governance," in M. Moore and L. Rakner (2002) (eds).

Brautigam, D. and S. Knack (2002): "Foreign Aid, Institutions and Governance in Sub-Saharan Africa", *Economic Development and Cultural Change* Vol. 52, no. 2 (Jan. 2004, Forthcoming).

Brautigam, D. (1999): *Aid Dependence and Governance.* Stockholm: Almquist and Wicksell International.

Brautigam, Deborah (1991): "Governance and Economy: A Review", *Policy Research Papers,* no. WPS 815, The World Bank.

Geoffrey Brennan and James Buchanan: *The Power to Tax: Analytical Foundations of a Fiscal Constitution* (Cambridge: Cambridge University Press, 1980).

Department of International Development (DFID) (2000): *Making Government Work for Poor People.* London: Department of International Development

Department of International Development (DFID) (2001): *Evaluation of Revenue Projects. Evaluation Summary EV 636* (February).

Fjeldstad, Odd Helge (2002): "Fighting fiscal corruption: The case of the Tanzania Revenue Authority," *CMI Working Paper* WP 2002:3. Ch2. Michelten Institute, Beyen, Norway.

Fjeldstad, Odd Helge, Ole Therkildsen, Lise Rakner, and Joseph Semboja (2000): "Taxation, Aid and Democracy. An Agenda for Research in African Countries," *CDR Working Paper* no. 5 Copenhagen: Centre for Development Research, (June).

Friedman, S. and D. Hlope (2002): " . . . And their hearts and minds will follow . . . ? Tax collection, authority and legitimacy in democratic South Africa" in M. Moore and L. Rakner (2002).

Gariyo, Zie (2000): "The politics of the introduction and implementation of VAT." Report submitted to the Taxation, Aid and Democracy research program.

Gauthier, B. and R. Reinikka (2001): "Shifting tax burdens through exemptions and evasion: An empirical investigation of Uganda." *Policy Research Working Paper,* no. 2735. Washington, D.C.: The World Bank (December).

Ghura, D. (1998): "Tax revenue in sub-Saharan Africa: effects of economic policies and corruption." *IMF Working Paper* 98/135. International Monetary Fund Washinton D.C.

Glenday, G. (1997): "Capacity building in the context of the Kenya Tax Modernization Program," in Grindle, M. S. (ed.) *Getting Good Government: Capacity Building in the Public Sectors of Developing Countries.* Harvard: Harvard University Press.

Gray, J., F. Shera, and A. Condy (2001): "Evaluation of the Zambia Revenue Authority consolidation project." Evaluation Study carried out by Department of International Development (DFID) (February).

Gray, J., J. Karuga and G. Ssemogerere (2001): "Evaluation of the Uganda Revenue Authority project." Evaluation Study carried out by Department of International Development (DFID) (February).

Guyer, J (1992): "Representation without taxation: An essay on democracy in rural Nigeria, 1952–1990" *African Studies Review*, vol. 35, no. 1 (April).

Harvey, C et al. (1996): "Taxation policy in Bangladesh, Sri Lanka, Uganda and Zambia." *Working Paper No 8 Task Force on Poverty Reduction*. Swedish International Development cooperation Agency (SIDA): Stockholm.

Joshi, A. and J. Ayee (2002): "Taxing for the state? Politics, revenue and the informal sector in Ghana," in M. Moore and L. Rakner (2002).

Kasimbazi, Emmanuel (2002): "Taxpayers' rights and obligations: analysis of implementation and enforcement mechanisms in Uganda." Report, submitted to the Taxation, Aid and Democracy Research Programme. Chr. Michelsen Institute, Bergen, Norway.

Kjær, M. (2000): Governance and the management of tax reform: The Ugandan case." Mimeo. Department of Political Science, University of Århus, Denmark, pp. 1–17.

Levi, Margaret, 1988, *Of Rule and Revenue*. Berkeley: University of California Press.

Luoga, F. F. (2001): "Taxpayers' rights and obligations: A survey of the legal situation in Tanzania." Report submitted to the Taxation, Aid and Democracy Research Programme. Chr. Michelsen Institute, Bergen, Norway.

Moore, Mick (1998): "Death without taxes," in Mark Robinson and Gordon White (eds.) *The Democratic Developmental State. Political and Institutional Design*. Oxford: Oxford University Press.

Moore, Mick and Lise Rakner (eds.) (2002): "Introduction: The New Politics of Taxation and Accountability in Developing Countries," *IDS Bulletin* 33 (3) (July).

O'Donnell, G. (1999): "Horizontal Accountability in New Democracies" with comments by R. L Sklar, P. Schmitter, and M. F. Plattner in Schedler et al. (eds.), pp. 29–71.

Obwona. M. and A. Muwonge (2001): "The efficiency and effectiveness of the revenue administration in Uganda." Report, submitted to the Taxation, Aid and Democracy Research Programme. Chr. Michelsen Institute, Bergen, Norway.

Rakner, L (2001): "Tax policies in Tanzania in the 1990s: Relations between state, interest groups and donors" (in Norwegian). *Den Ny Verden* vol. 34, pp. 79–93.

Rakner, L. and L. Svåsand (2002): "From dominant to fragmented party system: Zambia 1991–2001." Paper presented at "Analysing political processes in the context of the 2001 Zambian elections" workshop. Lusaka, Zambia June 5–6, 2002.

Schedler, Andreas. (1999): "Conceptualizing Accountability," in Schedler Andreas, and (eds,) *The Self-Restraining State.* Lary Diamond and Marc Plattner Boulder, Col.: Lynne Rienner Publishers, pp. 13–29.

Schumpeter, Joseph A. [1918] (1954): "The crisis of the tax state," *International Economic Papers* No. 4 eds. A peacock et al. London: Macmillan Ltd.

Ssewakiryanga, R. (2000): "No representation without taxation! Reflections on tax as site of socio-political struggles in the Ugandan 1996 VAT strike." Occasional paper, *Centre for Basic Research*, Kampala, Uganda.

Steinmo, Sven, 1993, *Taxation and Democracy. Swedish, British and American Approaches to Financing the Modern State*, New Haven Conn.: Yale University Press.

Stotsky, J. G. and Mariam Wolde A. (1997): "Tax effort in sub-Saharan Africa." *IMF Working Paper*, WP 97/107 (September).

Taylor, M. and D. Aarnes (2002): "Rebuilding confidence. Business attitudes to the electoral process in Zambia." Paper presented at workshop. Analysing political processes in the context of the 2001 Zambian elections workshop Lusaka, Zambia June 5–6, 2002.

Temu, A. and J. Due (2000): "The business environment in Tanzania after socialism: Challenges of reforming banks, parastatals, taxation and the civil service," *Journal of Modern African Studies*, vol. 38, no. 4, pp. 683–712.

Therkildsen, O. (2002): "Uganda Revenue Authorities: the limits of autonomy." Paper presented at the Taxation, Aid and Democracy Workshop, Windhoek, Namibia 4–5 April.

Therkildsen, O. (2001): "Understanding taxation in poor African countries: A critical review of selected perspectives." *Forum for Development Studies*, vol. 28, no. 1, pp. 99–125.

Therkper, S. (1999): "Revenue authorities—a comparison of the experience of Ghana and East African Countries." Bulletin for *International Fiscal Documentation* vol. 53. no. 4 (April), pp. 171–179.

Tilly, Charles, 1992, *Coercion, Capital and European States, AD 1990–1992.* Oxford, UK: Blackwell.

Van de Walle, N. Colas. (2001) *African Economies and The Politics of Permanent Crisis, 1979–1999* (Cambridge: Cambridge University Press).

World Bank (1998): *Assessing Aid: What Works, What Doesn't, and Why.* New York: Oxford University Press.

CHAPTER 4

AFRICAN GOVERNANCE AND CIVIL SERVICE REFORMS

DELE OLOWU

INTRODUCTION AND OVERVIEW

African civil services—as well as other components of the public service: parastatals and local governments—were created in the colonial period and patterned after the models of the colonizing power. The poor fit between expectations and actual performance has made them perpetual objects of reform in the post-independence era in most countries. In the wake of the economic and fiscal crises of the late 1970s, special attention has focused on revitalizing African civil services, originally as a part of programs of structural adjustment and state cutback. African civil services were perceived as bloated and a drain on the state's scarce resources. Even the state was seen as an obstacle to development. It was an institution that constrained the private sector from unleashing its productive potentials. Civil Service Reform (CSR) was thus a part of the program of rolling back the state.

Over time, it became clear that this approach to Africa's institutional reform was flawed. First, Africa's capacity for development and policy management already low (due to historical reasons of being a late starter in development), further declined in the two decades (1980s to 2000) of state rollback. Civil Service Reforms had contributed to the decline of state capacity at a time when it had become evident even to International Finance Institutions (IFIs), which increasingly took responsibilities for setting and managing Africa's development agenda, that the state was important for development. Hence, in its famous *World Development Report 1997*, The World Bank conceded that economic reforms—including structural adjustment—were not enough to bring about sustainable development. The state's capacity for promoting development needed to be enhanced especially in the face of the relentless pressures towards democratization and globalization. The civil service, recognized as the "core" public service, was an instrument of the state whose capacity must be substantially increased. The historical experiences of western industrialized countries and the newly industrializing countries of East Asia were used to highlight the type of strategies needed to boost the performance and capacity of the civil service. These perspectives were, however, not incorporated into most of the African CSR programmes—even though most of these were influenced and/or managed by the bank.

I intend to evaluate what has been referred to as the first- and second-generation reforms of African civil-service reforms as promoted by bilateral donors and especially The World Bank in the region since the late 1970s. Second-generation reforms, like those of the first, have not substantially improved the quality of the African civil services (Numberg 1996; Lienert 1998; Haq and Aziz 1999). I will review this evidence—as well that as of other reforms undertaken by national governments in the region with minimal external inputs—and provide an explanation for the perpetual poor performance of civil-service reforms in Africa. The argument made is that civil service as social institutions operate in three worlds of action: at operational, collective choice, and constitutive choice levels. At the *operational level*, choices regarding day-to-day operations are made. The structures, which make these decisions, are set at a deeper level, at the level of *collective choice* in which rules on how decisions will be made at the operational level are set. Finally, at the deepest level, *the constitutive level*, fundamental rules governing the structures of collective choice institutions are set (Kiser and Ostrom 1982; Bekke et. al 1996). Current CSRs restrict their analysis of civil services to the operational level. Proponents of reforms are yet to appreciate the governance and constitutive roles of civil services. This chapter therefore takes as its departure point two fundamental contentions. First, that the failure of CSRs is due more to poor policy and program design rather than poor implementation, as is often contended by proponents of reform. This is not to deny the existence of implementation problems—which can also be quite real—but only to place them in proper perspective. Civil Service Reforms are designed to respond mainly to quantitative questions ignoring important qualitative problems and roles of African civil services. Second, therefore, this chapter takes an institutional analytical perspective that views civil service institutions in terms of their three worlds of action: as personnel agencies of the state (operational choice), as institutions of policy making by societal stakeholders (collective choice) and as institutions that mediate the fundamental (governance) relationships between the rulers and the ruled (constitutional choice).

The chapter starts by defining civil service as institutions of the state and of the society. It then goes on to evaluate the first two generations of civil service reforms in Africa. After this, it identifies the major weaknesses in the current approach to CSR and suggests an alternative. The chapter is thus developed under the following subheads:

- The Role of the State in Development: Civil Services as State and Society Institutions
- Evaluation of Civil Service Reforms Since the 1980s
- Explaining the Failure of African CSRs
- Towards a New Genre of CSRs

The Role of the State in Development: Civil Services as State and Society Institutions

A major debate that civil service reform subsumes is the role that the state should play in development. Two schools of thought have developed on this subject. The first school, subscribed by many African states at the time of their independence is a *maximalist state*, for want of a better concept. It is a state, which stands above society and is responsible not only for law and order and major social and economic management but is also in charge of the "commanding heights" of the economy. The key instruments of the state in achieving its objectives were five-yearly dirigiste development plans, import substituting industrialization, socialization and nationalization of the economy and rapid indigenisation of the top personnel of the public sector (Adedeji 1981). Unfortunately, this activist role for the state was poorly performed and in the midst of the crisis associated with the oil shocks of the 1970s, a second school of thought emerged—led by Elliott Berg and the World Bank (1981).

This school recommended a *minimalist* role for African states as the state was perceived not only as incompetent its developmental roles but had become an obstacle to economic growth in that it repressed the productive forces in society—namely the private sector, the engine of growth and civil society organs. The task of reform is to remove this obstacle through programmes of cutback management. However, years of structural adjustment underscored the fact that in spite of the several failures of the state, it was still essential for providing the enabling environment for other institutions to emerge as productive institutions (given an equally systemic market failure). What was needed was not state reduction as such but state transformation.

Analysis of the experiences of the industrialized states and the high performing (Southeast) Asian economies (HPAEs) note the inappropriateness of the minimalist state in a developmental context. The crisis of production, which underlined the fiscal and economic crises that many countries confronted in the late 1970s, represented indeed a crisis of the state. The problem was not with state intervention but with the quality of that intervention. Paradoxically, in the Bank's study on HPAEs, it argued that "economic contests require competent and impartial referees—that is, strong institutions ... a high quality civil service that has the capacity to monitor performance and is insulated from political interference is essential to contest-based competition" (WB 1996: 11). A year later, the World Bank extended this argument when it argued that: *An effective state is vital for the provision of the goods and services—and the rules and institutions—that allow markets to flourish and people to lead healthier, happier lives. Without it, sustainable development, both economic and social, is impossible* (WB 1997: 1). It then went on to identify what constituted the basic functions of an effective (or more appropriately, a developmental) state as including—the provision of (a) the foundation of law, (b) a non-distortionary policy environment including macro-economic stability, (c) investments in basic social services and infrastructure and (d) protection of the vulnerable and (e) of the environment.

CIVIL SERVICE AND DEVELOPMENT

Each of these functions requires states, which have the necessary political, technical and administrative capacities. Table 4.1 shows the capacities required by states and the civil services to perform the basic roles expected by citizens. Democratization in the Africa region has placed even greater premium on these roles for open and technically sophisticated policies that achieve predetermined objectives (Grindle 1996). Besides, civil services are often called upon to help develop the capacities of the private sector, non-governmental organizations and actively engage external actors (including) donors at all levels of governance (UNDP 1996). The recommendation that countries with minimal capacity pursue limited state roles (as argued in the WDR 1997) is therefore not only counterproductive but may actually provide the justification for policies which rob these states of their scarce human resource capacity. Table 4.2 suggests that contrary to the impression that African civil services are too large in their total numbers, they are actually smaller than civil services in any of the world's regions. The problem is therefore not of numbers but the quality of those serving as civil servants. Data in Table 4.2 confirm other research on African public services that

Table 4.1 Governance Capacities—SSA

Capacity	Attributes	Possible Measuring Indices	SSA Situation Report
Political	Effective and legitimate channels for societal demand making, representation and conflict resolution.	• Legislative Effectiveness in audits	Weak but improving
	Responsive political leaders and administrators. Societal participation in decision-making.	• Voter Turn-out	
Regulatory	Establishment & Enforcement of State rules that regulate & supersede societal behavior/ rule of law	• Alternative claimants to sovereign power • Black Markets • Central Bank autonomy/effectiveness	Weak
Administrative	Routine management of state personnel & resources efficiently & accountably	• Turn-over/stability of top officials • No of govt accountants • Public/private sector wage ratio • Access to safe water	Weak
Technical	Expertise to make/ implement technical decisions	• Ratio of expatriate personnel • Ratio of science graduates/students • Literacy rate	Weak/Degrading
Extractive	Raise revenues for state needs	• Revenue:GNP • Direct:indirect tax • Ratio of fiscal reliance	Low
Delegational	Delegation of governance to regions, localities or judicial, legislative, CSOs	• CSOs role in budget making • LGs size (expenditures/ employees	Small

Source: Adapted from Brautigam, 1996; Grindle, 1996

Table 4.2   Government Employment as % of Population, 1997

Region	No. of Countries in Sample	Total Govt	Central Govt	Local Govt	Teaching & Health	Wages as % of GDP
Africa	20	2.0	0.9	**0.3**	0.8	6.7
Asia	11	2.6	0.9	**0.7**	1.0	4.7
Eastern Europe & former USSR	17	6.9	1.0	**0.8**	5.1	3.9
Latin American & Caribbean	9	3.0	1.2	**0.7**	1.1	4.9
Middle East & North Africa	8	3.9	1.4	**0.9**	1.6	9.8
OECD	21	7.7	1.8	**2.5**	3.4	4.5
Total	86	4.7	1.2	**1.1**	2.4	

Source: Schiavo-Campo, 1998

they are few not only in absolute numbers per population but also in terms of effective, well-resourced local governments close and responsive to citizens (United Nations 1992, Ginnekken 1991).

It is at the most critical level—the higher civil service (HCS)—in which African civil services are weakest. HCS are critical to the performance of any civil service (see for instance a good discussion of the French and British civil services respectively in Rouban 1996, Pilkington 1999 and Table 3). The issue is best captured by a review of the crucial role that this crop of officials have played in the Japanese development experience:

> Top civil servants have to bridge the world of administration and the world of politics, and to monitor the traffic back and forth, ensuring that the people reporting to them understand that they have to meet political goals and needs. At the same time, they also have to protect the administrative bureaucracy from day-to-day interventions by politicians who want to, for example, make sure that the new bridge is built in their district or constructed by their relatives' companies. (Kim 1996:5).

Several studies on the subject demonstrate the tendency for African public services to be "understaffed at the top but overstaffed at the bottom" (UN 1992: 16). Generally, the combination of economic and political factors has led to a severe hemorrhage of the best and brightest from African civil services. Poor economic performance sets severe limits to how much the state can pay its officials—a factor that led to severe wage erosion. But it is poor politics that aggravates matters as these introduce other more pernicious problems confronted by African civil services—severe wage compression, politicization and poor accountability regimes at the very top (Lindauer and Numberg 1994, Adamolekun 1999). These emanate from the symptoms of bad politics or bad governance, some of which have survived the second wave of democratization: the breakdown of the public realm due to personalization of power either by single parties or military regimes, prevalence of neo-patrimonial forms of rule, non-delegation by central authorities to other governance organs, withdrawal from politics by the masses and the resurgence of external forces (Hyden 1992, 1999, Baker 1998). For instance, the personalized nature of rule "means not only that public policy making lacks logic and empirical content that typically characterizes such an activity in other contexts but also that governance structures are largely informal and subject to arbitrary change" (Hyden 1992: 23).

Similarly, politicization of the most senior positions in the civil service lowers morale and undermines performance of those who work in the civil service. It is these trends that make the state to perform poorly in terms of internal, fiscal and economic management, policy implementation and revenue mobilization—and any attempt at CSR which focuses on numbers and cost alone is bound to miss out on the embeddedness of the civil service. I return to these issues again later in the paper. But the point being made here is that African states were not only suffering from the lack of capacities. Indeed, a major reason why they lacked essential capacities was because of the quality of governance. Of the greatest importance is therefore the need for political capacity to sustain a democratic climate, ensure the capacity to regulate and work with other institutional actors in policy management and to provide and sustain the wide array of public services required by a modern state.

The forces of globalization and democratization provided further rationale for the existence of states with reliable civil service capacities. While globalization underscores the importance of technical prerequisites of the civil service, democratization calls for civil services, which are at the same time subservient to and relatively autonomous of the political leadership (Etzioni-Halevy 1983, Suleiman 1999). This category of civil servants—professional, objective, rational and neutral—have always been scarce in African civil services. How to attract, retain and motivate them—not only at the centre but also in the localities and other centers of a polycentric state—ought to have become a major preoccupation of the CSR goals but this has not been the case. Rather,

African CSRs failed to recognize the important differentiation in the civil service—between the cadres at the base, which had a surplus, and the topmost cadre, which had a large number of vacancies—as a result of a mixture of supply and demand factors. Primary focus was on the lowest levels where progressive compression of civil service salaries over the years had produced a large and unnecessary oversupply of employees.

The above casts aspersion on the theoretical basis of the reforms. CSRs assumed a minimalist state with strong rhetoric on the power of the market, whereas the reality of development experience dictated the need to nurture developmental states, which works actively with all other institutional actors in society. These two models are poles apart. But this raises important questions of the expected roles of the civil service within the state and society.

Civil Service and Democratization

Some scholars argue that civil services are not linked to any identifiable theory of the social sciences, but renewed interest in the concept and role of the state in development, in institutional analysis and bureaucratic and post-bureaucratic models provide us with a wealth of insights into this crucial institution (Bekke et.al 1996). Significantly, most of the policy interest in reforming African civil services in recent years has come from economists and international finance institutions in their efforts to help resolve the fiscal crisis of the state from the late 1970s. CSR packages have thus been conceived as a part of structural adjustment programmes (SAPs) with three unfortunate results. This approach has had three results from the point of view of institutional design. First, civil services are perceived almost exclusively as instruments of the state and hence, secondly, CSRs are designed as a part of the programme of state-cut-back. Thirdly, the approach has also led to a pre-occupation with the quantitative aspects of the civil service—the numbers of persons in the civil service and their cost. Indeed, the primary objective of CSR, as originally conceived within SAP, was the reduction of the cost and numbers of people in the civil service. This confines CSR to the operational level of analysis. However, as noted above, the World Bank now identifies the civil service as one of the crucial institutions of an effective state. Three of the reasons it gave for the importance of the civil service were its roles in policy making, in ensuring accountability and transparency between the rulers and the ruled and through this arrangement, in the delivery of services at least cost (World Bank 1997:79–98). These roles require discussion.

Civil servants do not make policies as such but senior civil servants assist in formulating alternative options for the formal decision-makers— the elected politicians. As people with specialized skills and often with a lifetime commitment to their career, they bring into the policy process information and expertise, which inform the decisions of politicians and other social actors. Different countries combine the technical and political functions and expertise differently—depending on their social ideology, but the idea that civil servants provide technical information is one that is universally subscribed (Aberbach et. al 1981, Adamolekun 1986, Suleiman 1999). Education, long training, and tenure are powerful advantages in favor of especially the senior civil servants, facts that lead to a tendency for them to exercise more power in the policy process in some developing countries (Riggs 1964, Hyden 1984). This critical role of the civil service as institutions engaged in policymaking is often lost to those who are preoccupied with numbers and cost. They thus focus on the lower cadres—where there are often substantial surpluses—whereas it is the top layers of the civil service (formally referred to as the higher civil service [HCS]) that is tasked with policy formulation responsibilities. Unfortunately, civil services under current reforms are treated as if they were undifferentiated entities. The HCS comprises highly skilled people and are expensive to groom, attract, keep and manage especially in all countries, not less so in developing countries (Rouban 1998, Pilkington 1999). The result of two decades of CSRs which have been preoccupied with the reduction of numbers and costs has led to a situation in which the civil services of these countries have been denuded of the brightest and best HCS and the policy process has been abdicated by default to consultants, international financial institutions and expatriate technical advisers. (Jaycox 1983, Court et al. 1999). One response has been to import very expensive short-term technical assistance to replace lost indigenous manpower—at multiples of the cost of retaining the latter (Klitgaard 1989, Haq & Aziz 1999).

In addition, civil service systems also symbolize aspects of a society's constitutional order—as mediators and as instruments of asserting accountability between the rulers and the ruled. Civil service systems are organized in such a way that they are subordinated to the political class—who are the representatives of the public. The political executive is accountable to the legislature and the public for the overall performance of each department of the civil service. Different political systems have evolved diverse ways of expressing this relationship, but universally, they serve as symbols of constitutional order and the fundamental constitutive choices made by a society in respect of its governance (Bekke et al 1996). Even though subordinated to political executives, HCS are required to serve as neutral political actors in helping to resolve the tension between the partisan and state interests of their superiors. They do this by developing principles or criteria for distributing policy benefits which are rational, objective, non-partisan and reflect society's fundamental values of equity, justice, efficiency and effectiveness (Haque et al. 1997).

Eva Etzioni-Harlevy (1983: 90–92) argues that the role of top civil servants as rational, objective actors in the policy process is critical to maintaining the balance between political party leadership and the pursuit of the public interest in a democracy. HCS acts as a counterbalance to purely political and partisan pressure in the allocation of scarce resources, which is the essence of all political activities. Such ideas are being echoed today in the analysis of efforts to rebuild democracy in the former soviet republics (Suleiman 1999). These two roles of the HCS— the constitutive and policy roles—are distinct from the civil service's role of regulating and delivering public services at least cost—using a variety of agencies within and outside the public sector.

The above points underscore the fundamentally political roles of the civil service in any culture but often times, it is their economic roles as agents of production that gets the greater attention.

Evaluation of Civil Service Reforms Since the 1980s

As already noted above, African civil services have been subjected to reforms since the colonial period. This section reviews the experiences of the post-1970 period for two reasons. First, reforms of the immediate post-independence period have been extensively reviewed. They were premised on the growth, expansion and dominance of the public sector within the national economy (see AAPAM 1984, Mutahaba et al 1991, UNECA 1996). Secondly, the failure of this centralizing governance model and of their degeneration into patrimonial rule is also well researched (Wunsch & Olowu 1990, Davidson 1993, Hyden 2000).

African CSRs since the fiscal crisis of the late 1970s have been conventionally classified into two generations of reforms. First generation reforms took place in the late 1970s up to the mid-1980s as a part of the first set of structural adjustment programmes while the second generation ones were designed and implemented from the later parts of the 1980s to the 1990s. For instance, the Ghanaian CSR, which started in 1983, is regarded as an example of a first generation reform whereas the Ugandan CSR, which began in 1989, is widely referred to by its protagonists as an example of a second generation CSR. The key elements of first and second-generation reforms are highlighted in table 4.3. The elements of first generation reforms include: the elimination of ghost workers, downsizing, privatization and contractorization, departmental restructuring, improved budgeting expenditure controls and reform of pay and grading—essentially the consolidation of diverse remuneration systems. (See Olowu 1999). The overall rationale of these reforms was to cut public expenditure and revive the private sector. They were also managed as individual projects with premium placed on technical solutions by external consultants.

The World Bank was responsible for most of the first generation reform efforts and most of its Structural Adjustment Loans (SALs) were directed at revitalizing the civil service were carried out in Africa. Its own internal reviews showed that these reforms were not achieving their objectives (Numberg 1996). The most important achievement of these early CSRs—the reduction of numbers—was compromised by the fact that many states brought back some of the employees already laid off into other departments, referred to as the "revolving door" problem (Lindauer & Numberg 1984). On the other hand, the capacity of the civil service degenerated. A new set of reforms was proposed (see table 4.4).* The Uganda CSR for instance, included, not just the civil service but the local governments as well. The overall objective was also changed—to the improvement of management and efficiency and

Table 4.3   Roles, Expectations and Performancer of the Higher Civil Service

Essential State Function	Required Skills	Actual Performance (Africa)
Service Delivery Policy	Administrative	Medium
• Institutional Delivery Mechanisms • Scope of Services • Criteria for Evaluation		
Policy Management	Technical	Medium
• Information Processing • Articulation of Alternatives • Consultations with key stakeholders • Regulation of Service • Performance Evaluation/Reporting		
Accountability	Political	Low
• Managing Internal & External Accountability—Anti-Corruption • Liaison with external agencies & interest groups/conflict resolution		

Table 4.4   The Evolution of Civil Service Reform Programmes

RATTIONALE	Cut Public Expenditure Revive the Private Sector	Improve Government Efficiency & Effectiveness
CONTENT	• Elimination of ghost workers • Downsizing • Privatization & Contractorisation • Departmental Restructuring • Improved Budgeting & Expenditure Controls • Reform of Pay & Grading	• Creation of Semi-autonomous central government agencies • Decentralization • Human Resource Management Reforms-recruitment, selection, performance management • Anti-corruption Measures
MANAGEMENT	• Individual Projects • Technical Solutions devised by external consultants	• Comprehensive CSRs • Local Ownership, supported by external technical expertise

Adapted from D. Goldsworthy, 2000, p. 11

effectiveness in government rather than simply cutting back numbers, size and cost, although these continued to be key objectives of such CSRs. This was what was referred to as comprehensive civil service reform, and great emphasis was placed on local ownership. East African countries benefited more from these second-generation reforms. The Ugandan and Tanzania CSRs were generally regarded as the paragons of this new (second-generation) CSR effort. Table 4.5 shows the major gains of the Ugandan civil service reforms while Table 6 gives a sense of the key elements of the Tanzanian reform.

A close look at the Ugandan CSR (Table 4.5) shows some remarkable achievements. The total number of employees was reduced from 239,000 to 159,000, from a ratio of 1.5 to 0.7 civil servants to the total population between 1986 and 1996. On the other hand, the real wages of civil servants increased from 173 to 958, an increase of almost 900 percent. This caused the wage bill to rise from 1.4 percent of GDP to three percent of GDP between 1986 and 1996. Wage bill as a percent of current expenditures rose from almost 20 percent to approximately 25 percent within a decade from 1986. This meant that the reform substantially reduced employee numbers and also succeeded in raising the employee wage levels, regarded as excessively low at their pre-reform levels. However, the Ugandan case was a special case in that there was a consensus among all the donors that there was a need to raise wage lev-

Table 4.5 Uganda Civil Service Reforms & Costs (with Zambian comparators)

		1986	1991	1996
UGANDA	Civil Service Employment as % of Pop	1.5	1.4	0.7
	Central Govt. Employees '000s	239	269	159
UGANDA	Real Wage Per Civil Servant	–	173	958
UGANDA	Wage Bill as % of GDP	1.4	1.3	3.0
UGANDA	Wage Bill as % of Total	19.8	17.6	24.7
UGANDA	Revenue			
	% of Current Expenditures	15.2	18.7	29.7
ZAMBIA	CS/Pop	–	1.4	1.3
	Govt. Emp	–	116.9	130
	Real Wages	–	114	66
	Wage Bill/GDP	5.1	6.1	4.4

Source: IMF, Fiscal Affairs Department, 1997

els that had fallen to precipitous levels during the Ugandan civil war period. Uganda was also fortunate to experience strong economic growth about this time. More importantly, Uganda benefited from the new initiative on highly indebted poor countries' (HIPC) debt relief initiative. The latter released resources to enable it raise pay levels, independent of the entrenchment program. Even then, as in other countries, (Ethiopia, Tanzania) many of the retrenched teachers were re-deployed to district authorities (McCourt, 1998).

In general, African CSR protagonists claim some outstanding achievements. First, CSRs succeeded in the quantitative aspects of the reforms—the reduction of numbers of people who worked in the civil and public services. Six countries reduced their civil services by more than 10 percent between 1986 and 1986. These were Benin, the Central African Republic, Guinea, Madagascar, Mali, and Uganda. Sierra Leone and Tanzania also witnessed sizeable downsizing during the same period. Most of these reductions were achieved by the combination of measures: early retirements, voluntary retrenchment with generous severance payments, audits and organizational restructurings, wage freeze and attrition. Donors were particularly eager to finance severance packages. The result is that Sub Saharan Africa has the least number of civil servants per population in the world. Compared to other developing countries that have a civil service size per population of three percent, Africa's had declined to one percent by 1996 (Lienert, 1998, 5 and table 4.2).

Table 4.6   The Tanzanian Civil Service Reform Programme—1991–1999

Main Components:

- Redefinition of the Role of Government: Progressive withdrawal from direct production of goods and services
- Public Service Reduction: From 335,000 in 1992 to 270,000 in 1999
- Pay Reform: Progressive increases in pay levels; consolidation of non-transparent allowances and basic salaries; salary scales compressed from 1:9 in 1972 to 1:17 in 1999
- Decentralization of local government: restructuring of regional administrations
- Creation of Executive agencies for non-core and executive central government functions
- Code of Ethics

Upper	Middle	Lower	Total
2,095	25,924	114,147	142,166
1.47%	18.24%	72%	100%

Source: Adapted from D. Goldsworthy 2000, p. 10; United Nations 1992. *Size and Cost of the Civil Service: Reform Programs in Africa.* New Yark: Department of Economic and Social Development, p. 88

A second major achievement credited to first and second generation CSRs is the lowering of nominal and real wages in the region. Average wage bill for 32 African countries fell from 7 percent of GDP to 6 percent of GDP between 1986 and 1996. The devaluation of the CFA franc led to further decline of the wage bill in the Francophone countries by some 3 percent of the GDP. In actual fact, real wage bills fell for most of the region irrespective of their efforts at raising wages through CSR. According to Lienert (1998, 3–4): "Although reforms aimed at improving the level of real wages and the salary structure, very few countries achieved these objectives. On the contrary, real wages have continued to decline, by 2 percent a year on average during 1990–1996. . . . In the countries experiencing strong declines in real wages, the evidence suggests that there was a further compression of upper-grade salaries. For example, in Cameroon, the highest salary in 1994 was six times as large as the lowest salary, during 1984–1992; it was ten times larger."

Schiavo-Campo (1998) who has studied the data for different countries of the world summarized the changes in the decade 1980 to 1990 as follows:

- Globally, the relative size of central government shrunk by about 40 percent when measured by employment and by one third when measured by the wage bill. The reduction in central personnel reflected in some LDCs (especially Latin America) "a vast shift from central to local government." *In contrast in Africa, "the reduction in employment was reinforced by a shrinkage in local government as well"* (ibid. emphasis added).

- Relative or real wages fell slightly in OECD, held constant in Latin American countries and actually increased in Asia. Africa, however, experienced substantial cuts. He noted: "*it is developments in Africa which are largely responsible for the global decline in relative government wage. And that . . . while the economic welfare of the average civil servant improved slightly worldwide, it declined sharply in Africa*" (italics in the original).

- Only in Africa has there been a reduction in central government employment as well as in the central wage bill as a proportion of the GDP. And he concluded that "while the contraction of government in the decade of adjustment" is well known, the magnitude of that contraction is indeed remarkable. Yet, according to table 4.2, Africa already has the least number of civil servants per population among the world's regions.

The reduction in size or numbers and cost are usually the main claims made for the success of CSR in Africa. In reality, the real success of these reforms must lie elsewhere. First, they have helped to sanitize the system of human resource and fiscal management in states where the system of accountability had all but collapsed. The IFIs became the major instrument for asserting some controls on public expenditure—although the interest was to ensure that debts were paid up a times at the expense of social services. Nevertheless, the initiative was important, in that it placed constraints on states that perceived their sovereign authority as total and completely unchallengeable irrespective of their performance in governance. (See Baker, 1998.)

The reforms also put in place systems of performance monitoring for the civil service. CSRs led to the conduct of audits of civil and public service personnel in countries where the number of those working in the civil services were not known, and where these numbers have been deliberately infiltrated with large numbers of "ghost workers." In addition, staff and organizational audits led to major re-organizations and the privatization of some services that were being poorly performed by government agencies. Moreover, some of the reforms spearheaded governance improvement programs—e.g. helping to decongest the center through support for devolutionary decentralization programs to local governments and to executive agencies (Uganda, Tanzania). A state like Tanzania had in the 1970s abolished its local government system and replaced it with deconcentrated structures. The result as in other countries (Kenya, Malawi, Ethiopia, etc.) was disastrous and CSRs (especially of the second generation variety) have been accompanied by a revival of democratic local government systems (Olowu, 1990, 2001). There were also important initiatives to assist parliaments, judiciary, anti-corruption, and executive agencies (Organization for Economic Cooperation and Development, 1997; Goldsworthy, 2000).

Thirdly, these CSRs brought an end to practices that were no longer sustainable. These include, for instance, the use of the civil service as an employer of the last resort and the practice of automatic employment in the civil service for graduates of the secondary and higher educational institutions. Finally, the reforms released substantial inputs—especially manpower and equipment—for tackling substantive problems (Kiggundu, 1998).

However, the reduction in numbers and costs—what constituted the core of the reforms—must be regarded as a dubious success, at best. Cut-back management led to sharp reductions in the numbers of the civil services, but in many cases, the ones that left were the most needed in the civil service—the professionals in skilled categories who took the opportunity for alternative employment that they could compete for outside the public sector—and, in some cases, outside their countries. On the other hand, the large pool of the lower cadre officials stayed. This was because compression levels remained high—the "salaries for this (junior) group was higher than they could obtain in the private sector" (Lienert, 1998). For instance, it is easy to see in Table (4.6) that the Tanzanian civil service has a disproportionate size in the lowest cadres with negative implications for supervision and accountability by senior personnel.

Authors like Lienert—an official of the IMF—accept that more progress has been made in the quantitative aspects of CSR, "often to the detriment of civil service quality." However, Haque and Aziz (1999)—also both from the IMF—have demonstrated the horrible effects of these reforms on the out migration of skills from countries with scarce skills to other countries (brain drain, see table 4.7) accompanied at about the same time with the sharp increase in the flow of technical assistance expatriates into the region. They cited a study by Danso, which shows that technical assistance has increased by 50 percent between 1984 and 1987, and by 1995 was estimated to cost US four billion annually. On the other hand, nationals are prevented, as a policy of all United Nations agencies, from earning salaries at international levels in their own countries. Moreover, they proposed that at the same levels of compensation, technical assistance programs would attract higher skilled indigenes (who migrate) than residents of a higher income country.

Table 4.7 Commonly Cited Causes of Civil Service Ineffectiveness

Gambia	Ghana	Tanzania	Uganda
1. Overstaffing and poor resource allocation	1. Poor morale	1. Poor management of financial resources	1. Poor organization, departmentation, coordination & interfacing
2. Ineffective leadership at senior levels	2. Poor pay, benefits & incentives	2. Lack of accountability framework	2. Lack of proper planning
3. Weak management at senior and middle levels	3. High levels of absenteeism	3. Lack of accountability enforcement	3. Improper staffing
4. Little delegation of authority	4. Inadequate supervision & accountability	4. Lack of good records, data & management	4. Extreme laxity & indiscipline
5. Lack of proper organization of ministries	5. Ineffective promotion & career devt policies & procedures	5. Laxity at work	5. Bureaucratic Redtape
6. Imbalances in the distribution of resource	6. Poor performance appraisal practices	6. Lack of clear performance targets & standards	6. Undue Secrecy & Confidentiality
7. Outdated general orders & regulations	7. Poorly designed jobs	7. Job dissatisfaction	7. Institutional Inflexibility, rigidity & inert admin
8. Poor reporting relationships	8. Poor human resources management	8. Poor pay	8. Vague authorities
9. Lack of proper staff appraisals	9. Hostile Environment	9. Lack of effective appeals system	9. Poor attitudes & work ethics
10. Emphasis on operations not policies		10. Poor management of budgetary flows	10. Corruption, nepotism, tribalism, bad leadership
		11. Poor personnel management	
		12. Bribery & favoritism	

Source: United Nations, *Size & Cost,* 1992, p. 95.

They concluded their study by noting that "one explanation for the weak performance of the public sector in Africa may be the lack of attention to African talent in the design of reform. While many reforms were being planned and implemented badly, African talent, unable to find a place at home, was migrating abroad." They argued that the reason why many of the expatriate CSR protagonists were not able to see the implications of this development is to the fact that: *"civil service reforms have primarily been concerned with cost cutting and containment. The issue of productivity and the need for appropriate human capital for it have largely been secondary"*. (Haque and Aziz, 1999, 101; italics in the original)

EXPLANATIONS FOR THE FAILURE OF AFRICAN CSRs

It should be readily evident from the expose in the last section why African civil services have not led to the type of success that will turn the continent's circumstances around. In this section, I want to further elaborate on why this is the case. I shall argue that:

- CSRs are based on the wrong premises—on the idea of "affordable" civil services rather than "required civil services" dictated by the logic of a democratic, developmental state articulated in The World Bank's publication on the subject.
- CSRs are based on Poor Diagnosis—that African civil services are overbloated—a fact that cannot be empirically established for the totality of the African civil service profile. These civil services—as those who have studied the African civil service readily find—are poorly structured and concentrated. They have surpluses at the base but substantial shortages at the professional levels. Skilled personnel are also not well distributed in space, as there is a tendency to over-concentration at the centre.
- Finally, CSRs constitute a wrong prognosis: they represent the application of a wrong prescription to the problem confronting African countries.

CSRs AND STATE MODELS-NATURE AND ROLES OF THE AFRICAN STATE

One reason for the above errors is that the original CSRs were conceived primarily to reduce rather than empower a state that in many countries had become anti-developmental and patrimonial. Instead of seeking to transform the state, CSRs pursued a strategy of state denigration and denial. This point has already been highlighted, but it is useful to note here that this model of the African state is not only outmoded, the factual basis of CSR design has also been challenged as reviewed in the next section.

FACTUAL BASIS OF POLICY: ARE AFRICAN CIVIL SERVICES TOO LARGE?

For a variety of reasons, it is often difficult to come by comparative national statistics on civil services and especially for African countries. Nevertheless, the IMF and the World Bank have made great strides in this respect. In the first published statistical analysis on the subject, Heller and Tait (1983) demonstrated that developing countries generally had fewer civil servants per population than industrialized countries of the world. Among the developing countries, African countries had the least number of civil servants per their total population. Since civil servants are expected to provide service to their total population, this is the most important measure. And African countries have generally the least ratios (Table 4.2 is an updated version of this earlier study). But the problem is not only a quantitative one. There is a qualitative side to it as well. Most of the data on African civil services shows a bell-shaped structure, with the civil services narrow at the top but broad at the base (United Nations, 1992; Ginnekken, 1991). There are few skills available nationally because of Africa's late start in education but also because of low economic performance and of poor human resource policies that make civil services unable to compete with the nascent private sector, often a multi-national and even the public enterprises (that draw huge resources from the state if unsuccessful or from consumers if successful) and the growing number of non-governmental organizations (NGOs). Many of the latter organizations receive their funding from northern NGOs and their governments.

Strangely, The World Bank did commission a major study in the early 1980s on this subject. The study confirmed that developing countries did not have larger civil service populations than their developed counterparts, and that comparatively Africa had the least civil service population size per its citizens (Ozgediz, 1983). Schiavo-Campo (1998) has compiled more recent data as we saw above and has confirmed the same patterns up to the 1990s—that was reproduced as table 4.2 here. African countries have the least number of civil servants per their total populations and the CSRs of the 1980s and 1990s have helped to reduce these further. Selcuck Ozgediz's findings are worth reviewing in greater detail

Drawing on the work of Heller and Tait (1983), he found that the empirical evidence for 75 countries supports the thesis that "as per capita income rises, government employment increases on a per capita basis . . .

thus OECD now have more than twice as many public employees as the developing countries." He noted also that "African countries on the average, have fewer public employees per capita than Asian and Latin American countries." He concluded that "the public service in developing countries are not 'too big' at least not bigger than what would be expected on the basis of their population and level of income" (p. 3). He noted, however, that there was a tendency for the service to be concentrated in the central government level, helping to fortify the "big bureaucracy" perception in these countries. He also dismissed the idea that developing countries' public services were growing too fast. According to the available evidence, all states including today's industrialized countries tended to use the state as the machinery for producing essential goods and services pending the institutionalization of other private and civil society organizations—the famous Wagner thesis.

Hence, even though African civil services have excess personnel in some categories, they also have huge gaps in the skilled categories. Furthermore, the available personnel are excessively concentrated in the central government and the decentralized structures remain much weaker than in any other region of the world. These critical shortages and lopsided civil service structure are the problem and the proposals for reform have not defined the problem in this manner.

But protagonists of reform argue that the size of the civil service should be measured relative to the GDP or to the total public revenues. Defined in this way Africa's civil service is oversized—perhaps more oversized than any other continent of the world. However, there are two serious problems with the policy response of retrenchment. First, if economic performance was the problem, the focus of CSR should be on how to improve GDP or boost the revenue base. As the experiences of revenue enclaves in many countries in the region have shown, these would have called for different package of reforms rather than retrenchment. They call for strategic institution-building efforts focused on governmental organizations that can raise resources. Such units require more resources and autonomy and have successfully turned around revenue intakes in many countries (Devas and Hubbard, 2001). Furthermore, the prevailing prescriptions fly in the face of the effort to define the normative requirements for developmental states (Leftwich, 1996). Expenditure reduction—including developmental, and welfare expenditures, as well as civil service costs—have further aggravated recession in several African countries (Goldsmith, 2000). What civil services in these states require is more muscle and incentives that will enable them to provide the basic services necessary for economic growth.[1] Hence, even though there is the need for structural reforms within the civil service, there is a more pressing need to attract and retain skilled HCS who, with effective performance incentives in place, can provide the technical inputs to reinvigorate, lead, and raise the moral authority of the civil service and other parts of the public service in increasing economic performance and revenue mobilization. This is important in view of the recognition that African tax systems have not succeeded in netting the new rich (resulting from economic reforms) who are in the informal, non-official sectors—and in some cases in the organized private sector (Fjeldstad, 2001). These may lead to higher costs in the short run, with high dividends in the medium to long term. In other words, the emphasis of CSRs should be on how to generate resources to support CSR over a dynamic future time frame.

Approached this way, resources made available through donor-support and development finance for CSR should have been utilized to support improved wage levels for the scarce skills rather than spent almost wholly on removing excess (junior-level or surplus skill) staff. This is because an analysis of the problems of these civil services highlight the need to address issues relating to weak scarce skills at the top—a void that has compounded problems of supervision, accountability, and performance measurement—in view of the high external brain drain that has afflicted the continent. For instance, it is estimated that whereas there were only 40,000 African experts in the West between 1975 and 1984, this number rose to 80,000 in the 1986–1990 period. The estimate suggests that 50,000 to 60,000 African middle and high-level managers had emigrated by 1990 (UNDP, 1992 in Haq and Aziz, 1999). This issue is further explored in the next section.

MISLEADING PROGNOSIS-RETRENCHMENT BENEFITS TO PAY FOR THE COSTS OF CAPACITY BUILDING

One evidence that CSR diagnosis and prognosis are flawed is the glaring misfit between expected policy and actual outcomes. A recent review by the World Bank of its CSR program was not flattering in this respect:

"The review found that Bank-supported CSRs were largely ineffective in achieving sustainable results in downsizing, capacity building, and institutional reform" (1999). But it went on to blame this on "the political difficulties in implementing CSRs," although it conceded that "the relevance and ownership of the reforms were also weakened by a technocratic approach that failed to mainstream institutional analysis" in its administrative reform work.

Apologists of these CSRs have argued that perhaps the problem was the over-ambitious expectations of the reforms in terms of the time-frame allowed for implementation. Some others have pointed to the one or two outstanding reform success cases, already cited above (Uganda, Tanzania) (Goldsworthy, 2000).

In an earlier publication on this subject, I tried to demonstrate—drawing mainly on WB data—that the prescription that retrenchments will lead to savings, which will be used to raise the capacity of those who remain in the civil service, is flawed. Severance costs were often quite costly financially. More importantly, retrenchment led to a situation in which it was the most able that left first, where it was voluntary, leading to a further weakening of civil service capacity (Olowu, 1999, a) or b)? 15). Other analysts of the available data have come to the same conclusions (Lienert, 1998, Haque and Aziz, 1999).

I want to take this argument a little further here. The above prognosis was based on the faulty assumption that the African civil services were generally over-expanded. However, as already shown above, there is no empirical basis for this assertion other than civil service population as a ratio of GDP or total revenues. First, it is easy to note that this is not the manner in which civil services optimality is measured. In economic, as in administrative tradition, total Civil Service (CS) population to total population is used to measure civil service size. The logic behind this is that civil servants, by definition, are expected to serve the population. The second point is that the reforms completely neglected the differentiated structure of African civil service both in term of hierarchy, skills, and most importantly, the strategic function of the higher civil service as institutions for policy making and for ensuring accountable management of a bureaucracy.

In addition, besides discharging its policy development and regulatory functions, a developing state has to take on the responsibilities of helping to nurture the capacities of both for-profit and not-for-profit nongovernmental organizations. Any programs of assistance should therefore take this time dimension into consideration—the short-to-medium term when a state must be assisted to develop the institutional capacity to generate resources and spend it rationally, and the longer term when these capacities would be in place. Unfortunately, many CSR assistance are reluctant to provide salary support to remaining staff but would prefer to use these funds for downsizing and even redundancy programs.

The above points underscore a major challenge confronting African CSRs: their heavy dependence on external actors who seem to have a different approach to reform compared to the real needs of these countries' civil services. By systematically destroying the available capacity, these reforms seem to increase rather than decrease external dependency of the recipient states. This has led to an increasing tendency for donors to dominate the agenda for policy making with respect to reforms and other areas of policy—in spite of the avowed commitment to increasing local ownership (Court et al., 1999). A recent study on the nature of the problem of the African state came to the conclusion that African states are weak not in terms of their errors of commission—doing what they ought not to do—but more in terms of the errors of omission—not doing what they ought to do. The reason why they have failed in this area is that they have not developed their capacity to collect taxes and account to their own citizens. Most of them have been reliant on donor funds or mineral payments that do not require them to relate to their own people on the basis of a fiduciary contract. All these factors tie up with the governance problems highlighted earlier and explain the weakness of many states in developing more effective strategies for tackling corruption, protecting civil and political rights, and securing the legal environment for business (Goldsmith, 2000; see also Moore, 1998).

This last point raises the issue of whether reforms financed without additional external resources are different from the ones described above. Generally, there are few of these, but they have occurred mainly in countries that have or have recently undergone major democratic governance changes. Such countries include Botswana, Mauritius, Nigeria, Ethiopia, Namibia, and the Republic of South Africa. For instance, post-apartheid South Africa has pursued policies for re-dynamizing its public service that stressed rightsizing (not only downsizing), efficient service delivery, and accountability to the citizens as part of its *Batho Pele* (People First) program (Cameron and Tapscott, 2000, 84). These, together with concern for continuity of the state, are key areas in which HCS as an institution can make important contributions. Some of these countries have sought external assistance, but in a way that is focussed and enables them to utilise demand—driven technical inputs in building their own capacities (Adamolekun, 2002; Brautigam, 2000).

The above—mentioned experiences underscore the need to include the governance context in the analysis and reform of African civil services. Governance is the quality of rules that regulate relationships between the governors and the governed. Constitutive rules have been abused by authoritarian leaders in many African countries—they have been used to undermine the civil service, especially in terms of the exercise use of patronage in filling top positions, the reluctance to delegate or devolve power to other organs of state and non-state institutions other than the central executive (Hyden, 1999; Olowu, 1999b; Olowu and Sako, 2002). Governance reform thus becomes a *sine qua non* for effective states and effective CSRs. Fortunately, there is a renewed interest in governance in recent years, but the relationship between effective CSRs and good governance remains tenuous. One close student of the subject has suggested the fundamental restructuring of African civil services in a way that sets the HCS apart from the operational groups within the civil service and also from the parastatals and the local governments. He has suggested that HCS should be a small, highly resourced group who are recruited initially by contract with clearly articulated performance expectations—of providing leadership and achieving specified goals of their respective ministries. The tenure will be insulated by law and an independent commission, along the lines of the US Senior Executive Service (SES). A number of countries—Ghana is an early example—have adopted the principle, but have not fully implemented the concept as a crucial aspect of their CSR program (Adamolekun, 2002).

Conclusion: Towards A New CSR Genre

In spite of the differences in approaches to reform of the African civil service in the last couple of years, there are also considerable similarities among the countries in the continent. Francophone country experiences seem, since the devaluation of the CFA, to have followed the logic of the Anglophone and Lusophone experiences (Doe, 1998). Yet, such similarities mask considerable differentiation in the quality of civil services by region and by country. One research provides data that shows that bureaucratic quality is highest in the southern African region (47.4 percent) followed by West Africa (38.1 percent), with Eastern and Central Africa lagging behind (the average for Africa was 40 percent (Ali, 2001).

A new CSR must therefore learn several mistakes from past experience. Firstly, it should be sensitive to the differentiated nature of the African civil service. It is not only differentiated regionally as noted above, it is also differentiated in terms of its expected roles, class structure, and of its multiple capacities for effective governance. Efforts aimed at improving the political segment would be those that could be referred to as governance improvement components of the civil service. The commitment to reducing numbers and size in the civil service will still continue, but it will be focussed on those levels of the government civil service where there is excess—without the illusion that this will necessarily lead to cost reduction. On the other hand, there will be a need to vigorously enhance the capacity of the civil service to relate to other institutional actors within and outside the state as partners. These include local governments, residues of unprivatised parastatals, the private sector, NGOs, churches and mosques, besides the legislative, judicial, and other regulatory agencies. Clearly, there is a need to evolve new arrangements for governing, attracting, and retaining this scarce category of skills in African public services as a part of the effort of qualitative as well as quantitative re-orientation of Africa's civil services. This has supply and demand sides. On the supply side, it has implications for the selective reform of the continent's higher education system. On the demand side, reforms must give greater prominence to how to mobilize and increase the inputs of civil society and non-state actors in the policy and reform processes.

Second, a new African CSR will require new partnerships between Africans governments and their citizen groups on the one hand, and with donors and other external actors on the other. Both groups need to bring their skills to bear on the issue of CSR while paying respect for each other's concerns. One implication of this position is that CSR should not be part of a program of assistance to countries that are not ready to carry out major reforms of their governance architecture. But perhaps the most important issue is on how to finance the ambitious reforms in this paper. Current reforms seem to pay too much attention to the expenditure side and much less to the revenue side. Evidence has been adduced in the paper that African states can mobilize much better resources than they do at present. Some interesting case studies show what happens when the regulatory environment for private sector performance is improved—although key problems remain in that critical financial institutions have not been properly positioned to perform their roles of assisting the ongoing economic and political reform processes (Temu and Due, 2000 on Tanzania). In addition, substantial numbers of income—earners are still outside of African government's tax nets—especially those in the private and non-governmental sectors. Local governments in the cities are still awaiting major reforms that would tap into property rates that are not utilized in many countries in western, central, and eastern Africa. There is increasing evidence that African countries deliberately shy way from improving their tax-collection (preferring donor funds and externally generated revenue earnings instead) because of the likely political and accountability implications (Guyer, 1991, Moore et al., 1998).

Moreover, it is estimated that retrenchment exercises and technical assistance used in undertaking them cost huge sums. In Uganda it cost over US$20 million over a five-year period. Such resources could have been better utilized in attracting and retaining high-level officials on a contract basis to undertake such functions. For instance, a few countries in Africa (Ghana and Zimbabwe) have utilized the Senior Executive Service (SES) option, that has been successfully applied in other countries (Adamolekun, 2002; Adamolekun and Kiragu, 1999). Two other options are the use of donor assistance funds to pay for salary upgrades over a period of time as an incentive to stimulate strategic HCS in improving economic management. Finally, much more attention could be given to improving accountability and transparency in public service reforms. A lot of resources are lost to Africa through cases—not of petty corruption—but of grand corruption that involves heads of states, top political executives and officials (Moody-Stuart, 1997; Olowu, 1999b; Hope, 2000). African civil services are still needed to play these critical roles, not only in service delivery but also in policy advice and effective accountability at all levels of governance.

The upshot is that the African civil service viewed in its historical context remains largely uninstitutionalised. Its colonial heritage bequeathed positive and negative legacies, but post-independence developments in the form of reforms have often further aggravated problems rather than tackle them because of the tendency to rely less on facts or informed theory than ideologies of state roles and capacity. The hope is that the ongoing democratic re-awakening and the pressure towards global competition will compel national leaders and donors—who are currently championing reforms—to rethink current reform approaches and agenda as partners rather than as protagonists.

NOTES

1   Data provided by van de Walle (2001:16) using IMF data suggests that countries with higher incomes in the region have higher primary school enrolment rates and their populations are likely to live five years longer, though immunization is not higher and have higher employee levels.

REFERENCES

Aberbach, J. D. R. D Putnam, and B. A. Rockman (1981) *Bureaucrats and Politicians in Western Democracies* Cambridge, Mass.: Harvard University Press.

Adamolekun, L (1986) *Politics and Administration In Nigeria*. London: Macmillan.

Adamolekun, L (1993) "Note on Civil Service Personnel Policy in Sub-Saharan Africa" *Public Sector Management* vol. 68, no. 3, pp. 38–46.

Adamolekun, L and K. Kiragu (1999) "Public Administration Reforms" in L. Adamolekun, ed, *Public Administration in Africa: Main Issues & Selected Country Case Studies*. Boulder, Colo.: Westview Press, pp. 159–176.

Adamolekun, L. (2002) "Africa's Evolving Career Civil Service Systems: Three Challenges—State Continuity, Efficient Service Delivery and Accountability." *International Review of Administrative Sciences* vol. 68, no. 3, pp. 373–388.

African Development Bank (2001) *African Development Report 2001* Oxford, Oxford University Press.

Ali, G (2001) "Africa's Children and Africa's Development" Mimeo UNICEF, New York.

Baker, B (1998) "The Class of 1990: How Have the Autocratic Leaders of Sub-Saharan Africa Fared Under Democratization." *Third World Quarterly* vol. 19, no. 1, pp. 115–128.

Bekke, H. A. G. M, J. L Perry and T. J. Toonen, eds (1996) *Comparative Civil Service Systems in Comparative Perspective*. Bloomington: Indiana University Press.

Beyene, A (1999) "Ethiopia" in L. Adamolekun, ed. *Public Administration in Africa: Main Issues & Selected Country Case Studies*. Boulder, Colo.: Westview Press, pp. 227–249.

Brautigam, Deborah (1996) "State Capacity and Effective Governance" in B. Ndulu and N. Van de Walle, Eds, *Agenda for Africa's Economic Renewal*. Washington D.C.: Overseas Development Council, pp. 81–107.

Brautigam, D (2000) "Foreign Aid and the Politics of Participation in Economic Policy Reform". *Public Administration and Development* vol. 20, no. 3, pp. 253–264.

Cohen, J. M and J. R. Wheeler (1997) "Building Sustainable Professional Capacity in African Public Sectors: Retention Constraints in Kenya" *Public Administration and Development* vol. 17, pp. 307–324.

Court, J. P. Kristen and B. Weder (1999) "Bureaucratic Structure and Performance: First Africa Survey Results" Tokyo: United Nations University Press.

Devas, N. S. Delay and M. Hubbard (2001) "Revenue Authorities: Are they the Right Vehicle for Improved Tax Administration?" *Public Administration and Development* vol. 21, no. 3, pp. 211–222.

Dia, M. (1996) *Africa's Management in the 1990s and Beyond*. Washington D.C.: The World Bank.

Doe, L. (1998) "Civil Service Reform in the Countries of the West African Monetary Union" *International Social Science Journal* vol. 155, pp. 125–144.

Etzioni-Harlevy, E. (1983) *Bureaucracy and Democracy: A Political Dilemma* London: Routledge & Kegan Paul.

Goldsmith, A (2000) "Sizing Up the African State" *Journal of Modern African Studies* vol. 38, no. 1, pp. 1–20.

Goldsworthy, D (2000) *Public Service Reform: A Pro-Poor Perspective* Part 1, (Draft), Workshop on Public Service Reform, Ministry of Foreign Affairs, The Hague, Netherlands, 15–16, June 2000.

Grindle, M (1996) *Challenging the State: Crisis and Innovation in Latin America and Africa*. Cambridge: Cambridge University Press.

Haque, N. U and J. Aziz (1999) "The Quality of Governance: `Second Generation' Civil Service Reform in Africa," *Journal of African Economies* vol. 8, no. 1, pp. 68–106.

Heller, P. S. and Alan A. Tait (1983) Government Employment and Pay: Some International Comparisons. Washington, D.C.: International Monetary Fund.

Hope, K. R. (2000) "Corruption and Development in Africa" in K. R. Hope and B. C. Chiculo, Eds., *Corruption and Development in Africa: Lessons from Country Case Studies.* London, Macmillan, pp. 17–39.

Hyden, G. (1984) "Politics and Administration" in Barkan J. and J. Okumu, Eds., *Politics and Administration in Kenya and Tanzania* Berkeley, University of California Press, pp. 93–113.

Hyden, G (1999) "The Governance Challenge in Africa" in G. Hyden, D. Olowu, and W. Okoth-Ogendo, Eds., *African Perspectives on Governance* Trenton, Africa World Press, pp. 5–32.

Grindle, M (1996) *Challenging the State: Crisis and Innovation in Latin America and Africa* Cambridge, Cambridge University Press

Guyer, J (1992) "Representation without Taxation: An Essay on Democracy in Rural Nigeria, 1952–1990." *African Studies Review*, vol. 35, no. 1, pp. 41–80.

Kiggundu, M (1998) "Civil Service Reforms: Limping into the 21st Century" in M. Minogue, C. Polidano, and D. Hulme, eds., *Beyond the New Public Management: Changing Ideas and Practices in Governance* Cheltenham: Elgar, pp. 155–171.

Kim, Hung-Ki (1996) *The Civil Service System and Economic Development: The Japanese Experience* Washington D.C. Economic Development Institute

Kiser L. L. and E. Ostrom (1992) "The Three Worlds of Action: A Metatheoretical Synthesis of Institutional Approaches" in E. Ostrom, ed., *Strategies of Political Enquiry* Beverly Hills Calif.: Sage, pp. 179–222.

Klitgaard, R (1989) "Incentive Myopia" *World Development* vol. 217, no. 4, pp. 447–489.

Leftwich, Adrian, ed. (1996) Democracy and Development: Theory and Practice. Cambridge, MA: in association with Blackwell Press.

Lienert, I (1998) "Civil Service Reform in Africa: Mixed Results After 10 Years" in *Finance and Development* Vol. 35, No. 2, pp. 1–7.

Lindauer D and B. Numberg, eds. (1994) *Rehabilitating Government: Pay and Employment Reform in Africa* Washington D.C.: The World Bank.

McCourt, W (1998) "Civil Service Reform Equals Retrenchment? The Experience of 'Rightsizing and Retrenchment' in Ghana, Uganda and the UK" in M. Minogue et al., eds, *Beyond the New Public Management.* Cheltenham: Elgar, pp. 172–187.

Moody-Stuart, George (1997) Grand Corruption: How Business Bribes Damage Developing Countries. Oxford: World View.

Moore, M. (1998) "Death Without Taxes: Democracy, State Capacity & Aid Dependence in the Fourth World" in M. Robinson and G. White, eds *The Democratic Developmental State: Politics and Institutional Design.* Oxford: Oxford University Press, 84–121.

Numberg, B. (1996) "Rethinking Civil Service Reform: An Agenda for Smart Government." Draft. Washington, D.C.: The World Bank, PSPD.

Odd-Helge, Fjeldstad (2001) *Fiscal Decentralization in Tanzania: For Better or for Worse?* Bergen, Norway: Chr. Michelsen Institute.

Olowu, D (1990) "The Failure of Current Decentralization Programmes" in J S. Wunsch and D. Olowu, eds., *The Failure of the Centralized State: Institutions for Self-Governance in Africa* Boulder Colo: Westview Press, pp. 74–99.

Olowu, B (1999a) "Redesigning African Civil Service Reforms" *Journal of Modern African Studies* Vol. 37, No. 1, pp. 1–23.

Olowu, D (1999b) "Accountability and Transparency" in L. Adamolekun, ed., *Public Administration in Africa*, pp. 139–158. (Boulder, Colo: Westview Press)

Olowu, B (2001) "Pride and Performance in African Civil Service—the Experiences of Nigeria and Uganda" *International Review of Administrative Sciences* vol. 67, no. 1, pp. 117–134.

Olowu D. and L. Adamolekun (1999) "Human Resources Management" in L. Adamolekun, eds., *Public Administration in Africa:* Boulder, Colo.: Westview Press, pp. 86–106.

Olowu, D and S. Sako (2002) *Better Governance and Public Policy: Capacity Building for Democratic Renewal in Africa.* Kumarian Press Bloomfield, CT.

Ostrom, E. L. Schroeder, and S. Wynne (1992) *Institutional Incentives and Sustainable Development: Infrastructure Policies in Perspective* Boulder, Colo.: Westview Press.

Otobo, E (1999) "Nigeria" in L. Adamolekun, ed., *Public Administration in Africa: Themes and Country Cases.* Boulder, Colo.: Westview Press, pp. 292–310.

Ozgediz, S (1983) *Managing the Public Services in Developing Countries: Issues and Prospects.* Staff Working Paper no. 583 Washington D.C., The World Bank.

Pilkington, Colin (1999) *The Civil Service in Britain Today.* Manchester University Press. Manchester, UK.

Rouban, Luc (1998) *The French Civil Service* IIAP, La Documentation Francaise, Paris, France.

Schiavo-Campo, S (1998) "Government Employment and Pay: The Global & Regional Evidence," in *Public Administration and Development* vol. 18, no. pp. 457–478.

Suleiman, Ezra (1999) "Bureaucracy and Democratic Consolidation: Lessons from Eastern Europe" in L. Anderson, ed., *Transitions to Democracy* New York: Columbia Press, pp. 141–167.

Temu, A. E and J. M. Due (2000) "The Business Environment in Tanzania after Socialism: Challenges of Reforming Banks, Parastatals, Taxation and the Civil Service." *Journal of Modern African Studies* vol. 38, no. 4, pp. 638–712.

United Nations Economic Commission for Africa (1996) *Political and Administrative Efficiency in Africa: Emerging Trends, Prospects and Appropriate Policy Responses,* Addis Ababa. New York: UNECA.

United Nations (1992) *Size and Cost of the Civil Service: Reform Programmes in Africa* New York: Department of Economic & Social Development.

van de Walle, Nicolas (2003 forthcoming) "The Economic Correlates of State Failure." in Robert Rotberg, ed., When States Fail Princeton, NJ: Princeton University Press (2001) "Economic Correlates of State Collapse" Paper for Failed States Project.

van de Walle, Nicolas (2001) "Economic Correlates of State Collapse" Paper for Failed States Project. Mimeographed.

Van Ginneken, Wouter, ed. (1991) Government and Its Employees: Case Studies of Developing Countries Brookfield, Vt: Gower Publishers.

World Bank (1993) *The East Asian Miracle: Economic Growth and Public Policy* Oxford, Oxford University Press

World Bank, *World Development Report* (1997) Oxford: Oxford University Press.

Wunsch J and D. Olowu, eds., (1990) *The Failure of the Centralised State* Boulder, Colo.: Westview Press.

CHAPTER 5

FORGING DEVELOPMENTAL SYNERGIES BETWEEN STATES AND ASSOCIATIONS

AILI MARI TRIPP

Studies of associational life in Africa have looked at associations as filling gaps where the state has failed in the provision of social and welfare services or as a guarantor of economic well-being. They have shown associations as more efficient service deliverers than the state, as challengers to state authority, or as competitors with states for donor funds. Associations have also been seen as channels for party and state patronage, as coopted by ruling parties or regimes, or as victims of state suppression. These many faces of associational life, as important as they are, sidestep one of the more intractable problems in African governance. At the end of the day, it is not a question of whether societal groups or the state can deliver public goods and services or who can do it better, but rather, it is a question of *how* they can best do it together, possibly even with the private sector. It is inconceivable given the strengths and weaknesses of both sectors that either could be the sole engine for development. Nor is it feasible for one to do it at the expense of the other. The state frames the possibilities for associational agency, while much of the best energy, most creative practices, and developmental impetus has come from societal groups. For this reason the solutions have to be thought of as a combined effort between at least two if not three sectors where possible.

This paper discusses some of the changes in thinking about the role of voluntary associations within academic, policymaking, and donor circles over the past couple of decades. It examines the reasons for creating state-society synergies. It also looks at both the possibilities and problems with synergies between the state and those informal and formal organizations in Africa that provide welfare and public services, as well as organizations that promote economic development broadly defined.

By economic associations, I am referring to savings and credit associations, cooperatives, marketing and trading associations, and other such business oriented groups. The paper, for the most part, does not deal with professional, cultural, religious, political, or advocacy associations, unless they are also working on development issues. It is also not concerned with public institutions, except in relation to these non-governmental organizations.

The paper is primarily focusing on private associations at various levels, drawing on Norman Uphoff's categories.[1] It discusses national non-governmental organizations (NGOs) and regional private voluntary organizations (PVOs), district level organizations (hometown associations), sub-district initiatives (non-profit hospitals and cooperatives), local initiatives (market organizations, service clubs), community organizations and village-level associations, and group-level or neighborhood associations (rotating credit associations, groups based on ethnicity, age, gender). It also briefly mentions international non-governmental organizations (e.g., Red Cross, Oxfam).

An important distinction must be made between national and regional PVOs or NGOs, which are often run out of urban areas and are heavily dependent on foreign aid and a professional staff. As one moves down to the local, community, village, and neighborhood level, organizations are likely to be more membership based, more inclined to rely on membership funds and less on donors, and more participatory in orientation. They are also more likely to be informal and not registered as an official organization. It is these activities where one finds the most participation and voluntary activity, but it is also these organizations that have received the least serious empirical consideration. Many of the generalizations that apply to NGOs are not necessarily true of this level of mobilization.

NGOs and grassroots organizations have become increasingly important as a means through which development is promoted in Africa, in part because of state decline, economic crisis, shifting donor strategies that have moved towards greater supports for voluntary and NGO service provision, and the widespread realization that the state in Africa does not have the capacity to fulfill all the functions it had set for itself at independence. Government openness to voluntary activity has also increased.

CHANGING PERSPECTIVES ON THE ROLE OF ASSOCIATIONS

Today it is widely acknowledged by governments, donors, and academics alike that voluntary associations have a key role to play in the provision of welfare and public services and in promoting development. Remarkably, the consensus even spans the political spectrum from those who advocate a greater role for the state to neo-liberals.

In the 1980s and early 1990s a major focus of the development literature explored the potential of non-governmental organizations as alternatives to the failures of the state-directed development initiatives (Drabek, 1987; Korten, 1990). It showed how we were witnessing in many developing countries a return to collective action solutions that existed for centuries before the state displaced, constrained, and distorted the local and informal institutions that had met people's needs. NGOs and grassroots organizations were seen as often more in touch with the needs of ordinary people, having knowledge of local conditions and being responsive to local needs (Uphoff, 1993, 619). They were also perceived of as being "smaller, more participatory, more flexible, less bureaucratic, more cost effective," and able to reach the poor and most needy more easily (Robinson and White, 1997, 4).

In the West, scholars sought to explain the worldwide growth of the voluntary sector as a consequence not only of state failure, but also of market failure. There was an understanding that the market could not ensure equitable provision of services, nor could it guarantee comprehensive coverage throughout the country. In Africa, market failure was simply taken for granted.

This "New Policy Agenda" that emerged after the 1980s around the world saw markets and private sector initiatives—even with all their deficiencies—as the most efficient means for achieving economic growth. Similarly, the new consensus saw NGOs as more efficient and cost effective than the government in addressing development concerns as they relate to education, public health, family planning, infrastructure improvement, agricultural production, and micro-finance. NGOs, especially churches, have a long and proven track record in the area of service delivery and were seen as especially adept at reaching the poor (Edwards and Hulme, 1996, 961).

The other part of this emerging new consensus was an emphasis on good governance and democracy. In a reversal of what political scientists had generally taken for granted, that is, that development preceded or was a precondition for democracy, a new normative orthodoxy came to dominate official Western aid policy and development thinking. It saw good governance and democracy as essential conditions for development in all societies (Leftwich, 1996). This view became particularly prevalent in Africa, in which it was thought that democratization could break the development impasse.

Thus, with the end of the cold war and the spread of democratization in Latin America, Eastern Europe, former Soviet Union, and Africa, foreign donors adopted a new interest in democracy. First, they directed their energies toward promoting free and fair elections. Soon the emphasis shifted toward support for civil society activities aimed at contributing to democratization, giving rise to differences over whether assistance to developmentally oriented NGOs had an impact on democratization. Some believed that support for NGOs that focused on civic education and advocacy would best advance democratization. Others felt that developmentally oriented organizations contributed to a vibrant civil society and active citizenry, which in turn would serve as a basis for democracy. They were concerned with how the plurality of associations could be a training ground for democracy, promoting accountability of the state, and playing a watchdog role by checking state abuses (Bratton, 1989, 104; Brown and Korten 1991, 53; Korten, 1990, 99; Ottaway and Carothers, 2000, 13). At the same time, there have been studies highlighting the weakness of civil society in Africa, the lack of coordination among groups within civil society, and the donor dependence of NGOs. All these factors diminish the ability of civil society to put pressure on the state and play its expected watchdog role (Dicklitch, 1998).

More recently there has been an interest in the extent to which voluntary organizations can be seen as part of civil society, as they contribute to democratization by creating social capital, i.e., by building trust and reciprocity and by establishing horizontal linkages rather than vertical ones (Putnam, 1993; Rice and Sumberg, 1997). There is an interest in how ties based on ethnicity, clan or another ascriptive identities are gradually replaced by organizations that cut across these affiliations and create linkages and networks that bring people together around larger causes (Diamond, 1994, 9). This latter concern has evolved into debates about the usefulness of the concept of "social capital" (see Foley and Edwards, 1997; Newton, 1997; Widner and Mundt, 1998).

With the demise of the welfare state, Western governments shifted much of their social spending in their own countries from what had previously taken the form of unconditional block grants to contracts with NGOs for specific tasks, leaving less room for voluntary activities of organizations, communities, and the family. This gave rise to an "institutional choice" literature that focused on questions having to do with the appropriate mix of state, market, informal and voluntary non-profit sector in service provisioning. This literature examined the relative advantages of non-profits as service providers and the role of government in financing non-profit organizations.

However, these questions of the state-NGO mix have a slightly different flavor in Africa when compared to other parts of the world in which the state has been much more central to social service provisioning. In no other world region has there been as much societal involvement in the provisioning of social services as in Africa, especially in the areas of health and education, where churches, NGOs, and self-help groups have been especially active (Robinson and White, 1997, 9). Under colonial rule, for example, much of health provisioning was taken over by church missions and it was not until late colonial rule that the state began to invest in health facilities, especially in urban areas. Missions remained the major providers of health even at independence. Even today at the community level, various forms of community health groups, NGOs that run non-profit clinics, parent-teacher associations, grassroots groups, and religious institutions remain important in the provision of social and public services. For these and other reasons, African states have tended to treat NGOs as potential competitors in accessing donor funds.

Forms of State-NGO Synergy

It is generally recognized that those countries that have the best linkages between central government and communities through a network of local institutions have fared the best in agricultural performance, in social indicators, and in achieving higher levels of welfare (Ostrom, 1996, 1082; Uphoff, 1993, 613). Even though it is crucial that communities participate in shaping and contributing to social and public services to ensure universal access to services and goods, the state needs to play a coordinating role and establish the broader environment to facilitate such provisioning. The question is how does one create an adequate mix that does not stifle local participation and yet addresses the good of the whole and the particular needs of marginalized groups. Several scholars have sought to explain what accounts for such productive synergies (Evans, 1996; Ostrom, 1996; Robinson and White, 2001).

Some have suggested the linking of public and societal associations through intermediary organizations like boards or trusts that lean toward corporatist models found in Western Europe, Latin America and, East Asia (Hyden, 1995). Another model involves government organized NGOs, or GONGOS of the type found in China, where state control coexists with societal participation. Or there could be shared financing of services, joint policy making or collaborative administration of a service. Alternately, the government could carry out a devolution of funds earmarked for a particular activity, with community organizations deciding how to spend the money. With delegation, the state would determine the service to be provided but delegate the responsibility of organizing the service to a community organization. More commonly, states contract services out to community organizations on a competitive basis (Robinson and White 1997, 32).

One public-private model adopted in Africa in the context of structural adjustment was the use of fees for service, in which the state provides a service, but requires fees from community organizations and individuals. In the area of health service, user charges were to improve service quality by increasing funds going into health facilities. However, this outcome was evident in all but a few cases. Although there were some examples of improved care, for the most part problems emerged because governments took long to approve improvements in health facilities, and because of delays in setting up financial management systems at health facilities (Mwabu, 2001, 200). The end result was a decline in health provisioning, with the poorest members of society suffering disproportionately. Even introductions of small fees resulted in drastic reductions in the use of health services (Watkins, 2001, 229).

All of these public-private cooperation models come with their own set of problems involving coordination and duplication of efforts. They still face persistent problems of corruption and nepotism; problems of communication and cooperation between international NGOs and local civic organizations; ideological differences, e.g., the dispute between Catholic church and national family planning policy regarding use of contraception; and problems relating to NGO and government dependence on donors (Robinson and White 1997, 32).

Need for Synergy

Numerous important problems could be solved through a variety of state-associational synergies. For example, imbalances created by uneven regional capacities in wealthier regions could be equalized by focusing state interventions in regions that have a weaker associational base. State funding for associations could privilege poorer areas to ensure more even development.

Problems of Sustainability

Because NGOs are so dependent on the vagaries of external funding, which is generally limited in duration, NGO projects can not always be sustained over long periods of time. This is problematic because there are no guarantees that government funding or self-supporting strategies would be able to sustain an initiative previously funded from the outside. Moreover, high levels of donor dependency make NGOs susceptible to changing donor strategies and fads, which tend to be short-term. Donors might withdraw support from an NGO after deciding to shift their funding priorities or having found that an NGO was not meeting contract expectations. This leaves potential recipients with little recourse and at the mercy of shifting donor trends and agendas.

States can also play a positive role in the coordination of activities to prevent duplication of efforts. Any oversight role must not be used as an excuse for monitoring and curtailment of freedom of association, but rather should be carried out collaboratively with the aim of avoiding overlaps in activities of government, NGOs, foreign donors, and local associations. This danger of cooptation and being swallowed up by state intervention is ever-present as Lillian Trager warns in the Nigerian context of Yoruba hometown associations in Ijesa (2001, 259).

PROBLEMS OF REGIONAL IMBALANCE

One common oversight in the NGO/associational literature relates to the political dynamics of communities in which they work. Communities do not exist in a vacuum even though much of the institutional literature treats communities as though they were homogenous, egalitarian, ahistoric, sharing common values, interests and goals (Agrawal, 1997). Time and again studies are done without sufficient attention to who gains and who loses in various NGO interventions. Which groups are politically marginalized? Who are the real power brokers behind the scenes? The politics of gender, class, clan, ethnicity, even age is often ignored in contexts where it may have everything to do with why a particular initiative failed or proved divisive.

Related to this is the larger dilemma posed by NGO or local self-help initiatives. If left uncoordinated and not tied into a national plan, inequalities can easily result because wealthier communities are going to have greater access to resources to work with as they seek to address various community needs. On the one hand, self-help initiatives can have important developmental outcomes where the state has failed to provide services. On the other hand, isolated and uncoordinated responses create imbalances that may have uninvited consequences further down the road of ethnic tensions and regional antagonisms.

One example of an organizational mode that has introduced new regional imbalances are hometown associations. Already studies of hometown and migrant associations from Nigeria, Mali, and Côte d'Ivoire have alerted us to these potential dilemmas (Trager, 2001, 258; Dubresson, 1993, cited in Trager, 2001; Pratten, 1996). Hometown development associations have existed since the colonial era but gained in importance after the 1980s. In some countries they had diminished in importance or disappeared altogether after independence. However, in many parts of Africa we are witnessing a resurgence of these groups that link the urban and rural sectors and are often led by urban members with greater resources. Most home-town development associations emerged specifically to respond to collective community needs that were no longer being met by the government.

The range of activities hometown/development associations are involved in is enormous, including cooperative based agriculture; water development; initiation of business enterprises; electrification and the provision of solar electricity; the establishment of telephone and postal facilities; support for micro-entrepreneurs, women's income generating groups and market sellers; rehabilitation and building of schools, roads, medical facilities and libraries; AIDS support; care of orphans; the establishment of projects to conserve the environment; and raising funds in crisis situations for flood relief and other such causes. In Nigeria, hometown associations form community banks to support entrepreneurs and serve as a support for local industrialization (Trager, 1998; Barkan et al., 1991).

Membership is open to members of the community who participate in meetings and planning. The associations may tax members to finance projects, ensuring compliance through social pressure. In some areas they have become the apex organization for all the communities' associational activities. They often play an intermediary role, mediating between local and national interests and enjoying a high level of legitimacy among the communities they operate in.

In Tanzania, the development associations emerged in the late 1980s as a revival of older ethnic unions that were banned at independence in an effort to undercut ethnic bases of political action. Today they operate from the level of districts down to the local village level. As in Nigeria, they have assumed many of the former functions of government and have even improved on many of the public services provided by government. At the present they cooperate with local government, complement their activities, and push local governments to take action in various arenas. But this congenial relationship may not continue as they increase in strength since they gradually are replacing the functions of local government, for example, taxing coffee and cotton growers, building schools, roads, hospitals, wells.

Some are organized by urban dwellers to give assistance to their home areas. Others are organized exclusively by people living in rural areas, while some organizations are formed through rural-urban collaboration. Some are explicitly ethnically based, while others avoid such distinctions. Hometown associations may be formed as trusts to which rural dwellers apply for support. In other associations, councils of elected officials decide on how to spend their resources. While they overwhelmingly rely on their own resources, a few receive from foreign religious associations, and some receive modest support from bilateral donors for specific projects.

Hometown associations are usually begun by wealthier well-educated, and well-connected individuals involved either in business, politics or the church. Often they are led by civil servants or business managers who have returned or plan to return to their home village to retire. Not infrequently, Members of Parliament will either start or involve themselves in these associations both to help their home areas but also as a way of garnering votes. As political patrons, MPs can often find ways to direct government or even donor funding to assist their constituents. In Benin such Local Development Associations or Associations locales de développement (ALD) are set up at the neighborhood, village, commune, or district level. A study of them found that out of 64 Deputies in the first National Assembly, 39 were president of an ALD or a member of the executive committee, and the remaining 25 were members of such an organization (Bako-Arifari, 1995, 16). Hibou and Banégas (2000) argue that one reason for the rise in popularity of hometown/development associations in the 1990s has to do with the introduction of multipartyism and the increased importance of local and rural politics in constituency building. With heightened political competition it became all the more important to be perceived as doing something for one's home area and demonstrate their devotion to a citizens' association through concrete contributions to development.

These development associations are indicative of some of the new and creative development strategies that are evolving in Africa today, often quite apart from international NGO and donor initiatives. They have evolved to respond to state failure and even state suffocation of popular initiative. Nevertheless, their vitality also raises questions of regional balance. Clearly, communities with members who are wealthier and better educated are going to do better than communities with more limited endowments. In Tanzania, for example, the most vital development associations are found in the northern Kilimanjaro Region, while the poorest regions like Dodoma have no organizations of this kind. Even within communities and locales there are imbalances in access to wealth.

The question for the state is how to create productive synergies that can even out those imbalances without killing the spirit of self-reliance and initiative and without coopting or destroying the independent initiative that has been so critical to the success of these associations. This problem of synergy is especially challenging given that these development and hometown associations emerged in response to state failure and have often taken over local government functions out of necessity, potentially placing them in direct competition with the state for authority. Uniform policies regarding such associations may destroy these important developmental initiatives. But state support for poorer regions with weak or non-existent autonomous development associations would be welcome and could provide important incentives to generate similar initiatives.

PROBLEMS OF ACCOUNTABILITY

Although many organizations like hometown associations are locally funded, donor-funded NGOs, both indigenous and international, pose another set of problems. Donor-funded NGO substitution for the state provisioning has the potential to undercut state accountability to its citizens. NGOs are not elected by the people and therefore are not accountable to them in the same way as an elected representative might be. They can set an agenda with little popular mandate and far fewer political consequences if they fail. In the late 1990s in Tanzania and Uganda, the World Bank and IMF were negotiating directly with what they refer to as "Civil Society" (leading indigenous and foreign NGOs) regarding a Poverty Reduction Strategy Programme in Tanzania and a Poverty Eradication Action Plan in Uganda. There was no involvement on the part of parliamentarians in these negotiations. Although the NGOs do excellent work and their involvement constitutes popular participation, they are not, however, elected representatives of the Tanzanian and Ugandan people and are self-appointed spokespeople for the citizenry in those countries. This raises questions about who they are accountable to regardless of how much one agrees with their goals.

Accountability comes up in other ways as well. Were NGOs to eliminate a service due to changing donor priorities, it is difficult to hold them responsible in the same way accountability is required of the state. Moreover, short-term donor funding of NGOs does not always permit the kind of painstaking and slow but necessary institutional development to occur of the kind that states can provide ideally. States need to find ways to incorporate this kind of more unpredictable temporary NGO assistance into long-term efforts to establish a more stable state-run provisioning of a service.

Yet another dilemma of NGO accountability is related to their focus on process rather than outcomes. External donors and NGOs often superimpose their agendas on communities in a pre-defined way that they believe corresponds to the needs of local people. By not taking local priorities seriously, then often end up with disappointing outcomes and recriminations from donors and constituents alike. According to James Igoe's (2000) study of the pastoralist NGO movement in Tanzania, the NGOs had leaders who knew what Western partners were interested in funding. To receive funding they appealed to various stereotyped Western conceptions of pastoralists that had to do with ethnicity, human rights, conservation, and service delivery. Thus they sidestepped some of the major concerns of the Maasai that had to do with access and rights to land. Certain kinds of women's projects were introduced because they were thought to appeal to donors, rather than arising out of needs women had identified for themselves. The local NGO leaders were well-versed in the discourse of international organizations and were able to effectively appeal to those interests. In particular, they were able to form a network of Pastoral Indigenous NGOs called PINGO, which brought together very diverse pastoral peoples (Maasai, Barabaig, and Hadzabe). In spite of rhetoric of participation and community empowerment, this was in relative short supply, given the autocratic way in which the organizations were run in order to meet donor objectives. The program had the result of further marginalizing the people they were intended to assist. Numerous recent studies of donor-NGO-local interactions in other parts of Africa tell much the same story (Botchway, 2000; Benjamin, 2000; Tripp, 2000; Whitaker, 1996).

Such externally devised programs often do not correspond to needs and concerns of local people and are developed with little regard for pre-existing organizations (Howes, 1997, 832), interests, local sources of authority, forms of organization, local forms of accountability, and power dynamics in the community, including class and gender dynamics. As the Igoe example of the pastoralists shows, local actors can shape their appeals to meet donor guidelines, but this does not ensure that community priorities are addressed. Rather than pre-determining what the communities' goals ought to be and trying to shoehorn local realities into their externally driven mandate, NGOs should start by asking residents what they would like to see changed in a particular area, how it should be transformed, and they should work with local associations and resources for change.

State development initiatives failed for ignoring local conditions. Today we see the replication of these same mistakes with NGOs. Well-meaning international and domestic NGOs promote funding in the areas of human rights, the environment, and women's rights in ways that do not always correspond to local priorities or ways of formulating the issues. This dilemma is compounded by the fact that there are inadequate mechanisms through which local residents can demand accountability and express their needs regarding the NGOs. This lack of transparency in such power dynamics can be highly problematic (Tandon, 1991, 142). The lack of mechanisms for NGO accountability is far more problematic than the existence of the much-touted "briefcase NGOs" that are nothing more than scams. It is here where in an ideal world, the state could intervene to open up space where communities could express their own priorities and frustrations with NGOs. The state could ensure that NGOs find mechanisms that allow them to be accountable to the people they intend to help.

It is striking how little attention is paid to such dynamics time and again with predictably disastrous results. Mixed gender organizations are often introduced, without considering pre-existing gender relations and associational forms. Often men and women may have had their own separate organizations and women may have been much more active and experienced in running organizations. A mixed organization under such circumstances often means that men run the organization and a whole series of pre-existing power dynamics are replicated, leaving the women on the sidelines.

NGOs and donors often end up unwittingly creating community organizations led by wealthier, male, better educated, and politically connected local elites who know how to interact with donors. Underlying these developments is the assumption that the poorest members of the community are going to automatically benefit regardless of who is in control of the association and whether or not they are in a position to demand accountability without adequate mechanisms to do so (Howes, 1997, 832).

Problems of Duplication

Problems related to the duplication of efforts by various NGOs is another area that requires some state coordination and oversight given the limited resources available. Already there is a considerable experience in Africa in how to offset the dilemma of coordinating services to avoid duplication of efforts, unnecessary competition for resources and inconsistencies between different NGO approaches. National networks or umbrella organizations have helped minimize some of these problems. For example, the Private Health Association of Malawi and the Christian Hospital Association in Ghana facilitate cooperation between NGOs by promoting technical support, information sharing, and cost effective practices as well as coordinating participation in influencing national policy (Gilson et al., 1994). But at times such voluntary efforts are insufficient, especially when the NGOs are many and the areas of coverage varied.

In Tanzania, government-NGO efforts to jointly tackle the AIDS crisis are in many ways a model of such synergies. Initially a national AIDS

Task Force was formed in 1985, followed by the establishment of the National AIDS Control Program (NACP) in 1988. The NACP focused on promoting safer sex to the general population, youth, and people who traveled a lot through popular media and education campaigns as well as condom promotion and distribution (Msamanga and Swai, 1999). Government initiatives declined in the early 1990s and a United States Agency for International Development (USAID) funded Tanzania AIDS Project (TAP) formed in 1993 to strengthen the capacity of indigenous NGOs in HIV/AIDS-related activities. TAP's target populations were broader than the earlier high-risk groups identified by NACP. TAP went beyond NACPs focus on prevention to address the health and social consequences of AIDS by delivering services to people living with HIV/AIDS, to their families, and orphans. They also supported activities that would encourage broad-based community involvement rather than NACPs interventions targeting at risk populations. TAP supported nine regional NGO clusters or coalitions working on HIV/AIDS issues. These clusters linked up with 200 pre-existing local NGOs, some of which were health related, but others were involved with environmental issues, small scale industry, religion, and multipurpose concerns. This allowed TAP to link health issues to broader community concerns. TAP cooperated closely with the NACP, but also sought to reduce competition for resources between NGOs and government and prevent an overlap of activities. It sought to build capacity of NGOs, provide them with educational resources and information, offer technical training, peer education, as well as communication, leadership, and management skills. It was especially concerned with how to help communities realize their needs and define their problems accurately. Its coordinating efforts helped avoid wasting resources.

TAP worked closely with regional and district authorities to coordinate activities. It also saw its role as coordinating NGOs to help draft the National AIDS Policy and to keep "pestering the government to pay attention to the HIV/AIDS epidemic," as Dr. Justin Nguma, TAP director, explained to me in an 1999 interview. The government leadership had not been proactive when it came to the AIDS epidemic, and so TAP and other organizations had to fight tooth and nail to get the government to treat AIDS as a priority issue. They fought to get AIDS issues onto the school curriculum, although it was never made mandatory or a systematic part of the curriculum, partly due to a lack of funds to retrain teachers and provide materials.

Slowly changes became evident as seen in the declines in HIV infection rates nationwide. At a local level behavioral changes were palpable. TAP had worked with local healers, traditional birth attendants, traditional circumcisers, and trained them in several regions. The mobilization of traditional birth attendants in Dodoma meant that they began to require that expectant mothers provide rubber gloves. TAP affiliated Dodoma groups worked with local authorities to ensure sufficient availability of gloves. Similarly, community pressure in Iringa resulted in the adoption of specific regulations to discourage high risk behavior patterns.[2]

This community-based focus combined with the networking of clusters at the national level around particular issues and events was highly successful. Because it allowed for issues to be defined by the communities, implementation came much easier than initiatives driven simply from the outside. Moreover, having a supportive national policy that encouraged local level initiatives was critical. Although the government was not proactive around the AIDS issue, it was not prohibitive and was basically supportive, making it possible for communities to mobilize unimpeded.

This example and the above mentioned models of public-voluntary sector collaboration assume a basically cooperative relationship between state and society. However, such assumptions do not always reflect the realities of African state-society relations, which have at times been conflictual, competitive, and based on mutual suspicion.

Constraints on Synergy

The debates regarding the mix, overlap, and interaction between state, market, and the third sector are not as straightforward in Africa as in many other parts of the world. In Africa, the third sector has already been involved in filling gaps where state and market coverage was deficient. And yet it is constrained in ways not experienced as much in other parts of the world. Many have debated whether the third sector should function as a catalyst in initiating facilities, leaving maintenance to the private sector or the state. In many parts of Africa there is no guarantee that the state, let alone the private sector, is in any position to fulfill such a role.

In Latin America and India the third sector plays an advocacy role for services. Again, this seems unlikely to become a major function of the third sector in Africa, at least in the near future. This is, in part, because of the unresponsiveness and weakness of African states to respond to societal demands, but also the tendency among states to see associations as threats and competitors rather than as collaborators. Moreover, the third sector is extremely vulnerable to changes in the political and economic climate and to the amount of political space it has been afforded by the state. For example, in the 1990s, political liberalization and democratization in Africa, the shift away from military to civilian rule, and the trends away from one-party to multi-party rule created conditions conducive to greater civic activity and grassroots mobilization. However, these conditions are susceptible to change, given the tenuousness of the democratization processes in Africa. The third sector is extremely vulnerable to changes in state policy regarding services and to economic reform, i.e., liberalization, privatization, and macro-economic interventions.

A growing literature has challenged the earlier assumptions that took for granted the greater efficiency of NGOs in Africa and has shown them to be riven by corruption and their own clientelistic circuits built along ethnic and other lines. Some have raised questions about the comparative advantage of NGOs in reaching the poor, their cost effectiveness, popular participation, flexibility, and innovation. A few have even argued that were states to have access to the large amounts of funding NGOs have at their disposal, they too might be able to provide services as cost-effectively and might be able to better ensure more even coverage nationwide (Fowler, 1991, Edwards and Hulme, 1996; Tendler, 1989). But since states already have had far greater resources at their disposal (the most optimistic estimates suggest that NGOs account for about 5 percent of OECD aid to developing countries), the bigger question is why are states so inefficient. Moreover, one has to look not only at the differentials between NGOs and states but also at the overall problem of declining foreign aid. According to the IMF, development aid to Africa has fallen from $32 per capita in 1990 to $19 in 1998, despite evidence that such assistance has been effective in countries with sound economic and social policies (IMF, 2001).

THE POLITICS OF COOPTATION AND AUTONOMY

What seems to be underestimated in many discussions over how to create productive state-society synergies is the influence of politics, and in particular, the politics of state cooptation and societal autonomy. Creating these synergies is not simply a technical problem or an administrative dilemma. The extent to which such collaborations can succeed is highly dependent on political factors. If the state is not inclined to encourage full autonomous participation, the synergies are flawed from the outset.

The openness of the regime to non-state actors matters as does the legal environment within which they operate. How much autonomy associations are granted by the state also influences the extent to which they can flourish. The political environment has improved to varying degrees as African countries shifted from military to civilian rule and from single party rule to multipartyism. The new political spaces permitted an exponential increase in independent NGOs. Democratizing and semi-authoritarian states allowed for a much freer media. Organizational forms that had been banned in the past were now permitted. Cooperatives, trade unions, student and youth groups, women's organizations and associations focused on welfare, business and various professional associations that had been tied to the regime or ruling party under single-party rule diminished in importance, as new independent organizations sprang up (Woods, 1999; Thioub et al., 1998). This often placed the old politically oriented groups into direct competition with the newer NGOs in seeking supporters and donor funds. Some of these mass organizations subsequently delinked from the party or became semi-independent. The open repression and banning of organizations became less common and was replaced by a new repertoire of tactics to monitor, regulate, undermine, and in some cases, destroy, autonomous organizations that were perceived (usually quite erroneously) as having the desire and potential to undermine state authority.

Most national level autonomous associations formed in the mid-1980s and 1990s. NGOs have often had to adopt a defensive posture in defending their autonomy. In the late 1980s and 1990s NGOs found themselves opposing governmental legislative efforts to create agencies for the monitoring and control of NGO activities in Tanzania, Botswana, Ghana, Kenya, Zimbabwe, and Uganda (Gyimah-Boadi, 1998, 22; Ndegwa, 1996; Bratton, 1989, 577). Some of the best NGO-government relations in Africa can be found in Uganda, where NGOs are invited to participate in many government commissions and help plan the work of various ministries. The problems NGOs face in Uganda are, nevertheless, emblematic of the kinds of restrictions NGOs face even under the best of circumstances. In 2001, the network organization Development Network of Indigenous Voluntary Organisations (DENIVA) in wide consultation with other NGOs sought to get an amendment passed to the 1989 NGO Registration Statute that would enhance freedom of association. They were trying to preempt what they feared would be even harsher restrictions on NGOs by opening up the debate on the future of NGOs by engaging in dialogue with the government. Currently the Statute situates the NGO Registration Board in the Ministry of Internal Affairs alongside other internal security organs, making the government's primary interest in NGOs appear to be one of security rather than development. NGOs have agreed that the Statute interferes with their work and demoralizes the communities in which they work. Meetings of hundreds of NGOs found that the Statute subjected NGOs too much to the whims of the Minister, who had the power to revoke their permits in a way that infringed on the freedom of expression and association. They found that requiring the annual renewal of registration was cumbersome given the slowness of the wheels of the bureaucracy. Moreover, the focus on security was seen as undermining associational autonomy. As DENIVA leader Jessy Kwesiga (2001) put it: "As for denial of registration on the basis of incompatibility with Government policy, plans and public interest, what if the NGOs are expressing the will of the people that may be at odds with Government policy and Government definition of public interest? History in Uganda and elsewhere is full of many state-inspired undemocratic misfortunes in the name of public interest."

What is interesting about this particular debate, is the explicit articulation of how the society-state partnership ought to be configured. State and society are seen as complementing one another in development efforts, but this "social contract" will not work if the state sees fit to arbitrarily suppress the popular will of the people. Rather, state and society need to respect the "independence, rights and obligations of the other," writes Kwesiga.

In other instances, states have felt threatened by increasing donor attention to NGOs and have sought to eliminate NGOs altogether. In Tanzania, the independent Tanzanian Women's Council (BAWATA) was suspended by the courts in 1996 under pressure from the Tanzanian ruling party's women's organization, Umoja wa Wanawake (UWT) and the Ministry of Community Development, Women's Affairs and Children. BAWATA had been formed by the UWT to become a semi-independent organization to gain access to donor monies. When the BAWATA leadership unexpectedly steered it toward complete independence, the ruling party and the UWT turned against the organization. President Mkapa, who had the possibility of running for a second term, succumbed to UWT pressure to ban BAWATA, no doubt having calculated that the UWT delivers a large proportion of the Chama Cha Mapinduzi (Revolutionary State Party) (CCM) vote. Other women's organizations in Tanzania have also faced difficulties getting registered under various pretexts. Part of these tactics involved efforts to suppress existing independent organizations or prevent the emergence of organizations that might pose a challenge to the government and the ruling party. BAWATA took the matter to the High Court to challenge Societies Ordinance on the grounds that the government action was unconstitutional and in violation of international human rights conventions to which Tanzania is a signatory. Although BAWATA won its case, the entire debacle killed the nascent organization.

But even autonomous community funded organizations have posed threats to the state. In Uganda, for example, Parent Teacher Associations

(PTAs) represented one of the largest areas of independent community mobilization. They were not formed into a national or even regional or district-wide network, but rather, each PTA operated independently in its own respective school. Formed after independence, they became especially important under Idi Amin's rule as the country fell into civil war in the 1970s and government sponsorship of the educational system unraveled. The responsibility fell to parents to raise the funds and run the schools, which they did through the head teacher and a board of governors or management committees. This parental responsibility continued throughout the years of conflict and continued after Yoweri Museveni and his National Resistance Movement took over the country in 1986 after years of guerrilla war. From the 1980s up until 1996, 90 percent of the funding for the schools came from PTAs, which paid for school maintenance, salaries, educational materials, and furniture. Parents not only raised tuition fees, but they also provided school transport, midday meals, school supplies, textbooks, buildings, dormitories, teachers' houses, equipment, animals, and school farms that supplemented the teachers' salaries (Senteza-Kajubi, 1991, 324). In the process, imbalances arose because poorer parents could not afford the fees and hence were unable to school their children.

In a bid to gain votes in the 1996 presidential elections, Museveni announced the abolition of the PTAs and introduced Universal Primary Education (UPE). UPE was popular when it was initially announced, because it promised to allow poorer households to send their children to school. However, the government did not have the resources to deliver quality education to the majority of school children overnight. Teachers were not paid for months at a stretch, and large numbers of schools did not have adequate numbers of teachers or school supplies. Classrooms increased in size from 40 students to 110 on the average.

The political calculations were such that Museveni could ill afford such a large associational base that could potentially turn against him. Nevertheless, none of the major donors funding the UPE, including the World Bank and USAID, seemed to find the dissolution of PTAs in the rural areas problematic, nor did they seem to be particularly bothered by the political nature of the decision to ban the PTAs and introduce UPE so rapidly without almost any planning. The provision of education was being treated as a technical problem rather than as a political one. The PTAs were eventually allowed to return in the more politically volatile urban areas, but their rural counterparts remained banned.

Cooptation and coercion are directed at key NGO leaders, but also at organizations themselves. Although the largest women's organization in Kenya, Maendeleo ya Wanawake in Kenya (MYW), had separated from the ruling party Kenya African National Union (KANU) in 1992, the party continued to control its elections and leaders. It is no accident that the current leadership is pro-KANU and the leader, Zipporah Kittony, is a KANU loyalist and belongs to the same Kalenjin ethnic group as the president. These measures were aimed at ensuring MYW political support for KANU and keeping the organization's agenda depoliticized.

Such curtailment of autonomy keep organizations from resisting the state and make it difficult for them to articulate and advance their own organizational interests through advocacy. Instead, they are forced to become more dependent on patronage because this is one of the only avenues for influence and access to resources. State authorities often select their leaders and set or delimit their agendas. Societal differences are exacerbated when such a patronage system is superimposed upon a local community fragmented by differences that might determine access to patronage, i.e., ones' wealth, education, gender, ethnicity, religion. Amy Patterson, for example, found in her study of villages in Diourbel region of Senegal, that patronage kept local leaders from challenging state actions and from demanding better services (Patterson, 1998, 439).

My findings in Uganda were much the same as Patterson's, where autonomous associations gained leverage because of their independence. I conducted a series of case studies in Uganda in the 1990s of local level conflicts between women's organizations and local government officials over access to market space in one case; over the direction of a Kampala City Council infrastructure project in another; over the building of a health clinic in a rural area; and over the fate of a large network of women's organizations that had been taken over by a corrupt leadership. In all these cases and others, the women's associational autonomy kept them outside of patronage networks, but it was also the very reason they were able to resist the status quo, demand accountability and promote their developmental interests (Tripp, 2000). The fact that they were ultimately only partially successful in their endeavors was related to their status as women and the overwhelming power of the patronage networks. Nevertheless, they would not have even attempted to challenge the authorities, had they been part of those networks.

WHAT FALLS OUT

Much of Africa's associational life and development potential is left out of the government, donor and NGO development planning, not to mention scholarly debates on civil society. There are many organizational forms relevant to development concerns that do not even enter the debate because they are structured in ways that do not easily fit into Western-developed models of development. Too much of the discussion on societal input is focused on urban-based, donor-funded NGOs led by educated middle-class people. Yet the more informal, localized, sometimes smaller, often multipurpose, and more "traditional" looking organizations are left out of the picture. These are membership-based organizations that draw widespread participation, unlike the NGO sector.

These local level indigenous organizations involve rotating credit and savings associations, burial societies, a myriad of multipurpose self-help groups run by women, marketing and trading groups, local credit unions and cooperatives, ad hoc organizations to carry particular functions like build a bridge or a well, hometown and local level development associations, women's and men's councils, parent-teacher organizations, orphan assistance groups, and a variety of other organizations that provide social and public services and serve local development needs. The fact that they do not attract significant attention from the authorities may not be necessarily a problem, especially if intervention ends up destroying their self-help spirit. But it does mean that they are not given adequate recognition, as a source of development nor they are generally able to scale up and become larger more influential organizations.

Were these associations given more attention, we might be asking why so many community development banks have failed while rotating credit associations thrive as an institution throughout Africa and invariably have far lower default rates. Similarly, local organizations that do not rely on government and donor funding often seem to have a better track record, depending on their objectives and prexisting resource endowments (Botchway, 2000; Binns, 1999). In general, there has been poor integration between formal and informal financial systems with few efforts to address this concern. The two types of institutions co-exist but with divergent developmental outcomes.

For example, rotating savings and credit associations (ROSCAs) are enormously popular throughout Africa as a source of savings and credit. While formal financial institutions responded poorly to economic reform measures in countries like Malawi, Nigeria, Tanzania, and Ghana, informal financial agents responded dynamically and have proven to be more efficient.[3] Default rates for small-scale creditors in Tanzania, for example, were 0.1 percent and 2.5 percent for ROSCAs, while for commercial banks they were 80 percent (Aryeetey et al., 1997, 198, 205). Studies in Liberia, Côte d'Ivoire, Togo, Cameroon, and Nigeria found that participation in ROSCAs ranges from 50 to 95 percent (Bouman, 1995b).

A study of microfinance in Kenya, Ghana, and Malawi found that ROSCAS are highly efficient. Group solidarity forms the basis for risk management. Defaulters are punished by not being paid in future rounds, but the use of social sanctions can be limited because participants understand each others life situations and realize that they may be in need of forgiveness at a later date (Gugerty, 2000, 7). Money flows from one member of the group to the other in a way that savings match credits without any need for interest rates or collateral and where transaction costs are kept at a minimum (Buckley, 1997, 1085). Some ROSCAS serve as a kind of Rotary Club, allowing business people to network, exchange relevant information and build goodwill (Haggblade, 1978, 48–9). They are generally durable because they meet all the criteria of successful long standing-resource management organizations: They establish clear organizational rules, use graduated sanctions, and establish low-cost mechanisms to resolve disputes (Gugerty, 2000; Ostrom, 1990).

Another example of a developmental organization that has remained outside of scholarly, state and donor purview is the dual sex governance structure that has been revived in various parts of Africa, including the Igbo areas of Nigeria. A dual sex political system is one in which representatives of each gender governs their own members through a Council. In much of former Eastern Nigeria most communities have a broad based Women's Governing Council that has sole jurisdiction over wide ranging political, economic, and cultural affairs of women (Nzegwu, 1995). These organizations, according to Nzegwu, are autonomous of the state, yet their decisions are binding regardless of social status, education, or income level. Moreover, the local councils can represent women living as far as Lagos, Kano, or New York.

They are distinct from organizations modeled along Western patterns in that they promote a sense of "shared communitarian values rather than perceived divisive individualistic values," as Nzegwu puts it. Their flexibility and capacity to respond to changing situations accounts for their durability. The Igbo Women's Councils, for example, intervene in matters that concern the market, ensure moral behavior, sanction men who violate women's rights in the community, govern multiple smaller organizations, and lobby for women's interests at the national level. Nevertheless, according to Nkiru Nzegwu, organizations like these have been consistently overlooked and dismissed by development agencies because of preconceived notions of women's roles, a bias in favor of elevating literate people in leadership roles, and the misguided notion that men are the only experts when it comes to water supply systems, food production, mechanized farming, and business investment. Yet as

Nzegwu has forcefully argued, these activities are mostly the prerogative of women in Nigeria.

Nzegwu shows that these women's councils are enormously important to local women because they have a strong community orientation and claim to legitimacy. Their diverse membership means that the council can draw on a wide variety of skills and know-how for advice. Accountability is maintained by a strict monitoring system where nothing is hidden and the threat of public humiliation and ostracism weighs heavily as a deterrent to violations of council norms. Accountability is tied to community validation, which is an extremely effective constraint on corruption in this context. The complex and efficient administrative structures that can also adapt to new situations speak to the resiliency of these associations.

Their leaders service a wide range of associations and therefore are multifaceted in their approach, since they are concerned with social, cultural, religious, economic and political issues simultaneously, giving them a virtual "encyclopedic knowledge of their community." Their extensive vertical linkages that extend from the poorest of women to highly educated professional women and to Ibo women in cities around the world, give them an enormous network of financial, legal, informational resources on which to draw. The bottom line is that these kinds of organizations are viable and have enormous potential that has yet to be tapped by the development community, because the organizational structures do not fit the NGO patterns they are more accustomed to.

While the Women's Councils started in precolonial times, not all such indigenous organizations are old. Some have formed to respond to new contingencies. Some groups have taken over public service provision from the state such as the urban youth associations in Dakar and Kampala, which became frustrated with the lack of government public services and began to take matters into their own hands. Dakar young people who were part of a "Clean, Make Clean" movement formed groups to collect garbage, clean and paint buildings, shaming community leaders and public officials into making their own improvements in the city (Landell-Mills, 1992, 558). A similar association of youth in Kampala started on a voluntary basis cleaning public toilets, market places and painting pedestrian crossing near schools, similarly challenging the city authorities to do more in the provision of basic services.

Likewise in Ghana another group of 95 women in Ayirebi responded to economic crisis and structural adjustment in the 1980s by forming a cultivating group. They were able to pool resources to buy land and sell crops to purchase more land for individual and collective farming ventures. They also used a portion of their resources for community development. The women attribute their success over the years to their ability to rebuild and maintain strong social relations, to find alternative sources of income for the household, and to rely on local resources to meet the demands of local markets. Part of their success was also attributable to their capacity to define their own needs and come up with their own strategies to respond to national economic contraction. They conceived of economic opportunity in terms of mutual benefit rather than the individual benefit of one individual. Their economic successes and contributions to community welfare eventually brought them political recognition and a greater voice in household and community concerns (Dei, 1994, 126–127, 139–140). Dei explained that "The Ayirebi case study shows that local strategies of development must aim at achieving a diversified economy, but in a manner that prioritizes meeting local needs first." Thus, the challenge is to start with people's local needs and look at how people themselves are coping with economic stress to meet these needs. More attention needs to be paid to local understandings of problems, local resources, local markets, and local solutions.

CONCLUSIONS

This chaper has explored some of the challenges in creating viable state-society synergies in delivering public services and promoting development. The question is no longer should states and autonomous associations cooperate in development initiatives, but rather *how* should such cooperation occur and on what basis can it be built. These are especially salient questions in Africa, where the relationship between states and associations has been strained in both one party and multiparty contexts, and by state efforts to curtail autonomous mobilization through use of patronage, cooptation and repression. The need for such synergies is abundantly evident in situations where the state actively defines the limits of agency. They are also important as NGOs are not permanent institutions but are instead dependent on changing donor fads and interests. Under these circumstances, states need to play a backup role.

Where associations reify differences in society that reflect unequal access to resources, states should play an equalizing role. Communities may find it difficult to demand accountability from NGOs, as they may be providing social and public services but they are not elected representatives. Communities cannot easily throw NGOs out, nor are there generally viable mechanisms through which NGOs can be influenced by grassroots forces. The state can demand accountability where this becomes a problem and it has the authority to close down or investigate scam organizations. States could also play more of a backup role where

NGOs fail and donors withdraw. NGOs often have short-term agendas that are vulnerable to the vagaries of donor funding. The state needs to ensure that people are not left without services when unexpected changes occur. States can also play an important coordinating role by preventing a duplication of NGO, donor and governmental efforts. The danger in all such interventions is the concern that associational autonomy will be compromised by the state.

While there are numerous models for state-NGO synergies, the state-local association synergies are less easily configured, given that associations at this level are fluid, informal, and often have been created with the expressed purpose of evading the state. Yet they play important developmental roles that go unrecognized by government leaders, donors, and scholars alike. New ways need to be created that will simultaneously recognize the role these local associations play in development, while protecting their initiative, energy, flexibility, and creativity.

Notes

1   Norman Uphoff identifies three sectors—the public, collective action, and private sector—which are each represented at the following levels: international, national, regional, district, subdistrict, locality, community, and group.

2   "Final Report for the AIDSCAP Program in Tanzania," October 1991 to September 1997.

3   They go by many names in different parts of Africa. They are known as: Benin: *Asusu, Yissirou, Ndjonu, Tontine*; Botswana: *Motshelo*, beer parties; Burkina Faso: *Tontine, Tibissiligbi, Pari, Song-taaba*; Burundi: *Upato* (in Kiswahili); Cameroon: *Jangi, Ujangi, Djana, Mandjon, Djapa, Tontine, Djanggi, Njanggi, Ngwa, Ntchwa*; Egypt: *Gameya, Jam'iyya*; Ethiopia: *Ekub, Ikub*; Gabon: *Bandoi*; The Gambia: *Osusu, susu, esusu, Compin*; Ghana: *Susu, Nanamei akpee, Onitsha, Nnoboa*; Ivory Coast: *Tonton, Tontine, Moni, Diaou Moni, War Moni, Djigi Moni, Safina, Akpole wule, Susu, Aposumbo, Kukule, a tche le sezu, Komite, n'detie, m'bgli sika, Monu, mone*; Kenya: *Mabati, Nyakinyua, Itega, Mkutano ya wanawake, Mkutano ya wazee*; Liberia: *Esusu, susu, sau*; Madagascar: *Fokontany*; Mali: *Pari*; Mozambique: *Upato, Xitique*; Niger: *Adasse, Tomtine, Asusu*; Nigeria: *Esusu, Osusu, Enusu, Ajo* (Yoruba), *Cha* (Ibo), *Oha, Oja, Adashi* (Haussa, Tiv), *Bam* (Tiv), *Isusu* (Ot), *Utu* (Ibo), *Dashi* (Nupe), *Efe* (Ibibios), *Oku* (Kalabari Ijawas), *Mitiri, Compiri, Club* (Ibo); Congo, PR: *Temo, Kitemo, Ikilemba, Kikedimba, Kikirimbahu, Likilimba, Efongo Eambongo, Otabaka, Ekori, Otabi*; Senegal: *Tontine, Nath*; Sierra Leone: *Asusu, Esusu*; Somalia: *Haghad, Shaloongo, Aiuto*; South Africa: *Chita, Chitu, Stokfel, Stockfair,*

Mahodisana, Motshelo, Umangelo; Sudan: *Khatta, Sanduk, Sandook Box*; Swaziland: *Stokfel*; Tanzania: *Upato, Fongongo*; Tchad: *Pare*; Togo: *Soo, Tonton, Sodzodzo, Sodyodyo, Abo*; Tunisia: *Noufi, Sanduk*; Uganda: *Chilemba, Kiremba, Upato, Kwegatta*; Zaire: *Ikelemba, Osassa, Bandoi, Kitemo, Kitwadi, Adashi, Tontine, Bandal*; Zambia: *Icilimba, Upato, Chilenba*; Zimbabwe: *Chilemba, Stockfair, Kutunderrera* (www.gdrc.org/ icm/rosca-names.html; Bouman 1995a, 129).

REFERENCES

Agrawal, A. (1997). *Community in Conservation: Beyond Enchantment and Disenchantment.* Gainesville, Fl. Conservation and Development Forum.

Aryeetey, E., H. Hettige, M. Nissanke, and W. Steel. (1997). "Financial Market Fragmentation and Reforms in Ghana, Malawi, Nigeria, and Tanzania." *The World Bank Economic Review* 11(2): 195–218.

Bako-Arifari, N. (1995). "Démocratie et logiques du Terroir au Bénin." *Politique africaine* 59 (October).

Barkan, J. D., Michael L. McNulty, and M. A. O. Ayeni (1991). "'Hometown' Voluntary Associations, Local Development, and the Emergence of Civil Society in Western Nigeria." *Journal of Modern African Studies* 29(3): 457–480.

Benjamin, M. (2000). *Development Consumers: An Ethnography of "The Poorest of the Poor" and International Aid in Rural Tanzania.* Anthropology. Ph.D. Thesis. New Haven Conn.: Yale University.

Binns, T. and E. Nel (1999). "Beyond the Development Impasse: The Role of Local Economic Development and Community Self-reliance in Rural South Africa." *The Journal of Modern African Studies* 37(3): 389–408.

Botchway, K. (2000). "Paradox of Empowerment: Reflections on a Case Study from Northern Ghana." *World Development* 29(1): 135–153.

Bouman, F. J. A. (1995a). "ROSCA: On the Origin of the Species." *Savings and Development* 19(2): 117–46.

Bouman, F. J. A. (1995b). "Rotating and Accumulating Savings and Credit Associations: A Development Perspective" *World Development* 23(3): 371–384.

Bratton, M. (1989). "The Politics of Government-NGO Relations in Africa." *World Development* 17(4): 569–587.

Brown, L. D. and D. C. Korten (1991). *Working Effectively with Nongovernmental Organizations. Nongovernmental Organizations and the World Bank: Cooperation for Development.* S. Paul and A. Israel. Washington, D.C.: The World Bank, 44–93.

Buckley, G. (1997). "Microfinance in Africa: Is it Either the Problem of the Solution?" *World Development* 25(7): 1081–1093.

Dei, G. J. S. (1994) "The Women of a Ghanaian Village: A Study of Social Change," *African Studies Review* 37(2): 121–45.

Diamond, L. (1994). "Rethinking Civil Society: Toward Democratic Consolidation." *Journal of Democracy* 5(3): 4–17.

Dicklitch, S. (1998). *The Elusive Promise of NGOs in Africa: Lessons From Uganda*. New York: St. Martin's Press.

Drabek, A. G. (1987). "Development Alternatives: The Challenge for NGOs." *World Development* 15 (Autumn Special Issue): pp. ix–xv.

Dubresson, Alain. (1993). "Urbanistes de l'interieur: les cadres de la prefecture de Toumodi (Côte d'Ivoire)." In *Pouvoirs et Cites d'Afrique Noire: Decentralisations en questions*, ed. Sylvy Jaglin and Alain Dubresson. Paris: Karthala, pp. 259–284.

Edwards, M. and D. Hulme (1996). "Too Close for Comfort? The Impact of Official Aid on Nongovernmental Organizations." *World Development* 24(6): 961–973.

Evans, P. (1996). "Government Action, Social Capital and Development: Reviewing the Evidence on Synergy." *World Development* 24(6): 1119–1132.

Foley, M. W. and B. Edwards (1997). "Escape from Politics? Social Theory and the Social Capital Debate." *American Behavioral Scientist* 40(5): 550–561.

Fowler, A. (1991). "The Role of NGOs in Changing State-Society Relations: Perspectives from Eastern and Southern Africa." *Development Policy Review* 9: 53084.

Gilson, L., P. Kilima, Lucy Gilson, Peter Kilma, and Marcel Tanner. (1994). "Local Government Decentralization and the Health Sector in Tanzania." *Public Administration and Development* 14: 451–477.

Gugerty, M. K. (2000). *You Can't Save Alone: Testing Theories of Rotating Savings and Credit Associations*. Cambridge, Mass.: Harvard University.

Gyimah-Boadi, E. (1998). "The Rebirth of African Liberalism." *Journal of Democracy* 9(2).

Haggblade, S. (1978). "Africanization from Below: The Evolution of Cameroonian Savings Societies into Western Style Banks." *Rural Africana* 2(fall): 35–55.

Hibou, B. and R. Banégas (2000) "Civil Society and the Public Space in Africa'" *(CODESRIA Council for the Development of Social Science Research in Africa) Bulletin* 1.

Howes, M. 1997. "NGOs and the Institutional Development of Membership Organisations: A Kenyan Case." *The Journal of Development Studies* 33(6): 820–847.

Hyden, G. (1995). "Bringing Voluntarism Back In: Eastern Africa in Comparative Perspective." In *Service Provision under Stress in East Africa*, ed. J. Semboja and O. Therkildsen. Portsmouth, NH: Heinemann.

Igoe, J. J. (2000). *Ethnicity, Civil Society, and the Tanzanian Pastoral NGO Movement: The Continuity and Discontinuity of Liberalized Development*. Ph.D. Thesis. Boston, Mass.: Boston University.

International Monetary Fund (IMF) http://www.imf.org/external/np/vc/2001/031401.htm.

Korten, D. C. (1990). *Getting to the 21st Century: Voluntary Action and the Global Agenda*. West Hartford, Conn.: Kumarian Press.

Kwesiga, J. (2001). "NGOs Call for Change." *Monitor*. Windhoek, Nambia.

Landell-Mills, P. (1992). "Governance, Cultural Change and Empowerment." *Journal of Modern African Studies* 30(4): 543–567.

Leftwich, A., ed. (1996). *Democracy and Development*. Cambridge, Mass.: Polity Press.

Msamanga, G. and R. Swai (2000). *Monitoring and Evaluation of National HIV/AIDS/STD Program in Tanzania: A Case Study*. Published by MEASURE (Monitoring and Evaluation to Assess and Use Results) Evaluation Project. The University of North Carolina at Chapel Hill.

Mwabu, G. (2001). "User Charges for Health Care: A Review of the Underlying Theory and Assumptions." In *Social Provision in Low-Income Countries*, eds. G. Mwabu, C. Ugaz, and G. White, Oxford: Oxford University Press.

Ndegwa, S. N. (1996). *The Two Faces of Civil Society: NGOs and Politics in Africa*. West Hartford, Conn.: Kumarian Press.

Newton, K. (1997). "Social Capital and Democracy." *American Behavioral Scientist* 40(5): 575–586.

Nzegwu, N. (1995). "Recovering Igbo Traditions: A Case for Indigenous Women's Organizations in Development." *Women, Culture and Development: A Study of Human Capabilities*. M. Nussbaum and J. Glover. Oxford: Clarendon Press, 444–465.

Ostrom, E. (1990). *Governing the Commons*. New York: Cambridge University Press.

Ostrom, E. (1996) "Crossing the Great Divide: Coproduction, Synergy, and Development," *World Development* 24(6): 1073–1087.

Ottaway, M. and T. Carothers, eds. (2000). *Funding Virtue: Civil Society Aid and Democracy Promotion*. Washington, D.C.: Carnegie Endowment for International Peace.

Patterson, A. S. (1998). "A Reappraisal of Democracy in Civil Society: Evidence from Rural Senegal." *Journal of Modern African Studies* 36(3): 423–441.

Pratten, David T. (1996). "Reconstructing Community: The Intermediary Roile of Sahelian Associations in Processes of Migration and Rural Development." *African Rural and Urban Studies* 3(1):49–78.

Putnam, R., R. Leonardi, and R. Nonetti (1993). *Making Democracy Work: Civic Traditions in Modern Italy*. Princeton, N.J.: Princeton University Press.

Rice, T. and A. Sumberg (1997). "Civic Culture and Government Performance in the American States." *Publius: The Journal of Federalism* 7(27): 99–114.

Robinson, M. and G. White (1997). "The Role of Civic Organizations in the Provision of Social Services: Towards Synergy." Helsinki, UNU World Institute for Development Economics Research. (A longer version of the chapter appears in Mwabu, Ugaz and White [2001].)

Robinson, M. and G. White (2001) "The Role of Civic Organizations in the Provision of Social Services: Towards Synergy." In *Social Provision in Low-Income Countries*, eds. G. Mwabu, C. Ugaz, and G. White, Oxford: Oxford University Press.

Senteza-Kajubi, W. (1991). "Educational Reform During Socio-Economic Crisis." In *Changing Uganda: The Dilemmas of Structural Adjustment and*

Revolutionary Change, eds. H. B. Hansen and M. Twaddle. London: James Currey Publishers, 322–333.

Tandon, Y. (1991). "Foreign NGOs, Uses and Abuses: An African Perspective." *Associations Transnationales* 3: 141–145.

Tendler, J. (1989). "Whatever Happened to Poverty Alleviation?" *World Development* 17(7): 1033–1044.

Thioub, I., M.-C. Diop, and C. Boone. (1998). "Economic Liberalization in Senegal: Shifting Politics of Indigenous Business Interests." *African Studies Review* 41(2): 63–89.

Trager, L. (1998). "Home-Town Linkages and Local Development in South-Western Nigeria: Whose Agenda? What Impact?" *Africa* 68(3): 360–382.

Trager, L. (2001) *Yoruba Hometowns: Community, Identity and Development in Nigeria*. Boulder, Colo.: Lynne Rienner Publishers.

Tripp, A. M. (2000). *Women & Politics in Uganda*. Madison: University of Wisconsin Press.

Uphoff, N. (1993). "Grassroots Organizations and NGOs in Rural Development: Opportunities with Diminishing States and Expanding Markets." *World Development* 21(4): 607–622.

Watkins, K. "Cost Recovery and Equity in the Health Sector: The Case of Zimbabwe." In *Social Provision in Low-Income Countries*, eds. G. Mwabu, C. Ugaz, and G. White, Oxford: Oxford University Press.

Whitaker, C. N. C. (1996). The Impact of Women's Participation in an Income-Generation Program in Southwestern Tanzania. Anthropology. Ph.D. Thesis. Baltimore: Johns Hopkins University.

Widner, J. and A. Mundt (1998). "Researching Social Capital in Africa." *Africa* 68(1): 1–23.

Woods, D. (1999). "The Politics of Organising the Countryside: Rural Cooperatives in Côte d'Ivoire." *Journal of Modern African Studies* 37(3): 489–506.

Chapter 6

Democratic Decentralization of Natural Resources

Institutional Choice and Discretionary Power Transfers in Sub-Saharan Africa

Jesse C. Ribot[*]

Introduction

Researchers, development agencies, and non-governmental organizations (NGOs) around the world are promoting greater local public participation in the use and maintenance of forests, pasture lands, wildlife, and fisheries in order to improve local development and natural resource management.[1] Under the rubric of "decentralization," governments across the developing world are also transferring management responsibilities and powers from central government to a variety of local institutions (see Dillinger 1994:8, Crook and Manor 1998; UNCDF, 2000:5–11; World Bank 2000; Ribot 1999a:51; Fisher 1991). These reforms aim to increase popular participation to promote more equitable and efficient forms of local management and development. Such decentralizations across Africa are re-shaping the local institutions that manage natural resource, promising to increase participation in ways that will profoundly effect who manages, uses, and benefits from these resources.

The key to effective decentralization is increased broad-based participation in local public decision making. Theorists believe that *downwardly accountable* or *representative authorities* with *meaningful discretionary powers* are the basic institutional elements of decentralization that should lead to local efficiency, equity, and development

(Mawhood, 1983; Ribot 1996; Romeo, 1996; Crook and Manor, 1998; Agrawal and Ribot, 1999; Smoke, 2000; Mandondo, 2000).[2] Effective decentralization concerning powers over natural resources require these same elements. However, when examined in detail, community-based and decentralized forms of local natural resource management often lack representation, downward accountability and/or sufficient powers. The World Bank (2000, 107) has pointed out that "decentralization is often implemented haphazardly." This irregularity is apparent in projects and reforms related to the environment, in which poorly structured decentralizations threaten environmental management and equity as well as decentralization and local democracy writ large.

Decentralizations in Burkina Faso, Cameroon, Guinea, Malawi, Niger, The Gambia, and Zimbabwe, for example, are transferring decision-making powers to various unaccountable local bodies, threatening local equity and the environment (Schroeder, 1999; Ribot, 1999a; Delnooz, 1999; Oyono, 2002). Many governments, such as those of Burkina Faso, Senegal, The Gambia, Mali, Uganda, and Zimbabwe, are devolving insufficient powers and benefits either to constitute a decentralization or to motivate local actors to carry out new environmental management responsibilities (Ribot, 1999a; Mandondo, 2000; Conyers, 2001, 29; Engberg-Pedersen, 1995, 2; Ribot, 1995; Bazaara, 2002). Ghana has created local district management committees without sufficient funds to meet their mandates (Porter and Young, 1998, 515). In Zambia, decentralization of control over forests without sufficient environmental management and use guidelines reportedly has led to over-exploitation (Walker, 2000).[3] Across the board, the appropriate mix of powers and functions of different local actors is poorly defined at best (Onyach-Olaa and Porter, 2000). Further, there is little empirical data or experience from which to derive the best local institutional arrangements or to show which factors link decentralization reforms to improved social and ecological outcomes (Little, 1994; Brock and Coulibaly, 1999, 30; World Bank, 2000, 109; Conyers, 2001, 28–9).

Natural resources provide a lens into decentralization and the development of local democracy. Substantively, democracy is about the accountability of leaders to the people (see Moore 1997). Some degree of democracy—a locally accountable local institution—is the first element of effective decentralization. Discretion over natural resource use and management then become the power that makes that representation meaningful. This chapter examines the degree to which the choice of local institutions and the natural resource powers being transferred to them constitute even a degree of democratic decentralization. Are decentralizations of natural resources based on or supporting institutional arrangement that enfranchises local populations? Are they transforming subjects into citizens, and are they establishing the arrangements that theory tells us will provide equity, efficiency, development, and environmental benefits?

The next section examines democracy-natural resource inter-linkages by querying which actors that are being empowered with natural resource use and management decisions in current decentralizations. The third section looks at implications of the kinds of powers that local authorities receive and the means by which they are transferred. The fourth section explores several salient implementation issues. This is followed by conclusions and recommendations.

INSTITUTIONAL CHOICES: LOCAL DEMOCRACY AND THE LOCATION OF DISCRETION

Decentralizations are of great interest to environmentalists because they reshape the institutional infrastructure on which future local natural resource management will depend—potentially establishing institutions for sustainable and equitable community representation and inclusion. Natural resource management and use is of interest to promoters of decentralization and local democracy, because they are a source of revenue and power, and therefore potential legitimacy for new local government authorities. Whether, however, the transfer of natural resource powers within or into the local institutional landscape will promote or undermine representative, accountable and equitable processes depends strongly on which local actors are being entrusted with discretionary powers over natural resources.

Natural resources play a special role in local democratization because local populations rely on them for their daily livelihoods, and governments rely on them as a source of wealth. But, if allocated to non-democratic institutions, environmental powers can also play a counter-productive role. The colonial state, for example, used allocation of land control to legitimate and strengthen customary authorities, who served as their local agents, for the purposes of controlling and managing local people.[4] Today, environment is again becoming an arena of struggle for chiefly power (van Rouveroy van Nieuwaal, Adeiaan, and van Dijk, 1999, 6). As African countries democratize and decentralize, new and more representative forms of local government will also have to rely—at least partly—on natural resources to have an economic base to work from and to have meaningful powers on which to build their legitimacy. Allocating environmental powers to chiefs or other administrative or non-representative authorities can reinforce these less-systematically accountable actors at the expense of representative authorities, slowing democratic transition (Ribot, 1996; 1999a).

Decentralized natural resource management and use decisions can, conversely, be a fulcrum for democratic change. Natural resources are revenue-generating as opposed to other important public services, such as infrastructure, health and education, hence, they can provide revenues needed to make local government more independent, and they can give local governments allocative powers over lucrative opportunities, both of which can help build local government legitimacy. Local representative bodies need powers over the resources that affect their constituencies in order to become legitimate actors around which civic organizations and citizens rally for justice, sustainable livelihoods, and economic improvement. In some parts of Mali, for example, "farmers perceive decentralisation as a threat that may take their existing power to control resources in their *terroir* [commons] out of their hands and give it to the commune [the new elected local governments]." But, this fear may have a positive effect on local governance, since, "the village . . . is likely to play an active role in commune politics in order to retain control of decisions made about resources" (Brock and Coulibaly, 1999, 31). In Zimbabwe, funds from wildlife management can be invested by community institutions in projects of their choice. Conyers (2001, 24–5) observes that "the ability to fund activities in this way increases the status and legitimacy of local institutions and makes the concept of community planning meaningful." The placement of natural resource management decisions with representative local government engages local people with local government, given the importance of these resources in their daily lives. These environment-democracy linkages can be a source of strength for both environmental and democratic objectives.

In these ways, entrusting local institutions with environmental decision-making, rule-making and adjudication contributes directly to building local democracy. Without discretionary powers, local governments cannot gain the legitimacy they need to effectively represent local populations. Rural councilors in Senegal in the 1980s were embarrassed to hold their positions because with limited powers, they could do nothing for their constituents (Hesseling, n.d., 17; Ribot, 1993). Local people went instead to village chiefs or merchants for assistance and advice (Ribot, 1999a). In Burkina Faso, villagers went to merchants—who were powerful actors in the community—to resolve local problems, rather than to elected village presidents or village chiefs. They went to those authorities who had the power to respond (Ribot, 1999a). In these cases, recognition and legitimacy follow from power. Those holding powers become useful authorities.

In India, civil society organizations were observed to crystallize around empowered local government.[5] It is only logical that civic organizations form when there is a chance that they can have influence. A local government that has no powers, that is driven by mandates from above, or that is not downwardly accountable, is an ineffective rallying point for civil action. Creating an empowered, accessible, and responsive government can be part and parcel of enabling the emergence of strong civil society. But without empowered, accessible, and responsive local government institutions, civil organizations may be discouraged from engaging the state to get the things they need. They may be frustrated or simply irrelevant and may whither away.

Ironically, despite the benefits of decentralizations stemming from increased popular participation, many decentralization efforts are choosing to strengthen or reproduce top-down rural administration or non-representative local authorities (See Bigombe-Logo, 2001; Brown, 1999; Graziani and Burnham, forthcoming; Mandondo, 2000; Bazaara, 2002; Mapedza, 2002; Namara, 2001a; Ribot, 1999a; Schroeder, 1999). Power over natural resources is often being devolved to non-democratic and often unaccountable or upwardly accountable local institutions such as chieftaincies, religious orders, non-governmental organizations, and forest service or project-organized committees constituted mostly of private interests.

In forestry, almost all of the arrangements for decentralized or participatory natural resource management involve creation of management committees with some direct relation to local governments and to the forestry service. These committees are usually constituted to make decisions on behalf of the local community—although they often simply administer centrally prescribed management activities. The most common problems are that the committee does not represent nor is accountable to the local population, or that it is not constituted by or under the direct authority of local representatives. More often, they are constituted by the forest services, represent a few commercially interested parties or are under the control of the local elite. Representative authorities are often only one among many committee members, with no controlling role (Ribot, 1999a; Agrawal and Ribot, 1999).

There are notable, more democratic, exceptions to this pattern in Uganda where some management committees are created or constituted by the elected local government (Namara, 2001a; Bazaara 2002). Conyers (2001, 38) found that after bad experiences with one elected committee under the CAMPFIRE program in Binga, Zimbabwe, ". . . a new and more responsible CAMPFIRE committee had been elected. . . ."

She observed that the system of elected committees ". . . although not without its problems, has so far proved to be reasonably effective."

Even where elected local representatives exist (as in Senegal, Mali, Zimbabwe, South Africa, and Uganda), they are rarely entrusted to represent local communities in significant matters of natural-resource management. Their powers remain highly limited or are circumscribed by central agencies. Donors and NGOs pursuing decentralizing programs often sideline elected local authorities, owing to a general lack of confidence in any form of government (see Evans, 1997 and Tendler, 1997 who question the basis for the lack of confidence; cf. Romeo, 1996). In Mali, where new laws give local government control over forest management, many projects still circumvent them in favor of project-selected committees or "customary" authorities, where custom is often a pretext to engrain gender, caste, and ethnic inequalities. Outsiders often prefer to work with customary authorities to show sensitivity to "indigenous" claims. Central agencies also often support customary authorities because they can serve as vote banks for national elections, and are easier to integrate into patronage networks than are less-predictable elected local authorities. In this sense, the re-emergence of neo-traditionalism and customary authorities across Africa appears to be a serious backlash against local democratization.

When representative local government is in place, the empowering of alternative authorities undermines the function and ultimately the legitimacy of the new democratic local authorities. In short, governments and donors working on decentralized community-based natural resource management often choose not to reinforce forms of democratic decentralization that would be institutionally sustainable, spatially replicable (through legislation across a given nation's territory), and capable of embodying the institutional arrangements necessary for reaping the benefits that participatory and decentralized approaches promise (See Ribot, 1999a; Schroeder, 1999).

Empowering authorities that are not held downwardly accountable to local populations can imperil the long-term environmental well-being expected from more accountable local management. It can imperil democracy by taking resources away from emerging democratic structures while strengthening and helping to entrench the very non-democratic institutions that democratic reforms aim to replace. Successful environmental decentralization programs must take advantage of, support and work with democratic reforms. Successful democratic reforms will benefit from careful institutional choices within the natural resources sectors. In short, local institutional choice matters.

POWER AND THE RESTRICTION OF DISCRETIONARY DEMOCRATIC SPACES

In most African countries few discretionary powers are transferred to local authorities. Powers that could be devolved without any threat to forests, for example, remain centralized (Ribot, 1999b; Conyers, 2001, 29; Fairhead and Leach, 1996; Goldman, 2001). At the same time, forests are being privatized without concern for ecological or social implications. Management requirements are being set by central governments that far exceed necessary minimum standards. Forest services across Africa transfer non-commercially valuable use rights while retaining central control over the lucrative aspects of the sector (Ribot, 2001a; forthcoming). In addition, they set up complex prescriptive systems of forest management planning that require "expert" forester services before local governments can make any decisions as to how, when, where, or by whom forests should be used and commercialized. Only the most trivial decisions and the odium of management are devolved while the forest service maintains strict control over valuable aspects of forestry. Further, management obligations are rarely balanced with necessary fiscal resources or other benefits.

Under Mali's and Uganda's progressive decentralizations, democratically elected local governments have been established as recipients of decentralized powers. In Mali, however, the environmental service refuses to transfer powers to elected local government despite requirements of the new forestry laws.[6] Similarly, in Uganda, powers transferred to local institutions are limited by required restrictive management plans (Namara, 2001a; Bazaara, 2002). Uganda's proposed Forestry Law of 2001 does not specify either the guidelines for selecting powers that will be transferred, nor the levels of local government that will receive them (Republic of Uganda [ROU], 2001). In both cases the laws give local authorities the right to manage natural resources, but they are subject to restrictive requirements imposed by the central environmental agencies. Management plans to re-centralize any autonomy that might be implied by the transfer of rights to manage. Further, in both countries many forests previously in the public domain are being privatized in the name of decentralization (Muhereza, 2001; Ribot, 1999b). Taking public resources away from democratic institutions and transferring them to customary and other private bodies neither supports nor follows the logic of democratic decentralization.

The mix of powers and obligations to retain at the center and to be devolved to different political-administrative scales is a matter that requires critical analysis and informed public debate. Otherwise, environmental services around the continent are likely to continue to micro-manage environmental sectors. The principle of "subsidiarity" calls for decisions to be located at the lowest possible political-administrative level without negative effects at a higher level (Follesdal, 1998; Rocher and Rouillard, 1998). Following this principle, decisions that can be made by citizens without regulation should be established in the domain of citizen rights. Decisions that can be made by representative local government without jeopardizing social and ecological well-being should be retained at that level. The subsidiarity principle is not followed in any African environmental decentralization. Environmental subsidiarity principles need to be developed.

"Means of transfer" are another critical dimension of power transfer (Conyers, 1990:20; Ahwoi, 2000). Security and sustainability of decentralization reforms rests largely on the means used to transfer powers from central government to other entities. "Means of transfer" can be constitutional, legislative, or they may take place through ministerial decrees or administrative orders. Constitutional transfers are the most secure or sustainable (see Conyers, 2000). Ghana, Ethiopia, Mali, Senegal, South Africa, and Uganda all have constitutional clauses that assure some degree of decentralization (UNCDF, 2000, 6). While these clauses do not specify which powers are decentralized, they provide leverage for lawmakers to establish and maintain decentralized governance arrangements. The specification of the powers to be decentralized—whether or not there is constitutional support for decentralization—usually takes place through legislation or through decrees and orders, which are less-stable forms of transfer that can change with the balance of powers among parties or the whims of the party in power (Ahwoi, 2000).

In environmental legislation in Mali, Cameroon, Senegal, Guinea, Burkina Faso, South Africa, Zimbabwe and elsewhere, decisions concerning the allocation of important powers are left to be made by ministerial or administrative decree. In Mali, for example, decentralization is called for by the constitution, while decentralization of powers over natural resources is called for in environmental legislation, such as the forestry code. But, within the 1996 forestry code, the powers to be devolved are left to be specified by decree of the minister responsible for forests. The procedures to resolve disputes over forestry matters will be specified by order of the state-appointed governor of each region. Hence, decentralization in the environmental sector is ultimately reserved as a discretionary matter for the ministry responsible for forests and its administrative staff. In this manner, what appears to be a constitutional guarantee is transformed into an executive branch discretion (Ribot, forthcoming).

The distinction between rights and privileges is key in the construction of local autonomy, whether for governance units or for individuals. Privileges are open to the abuses of the allocating authority who may give them and take them away at whim. This is why delegated privileges do not constitute decentralization. As Oyugi (2000, 7) suggests, ". . . those receiving delegated authority act for those who delegate it, whether by law or administratively" (also see Bates, 1981). Effectively, they become subjects of those higher authorities—having little discretion of their own. The domain of local autonomy in which individuals and local authorities can act *freely* is defined by *rights* and protected through representation and recourse. This is precisely the domain of discretion that would allow local authorities to serve local needs—when they represent local people and are accountable to them. With such rights, local people are transformed from subjects to citizens, since they can shape the use of this domain of local freedom through representation and recourse (see Ribot, 1999a; Mamdani, 1996a). In short, the means of transfer is a defining aspect of decentralization and democracy more broadly: delegation subjects people to central government whims, while legislated transfer creates local rights, recourse, and a space for citizenship.

In sum, insufficient discretionary powers are being devolved in the environmental arena and these transfers are made through insecure legal means. Both insufficient discretion and insecurity restrict the creation of democratic space essential for effective decentralization.

Implementation and Sequencing

Sequencing for democratic and empowered local authorities requires a closer look at many factors. Salient among those impinging on institutional choice and power transfers are the 1) mechanisms of accountability, 2) the balance between technical requirements and democratic processes, and 3) the relation between power and capacity. Each of these are discussed below.

Mechanisms of Downward Accountability

In choosing or crafting local institutions for decentralized natural resource management, the objective is to empower the most broadly representative and downwardly accountable local institutions. Local authorities can be held downwardly accountable to local constituencies in numerous ways. The most commonly cited means of accountability are elections.[7] Elections alone are not sufficient, however, since many elected officials are not accountable to their constituencies—even when the electoral system is well crafted.[8] Many other legal, informational, social, economic, and political mechanisms can also help assure downward accountability—of elected or any other local actors.

Non-electoral mechanisms for increasing downward accountability—of elected or any other local actors—include recall, referenda, legal recourse through courts, third-party monitoring by media, NGOs or independently elected controllers, auditing and evaluation, political pressures and lobbying, media/NGO provision of information on roles and obligations of government, public local government reporting requirements, education, central oversight of local government, taxation, embeddedness of leaders in their community, belief systems of leaders and their communities, civic dedication and pride of leaders, performance awards, widespread participation, social movements, and threats of social unrest and resistance (see Tendler, 1997; Moore, 1997; Guyer, 1992; Scott, 1976; O'Donnell, 1998; Blair, 2000). Various "horizontal" relations among political or administrative units at the same level, "vertical" or upward accountability relations with the central state, and a systematic separation and balance of powers can also shape local authority downward accountability (Tendler, 1997; Porter and Onyach-Olaa, 1999; Oloka-Onyango, 1994, 463–518; Mamdani, 1996b; Blair, 2000; Mamdani, 1996a, 145–6). These and other mechanisms can all contribute to local accountability.[9]

While not subject to elections, authorities appointed by central government (deconcentrated authorities), customary authorities holding public powers or even private organizations can also be made more downwardly accountable, more democratic and therefore more apt to be socially and environmentally responsible through many of these mechanisms. The progressive and systematic application of these mechanisms could be a good alternative strategy for democratic reform where electoral mechanisms are too threatening to the central state (Mandondo, 2000).

BALANCING ACTS: ENVIRONMENTAL PLANNING AND MINIMUM STANDARDS

Tensions between national and local objectives—concerning, for example, foreign exchange, watershed management, conservation, commercial production, and local livelihoods—interfere with the decentralization of powers over natural resources and the environment (Namara, 2001, 1). Within state-local tensions, there is a common ". . . tension between the technocratic practices of development managers and the newly pluralistic political practices created by processes of democratization" (Shivaramakrishnan, 2000, 431; also see Engberg-Pedersen, 1995, 2–3, 26; Wollenberg et al., 2001). As observed in the early 1940s in U.S. grass-roots development efforts, "The pressure to 'get things done' has tended to encourage appointment rather than elections" (Lewis cited by Selznick, 1984 [1949]). Similarly, national environmental objectives often conflict with national objectives for establishing local democratic governance. National technical objectives may prescribe how natural resources can be used, while democratic objectives may call for local populations to set their own priorities for environmental quality and use. In both cases there is a problem of articulation between national objectives and local autonomy. Decentralization should seek to find the maximum degree of local freedom nested within higher-level economic, social and environmental objectives around the use and maintenance of natural resources.

Inter-sectoral planning processes involving elected local representatives are a common part of decentralization. Environmental ministries tend to avoid these integrative processes. Instead, they opt to manage the local arena through development and application of environmental management plans on a bilateral community-by-community basis, bypassing local integrative planning processes or even avoiding local democratic institutions and processes altogether. In Niger, the forestry service chose to create separate local decision-making processes from those developed in the more integrative rural code (Ngaido, 1994). In Guinea, the U.S. Agency for International Development's environment team refused to work with elected local governments because they felt it would be "inefficient" (Ribot, 1998; cf. Lippman, 2001, who omits this observation).

The complement to this avoidance pattern is a tendency for environmental services to create elaborate planning processes with local institutions they choose to work with or create. In Cameroon, for example, communities wishing to set up a community forest under the 1994 forestry law must create and register a community forestry management committee with a written constitution, cartographically demarcate their "traditional" territories, compare those boundaries with allowable zones in a Forest Service forest use plan (*Plan de Zonage*), determine the extent of forest accessible for the community forest, and establish a simplified forest management plan to be approved by the prefecture authorities and the Forest Department (see Graziani and Burnham, forthcoming, 3). Under pressure from donors concerning the difficulties these requirements posed, the Ministry of Environment and Forests set up a Community Forestry Development Unit to provide implementation assistance.

Management planning of this nature is becoming an increasingly important management tool for central environmental ministries. Unfortunately, planning processes where central ministries specify in great detail what plans must look like, undermine the notion of local autonomy and become new tools of executive-branch control. In Burkina Faso, Cameroon, Mali, Senegal, and Uganda, the forest service requires management plans for each jurisdiction that wishes to engage in commercial woodcutting. These plans are cumbersome to develop, in most cases unnecessary for ecological sustainability, and usually leave little decision making to the local authorities. Further, these schemes—usually construed as participatory and sustainable management—often *require* local communities to engage in extractive activities in order to supply international markets or meet national needs for forest products (Ribot, 1999a; 1995; Delnooz, 1999).

Several questions need to be addressed if a domain of "decentralized" local democratic use and management are to be nested within national and international objectives. First, which powers can be transferred without threatening the environment or without requiring any form of expert intervention or planning process? As mentioned earlier, there are many forestry decisions that can be transferred without any environmental implications (Ribot, 1999b). Many commercial decisions that have been kept central are political rather than technical decisions—such as *who* can hold permits to commercialize timber and woodfuels (Bazaara, 2002). Second, which forestry activities can be transferred without fiscal support? These might include expanded use rights, expanded commercial, revenue-generating rights, the right for local governments to tax commercial forestry, or decisions on who has local forest access.

Many environmental management techniques and objectives can be achieved without local planning. Minimum environmental standards, for example, are an alternative to planning. Under this approach a set of minimum guidelines and requirements are set out for individuals or communities. Within these restrictions, individuals or communities can plan or not plan, use or not use according to their local objectives and needs. The minimum standards define the domain of local autonomy. Planning processes then are an option for optimizing activities within the domain of autonomy. Under this model, the domain of autonomy is defined as a set of rights in law and not through a planning process that allocates powers and obligations under administrative environmental service discretion.

There is a great need in environmental circles to re-think the actual minimum requirements for sound environmental use and protection. It is time to scope out and create the maximum domain of local autonomy—through minimum standards. Planning may be a positive tool, if it is one that local populations can *choose* to use, if and when they decide to take on activities that require it.

Capacity and power-a chicken and/or egg problem

. . . It is frequently argued that decentralization should not take place until the necessary capacity exists; but this tends to be a "chicken and egg" type of argument, since more often than not it is only the pressure of decentralization which motivates the action necessary to improve capacity—and motivates the existing staff and the local level to recognize their own potential and demonstrate their real abilities.

Diana Conyers, 1990, 30

Ahwoi (2000, 4) lists lack of adequately trained human resources as a local government problem in Ghana. Similar arguments are still being made by Mali's and Senegal's forest services (interviews, March 2002). Indeed, "most often it is argued that until there has been a marked improvement in Local Government capacities and institutional practices, they will fail to respond to needs expressed by their constituencies, will tend to neglect national policy priorities and, in the main, behave in unaccountable and inefficient ways" (Onyach-Olaa and Porter, 2000, 3). The argument that powers cannot be devolved without capacity and resources is widespread and is often specious (Clauzel, 1995, 49; Oyugi, 2000, 10; Ribot, 1996).[10] As Conyers (1990, 30) and Fiszbein (1997) indicate, the relation between ability to receive power and local capacity is not unilinear. The "capacity" argument is often evoked to avoid transferring powers or reducing oversight.

Fiszbein (1997, 1), conducting research in Colombia, shows that ". . . what appears to some analysts and policy-makers as lack of capacity, might in fact be the reflection of a conflict in the objective function used, on the one hand, by those analysts/policy-makers and, on the other hand, by the local people." Fiszbein (1997, 3) attributes what is often perceived as "lack of capacity" to such conflict between national and local preferences, reporting that: "Many of those local governments might have usual or perverse preferences—at least from the national perspective—but they sure had no lack of capacity to achieve their objectives." I would add that central "objective functions" often include central actors' fears of losing economic and political powers.

Fiszbein further points out that the perception of poor capacity is fostered by poorly designed incentives. For example: "When fully accounted, the combination of earmarking and unfunded mandates represented for many municipalities [in Colombia] more than 100 percent of the untied portion of the automatic inter-governmental grant they were receiving. . . . Thus, the observation that few municipalities were complying with those mandates . . . was more a reflection on the absurdity of the policy than on the local capacity" (1997, 3). Similarly, as Onyach-Olaa and Porter (2000, 3) point out, research in Uganda has made it "increasingly evident that Local Government performance is greatly dependent on and is actually being constrained by inability of central government agencies and their donor partners to deliver on their mandated responsibilities." Local government performance appears to be as much a function of central government and donor accountability as local capacity per se.

Implementing decentralization may require coordination, civic education campaigns, orientation and training programs for local parties. Without powers, however, people are less likely to learn or to even engage in capacity building efforts. Risks must be taken to transfer powers *ahead of* capacity so that capacity building can have an empowering, rather than a controlling or punitive, meaning.[11]

Conclusions and Recommendations: Sequencing for Democratic Decentralization

Decentralization of environmental powers is in its early stages. Effective environmental decentralization involves local representative and downwardly accountable authorities who hold significant discretionary powers over natural resources. To date, however, local actors receiving environmental powers are rarely representative or downwardly accountable. The discretionary powers being transferred to local authorities are often limited. This general failure of African governments to establish democratic decentralization of natural resources appears to reflect a larger resistance to establishing local democracy. The natural resource arena should be compared with health, education, and infrastructure to see the degree to which these observations reflect sectoral peculiarities or a larger pattern of central governments, using institutional choice and retained powers to consolidate discretion in the executive branch.

Below are a few recommendations—many concerning sequencing—aimed at pushing the decentralization experiment along.

DEMOCRATIC LOCAL GOVERNMENT FIRST

The kinds of outcomes expected from decentralizations are predicated on some form of downwardly accountable local representation. Establishing locally accountable representative institutions is a priority—perhaps a pre-condition. This means querying the structures of local elections to see if they establish downwardly accountable bodies or just place party representatives in the local arena. Without systematic means for public participation and voice in local decisions, transfers of power to the local arena become deconcentration or privatization by default. Representation is an environmental issue if sustainable and effective decentralization of power over natural resources is to occur.

APPLY MULTIPLE ACCOUNTABILITY MEASURES

Accountability measures, in the presence or absence of representative local government can foster a degree of downward accountability of whichever authorities hold powers over natural resources. Elections are not the only means of accountability. Based on his observations in Zimbabwe's CAMPFIRE wildlife management program, Mandondo (2000, 15) argues for an incremental application of accountability measures for democratizing natural-resource governance where democratic institutions are not established. A series of accountability measures could be applied with or without more democratic forms of local government to improve the responsiveness of local authorities—including elected ones—to local people (see Ribot, forthcoming).

DISCRETION BEFORE OBLIGATION: FREEDOM WITHIN OVERSIGHT-ESTABLISHING A DOMAIN OF LOCAL AUTONOMY

With overbearing systems of environmental management planning and oversight by line, local government and interior ministries, how can local authorities develop capacity to operate independently and how can they develop legitimacy in their own communities? One of the priorities, indeed one of the defining characteristics, of decentralization is the creation of a domain of local discretion. In environmental decentralizations, this domain is constrained by 1) failure to transfer discretionary powers, and 2) restrictive oversight in the form of supervision, approval, and management plans. Without local autonomy or local discretionary powers, local authorities are unlikely to be respected and legitimate in the local arena, and they are less likely to be the channel of communication and action around which civil society will form. Local representation without a domain of discretion is neither democracy nor decentralization.

While the transfer of powers without accountable representation is a dangerous business, representation without power is empty.

POWER BEFORE CAPACITY

Central governments are reluctant to devolve powers before capacity has been demonstrated. But without powers there is no basis on which local authorities can gain experience needed to build capacity or demonstrate that capacity has been gained. "Catch-22" lack-of-capacity arguments are often excuses not to devolve powers. Arguments that local populations lack capacity to use and manage natural resources and to manage local conflicts are most often baseless. Many local natural resource decisions do not require any special capacities. To proceed with decentralizations, the risk of transferring powers before assessing or building capacities must be taken. Which transfers can be made without local "capacity" building? How can power transfers be used to build capacity? How can capacity claims by central ministries be challenged?

RIGHTS RATHER THAN PRIVILEGES: OPTING FOR SECURE MEANS OF TRANSFER

Powers delegated by central agencies to local authorities are *privileges* that can be taken away. Those who hold them are accountable to the delegating body—by dint of their insecurity and fear of losing those privileges. Powers that are transferred as *rights* are less easily given and taken away. Such rights establish a domain of discretionary freedom. Security of transfer depends strongly on whether powers are transferred to local authorities as rights spelled out in the constitution or through a legislative processes, or as privileges handed out through ministerial decrees, administrative orders, temporary licenses or permits. The degree to which the transfer is secure helps to determine the degree of independence that local authorities have in exercising their? powers. It also reflects the degree to which governments are serious about creating a domain of local discretionary power that is so basic to effective decentralization (Meinzen-Dick and Knox, 1999, 13). When constructing or observing decentralizations, considerable attention must be paid to the means of transfer being used. The key question is which powers can be transferred as rights without threatening higher-scale public interests.

MINIMUM ENVIRONMENTAL STANDARDS BEFORE PLANNING

A minimum environmental standards approach should be explored as an alternative to the current trend toward micro-management through elaborate planning. This approach specifies a set of restrictions and guidelines for environmental use and management. Any local government or individual operating within those restrictions needs no plan to use or manage resources. Some kinds of actions may require plans in order to maintain the minimum standards, but again, permission is not required from central environmental ministries, unless they violate minimum standards. Today's approaches require planning and supervision for any commercial use. More research and debate must go into identifying the boundaries between what can and cannot be done without the direct intervention of environmental service. The domain of action that does not transgress minimum standards is the domain of local autonomy that makes for effective decentralization.

Conclusion

The above observations and recommendations that take on meaning within a specific social, legal, and political-economic context. These are not design guidelines. They are observations about multiple and different processes currently going on across Africa. The meaning of power transfers in one place will be completely different than in another, depending on the nature of local authority and the central state. Like any power transfer, environmental powers transferred into the local arena will take on the contours of existing political and economic relations. If the authorities are democratic, then powers transferred can support democratic relations. If they are despotic, then despotic authorities will be strengthened. The path toward decentralization, then, must be carefully trodden. A deep sense of locality and of politics is needed to follow every turn. An awareness of the structure of actors, powers, accountability relations, means of transfer, and the meanings and uses of "capacity," as well as an awareness of the large gaps between discourse, law and practice, will be a useful map.

Acknowledgements

*Thanks go to Nathan Badenoch, Angelo Bonfiglioli, Juliet Kanyesigye, Paul Smoke, and Peter Veit for their insightful constructive comments on earlier drafts of this chapter. I also want express my gratitude to the Dutch Government grant the and U.S. Agency for International Development grant for supporting the Institutions and Governance Program at World Resources Institute to conduct the research that went into this chapter. I also greatly appreciate Roger Shotton and Kadmiel Wekwete at the United Nations Capital Development Fund (UNCDF) for inviting me to participate in Cape Town Symposium on which this volume is based and for which this chapter was originally written.

NOTES

*Correspondence to Jesse C. Ribot, Senior Associate, Institutions and Governance Program, World Resources Institute, 10 G Street, N.E., Suite 800, Washington, D.C. 20002 USA, *JesseR@WRI.org*.

1 The Rio Declaration on Environment and Development states: "Environmental issues are best handled with the participation of all concerned citizens, at the relevant level" (http://www.accessexellence.org/ AB/IE/Rio_Declaration_On_Envirmt.html). Also see Ostrom, 1990; Agrawal, 2001; Wollenberg et al., 2001; Fortmann et al., 2001 among many others.

2 For definitions and theoretical underpinnings of decentralization, see Ribot forthcoming.

3 Similar, but doubtful, claims are made by the Ugandan environmental ministry and by foresters in Ghana to justify re-centralization (personal comm. Dr. N. Bazaara 2001, and Aaron diGrassi 2002).

4 See Mamdani, 1996a:140; Chanock, 1991:64; Hesseling, n.d.; Watts, 1993; Bassett and Crummey, 1993; Downs and Reyna, 1988; Fisiy, 1995:50; Geschiere, 1993:166. Murombedzi, 1998.

5 Anu Joshi (personal communication, IDS, Sussex, 1999).

6 Personal communications, Yaya Tamboura, Directeur National, Direction National de la Conservation de la Nature, Bamako, Mali, November 2000 and meetings with forestry officials in Mali in March 2002.

7 Cf. Hesseling 1996. See Echeverri-Gent (1992) for a study of competitive local elections in West Bengal, India that helped make policy more responsive to the poor. For a similar argument from Colombia about the importance of competitive local elections, see Fiszbein (1997).

8 See for example Mehta 1996.

9 This list is further developed in Ribot forthcoming; Ribot, 2001b; 1999a.

10 There is evidence that capacity arguments are largely unjustifiable in the environmental arena (see Ribot, 1999a, Fairhead and Leach, 1998, Tiffen, Mortimore and Gichuki, 1994, Cappon and Lind, 2000; Murombedzi, 1998; Goldman, 2001; Graziani and Burnham, forthcoming:3; Ostrom, 1990; Peluso, 1992; Fairhead and Leach, 1996; Schroeder, 1999).

11 Based on their perceptions, members of the Colombian Congress argued " . . . no real benefit would be derived from transferring funds and responsibilities to local governments if their lack of capacity would not allow them to manage them effectively . . . " (1997:1). Opponents, however, argued " . . . that only if fiscal resource and responsibilities for service delivery were transferred to local governments would those capabilities develop . . . " (1997:2). The lessons learned in Colombia are relevant to Africa.

REFERENCES

Agrawal, A. 2001. "The Regulatory Community: Decentralization and the Environment in the Van Panchayats (Forest Councils) of Kumaon." *Mountain Research and Development* 21(3): 208–211.

Agrawal, A, and Ribot J, 1999. "Accountability in Decentralization: A Framework with South Asian and African Cases." *Journal of Developing Areas* 33(summer): 473–502.

Ahwoi, K. 2000. "Challenges Facing Local Governments in Africa in the 21st Century: An Executive Summary." *Local Government Perspectives* 7(3): 1–7.

Bassett, T, and D. Crummey (eds.). 1993. *Land in African Agrarian Systems.* Madison: University of Wisconsin Press.

Bates, R. 1981. *Markets and States in Tropical Africa.* Berkeley: University of California Press.

Bazaara N. 2002. Actors, Powers and Environmental Accountability in Uganda's Decentralisation. Paper presented at the World Resources Institute's Decentralization and Environment Conference, Bellagio, Italy 18–22 February 2002.

Bigombe-Logo, P. 2001. Décentralisation de la Gestion Forestière et Développement Local au Cameroun: Economie Politique de l'Accountabilite et de la Performance dans la Gestion Locale des Revenus Forestiers au Sud-Est Cameroun. Draft report to the World Resources Institute/Centre for International Forestry Research program on Decentralization and the Environment, Yaounde, Cameroon. February 2001, mimeo.

Blair, H. 2000. "Participation and Accountability at the Periphery: Democratic Local Governance in Six Countries." *World Development* 28(1): 21–39.

Brock, K, Coulibaly N. 1999. Sustainable Rural Livelihoods in Mali. Research Report 35, Sustainable Livelihoods Programme, Brighton, Sussex: Institute for Development Studies.

Brown, D. 1999. Principles and Practice of Forest Co-Management; Evidence from West-Central Africa. European Union Tropical Forestry Paper 2, Overseas Development Institute, London.

Capon, J, Lind J. 2000. Realities or Rhetoric? Revisiting the Decentralization of Natural Resources Management in Uganda and Zambia. Nairobi: African Center for Technology Studies Press.

Chanock, M. 1991. "Paradigms, Policies, and Property: A Review of the Customary Law of Land Tenure." In *Law in Colonial Africa*, Kristin Mann and Richard Roberts (eds.). Portsmouth, Oreg.: Heinemann, 61–84.

Clauzel, J. 1995. Données, enjeux et techniques de la décentralisation en Afrique. *La Decentralisation en Afrique de l'Ouest.* In *Conduit du processus dans les pays francophones et lusophones, Ouagadougou,* J. P. Elong Mbassi (ed.) Cotonou, Bénin: PDM and CEDA, 45–64.

Conyers, D. 2001. Whose Elephants Are They? Decentralization of Control over Wildlife Management through the CAMPFIRE Programme in Binga District, Zimbabwe. Working Paper, World Resources Institute, January 2001: 31.

Conyers, D. 2000. "Decentralisation: A Conceptual Analysis Part 1." *Local Government Perspectives: News and Views on Local Government in Sub-Saharan Africa* 7(3): 7–9, 13.

Conyers, D. 1990. "Decentralization and Development Planning: A Comparative Perspective." In *Decentralizing for Participatory Planning: Comparing the Experiences of Zimbabwe and Other Anglophone Countries in Eastern and Southern Africa*, P. de Valk and K. H. Wekwete (eds.); Aldershot: Avebury Press, 15–36.

Crook, R, Manor J. 1998. *Democracy and Decentralization in South-East Asia and West Africa: Participation, Accountability, and Performance*. Cambridge: Cambridge University Press.

Delnooz, P. 1999. *Gestion des Ressources Forestières: La Communauté, L'État et le Marché: Etude de Projets D'Aménagament au Burkina Faso*. Unpublished doctoral dissertation, Fondation Universitaire Luxembourgeoise, Louvain-la-Neuve, Belgium, December 1999.

Dillinger, W. 1994. *Decentralization and Its Implications for Urban Service Delivery*. In Crook and Manor 1998.

Downs, R. and S. P. Reyna (eds.) 1988. *Land and Society in Contemporary Africa*. Hanover: University Press of New England.

Echeverri-Gent, J. 1992. "Public Participation and Poverty Alleviation: The Experience of Reform Communists in India's West Bengal." *World Development* 20(10): 1401–22.

Engberg-Pedersen, L. 1995. Creating Local Democratic Politics from Above: The "Gestion des Terroirs" Approach in Burkina Faso. Drylands Programme Issue. Paper no. 54, April. London: International Institute for Environment and Development.

Evans, Peter B. 1997. "The Eclipse of the State? Reflections on Stateness in an Era of Globalization." *World Politics* 50 (October): 62–87.

Fairhead, J, Leach M. 1996. *Misreading the African Landscape: Society and Ecology in a Forest-Savanna Mosaic*. Cambridge: Cambridge University Press.

Fisher, M. 1991. *Indirect Rule in India: Residents and the Residency System, 1764–1858*. New Delhi: Oxford University Press.

Fisiy, C. 1995. "Chieftaincy in the Modern State: An Institution at the Crossroads of Democratic Change." *Paideuma* 41: 49–62.

Fiszbein, A. 1997. Decentralization and Local Capacity: Some Thoughts on a Controversial Relationship. Paper presented at the Food and Agriculture Organization/United Nations Capital Development Fund/World Bank Technical Consultation on Decentralization, Rome, 15–8 December 1997.

Follesdal, A. 1998. Survey Article: Subsidiarity. *Journal of Political Philosophy* 6(2):190–218.

Fortmann, L, E Roe, and Michel van Eeten. 2001. "At the Threshold between Governance and Management: Community-Based Natural Resource Management in Southern Africa." *Public Administration and Development* 21:171–185.

Geschiere, P. 1993. "Chiefs and Colonial Rule in Cameroon: Inventing Chieftaincy, French and British Style." *Africa* 63(2): 151–75.

Goldman, M. 2001. Partitioned Nature, Privileged Knowledge: Community Based Conservation in Massai Ecosystem, Tanzania. Draft Working Paper for the Environmental Governance in Africa Working Paper Series, Institutions and Governance Program of the World Resources Institute, July. Mimeo.

Graziani, Monica and Philip Burnham. 2002. "Legal Pluralism in the Rain Forests of Southeastern Cameroon." In Katherine Homewood (ed.), *Rural Resources and Local Livelihoods in Africa*. Oxford: James Curry.

Guyer, J. 1992. "Representation without Taxation: An Essay on Democracy in Rural Nigeria, 1952–1990." *African Studies Review* 35(1): 41–79.

Hesseling, G. 1996. Legal and Institutional Incentives for Local Environmental Management. Occasional Paper no. 17, Henrik Secher Marcussen (ed.), International Development Studies, Roskilde University.

Hesseling, G. (in collaboration with M. Sypkens Smit). n.d.[circa 1984]. Le Droit Foncier au Senegal: L'Impact de la Réforme Foncière en Basse Casamance, mimeo.

Lippman, H. 2001. Linking Democracy and Development: An Idea for the Times. Center for Development of Information and Evaluation, U.S. Agency for International Development, Program and Operations Assessment Report no. 29, June.

Little, P. 1994. "The Link Between Local Participation and Improved Conservation: A Review of Issues and Experiences. In *Natural Connections: Perspectives in Community-Based Conservation*, David Western and R. Michael Wright (eds.). Washington D.C: Island Press, 347–372.

Mamdani, M. 1996a. *Citizen and Subject: Contemporary Africa and the Legacy of Late Colonialism*. Princeton, N.J.: Princeton University Press.

Mamdani, M. 1996b. "Indirect Rule, Civil Society, and Ethnicity: The African Dilemma." *Social Justice* 23(1–2): 145–6.

Mandondo, A. 2000. Situating Zimbabwe's Natural Resource Governance Systems in History. Center for International Forestry Research Occasional Paper no. 32, December. Jakarta: CIFOR.

Mapedza E. 2002. Comanagement in the Mafungautsi State Forest Area of Zimbabwe—What Stake for Local Communities? Draft report to the World Resources Institute program on Decentralization and the Environment, United Kingdom, February, mimeo.

Mawhood, P., ed. 1983. Local Government in the Third World: The Experience of Tropical Africa. New York: J. Wiley and Sons.

Mehta, A. 1996. "Micro Politics of Voluntary Action: An Anatomy of Change in Two Villages." *Cultural Survival Quarterly* fall: 26–30.

Meinzen-Dick, R, Knox A. 1999. Collective Action, Property Rights, and Devolution of Natural Resource Management: A Conceptual Framework. International Food Policy Institute, Washington, D. C., Mimeo.

Moore, M. 1997. "Death without Taxes: Democracy, State Capacity, and Aid Dependence in the Fourth World, in *Towards a Democratic Developmental State*, G. White and M. Robinson (eds.). Oxford: Oxford University Press, 84–121.

Muhereza, F. 2001. Concept Note on the Need to Re-think the Issue of Private Forests. February, Kampala, Uganda. Mimeo.

Murombedzi, J. 1998. The Evolving Context of Community Based Natural Resource Management in Sub-Saharan Africa in Historical Perspective. Paper prepared for the International Workshop on Community Based Natural Resource Management, Washington, D. C.: The World Bank, 10–14 May.

Namara, A. 2001. Whose Interests Matter? Assessment of the Operations of Local Institutions in Natural Resource Management: the Case of Bwindi Impenetrable National Park, Uganda. Draft report to the World Resources Institute/Centre for Basic Research program on Decentralization and the Environment, Kampala, February, mimeo.

Ngaido, T. 1994. *Aino Kaino* (donne moi un peu) ou *Ainoma* (Cultivons): Un exemple de gestion foncière et de dégradation l'environnement dans le canton de Tamou (Niger). "Le Foncier dans le Processus de la Desertification: Cause ou Remede," Paper prepared for the workshop on L'impact des système fonciers et des modes de propriété et d'accés aux ressources sur la dégradation des terres et la désertification, organized by the International Development Research Center, Dakar Senegal 7–9 March 1994.

O'Donnell, G. 1998. "Horizontal Accountability in New Democracies." *Journal of Democracy* 9(3): 112–126.

Oloka-Onyango, J. 1994. "Judicial Power and Constitutionalism in Uganda: A Historical Perspective." In *Uganda: Studies in Living Conditions, Popular Movements and Constitutionalism*, Mahmood Mamdani and Joe Oloka-Onyango (eds). Kampala: Journal für Entwicklungspolitik and Center for Basic Research, 463–518.

Onyach-Olaa, M, Porter D. 2000. Local Government Performance and Decentralisation in Uganda: Implications for Central Governments and Donors. Ministry of Local Government: Kampala, Uganda, mimeo.

Ostrom, E. 1990. *Governing the Commons: The Evolution of Institutions for Collective Action*. Cambridge: Cambridge University Press.

Oyono R. 2002. Policy Change, Organizational Choices, "*Infraoutcomes*" and Ecological Uncertainties of The Decentralization Model in Cameroon. Paper presented at the World Resources Institute's Decentralization and Environment Conference, Bellagio, Italy, 18–22 February.

Oyugi, W. 2000. Decentralization for Good Governance and Development. *Regional Development Dialogue* 21(1): 3–22.

Peluso, N. 1992. *Rich Forests, Poor People: Resource Control and Resistance in Java*, Berkeley: University of California Press.

Porter, D, Onyach-Olaa M. 1999. "Inclusive Planning and Allocation for Rural Services." *Development in Practice* 9(1–2); 56–67.

Porter, G, Young E. 1998. Decentralized Environmental Management and Popular Participation in Coastal Ghana. *Journal of International Development* 10: 515–526.

Ribot, J. C. 2002. African Decentralization: Local Actors, Power and Accountability. Geneva: UNRISD, Paper 8.

Ribot, J. C. 2001a. Science, Use Rights and Exclusion: A History of Forestry in Francophone West Africa, Issue paper no. 104, International Institute for Environment and Development, London, May.

Ribot, J. C. 2001b. "Integral Local Development: 'Accommodating Multiple Interests' through Entrustment and Accountable Representation." *International Journal of Agricultural Resources, Governance and Ecology* 1(2–4): 327–351.

Ribot, J. C. 1999a. Decentralization, Participation and Accountability in Sahelian Forestry: Legal Instruments of Political-Administrative Control. *Africa* 69(1): 23–65.

Ribot, J. C. 1999b. "A History of Fear: Imagining Deforestation in the West African Dryland Forests," *Global Ecology and Biogeography* 8: 291–300.

Ribot, J. C. 1998. Memo on NRM-DG Linkages, Observations on the Democracy and Governance (SO4) components of USAID's NRM (SO1) activities in Fuuta Djallon Guinea. Washington, D. C.: World Resources Institute. January, mimeo.

Ribot, J. C. 1996. "Participation without Representation: Chiefs, Councils and Forestry Law in the West African Sahel." *Cultural Survival Quarterly*. Fall: 40–44.

Ribot, J. C. 1995. "From Exclusion to Participation: Turning Senegal's Forestry Policy Around." *World Development* 23(9): 1587–1599.

Ribot, J. C. 1993. "Market-State Relations and Environmental Policy: Limits of State Capacity in Senegal." In *The State and Social Power in Global Environmental Politics*, Lipschutz R, Conca K. (eds.). New York: Columbia University Press.

ROU (Republic of Uganda). 2001. The Forestry Act: Draft for Consultation. Ministry of Water, Lands and Environment, Uganda Forests, January.

Romeo, L. 1996. Local Development Funds: Promoting Decentralized Planning and Financing of Rural Development. United Nations Capital Development Fund, Policy Series.

Schroeder, R. 1999. "Community Forestry and Conditionality in the Gambia." *Africa* 69(1): 1–22.

Scott, J. C. 1976. *The Moral Economy of the Peasant: Rebellion and Subsistence in Southeast Asia.* New Haven, Conn.: Yale University Press.

Selznick, P. (1949) 1984. TVA and the Grassroots A Study in the Sociology of Formal Organization. Berkeley: University of California Press.

Shivaramakrishnan, K. 2000. "Crafting the Public Sphere in the Forests of West Bengal: Democracy, Development and Political Action." *American Ethnologist* 27(2): 431–461.

Smoke, P. 2000. Fiscal Decentralization in Developing Countries: A Review of Current Concepts and Practice. Geneva: United Nations Research Institute for Social Development.

Tendler, J. 1997. *Good Government in the Tropics.* Baltimore, Md.: Johns Hopkins University Press.

United Nations Capital Development Fund (UNCDF). 2000. Africa: Decentralisation and Local Governance Conference Concept Paper. for

Decentralisation and Local Governance Conference, Capetown, United Nations Capital Development Fund, March (Draft).

Tiffen M, Mortimore, M. and Gichuki, F. 1994. *More People, Less Erosion: Environmental Recovery in Kenya*; Chichester: John Wiley and Sons. not New York?

van Rouveroy van Nieuwaal, E. Adriaan B, and van Dijkm R. 1999. *African Chievtaincy in a New Socio-Political Landscape*. Hamburg: Lit Verlag.

Walker, P. A. 2000. Democracy and Environment: Congruence or Contradiction? *Commons Southern Africa* 2(1): 4–6.

Watts, M. 1993. "Idioms of Land and Labor: Producing Politics and Rice in Senegambia." In *Land in African Agrarian Systems*, Thomas J. Bassett and Donald E. Crummey (eds.). Madison: University of Wisconsin Press; 157–221.

Wollenberg, E, Anderson J, and Edmunds D. 2001. "Pluralism and the Less Powerful: Accommodating Multiple Interests in Local Forest Management. *International" Journal of Agricultural Resources, Governance and Ecology* 1(3–4): 199–223.

World Bank. 2000. Entering the 21st Century: World Development Report 1999/2000. Oxford: Oxford University Press.

Chapter 7

Foreign Aid and State Administrative Capability in Africa[1]

Arthur A. Goldsmith

Introduction

In its 1997 *World Development Report*, the World Bank argued that a capable state is the foundation stone of social and economic progress. This report represents belated official recognition that the minimal state of neoclassical economics is never going to promote a vigorous marketplace or eradicate widespread poverty in developing countries. Or, as North (1997: 8) expressed his bemusement at the same idea, "you can't do with the state but you can't do without it either." In the more balanced view of development strategy that is emerging, successful societies have states that harness the energy of business and individuals, and act as their partner on the path to greater prosperity for all. Such states catalyze development by performing so-called "core" state functions, especially establishment of groundwork of law, provision of a stable macroeconomic environment, and investment in basic social services and infrastructure.

Official acknowledgment of the critical role of the state in development recalls arguments made by Hobbes in the seventeenth century. His Leviathan grew out of the profound uncertainty people experience when central authority is absent. To escape this "state of nature" and gain opportunities for "commodious living," Hobbes (1991: 90) thought that people had agreed to submit themselves to an independent political authority. The formation of the Leviathan allowed citizens to possess property and enjoy of a modicum of personal liberty (ibid. 171). Though Hobbes' account of the origins of the state is doubtful on historical grounds, he was right to point out that sovereignty is a precondition for modernization. Nevertheless, carrying out the Leviathan's core activities is no negligible task—especially if they are done with a spirit of client responsiveness and citizen empowerment, as most multilateral agencies and bilateral donors now specifically recommend (ECA, 1999, DAC, 1993).

Few states in Sub Saharan Africa (hereinafter simply Africa) meet up to the donors' demanding standards for governing, according to other expressions of official thinking (World Bank, 1989, 1997, 2000a). Yet, the foreign aid establishment has been implicated in the very problem of state weakness. Critics charge that aid donors have usurped national policy making in the region, and they see excessive aid as killing any incentive African states have to rule effectively. Instead of helping Africans to build the sort of capable states they need for development, the international financial institutions and bilateral foreign assistance agencies stand accused of inadvertently encouraging a system of fragile, powerless states that trap the region in economic backwardness (Aron, 1996, Moore, 1998).

This chapter questions two articles of faith about African states, namely that most are losing capacity, and that foreign aid has an unintended destructive effect that is partly responsible for the loss of capacity. I do so by looking for correlations between heavy use of aid over the past several decades and low public administrative capabilities. My approach differs from most studies of aid effectiveness which traditionally emphasize economic consequences not administrative outcomes. The universe is 48 states located south of the Sahara, including several island states. Central government is the focus, as opposed to regional or local governments.

I start by defining state capability and foreign aid and by reviewing arguments about the relationship between the two. Then I consider two approaches for gauging general state capability, one based on public and expert opinion, the other on objective proxy variables. Both approaches suggest that the various African states exhibit a greater range of capability than is commonly understood, and that the trends in some countries may be to acquire more capability, not simply to lose it. Foreign aid's administrative impact—for good or ill—appears to be exaggerated by both supporters and detractors of aid. The driving factors behind decay or development of public institutions are mainly local.

STATES AND STATE CAPABILITY

The standard social science definition is that a state is a compulsory organization that makes rules for, and sustains itself by extracting resources from, the population within its territorial domain. Many observers rightly question the extent to which African states can actually meet these criteria. Jackson and Rosberg (1982), for example, see a pattern of make-believe states in the region. Aside from having sovereignty under international law, many of these entities are short of the real power it takes to make and enforce public policy within their formal boundaries. Sovereignty thus is a continuum, extending from very weak states that are little more than legal fictions accepted by the world community to stronger states that wield authority over almost all their people and that have the means to promote national development on their own.

The polar cases of weakness are manifested in state failure or collapse, when a large share of inhabitants refuse either voluntarily or through coercion to heed the laws and commands of state officials, and instead turn to some other agency for their protection (Zartman, 1995). Somalia and Sierra Leone are two spectacular examples of state failure in Africa. When the social contract starts to come apart, the state ceases to provide the public goods vital for Hobbesian "commodious living." Sporadic internal violence may escalate into unrestrained civil war, which in turn may destabilize neighboring states or trigger interstate conflict, as recently occurred in Rwanda and the Democratic Republic of Congo (DRC). Some African states like Uganda have recovered from collapse, but they still see their authority diminished in peripheral areas and displaced by ideologically or religiously motivated groups and by criminal syndicates. Elsewhere, in Nigeria for instance, personal security and property are threatened even in central locations due to pervasive petty and organized crime. The spread of small arms and the corruption and incompetence of the official security services heighten the danger. "Felonious" states, such as Liberia, have themselves degenerated into criminal enterprises, using whatever authority they retain to traffic in illegal drugs, gems, and other contraband, or to engage in money laundering (Bayart et al., 1999).

States on the more competent side of the spectrum avoid or curtail these risks and difficulties. Botswana, Mauritius, and Namibia are probably the best examples of relatively capable states in Africa. They usually turn up at the top of surveys of the region's national business climate (World Economic Forum, 2000) and tend to have relatively strong economic and social performance. These countries possess comparatively large public bureaucracies that are reasonably successful in carrying out tasks they set for themselves (Goldsmith, 1999, Court et al., 1999). The extent to which even Africa's best-run states are autonomous policy-making entities is another question, for they are apt to consult and cooperate with foreign powers and international lending agencies on economic matters (Mengisteab and Daddieh, 1999). Compromise of sovereignty, however, is nothing new in international relations (Krasner, 1999).

What is central state capability? For clarity, I find it useful to parse the concept, and isolate the state as a means to deliver services or carry out policies reliably and at reasonable price, from the state as a forum to engage citizens and clients in deciding what those services or policies should be. State capability entails both *efficiency* (sometimes thought of as "doing things right" so they are completed and do not cost too much) and *effectiveness* ("doing the right things" that people really want doing or that ought to be done anyway). To illustrate the distinction another way, an efficient state makes trains run on time; an effective state establishes a train schedule that meets travelers' needs.[2]

The international development establishment tends to combine these two aspects of state capability under the rubric of "good governance." The United States Agency for International Development (1998), for example, defines governance as the state's capacity to "develop an efficient and effective public management process . . . [and] to deliver basic services." Resistance to political corruption is often tossed into the definition as well (DAC, 1993, World Bank, 1994).[3] But such umbrella definitions of state capability muddy the waters for analysis.

Efficiency and effectiveness clearly are related, and over time, it may be impossible for a state to produce desired effects at reasonable cost without significant input and guidance from constituents. That said, efficiency and effectiveness are not identical and need not go hand in hand. Some states are reputed to be quite proficient at getting jobs done without being particularly democratic about deciding what they do (e.g., pre-1994 South Africa); conversely, other states get high marks for open procedures but low marks for carrying out routine technical and management tasks (e.g., post-1994 South Africa).

This paper will concentrate on state capability in the efficiency sense, that is, as an instrumentality by which state leaders try to put public decisions into practice, irrespective of the character of those decisions.[4] I specifically leave aside the effectiveness issues of democratization and citizen participation in those decisions. Nonetheless, it should be borne in mind that efficient administration is a means that can be devoted to desirable or undesirable ends. As Rose-Ackerman (1999, 179) points out, society is not made better off when a corrupt or brutal state becomes more efficient. The social welfare is improved when such a state also grows more effective at directing its energies toward socially useful ends.

FOREIGN AID

African states are important recipients of foreign aid, which, as noted above, many observers suspect of corroding their administrative capability (Bräutigam, 2000, Knack, 2000a, Therkildson, 2000, 69). Usually known as official development assistance or ODA, foreign aid is an international delivery of resources that takes place independently of market forces. Formally, ODA is defined as a net transfer in cash or kind that is administered with economic development in mind and that has a grant element of no less than 25 percent. The Organization for Economic Cooperation and Development (OECD) compiles annual figures that report the actual financial disbursement of aid from all sources, less any repayments of earlier loans during the same period. The figures also cover goods or services valued at cost, including technical assistance such as the provision of experts to help with particular problems. About one-third of Africa's ODA is technical assistance.

The formal definition of ODA only covers resources coming from public sources, however, not from private charitable activities. These latter may be significant for Africa—net grants from non-governmental organizations (NGOs) were the equivalent of one-eighth the world's ODA in 1999 (DAC, 2000). Private grants may free up other public funds and allow African states to spend less of their money on education, health, or other social services. ODA also does not include military aid and security assistance, though the amounts of this are modest for Africa in any case. Nor does it include the value of favored access to developed country markets, such as the Lomé Convention, which may indirectly subsidize African states. Finally, International Monetary Fund loans are not covered by the definition, despite the fact that IMF agreements often are the prerequisites for conventional aid programs. Thus, ODA may understate the true volume of "non-market" external resources accessible to African states at any moment.

In spite of that, ODA has also been criticized for exaggerating the scale of resource transfers by grouping together grants and loans. Even a subsidized loan has to be paid off. Recently researchers at the World Bank have devised a more conservative measure of foreign aid that they think is a better estimate of the public resources truly being donated to recipient countries (Burnside and Dollar, 2000, Chang et al., 1998). Called effective development assistance (EDA), it is the sum of grants and the grant-equivalent of official loans. EDA to the African region is consistently about two-thirds the level of ODA in any given year. Perhaps the "real" amount of aid lies somewhere between the two.

Whichever measure is deemed more accurate, we can see that development aid rose slowly in real terms in the early post-colonial era, and then exploded upward with the rush toward "structural adjustment" in the early 1980s. (See figure 7.1). Development aid (both ODA and EDA) leveled off when superpower rivalry ended in the late 1980s, however, and began dropping after the mid-1990s. Africa's total ODA in 1998 was three-quarters the level five years earlier. Measured as a share of Africa's GDP (excluding Nigeria and South Africa), aid has fallen in half during that period (World Bank, 2001). Not every country has lost that much, so the situation across the region is less dramatic than suggested by the aggregate figures. Nonetheless, it is likely that development assistance to Africa will fall further in real terms (O'Connell and Saludo, 2001).

Figure 7.1 covers the entire post-colonial era in Africa, during which total ODA for the region added up to nearly $300 billion (1996 prices). This is not an immaterial sum, though it amounts to no more than one-quarter of all ODA provided worldwide since 1960. To put the ODA figure in further perspective, the full tally only comes to about $450 per capita for all African countries between 1960 and 1998, or a little over $10 each year for each person in Africa.[5] Nonetheless, the modest all-Africa average conceals wide inter-country variations. A few heavily populated countries, notably South Africa and Nigeria, which received little development aid, pull down the regional mean. By contrast, some less populous countries got several thousands of dollars in aid per capita during the period. That is a great deal of money in places where the average yearly income may be measured in hundreds of dollars. Table 7.1

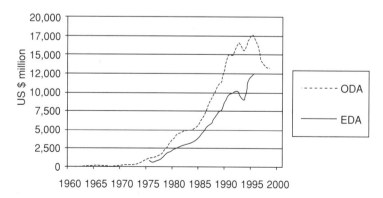

Source: World Bank 2000b, Chang et al. 1999.

Figure 7.1 Total Foreign Aid to Africa (1996 prices)

Table 7.1 African countries have received widely different amounts of foreign aid over four decades

Total Official Development Assistance per capita 1960–1998 (in 1996 prices)			
Least		*Most*	
South Africa	$58	Gabon	$4,512
Nigeria	$114	São Tomé and Príncipe	$6,525
Eritrea	$225	Cape Verde	$7,344
Ethiopia	$436	Djibouti	$9,913
Angola	$577	Seychelles	$12,343
All Africa average	$449		

Note: Eritrea and South Africa only received aid from 1993.
Source: Author's calculations based on World Bank 2000c. World Development Indicators 2000 on CD-ROM. Washington, D.C.: The World Bank.

reports representative data on aid intensity. Clearly, aid weighs very heavily in many African countries, particularly in the smaller countries.

Aid: Unproductive or Counterproductive for State Capability?

The question under consideration is what *net* effect all this aid has on central state capability in Africa. Donors have long tried to strengthen public institutions in developing nations. They are well aware that using aid for institutional development is difficult and subject to reversals when the aid is terminated. A major official review of aid effectiveness in the 1980s, for example, conceded that when it came to increasing institutional capacity in recipient countries, "the broad picture cannot be described as satisfactory" (Cassen and associates, 1986, 111).

Many critics outside the aid establishment, however, go further. The problem in their view is more than a failure of aid to live up to its promise of helping Africans build more capable states. The critics fault aid for actually making matters worse by undermining domestic administrative capability. In other words, they see well-intended activity by donors inadvertently weakening the recipient states. Two, somewhat contradictory arguments are often put forward to support this claim.

The first critique points to donor intrusiveness and to the loss of sovereignty that comes with acceptance of development assistance. Under the lending formula common since the 1980s, African states could borrow money at favorable interest rates, but the loans came with conditions designed to insure that they would be repaid. Debtor countries were required to deregulate their economies, privatize industry, emphasize exports, and restrain public spending to qualify for continued credit. Many observers see this as an unjustified handover of policy making powers to external agencies (Williams, 2000), which they blame for deforming African states and undermining their legitimacy among their constituents.

This somewhat patronizing line of reasoning tends to ignore the extent of African states' informal veto power in aid negotiations. Africa's international creditors regularly complain about the lack of "country ownership" of policies in the region adopted under pressure, leading to "policy slippage" and consistent failure to meet targets (van de Walle and Johnson 1996, 54–59). It is easy to overlook how much bargaining room even a bankrupt state has, especially with off-the-record decisions to ignore or impede stated plans and actions. The donor community often yields to this unspoken power by continuing to extend credit to defaulting states.

Thus, one should not exaggerate the degree to which African states have lost their capacity to set the policy agenda within their borders (Leiteritz, 2001).

The second argument about aid and state capacity concedes this point with regard to recipient bargaining room. In fact, the claim is that recipients have so much latitude when taking aid that a "moral hazard problem" emerges for the donors (Killick, 1998; Bräutigam, 2000). Moral hazard describes any situation in which risky or otherwise undesirable behavior is encouraged because risk takers believe a third party will bail them out of mistakes. In more formal terms, it entails actions by agents maximizing their own utility to the detriment of others where agents do not bear the full consequences of their actions. Aid is thought to create moral hazard by releasing other resources for African states to use as they see fit, without holding them to account for policy blunders or violation of loan covenants. Recipients are indirectly rewarded for reckless conduct that undercuts their administrative capability.

Moore (1998) makes the analogy to "rentier" states that have "unearned" sources of income, such as rents available from mineral wealth. Aid has become like a natural resource for many African states, providing them a regular and accessible revenue stream. These flows free states from having to preserve or improve their ability to tap domestic sources of funds. Nor do they need to establish a bargain with local constituencies whereby the recognized authorities will supply public services in exchange for taxes and fees. The fact that African states can survive or expand by taking aid, creates incentives for them to neglect their bureaucratic capability, which they no longer need to meet the demands of citizens and local interest groups.

But is it true that large amounts of aid delivered over long periods have systematically misdirected leaders' energies, fostered irresponsible public administration, and encouraged states to live beyond their means? Like many strongly stated arguments, this one has its place but has been made too much of by its advocates. States develop the way they do for multiple reasons. Rentier status, for example, has not prevented oil-rich Middle Eastern states from becoming fairly efficient at repressing or co-opting dissent (Saudi Arabia) or projecting military force (Iraq). Similarly, aid should not have the same bad effects everywhere in Africa.

PROJECT AID

For one thing, donated or borrowed resources are resources nonetheless. Even if they leave no lasting impression, gifts and loans can help to keep alive important state functions that would otherwise be abandoned. This is especially so when we look at special foreign aid projects to assure the supply of "merit goods" (things whose consumption is considered intrinsically desirable, such as food and shelter) to society. The market does not spontaneously generate these items for everyone. Providing merit goods regardless of citizens' ability to pay can be an important source of political legitimacy and economic stability, as states from Classical Greece onward have understood. The ancient city-states made regular, free distributions of corn to quell social unrest. In Africa, the contemporary equivalents include food-for-work schemes, child nutrition projects, community health clinics, and clean water projects.

Faced with financial constraints, many African states have discriminated in their budgets against health and social services, though they have tended to protect education spending (Gyimah-Brempong, 1998). Welfare-oriented undertakings for Africa have strong constituencies in the high-income countries and may be singled out for special consideration in foreign aid budgets. Donors have stepped in with money and expertise to replace some of the lost merit goods, buttressing the recipient states by encouraging social stability. Consequently, external agencies gain a major say in what social services African states provide and how they are delivered. Special implementation units may be set up to see that the resources are used as the donors want them to be used. This "bypass strategy" also is common with donors' endeavors in other sectors, producing foreign aid enclaves throughout the state administrative network in Africa.

To count these "islands of prosperity" as a loss of state sovereignty and capacity, however, assumes that the opportunity cost of the projects is positive—in other words, that African states give up more than they get back by accepting project aid. While we could never know the counterfactuals for sure, it is a stretch to think that these states would *generally* be better off without special foreign aid projects, at least in the near-to-medium-term. They would need systematically to find more efficient means of producing the same benefits with no outside help, or to identify substitute investments that would yield higher returns. Given the tendency of all states to "muddle through," I doubt that African states would regularly prove better at spotting and carrying out social or other types of projects on their own.

This is not to deny that recipient states pay a hidden price any time they agree to project aid. There are the transaction costs of having to negotiate the aid contract and comply with the sponsor's oversight requirements. The project may have been poorly conceived and have a negative demonstration effect on other domestically funded projects. Outside funding spawns perverse incentives, inducing the state to chase aid dollars and forgo other activities (Bräutigam, 2000, 24). New opportunities for graft may be created. Counterproductive gamesmanship occurs on the donor side too (McPherson, 2001).

Yet, these costs need to be set against the gains of having extra outreach or other activities that presumably serve the needs of some constituencies, which may help in a roundabout way to boost the state's claim to legitimate power. Legitimacy or the belief that a state has the right to rule, is an important element of state capacity. Stand-alone projects reinforce legitimacy in Africa, even if the projects are not sustainable on their own, without foreign input. Recipient states at least get to postpone the day of reckoning they would have to face, were they unable to vaccinate as many children, hire as many teachers, or build as many roads.

Withering Away of the State?

One specific charge against aid is that it has weakened the state through public sector downsizing. Structural adjustment lending usually requires containment of the public wage bill and reduction of government employment to meet near-term fiscal targets. In a sample of 20 African countries, central government employment as a share of the total population fell by 39 percent between the early 1980s and early 1990s. The central government wage bill as a proportion of GDP also fell by 21 percent. How much of this should be attributed to structural adjustment conditionalities is not self-evident, however. A sample of OECD countries experienced almost the same proportional decline in government employment and wages during this period (Schiavo-Campo et al., 1997, 9)—and obviously none of them took out structural adjustment loans.

Nor is it clear that the downsizing hurt government capacity as much as appearances suggest. Salaries and effective staffing (that is people who show up for work as opposed to just being carried on the payroll) had already fallen drastically in many African countries, so any aid-induced rationalization of the bureaucracy in the 1990s may have represented little incremental loss in real capability. Also, experience shows that when financial crises abate, public employment tends to re-expand due to the same pressures that caused it to grow in the first place.

Another fact worth remembering is how much of Africa's aid is technical assistance that offsets some of the decline in domestic human resources. Technical assistance is a broad category of activities, including consultancies by foreign experts, local training seminars, and overseas fellowships for African nationals. At last count, perhaps 40,000 expatriate technical personnel were resident in Africa supervising projects and providing guidance to local counterparts (Berg, 1993). Many of these people are working on civil service reform and "capacity building" activities. For example, the World Bank annually provides some $365 million to finance technical assistance (both stand-alone projects and technical assistance embedded in other projects) specifically to improve public sector performance. That is about 17 percent of its lending to Africa (World Bank, 2000b, 162).

Technical assistance is controversial. Donors like it because it provides jobs for their citizens and helps them monitor the recipient bureaucracy. However, foreign expertise is expensive and the individuals sent overseas are not necessarily suited for the tasks at hand. In some cases, foreign experts carry out their assignments with little training or involvement of host country personnel. There may be redundant skilled local workers who could do the same jobs at lower cost, though others dispute this (Cohen, 1992, 501). The training and education programs also have been criticized for adding to the "brain drain" of African bureaucrats who, after learning new skills, flee the state bureaucracy for employment in international agencies, in the local private sector, or, worse yet, in foreign countries. It bears repeating, however, that the client state does obtain new knowledge and technology in the bargain that it might not have obtained as quickly from alternate sources.

A point that sometimes gets lost in these debates over the impact of foreign aid on public administration is that a loss of sovereignty is not the same as a loss of administrative efficiency. A semi-sovereign or client state may still perform reasonably well, while being subject to outside advice and having to depend on outside funding and expertise to carry out the ordinary functions of government. Côte d'Ivoire was long thought to represent the success of such a model of development. So was Botswana. Much of the organizational capital in a dependent state is a wasting asset, that will be abandoned in the absence of further aid. Its heavy reliance on foreign human resources did not prevent Côte d'Ivoire from losing ground during the 1980s and 1990s. That said, temporary aid-induced improvements in administrative capability are not a setback for the recipient while they last. They add to the power of the state, even if only to prop it up for the moment. Pulling away this prop is probably not going to enhance bureaucratic efficiency any time soon.

THE RISE OF THE THIRD SECTOR

A specific way that project aid is alleged to perpetuate the weakness of African states is by funding of non-government organizations (NGOs) and community groups (Bräutigam, 2000, 36). Since 1989, nearly half of the World Bank's projects in Africa entail some NGO involvement. Many bilateral donors have partnerships that are even more extensive with private and voluntary groups. The availability of foreign funds has ignited an explosion in NGOs. The number registered in North-west Somalia, for example, burst from 40 to 553 in the eight years through 2000 (Hammond, n.d.). The belief among donors is that these "third sector" organizations are superior to government agencies in delivering community services. Whether or not that is so, aid-financing of NGOs is seen as having the potential negative byproduct of undermining state legitimacy (Fowler, 1991). Privatization of service delivery takes resources away from the central government and compromises public sector capability.

While subcontracting with NGOs is a sign of state collapse in Somalia, this need not be so in every country. An alternative scenario is when the privatization of service delivery merely represents an extension of the state's reach by other means. The state retains at least nominal control of its contractors' activities through legal and administrative regulations (Bratton, 1989). Even though NGOs may simply be filling a vacuum the state would leave vacant on its own, in many cases the state still may get much of the credit for the results. That tends to shore up its claim to legitimate power in the eyes of citizens (Sandberg, 1994, 11–12).

The amount of funding, in any case, is less than many people realize. Worldwide, only about 15 percent of ODA is channeled through NGOs, amounting to some $9 billion annually (Gibbs et al., 1999). This does mask considerable variety across countries and across sectors. In the social sectors of some Sahelian countries, for example, the proportion of aid going through NGOs may be much greater than 15 percent. Still, the preponderance of foreign aid usually remains at the disposal of national governments. This includes some of the resources directed to NGOs through so-called social funds, a minimum of 24 of which have been set up in Africa since 1991. Social funds are meant to overcome inefficiencies associated with the public sector, going around usual procedures to work with local and private organizations to take quicker action to reach poor people. Because these are freestanding operations, usually institutionally distinct from government line ministries, social funds can be seen as detracting from the central state.

Again, the sums involved are probably too small to have a major impact in most countries. According to a recent report, donor financing of social funds worldwide is projected to be merely $9 billion over the next five years (Fumo et al., 2000). Even these modest funds are not necessarily "lost" to the state in Africa. A central administrative entity, often a semi-autonomous unit set up for this purpose, is usually used to disburse money to intermediary organizations, which can include local governments. Therefore, the state continues indirectly to control the deployment of these resources. In some countries, Ethiopia for example, central authorities treat the social fund as an off-budget slush account. They can tap it to distribute patronage via approved "independent sector" organizations to favored regions and localities, thereby reinforcing not compromising state legitimacy and authority.[6]

Authentic non-partisan NGOs need not pose a threat to central authority either. According to interest group theory, a vibrant associational life is a source of state strength, not weakness. While some community organizations and voluntary associations have become disillusioned and may have given up on political lobbying, others are likely to put pressure on government officials to reduce waste and corruption in the delivery of public services. Channeling foreign aid through NGOs may thus have some indirect effect of helping to increase demand for improved administrative efficiency over the long term.

Ottaway (2000) argues that the NGOs fostered by foreign aid have not acted this way in Africa. She finds such organizations to be alienated from the communities they are supposed to represent, and thus ineffective in giving voice to local demands. There are exceptions, however. Over time, links to domestic bases of support may deepen and lead to better policy advocacy. Case studies in Ghana, Uganda, and South Africa find aid-supported NGOs can become key players in setting the course of national reform (Hearne, 1999). At least one of these countries— Uganda—is seen as having improved its bureaucratic capability since the 1980s (Langseth, 1995; Mose, 2002).

Measuring state capacity

Is it possible to assess African bureaucratic capability with precision? Specific administrative problems are easy enough to identify: budget offices do not manage the budget (Sekwart, 1997); central banks do not control the money supply (Fielding, 1996); tax departments fail to collect taxes (Bleaney et al., 1995). But how does overall capability look? Without some concrete indicators, state capability is little more than a debatable abstraction. One approach to operationalizing the concept has been to put together subjective ratings based on expert opinion or on the results of surveys of business leaders. Another is to identify objective proxies that indirectly represent the capacity of the state. Neither of these approaches are fully satisfactory, for reasons explored below. Nonetheless, they present an overall picture somewhat at odds with simplistic "Afro-pessimism" often voiced in the popular press and many scholarly reports.

Subjective indicators

Perhaps the most familiar subjective measure is the Bureaucratic Quality Index, put together by Political Risk Services Group of Syracuse, New York. It is widely used in international quantitative research (Keefer and Knack, 1995; Burki and Perry, 1998; Englebert, 2000). Purportedly an indicator of the professionalism and competence of the civil service, the dataset offers a time series going back to the early 1980s that make it possible to track improvement or decay in national administrative capacity.[7] For what the data is worth, and it may not be much, they portray Africa as having mixed yet generally *improving* administrative capacity. Half the African countries that were rated went up on the Bureaucratic Quality Index between 1982 and 1997, one-quarter stayed the same, and one-quarter supposedly lost quality (see table 7.2). The base rating is still quite low in most countries. Some of the specific scores are questionable. Is Cameroon really one of the best-run and improving states in Africa, for instance?

Few people looking at Africa from the outside would expect to see any sign of bureaucratic improvement under structural adjustment, though other domestic opinion surveys have uncovered the same perception of positive trends shown in the PRS Group data. A corroborating survey is the *Africa Competitiveness Report*. Business executives in more than half the countries studied reported a positive direction of change over the period from 1996 to 1999 (World Economic Forum, 2000, 11). Those results were confirmed in the African Bureaucratic Structure Survey (Court et al., 1999). It investigated the efficiency of the state bureau-

Table 7.2   State capacity is variable and improving in several African countries, according to one source

Score	1997 Bureaucratic Quality Index
4 and above	Cameroon↑, Côte d'Ivoire, Gabon↑, Ghana↑, Kenya↑, Namibia↑, South Africa↓, Zimbabwe↑
3 to less than 4	Angola↑, Botswana↓, Gambia↑, Mozambique, Nigeria↑, Senegal
2 to less than 3	Burkina Faso↓, Congo Republic, DRC↑, Ethiopia↑, Guinea↑, Guinea-Bissau, Madagascar↓, Malawi↓, Niger↓, Sudan↑, Tanzania↑, Togo, Uganda↑, Zambia↑
Less than 2	Liberia, Mali, Somalia↓, Sierra Leone↓
Not rated	Benin, Burundi, Cape Verde, Central African Republic, Chad, Comoros, Djibouti, Equatorial Guinea, Eritrea, Lesotho, Mauritania, Mauritius, Rwanda, São Tomé and Príncipe, Seychelles, Swaziland

Average rating: 2.1 in 1982, 2.6 in 1997.

Note: Bureaucratic quality scores range in value from 0–6, with higher values indicating better quality. High scores signify an established mechanism for recruitment and training, autonomy from political pressure, and strength and expertise to govern without drastic changes in policy or interruptions in government services when governments change. A "↑" indicates improvement in annual country rating since 1982 (or nearest available year). A "↓" indicates deterioration.

Source: Author's calculations, based on IRIS-3 File of International Country Risk Guide Data.

cracy in delivering services in 20 countries over the last ten years, and found no evidence of major across-the-board deterioration in service provision. Eritrea and Mauritius appear to have made significant progress, while Kenya and Nigeria declined, and other countries remained stable.

Additional subjective rating systems exist for national administrative capacity. The World Bank's Operations Evaluation Department assigns an annual grade to each of the Bank's borrowing countries, with a separate grade given for the performance of public sector institutions. These evaluations are confidential, but the 1999 data were leaked to *The Guardian* newspaper and subsequently made available over the Internet by anti-Bank activists. The Bank's ratings cover more countries than the PRS Group dataset, though the leaked information leaves out the less indebted (and probably better-run) countries of Africa. There is a similar range of state capability reported, however. Seventeen African countries got "As" and "Bs" for public sector management, three received "Cs," and twenty got "Ds" and "Fs" (Table 7.3).[8]

Table 7.3   The World Bank "report card" on public institutions: "grade curve" for Africa

Grade	Country Policy and Institutional Assessment (1999): Public Sector Management and Institutions Component
A	Cape Verde, Eritrea, Ethiopia, Ghana, Lesotho, Uganda, Zambia
B	Benin, Burkina Faso, Côte d'Ivoire, Malawi, Mauritania, Mozambique, Rwanda, Senegal, Tanzania, Zimbabwe
C	Madagascar, Mali, Niger
D	Burundi, Cameroon, Djibouti, Gambia, Guinea , Kenya, São Tomé and Príncipe, Togo
F	Angola, Central African Republic, Chad, Comoros, DRC, Congo Republic, Guinea-Bissau, Liberia, Nigeria, Sierra Leone, Somalia, Sudan
No information	Botswana, Equatorial Guinea, Gabon, Mauritius, Namibia, Seychelles, South Africa, Swaziland

Note: The World Bank's Operations Evaluations Department rates countries on current performance in criteria grouped into four categories, one of which is public sector management and institutions (including property rights and rule-based governance; quality of budgetary and financial management; efficiency of revenue mobilization; efficiency of public expenditures; and transparency, accountability, and corruption in the public sector.)
Source: World Bank, as reported by Globalization Challenge Initiative (2000).

Unfortunately, the Bank and the PRS Group do not seem to agree on which states in Africa fare well and which fare poorly. The unreliability of subjective measures of governance is underscored by yet another exercise in quantifying governance. Researchers at the World Bank recently assembled governance indicators based on several surveys of perceptions of the quality of governance taken during 1997 and 1998. National performance in Africa was reported to be quite low, but not unanimously so. There turned out to be a large degree of inconsistency in the underlying surveys, however. Some of the findings are bizarre—Sierra Leone, for example, got one of the best ratings for public sector effectiveness. The World Bank team concluded that it is misleading to try to rank countries precisely according to their level of governance (Kaufmann et al., 1999). Summary results for Africa are shown in Table 7.4.[9]

In the end, the subjective approach suggests that administrative systems are variable across the sub-continent, and provides tentative evidence that capacity may be getting stronger in *some* countries—though which ones is a matter of dispute. These are not trivial findings, for they tend to refute impressionistic accounts of region-wide administrative collapse (Dramé, 1996). That said, no evidence exists of significant

Table 7.4   Another recent effort from the World Bank to quantify state capacity

Rating	Composite Governance Indicator (1997–98): Government Effectiveness
Greater than 0	Botswana, Gambia, Mauritius, Namibia, Senegal, Sierra Leone
0 to −1	Benin, Burkina Faso, Cameroon, Central African Republic, Chad, Congo Republic, Côte d'Ivoire, Ethiopia, Ghana, Guinea, Guinea-Bissau, Kenya, Lesotho, Liberia, Madagascar, Malawi, Mali, Mozambique, South Africa, Swaziland, Tanzania, Togo, Uganda, Zambia
Less than −1	Angola, DRC, Gabon, Niger, Nigeria, Somalia, Sudan, Zimbabwe
Not rated	Burundi, Cape Verde, Comoros, Djibouti, Equatorial Guinea, Eritrea, Mauritania, Rwanda, São Tomé and Príncipe, Seychelles
Average rating: −0.532 (range −1.769 to 0.221)	

Note: The indicator is measured in units ranging from about −2.5 to 2.5, with higher values corresponding to better outcomes. Government effectiveness reflects factors such as the quality and competence of civil service, the quality of public services, and the credibility of the government. The composite indicator is constructed using an unobserved components methodology to combine information from different sources into aggregate governance indicators.
Source: Kaufmann et al. 1999. Aggregating Governance Indicators. World Bank Policy Research Working Paper 2195. Washington, D.C.: The World Bank.

broad-based administrative improvement, either. Nonetheless, a few states, notably Botswana and Mauritius, appear to have obtained and retained reasonably good state capability. A few others seem to be making some headway, impermanent though it may be.

OBJECTIVE YARDSTICKS

Can objective yardsticks of state capability yield deeper insights? Perhaps, though the quality and coverage of many African datasets limit this approach too. Jackman (1993) proposes easily measured indicators of state *political* capacity, which is somewhat different from the question of *administrative* effectiveness of primary interest here. Still, the results are worthy of note. Jackman defines political capacity as a function of continuity and regularity in state-society relations, that is, as the creation of legitimate public institutions. For objective proxies for political capacity, he suggests chronological age of state institutions (operationalized as the time elapsed since independence and since promulgation of the current constitution) and generational age of national leadership (as indicated by a demonstrated history of leadership transfers).

The date of independence is not particularly useful for differentiating among states within the African region, since most of these countries became independent at about the same time. The date of the latest constitution is potentially more revealing, though many countries adopted new, multiparty constitutions in the 1990s. Leadership turnover is problematic because it often results from extra-constitutional violence in Africa, so that a higher number of leaders may indicate political instability rather than increased political capacity. However, the number of coups has dropped sharply over the last decade, and the proportion of electoral-based successions is up (Goldsmith, 2001a). Keeping these caveats in mind, we can compare average 1985 and 2001 performance on the variables offered by Jackman (Table 7.5).

It is an arithmetic certainty that the mean age of the political systems would grow between the two periods. More significant is the fact that mean constitutional age in the region changed little over that time. This is due almost entirely to the recent flurry of democratic constitutional reforms. We also see that leadership turnover increased the second period. On two of three criteria, therefore, Africa's average state political capacity may have *strengthened* slightly. Perhaps more significant is the evidence of performance gaps among African countries. Botswana, Mauritius, and, to a lesser extent, Senegal perform relatively well on Jackman's indicators of institutional legitimacy and effectiveness, just as they do on the subjective measures of state performance discussed in the

Table 7.5   Indicators of "national political capacity" in Africa

	1985			*2001*	
Average time since independence	*Average constitutional age*	*Avg. no. of leaders in current constitutional period*	*Average time since independence*	*Average constitutional age*	*Avg. no. of leaders in current constitu period*
28.3 years	12.7 years	1.3	42.9 years	12.3 years	2.1

Note: Constitutional age is the number of years since the current constitution or major revision to it was adopted. Leaders are top policy makers, usually the president. Individuals who have held office for more than one term are counted once.
Source: 1985 data are from Jackman (1993, 164–65); 2001 are author's estimates.

previous section. Again, we need to remain cautious in interpreting these findings.[10] The importance of a new constitution or a history of leadership transitions may not be the same in all countries.

Returning to administrative capability per se, a good barometer is public finance. Hobbes asserted that "to levy money upon the subjects" was among Leviathan's most critical responsibilities.[11] The pursuit of revenue is a pressing concern for all states; capable states have the organizational wherewithal to extract revenue from society sufficient to respond to social needs and pursue collective goals. A system of collecting taxes is simultaneously a mechanism for gathering information on citizens and businesses, and forcing them to comply with the state's reporting requirements and allied regulations (Moore, 1998). A state that can collect a large amount of revenue thus proves it possesses administrative capacity. Tax collection data are available for many countries and can be reviewed to compare state capability. Then again, having this capability may not encourage economic development in the absence of public accountability. Putting in place a more efficient revenue collection system may simply add to rent seeking, by giving officials new opportunities to grant fraudulent exemptions in exchange for illegal payoffs. This is what happened with a tax reform program in the DRC (Rose-Ackerman, 1999, 207).

Migdal (1988, 286) proposes that another objective approach to measuring state capability is to look at school enrollment data. Enrollment as a percentage of the eligible population is a proxy for the state's power to mobilize its inhabitants into public institutions and make them submit to state rules. States that educate a high proportion of school-aged children thus implicitly demonstrate their general administrative capability.[12] As with public finance, enrollment is reasonably well-documented in Africa. In neither case, however, are the reported numbers to be fully trusted.

Do these last two objective indicators tell us more than we have already learned from the subjective data? Turning first to the question of taxes, some African states have broadened their tax bases and implemented tax reforms in recent years (Ramikrishnan, 1998). In the early 1980s, total tax revenues as a share of GDP in Africa was about 18 percent. By the late 1990s, the total tax revenues were slightly greater—19 to 21 percent of regional GDP. Individual countries varied greatly. Taxes amounted to only seven percent of GDP in Chad in 1999, though that was an improvement over the two percent reported for 1983. Total taxes as a percent of GDP fell in Botswana and Mauritius, though the rate remained fairly high for the region at 29 percent and 18 percent of GDP, respectively (World Bank, 2001).

The composition of revenue also is interesting. Income taxes are often considered the best test of state power because they are so invasive and difficult to collect. African states are apt to rely less on this type of tax compared with states in other regions (Herbst, 2000, 120). However, the share of GDP represented by these direct taxes has been trending modestly upward. Despite the problems of large subsistence and informal sectors, many African states look as if they are becoming more adept at imposing levies on income, profits, and capital gains. For example, Kenya's income tax receipts rose from 6.2 percent of GDP in 1972 to 9.1 percent in 1996. This may only reflect urbanization and economic modernization, rather than any enhancement in tax administration, and the improvement does not apply to all countries. In Uganda, income tax has dropped proportionately over the years for which we have readings, and in Ghana, income tax has maintained a constant share of GDP.

A more sophisticated approach is to estimate "tax effort," which is the ratio of actual tax receipts to some measure of "taxable capacity." Mining, for example, is easier to tax than agriculture, so, all other things equal, a country with a large mining sector would have greater taxable capacity than an agriculturally-based country. Stotsky and WoldeMariam (1997) find a large variation in tax effort among African countries, with some improving and some declining during the early to mid 1990s. The experience of many countries thus contradicts the idea that, as a rule, African states lack or are losing an important ability to generate revenue. World Bank and International Monetary Fund (IMF) projects may be partly responsible, having put in place independent revenue authorities with foreign experts in many countries.

Taking tax revenue as a measure of administrative efficacy, it thus would appear that several African states have grown *more capable* compared with the level thirty years ago. No universal depletion of bureaucratic capability is suggested by the tax revenue data, which reaffirms the spotty positive movement found in the PRS Group's subjective observations.

The other proposed objective marker of bureaucratic capability is school enrollment. Though again the quality of the underlying data is uneven, World Bank (2001) time series tend to underscore what is becoming a familiar pattern: wide national disparities amid slight regional improvement. Among enrollment statistics, primary school enrollment is probably the best proxy for state capability. Most African states aim for universal or at least widespread basic education. Primary enrollment thus captures the extent to which states are able to meet an important self-set goal. Average enrollment at the primary level has crept upward a bit since 1980 to a level of just over 60 percent of the school-aged population. Secondary enrollment, though it may be a lower stated priority, shows a parallel trend.

As with taxes, large variation occurs around the mean. Many countries do not report enrollment data—and these are probably the poorest performers as the ability to collect and disseminate statistics is itself an important marker of administrative efficiency. Among countries that do report, primary enrollment in the 1990s ranged widely. In Botswana and Mauritius, for example, the figures are generally well over 90 percent of the available population (though the reported figure dripped inexplicably in the latter part of the decade). Compare that with Niger at only 25 percent in 1996. There is obviously plenty of room for improvement in many countries, but most have been maintaining or raising their enrollment figures despite the austerity of recent years.

These accomplishments obviously say nothing about school attendance or learning outcomes. Clearly, it is out of place to make strong general inferences about state capability based on this slender reed. Still, two broad observations are possible: states in Africa differ greatly in their ability to mobilize children for school; and average capacity to provide schooling seems to be stable or heading upward, not downward, in many countries.

HOW MUCH DOES AID REALLY MATTER?

The last question for this paper is whether the states that have the *better* capability (as indicated by either subjective or objective criteria), are those that received the *least* foreign aid. In other words, are stronger state institutions and performance associated with lower aid intensity, as critics of aid predict?

An alternative hypothesis is that aid intensity is less important than the initial character of the state that gets the aid. A well-known paradox of aid is that it works best where it is least needed (Burnside and Dollar, 2000). Capable states can make good use of aid, but they might do as well without it. Incompetent states waste aid, though they need the help. The critical variable is not the volume of aid, but the underlying character of the beneficiary (Azam et al., 1999; Devarajan et al., 2001, 2).

Support for this line of reasoning can be seen in table 7.6, which suggests that undue amounts of aid are not directly implicated in the extreme cases of state collapse. The DRC (formerly Zaire), for example, is often cited as the paradigmatic client state that continued to exist for many years thanks to artificial life support provided by donors (Lancaster, 1999). Yet, since 1960 it has received only about one-sixth

Table 7.6   Africa's "failed" states often received less foreign aid than some relatively "efficient" states

Total ODA per capita 1960–1998 (in 1996 prices)			
Consensus "Failed" states		Consensus "Efficient" states	
Angola	$577	Botswana	$4,495
Congo, Dem. Rep.	$710	Cape Verde	$7,344
Sierra Leone	$988	Mauritius	$1,830
Somalia	$2,221	Namibia	$1,133
Sudan	$1,056	South Africa	$58

Note: Namibia only received aid from 1985, South Africa from 1993.
Source: Author's calculations based on World Bank 2000c.

the amount of ODA per capita received by Botswana, a state that is widely regarded as among the more efficient in Africa.

Admittedly, Botswana is now much richer than the DRC, so the larger absolute amount of aid is relatively less important for Botswana. However, this was not always so. If we go back to 1970, Botswana's per capita GNP was only $160 versus $200 in the DRC (World Bank, 2000a). Botswana received $77 in ODA per capita that year (current prices), far exceeding what the DRC received ($14 per capita). It would appear from the evidence that Botswana made productive use of these resources, the acquisition of which did not undermine its central administrative capability or prevent economic development. The DRC, by contrast, failed to take advantage of aid and neglected to build the public institutions that could hold the country together (admittedly a far more challenging task in this larger and further-flung territory).

Another interesting pairing is Sierra Leone and Mauritius. In the mid-1960s, Sierra Leone's per capita GNP was roughly half that in Mauritius. After independence, Sierra Leone received about half as much per capita ODA as Mauritius—that is, each country obtained a similar volume of aid resources in proportion to its national economy. Yet, three decades later, real per capita GNP in the West African country has dropped by 50 percent; in Mauritius it has risen by over 200 percent. The former state has degenerated into anarchy, whereas the second is one of Africa's most successful states. Again, it is hard to hold international donors responsible for these divergent national trajectories. The driving forces must be internal, not too much or too little foreign aid.

CONCLUSION

Only with trepidation would anyone venture to draw conclusions and policy advice from these questionable subjective and objective indicators of state capacity. Nonetheless, one interpretation is that long-run public bureaucratic capability is primarily endogenous and unmoved much by aid, one way or the other. A few African states function reasonably well on their own, irrespective of foreign assistance. Others consistently do very poorly, with or without a great deal of assistance. There is little evidence of general deterioration of state capacity across the region

In states that have nascent administrative capability in the first place, aid may do some good, though it is not needed over time. In states at the far end of the spectrum on bureaucratic efficiency, aid probably has little benefit other than as a stop-gap against famine or natural disaster. Along the broad middle range of state capability, aid would appear to have a positive, if transitory, influence. Donors aid may have produced these temporary salutary effects through a variety of mechanisms, such as technical assistance for civil service "capacity building" and "policy dialogue" over governance reforms. This is hardly a ringing endorsement of development assistance, whose long-term helpful impact has been inhibited by multiple factors, including faddism and conflicting strategies among the various international financial institutions and development agencies and lack of domestic political accountability among the recipients. Few African states are particularly well-managed as a result of aid, but the implication is that many would be managed still less well without external advice and supervision. There is nothing is these data to suggest that African states would generally perform better on their own.

If so, that raises the issue of what will happen if the crutch of aid is taken away from these countries. As noted, aid receipts are dropping in the region. Some experts are recommending an "aid exit" strategy (McPherson, 2001), and no one expects aid to return to the levels of the early 1990s. For Africa's better-managed states the effect of sharply lower aid would probably be immaterial. The same thing may be true of the collapsed states that receive mainly emergency relief at present. That leaves the wide range of remaining states. Forced to become more self-reliant, will they reconfigure themselves and discover how to better fashion conditions for national development? Or will less aid mean fewer books distributed, fewer wells drilled, and less health care provided—thereby raising the risk accelerated chaos and state collapse in the region?

Based on the evidence in this paper, the probability of the second scenario is greater. In the end, the phoenix of more effective states may emerge from the debris. That process will be slow and costly. The more desirable alternative may be to find ways of managing foreign aid so that it has a more pronounced and lasting positive effect on state capacity— a goal that has proved elusive to donors and recipients alike over the past several decades.

Notes

1 I am grateful to Clive Gray, Peter Lewis, and Nic van de Walle for comments on earlier drafts of this chapter.

2 Political scientists seem generally to prefer a fourfold definition of capacity that captures critical state functions, as opposed to the instrumental view offered here. Grindle (1997, 8) suggests that in addition to administrative capacity and political capacity (both implicit in my efficiency/effectiveness categories), capable states exhibit institutional and technical capacity. Migdal (1988, 4) presents a different fourfold list of essential state functions: the capacities to penetrate society, regulate social relationships, extract resources, and use resources in determined ways. Bräutigam (1996, 83) separates capacity into four similar dimensions: regulatory, administrative, technical, and extractive. My conceptualization of state capability is consistent with these detailed functional characterizations, but focuses more on the means for performing these functions. Looking at state capability in instrumental rather than functional terms seems to me to simplify the tasks of measurement and analysis.

3 Due to space constraints, I will not deal with the complicated question of political corruption in this chapter, though corrupt practices are both a cause and an effect of low state capability. Bribes and kickbacks raise the cost of implementing policies and reduce the probability of those policies accomplishing their stated ends, and they are most common in weak states. For evidence that foreign aid may increase corruption among recipients, see Alesina and Weder (1999) and Svensson (2000).

4 State capacity is arguably a more significant dimension than democracy for the comparative study of African political systems (Villalón, 1998, 6). Goldsmith (2000a, 2001b) presents empirical evidence that foreign aid has not setback but may have supported democratization in Africa in the 1990s. For a contrary view, see Knack (2000b) and Simon (2001).

5 My preferred way of measuring aid intensity is aid per head of national population. Other studies, including some of my work (Goldsmith, 2001b), take aid as a percent of national income or product. While it controls for the level of national development, that calculation has the disadvantage of being thrown off by misestimates of the GNP and by changes in the foreign exchange rate. The dollar figures for ODA, on the other hand, are more complete and reliable, and so are used here (prorated for size of population). For comparison, all-Africa, ODA represented 3.5 percent of GDP in 1999, way down from the high of 10.2 percent in 1992 (World Bank, 2001). The correlation between the two series is relatively high, however (0.54).

6 Personal communication from Steve Peterson, Harvard University.

7 The Bureaucratic Quality Index is one of six components of the PRS Group's overall political risk assessment, the other components being corruption in government, rule of law, ethnic tensions, repudiation of government contracts, and expropriation risk. The data are available in the IRIS-3 File of International Country Risk Guide Data, on sale by the PRS Group.

8 The World Bank's Country Policy and Institutional Assessment rates national performance on 20 equally weighted criteria that are grouped into four categories. In addition to public sector management and institutions (reported here), the other three categories are economic management, structural policies, and policies for social inclusion.

9 In addition to government effectiveness, reported in Table 7.5, five other composite indicators were assembled for voice and accountability, political stability/lack of violence, the regulatory framework, the rule of law, and control of corruption.

10 Englebert (2000) proposes a state "development capacity index" based on both subjective and objective criteria. This index is too highly aggregated and covers too many years to be of use here. It is noteworthy, however, that the same states do well on Englebert's rating system, especially Botswana and Mauritius, but also other southern African states such as Lesotho, South Africa, and Swaziland.

11 Cited in Bräutigam (2002).

12 A complicating factor is that churches and other private organizations supply much of the education in Africa. Since these entities usually work within state guidelines, however, they can be seen as a low-cost arm of state policy.

BIBLIOGRAPHY

Alesina, Alberto, and Beatrice Weder. forthcoming. "Do Corrupt Governments Receive Less Foreign Aid?" *American Economic Review.*

Aron, Janine. 1996. "The Institutional Foundations of Growth," in Stephen Ellis, ed. *Africa Now.* London: James Currey.

Auyeh, Mose. 2002. "African Efforts to Improve Governance: Civil Service and Decentralization Reforms in Uganda." Paper Presented at the Conference on Consolidation in New Democracies, Uppsala, Sweden, 8–9 June.

Azam, Jean-Paul, Shantayanan Devarajan and Stephen A. O'Connell. 1999. "Aid Dependence Reconsidered." Centre for the Study of African Economies Working Paper Series 99.5. Oxford, UK: Oxford University.

Bayart, Jean-François, Stephen Ellis, and Béatrice Hibou. 1999. *The Criminalization of the State in Africa.* Oxford: James Currey.

Berg, Eliot J. 1993. *Rethinking Technical Cooperation: Reforms for Capacity Building in Africa.* New York: United Nations Development Program.

Bleaney, Michael, Norman Gemmell, and David Greenaway. 1995. "Tax Revenue Instability, with Particular Reference to Sub-Saharan Africa." *Journal of Development Studies,* 31, 6: 883–902.

Bratton, Michael. 1989. "The Politics of Government-NGO Relations in Africa." *World Development*, 17, 4: 569–587.

Bräutigam, Deborah. 1996. "State Capacity and Effective Governance," in Benno Ndulu and Nicolas van de Walle, eds., *Agenda for Africa's Economic Renewal*. Washington, D.C.: Overseas Development Council.

Bräutigam, Deborah. 2000. *Aid Dependence and Governance*. Stockholm: Almqvist and Wiksell International.

Bräutigam, Deborah. 2002. "Building Leviathan: Revenue, State Capacity, and Governance," *IDS Bulletin*, 33, 3.

Burki, Shaheed Javi, and Guillermo E. Perry. 1998. *Beyond the Washington Consensus: Institutions Matter*. Washington, D.C.: The World Bank.

Burnside, Craig and David Dollar. 2000. "Aid, Policies, and Growth." *American Economic Review*, 90, 4: 847–868.

Cassen, Robert and associates. 1986. *Does Aid Work?* Oxford: Clarendon.

Chang, Charles C., Eduardo Fernandez-Arias, and Luis Serven. 1998. "Measuring Aid Flows: A New Approach." World Bank Policy Research Working Paper 2050. Washington, D.C.: The World Bank.

Cohen, John M. 1992. "Foreign Advisors and Capacity Building: The Case of Kenya." *Public Administration and Development* 12, 5: 493–510.

Court, Julius, Petra Kristen and Beatrice Weder. 2000. "Bureaucratic Structure and Performance: First Africa Survey Results." Tokyo: United Nations University.

DAC (Development Assistance Committee). 1993. *DAC Orientations on Participatory Development and Good Governance*. Paris: Organization for Economic Co-operation and Development.

DAC. 2000. *DAC Tables from 2000 Development Co-operation Report*. www.oecd.org/dac/htm/dacstats.htm#Dactables.

Devarajan, Shantayanan, David Dollar, and Torgny Holmgren, eds. 2001. *Aid and Reform in Africa: Lessons from Ten Case Studies*. Washington, D.C.: The World Bank.

Dramé, Tiébelé. 1996. "The Crisis of the State," in Stephen Ellis, ed. *Africa Now*. London: James Currey.

Economic Commission for Africa (ECA). 1999. *The ECA and Africa: Accelerating a Continent's Development*. New York: United Nations ECA.

Englebert, Pierre. 2000. *State Capacity and Development in Africa*. Boulder, Colo.: Lynne Rienner.

Fielding, David. 1996. "The Causes and Consequences of Central Bank Money Supply Decisions: Evidence from Africa." *Applied Financial Economics*, 6, 2: 121–41.

Fowler, Alan. 1991. "The Role of NGOs in Changing State-Society Relations: Perspectives from Eastern and Southern Africa." *Development Policy Review*, 9, 1: 53–84.

Freedom House. 2001. *Annual Survey of Freedom Country Scores* www.freedomhouse.org.rankings.pdf/.

Fumo, Claudia, Arjan de Haan, Jeremy Holland, and Nazneen Kanji. 2000. "The Social Fund: An Effective Instrument to Support Local Action for

Poverty Reduction?" DFID; Social Development Department Working Paper no. 5.

Gibbs, Christopher, Claudia Fumo, and Thomas Kuby. 1999. *Nongovernmental Organizations in World Bank Supported Projects: A Review*. World Bank Operations Evaluation Department. Washington, D.C.: The World Bank.

Globalization Challenge Initiative. 2000. *News and Notices for IMF and World Bank Watchers*, 2, 3; available at www.challengeglobalization.org/html/news_notices/fall2000/fall2000_02.shtml.

Goldsmith, Arthur A. 1999. "Africa's Overgrown State Revisited: Bureaucracy and Economic Growth." *World Politics*, 51, 4: 520–46.

Goldsmith, Arthur A. 2000. "Sizing up the African State." *Journal of Modern African Studies*, 38, 1: 1–20.

Goldsmith, Arthur A. 2001a. "Donors, Dictators, and Democrats in Africa." *Journal of Modern African Studies*, 39, 3:411–36.

Goldsmith, Arthur A. 2001b. "Foreign Aid and Statehood in Africa." *International Organization*, 55, 1: 123–48.

Grindle, Merilee S. 1997. *Challenging the State*. Cambridge: Cambridge University Press.

Gyimah-Brempong, Kwabena. 1998. "The Political Economy of Budgeting in Africa: 1971–1991." *Journal of Public Budgeting, Accounting and Financial Management*, 9, 4: 590–616.

Hammond, Laura. n.d. "NGOs: When Too Many Can Be a Bad Thing." (UNCHS) (Habitat) http://www.unchs.org/unchs/english/hdv6n2/viewpoint.html.

Hearne, Julie. 1999. "Foreign Aid, Democratisation, and Civil Society in Africa: A Study of South Africa, Ghana, and Uganda." *Institute for Development Studies Discussion Paper 368*.

Herbst, Jeffrey. 2000. *States and Power in Africa: Comparative Lessons in Authority and Control*. Princeton, N.J.: Princeton University Press.

Hobbes, Thomas. 1991. *Leviathan* (1651), ed. Richard Tuck. Cambridge: Cambridge University Press.

Jackman, Robert W. 1993. *Power Without Force: The Political Capacities of Nation-States*. Ann Arbor: University of Michigan Press.

Jackson, Robert H., and Carl G. Rosberg, Jr. 1982. "Why Africa's Weak States Persist: The Empirical and Juridical in Statehood." *World Politics*, 35, 4: 1–24.

Kaufmann, Daniel, Aart Kraay, and Pablo Zoido-Lobatón. 1999. "Aggregating Governance Indicators." World Bank Policy Research Working Paper 2195. Washington, D.C.: The World Bank.

Keefer, Phillip, and Stephen Knack. 1995. "Institutions and Economic Performance: Cross-Country Tests Using Alternative Institutional Measures." *Economics and Politics*, 7, 3: 207–227.

Killick, Tony, with Ramani Gunatilaka, and Ana Marr. 1998. *Aid and the Political Economy of Policy Change*. London: Routledge.

Knack, Stephen. 2001. "Aid Dependence and the Quality of Governance: A Cross-Country Empirical Analysis." *Southern Economic Journal*, 68, 2: 310–329.

Knack, Stephen. 2000b. "Does Foreign Aid Promote Democracy?" Working Paper 238. University of Maryland, Center for Institutional Reform and the Informal Sector, Available at www.inform.umd.edu/EdRes/Colleges/BSOS/Depts/IRIS/IR-S/docs/wp238.pdf.

Krasner, Stephen D. 1999. *Sovereignty: Organized Hypocrisy.* Princeton, N.J.: Princeton University Press.

Lancaster, Carol. 1999. *Aid to Africa.* Chicago: University of Chicago Press.

Langseth, Petter. 1995. "Civil Service Reform in Uganda: Lessons Learned." *Public Administration and Development*, 15, 4: 365–90.

Leiteritz, Ralf J. 2001. "Sovereignty, Developing Countries and International Financial Institutions." *Review of International Studies*, 27, 3: 435–40.

McPherson, Malcolm F. 2001. "An 'Aid Exit' Strategy for African Countries," in Malcolm F. McPherson, ed., *Restarting and Sustaining Growth and Development in Africa.* Cambridge: Harvard University.

Mengisteab, Kidane, and Cyril Daddieh, eds. 1999. *State Building and Democratization in Africa: Faith, Hope, and Realities.* Westport, Conn.: Praeger.

Migdal, Joel S. 1988. *Strong Societies, Weak States.* Princeton, N.J.: Princeton University Press.

Moore, Mick. 1998. "Death without Taxes: Democracy, State Capacity, and Aid Dependence in the Fourth World," in Mark Robinson and Gordon White, eds., *The Democratic Developmental State.* Oxford: Oxford University Press.

North, Douglass C. 1997. "Prologue," in John N. Drobak and John V. C. Nye, eds., *The Frontiers of the New Institutional Economics.* San Diego, Calif.: Academic Press.

O'Connell, Stephen A., and Charles C. Soludo, 2001. "Aid Intensity in Africa," *World Development*, 29, 9: 1527–1552.

Ottaway, Marina. 2000. "Social Movements, Professionalization of Reform, and Democracy in Africa," in Marina Ottaway and Thomas Carothers, eds., *Funding Virtue: Civil Society Aid and Democracy Promotion.* Washington, D.C.: Carnegie Endowment for Peace.

Ramikrishnan, Subramaniam. 1998. "Public Budgeting and Financial Management in Sub-Saharan Africa: A Critical Survey." *Journal of Public Budgeting, Accounting and Financial Management*, 10, 2: 221–54.

Rose-Ackerman, Susan. 1999. *Corruption and Government.* Cambridge: Cambridge University Press.

Sandberg, Eve, ed. 1994. *The Changing Politics of Non-Governmental Organizations and African States.* Westport, Conn.: Praeger.

Schiavo-Campo, Salvatore, Giulio de Tommaso, and Amitabha Mukherjee. 1997. "An International Statistical Survey of Government Employment and Wages." World Bank Policy Research Working Paper 1806. Washington, D.C.: The World Bank.

Sekwart, Alex. 1997. "Public Budgeting Deficiencies in Sub-Saharan Africa: A Review," *Journal of Public Budgeting, Accounting and Financial Management*, 9, 1: 143–60.

Simon, David J. 2001. "Aid and Democracy in Africa." Paper prepared for the Annual Meeting of the American Political Science Association, San Francisco, 30 August–2 September.

Stotsky, Janet G., and Asegedech WoldeMariam. 1997. "Tax Effort in Sub-Saharan Africa." IMF Working Paper 97/107. Washington, D.C.: Fiscal Affairs Department, International Monetary Fund.

Svensson, Jakob. 2000. "Foreign Aid and Rent-Seeking." *Journal of International Economics*, 51, 2: 437–461.

Therkildson, Ole. 2000. "Public Sector Reform in a Poor, Aid-Dependent Country, Tanzania." *Public Administration and Development*, 20, 1: 43–60.

United States Agency for International Development. 1998. Center for Democracy and Governance. "Democracy and Governance: A Conceptual Framework." Available at www.usaid.gov/democracy/pdfs/pnacd395.pdf.

Van de Walle, Nicolas, and Timothy A. Johnson. 1996. *Improving Aid to Africa*. Washington, D.C.: Overseas Development Council.

Villalón, Leonardo A. 1998. "The African State at the End of the Twentieth Century," in Leonardo A. Villalón and Phillip A. Huxtable, eds., *The African State at a Critical Juncture: Between Disintegration and Reconfiguration*. Boulder, Colo.: Lynne Rienner.

Williams, David. 2000. "Aid and Sovereignty: Quasi-States and the International Financial Institutions." *Review of International Studies*, 26, 4: 557–73.

World Bank. 1989. *Sub-Saharan Africa: From Crisis to Sustainable Growth*. Washington, D.C.: The World Bank.

World Bank. 1994. *Governance: The World Bank Experience*. Washington, D.C.: The World Bank.

World Bank. 1997. *World Development Report 1997: The State in a Changing World*. New York: Oxford University Press.

World Bank. 2000a. *Can Africa Prosper in the 21st Century?* Washington, D.C.: The World Bank.

World Bank. 2000b. *Reforming Public Institutions and Strengthening Governance*. Washington, D.C. The World Bank.

World Bank. 2000c. *World Development Indicators 2000 on CD-ROM*. Washington, D.C.: The World Bank.

World Bank. 2001. *Africa Database on CD-ROM*. Washington, D.C.: The World Bank.

World Economic Forum. 2000. *The Africa Competitiveness Report 2000/2001*. New York: Oxford University Press.

Zartman, William, ed. 1995. *Collapsed States: The Disintegration and Restoration of Legitimate Authority*. Boulder, Colo.: Lynne Rienner.

Chapter 8

Governance and the Private Sector in Africa

Linda Cotton and Vijaya Ramachandran

Introduction

The economic liberalization that has taken place in many Sub Saharan African countries over the last two decades has largely failed to bring about the dramatic growth needed to lift the countries out of poverty. Economic reforms have largely been in response to pressure from international financial institutions and bilateral donors. However, adjustments in Sub Saharan Africa have also been carried out in response to the widespread failure of command economies both at home and abroad, the reduction or cessation of support from former communist countries, and the pragmatism of some African leaders in the face of continually worsening economic conditions.

The standard stabilization and structural adjustment policies of fiscal deficit control, inflation reduction, positive real interest rates, foreign exchange deregulation, reduction of subsidies and other distorting incentives, privatization, trade liberalization, revision of tax systems, opening up of investment, and financial sector reform have been implemented, to varying degrees, in many African economies. Based on the evidence of almost three decades of reform, it is fair to say that the results have in general been disappointing. Although some progress has been made in terms of increasing life expectancy and literacy across the continent, the average GDP per capita (in constant prices) is *lower* now than three decades ago. Just to keep the number of absolute poor over the next 15 years constant, Sub Saharan Africa needs to grow at an average of more than 5 percent, almost twice the rate of the last three decades. To meet the Millennium Development Goal of halving the incidence of poverty by 2015, African countries will need to grow at a rate of 7 percent, with significantly greater equality in income distribution. It is highly unlikely that this rate of growth will be achieved.

Given the thinness of capital markets in African countries, any significant increase in growth, at least for the foreseeable future, can only be achieved through improvement in private sector investment and in particular, in foreign direct investment (FDI). The increase in FDI that helped spur growth in many developing countries during the last two decades largely bypassed Sub Saharan Africa. In 1999, Sub Saharan Africa's share of global FDI was just 1.2 percent and, of the FDI in all developing countries, the continent accounted for just 5 percent of flows. Absolute figures for FDI, however, did increase 25 percent from $8 billion in 1998 to $10 billion in 1999 (UNCTAD, 2000).

One recent study indicates that the blame for inadequate growth in reforming countries in the last three decades rests perhaps with (1) the slowing growth of Organization for Economic Co-Operation and Development (OECD) countries during the same period and (2) increased interest rates in OECD countries, raising the debt burden of the poorest countries (Easterly, 2001). These factors are extremely important in placing Africa's economic problems in context. However, the disappointing economic performance has resulted from a mixture of the international trade and monetary environment, the depth and speed of domestic reforms, and the institutional weaknesses preventing their implementation. Conflict and war in numerous countries undoubtedly precludes investment and creates a contagious bad reputation for all countries in the neighborhood from an investor's perspective, regardless of the real security risk involved.

Private sector actors encounter various types of risk attempting to do business in Africa. Some risks arise from macroeconomic policies, including debt management, the rate of economic growth, and the composition and volatility of a country's balance of payments. But investors often view factors such as political instability and policy reversals as the most important obstacles to investment in Africa. Political risk includes the propensity for governments to be overthrown or otherwise changed, and various phenomena of social unrest. A commonly used measure of risk is the Business Environment Risk Intelligence (BERI) index. This index measures the security of property rights in a country and other factors such as the strength of institutions that are relevant for private investment. The BERI index has a strong positive correlation with private investment in Africa. Other risk factors include high levels of public debt, macroeconomic volatility, real exchange rate instability, and volatility of average tax rates. Institutional factors include enforcement of property rights, as well as the regulation, organization, and liquidity of the stock market, the efficiency of the public sector, the legal system, the neutrality of the judiciary, corruption, and bureaucratic red tape. Fear of policy reversal looms large in many investor surveys of Africa (Collier and Pattillo, 2000). In other words, investors worry that policies once introduced will not remain in place for various reasons.

Yet another domestic element that investors take into consideration is the level of good governance. It was the change in the international context that enabled a serious examination of domestic governance issues by the international finance institutions, (IFIs). The end of cold war reduced the need of developed countries to support allies regardless of the nature of their regime. This enabled bilateral donors to more closely examine the political conditions surrounding economic reforms. "Good government" was the term used by IFIs during the late 1980s to imply that corrupt, inefficient regimes were inimical to free markets. Some analysts believe that this term was later changed to "governance" in order to make it less ideological and closer to a generic call for technically well-managed institutions (Crook, 1995).

"Good governance" as the term is used now is also closely linked to the consolidation of liberal democratic transitions that have taken place in some, but certainly not all, African states in the 1990s. It has become clear that for liberal democracy to exist it requires not just a series of fair elections and a smooth change of power from one leader to another, but also a fundamental change in the relationship of the citizen to the state, producing accountability and transparency (Levy, 1997). The institutionalization of democratic structures is a lengthy process that requires at least generations and has only just begun in those countries that have taken the first steps toward liberalization and democratic elections.

The private sector is one interest group among several that is attempting to expand its influence and operational space as certain countries consolidate their democratic systems of government. In particular, business groups can be rather proactive in creating their own political space and pushing governments to create the economic environments they require (Brautigam, 2000).

The extent of democratization and the impetus for the development of good governance varies from country to country across the continent. At times, measures taken to improve governance stem largely from international pressure and loan conditionalities. These pressures promote and support, for example, anti-corruption programs, civil service reform, and assistance with institutionalizing the rule of law. Changes in governance can also emerge from domestic forces (such as active non-governmental organizations or media exposure of corruption). Usually, governance reforms are the result of these mutually reinforcing sources of pressure. Governance reforms being sought by international and domestic actors alike could have considerable impact on the growth of the private sector.

Another important source of pressure for governance reform can be the presence of a broad-based class of entrepreneurs. However, this is missing in much of Africa. African entrepreneurs largely belong to minority ethnic groups. Entrepreneurs of European, Asian, and Middle Eastern descent control a major share of manufacturing resources in Sub Saharan Africa. Some researchers argue that these minority entrepreneurs have played an invaluable role in the growth of the private sector by bringing better skills, financial resources, and networking channels. However, these entrepreneurs are also accused of hindering the growth of indigenous private enterprise by engaging in rent-seeking and limiting the hiring of locals. Either way, the total number of entrepreneurs in any given country remains small. Understanding the reasons for this problem and finding a way to encourage entrepreneurship across all ethnic groups is a challenge that needs urgent attention, if governance reform and private sector growth are to pick up.

In some ways, the persistence of minority dominance in the private sector is a result of poor governance. Entrepreneurship in developing countries often entails overcoming inefficiencies in routine managerial functions such as interruptions in production, variance in quality, slow rate of output, and leakages of raw materials (Kilby, 1983). Minority entrepreneurs often have a superior initial endowment of capital, knowledge of markets and technology, and acquired traditions that help raise productivity. This is because they belong to communities that have historically engaged in trade and commerce and have built networks of credit and information over long periods of time across different regions and continents. Also, external environmental parameters such as limited occupational choice, the never-distant threat of expulsion, various manifestations of weak governance, including poor infrastructure, ad hoc tax policy, and political instability, have helped to build intra-community networks of trust that provide access to scarce information, risk-spreading arrangements, favorable terms of credit, and a larger pool of individuals to whom managerial responsibility can be delegated.

A study of Kenyan capitalists provides interesting anecdotal evidence to back up the above-mentioned theory (Himbara, 1994). This study shows that Asian entrepreneurs in Kenya have gradually built an extensive network of large enterprises in several different industries that fueled the growth of the private sector throughout the twentieth century. Collective efforts through industrial associations such as the Federation of Indian Chambers of Commerce of Eastern Africa and the Association for the Promotion of Industries in East Africa headed by prominent industrialists of Asian heritage were instrumental in formulating policies that helped to generate growth in the private sector.

More recent data from the World Bank also provide insights into the relative importance of minority entrepreneurs. Analysis of these data for four countries in Sub Saharan Africa—Zambia, Zimbabwe, Tanzania, and Kenya—shows that very small firms are mostly owned by indigenous entrepreneurs, while larger firms are owned by minority entrepreneurs (Ramachandran and Shah, 1999). Entrepreneurs of Asian descent own the large firms in Kenya, Tanzania, and Zambia, and Europeans own large firms in Zimbabwe. Asian entrepreneurs are between 5 and 10 times more likely to have parents in the same business as compared to indigenous African entrepreneurs. About 80 percent of African entrepreneurs established their own businesses; that number is closer to 60 percent for Asian and European entrepreneurs, demonstrating that community-based control of private enterprise thrives in the private sector. In general, the analysis of data from East Africa shows that Asian and European entrepreneurs have a clear advantage over Africans in terms of levels of education attained, work experience, size of firm, and rate of firm growth. Minority entrepreneurs have better access to financial and informational networks (Brautigam, 2000). Indigenous African entrepreneurs do not have access to the types of networks created by Indian- and white-owned firms that provide contractual mechanisms for access to credit, information, and other inputs that generate firm growth. In the absence of strong institutions and broad-based markets, network effects remain an important form of selection. An ethnic group may use close ties within the community to garner business-related information and to enforce credit contracts.

GOOD GOVERNANCE AND THE PRIVATE SECTOR

The underlying premise of this chapter is that the expansion of a diversified, broad-based, and well-regulated private sector is an important factor in economic growth, *a necessary but not sufficient condition for poverty reduction*. Given the low savings rates in Sub Saharan African countries, a considerable amount of this investment will need to come from foreign sources (Ramachandran, 2000). Numerous studies have outlined the factors that foreign investors take into account while considering investing in Sub Saharan Africa, among them resource endowments, political stability, productivity and cost of labor, access to credit, transportation costs, quality of utility provision, macroeconomic stability, taxes, and regulatory and business environment (UNCTAD, 1995;

Bennell, 1997; Sachs, 1998; McMillan et al., 1999; Pigato, 2000; Ramachandran, 2000). Most of these factors are also important to domestic investors, critical for creating broad-based growth, especially through linkages and technology transfer with foreign firms.

The scope of this chapter does not allow for discussion of subjects such as resource endowments, cost of labor, access to capital, and political stability. Rather, we have selected four elements of "good governance" that are directly controlled by the government: 1) the quality of business-specific laws; 2) policies and regulations; 3) the efficiency of the implementing institutions; and 4) the rule of law and corruption. In a sense we are surveying governance issues through the lens of the private sector. In the subsequent section, three African cases demonstrate the interdependence of these "good governance" elements and the difficulties that arise when there is progress in one or two elements but not in others. Finally, we conclude with some observations about the implications of striving for good governance and the growth of the private sector in Africa.

RATIONAL AND EFFECTIVE POLICIES AND REGULATIONS

Economic policy reforms can usefully be divided into two categories, distinguished according to the role of government (Goldsmith, 1998). Type 1 refers to activities in which the government should not be involved. Most of structural adjustment reforms, reducing the size and activities of the state, fall into this category. Type 2 refers to those public goods required of the government that Sub Saharan African states often fail to adequately provide. Of course, categorizing a particular failure is problematic in that it depends on the government's (and increasingly the public's) perception of the proper role of government in the economy.

While Type 1 "state interference" reforms have been attempted in many Sub Saharan African countries, the results have been mixed: "With liberalization, much of this structure has been done away with; however, many of the institutions survive, along with their procedures and requirements, even though today they serve little purpose" (Emery, 1999, 15).

Many barriers to private sector growth still exist despite the significant liberalization achieved in some Sub Saharan countries: excessive approvals, licenses, and registrations, lack of access to land and utilities, and undue operational requirements such as non-transparent tax systems and regulations on foreign trade and labor (Emery, 1999). These administrative barriers can negate many of the positive achievements made in maintaining macroeconomic stability and carrying out structural adjustments.

Often times overlooked is the fact that the private sector also has a significant, albeit indirect, interest in adequate government funds being dedicated to increasing social capital (education and health care). The productivity of workers, as well as that of the entrepreneurial class, depends directly on these types of public expenditures. In addition, certain industries (forestry, fishing, etc.), whether they realize or act upon it or not, have a long-term interest in the sustainable management of natural resources. The ministries and regulatory agencies overseeing these sectors have, at least in part, a responsibility to effectively promote the long-term availability of these resources.

Inherent to the concept of good governance is the idea that the private sector should be included in designing policies and regulations that affect them. Participation increases the likelihood of addressing the most urgent constraints on business. Of course, that is not to the exclusion of other groups with an interest in the impact of private sector activities, such as environmental groups and workers unions. This type of business-government interaction obviously increases in conjunction with political liberalization. The government of Mauritius and business groups have had institutionalized consultations for many years, but more recently business interest groups have pressed for reforms in Zimbabwe, Uganda, and Ghana (Brautigam, 2000). This development is encouraging in light of the experience of Korea and Taiwan where governments were autonomous in terms of initial reforms but continued reforms with the inclusion of feedback and input from the private sector (Evans, 1995).

CIVIL SERVICE REFORM

The quality of the civil service is related directly to the Type 2 reforms referred to previously—those areas where the state should be providing public goods. Inappropriate policies and regulations are often due to the lack of capacity in implementing agencies. Ineffective management and lack of human capacity or financial resources can reduce the value of even the best policies. There is a long-standing perception on the part of the civil service as well, that business must answer to them, instead of vice versa.

The civil service reform that accompanies structural adjustment programs in Sub Saharan Africa has been largely centered on reducing the nominal wage bill. Achievements in what has been called the "first-generation" of reforms have been modest. In 32 Sub Saharan countries, the average nominal wage bill was reduced from 7 percent of GDP to 6 percent from 1986 to 1996 (Lienert, 1997). But again, there is considerable variation among countries. In countries in the Communauté Financiere Africaîne (CFA) franc zone, there has been a reduction in real wages due to a lack of compensation for the 1994 devaluation. In non-CFA countries, real wages have increased since 1990, but this average is heavily influenced by increases in three countries—Uganda, Kenya, and Ghana—while most other countries have seen a decline in real government wages (Lienert, 1997). Some countries have achieved considerable downsizing, but overall progress has been modest. Often, the reduction in the nominal wage bill was not achieved through downsizing but by reducing salaries, leading to reduced worker morale, difficulties in recruiting qualified technical and professional staff, and increased incentives for accepting bribes (Lienert, 1997).

The connection between non-wage expenditures and efficiency has also been overlooked to a large extent. The ratio of wage to non-wage expenditure deserves more attention in future reform efforts. For the private sector in particular, lack of financial resources to carry out civil service responsibilities leads to delay and errors. Commonly cited problems are lack of money for printing registration and other forms, the lack of computerization of files, and the establishment of offices outside of the capital (Emery, 1999). In infrastructure provision especially, non-wage resources are critical to efficiency and effectiveness. Lack of resources can contribute to delays in essential services such as the installation, repair, and delivery of water, electricity, and telecommunications (Emery, 1999).

It has been acknowledged that the "first generation" or quantitative reforms of the last two decades in Sub Saharan Africa, as in other developing countries, have come largely at the expense of "second generation" or qualitative reforms (Lienert, 1997; Ul Haque, 1998; Goldsmith, 1998; Olowu, 2001). In particular, institutions have been slow to reform and have strongly adhered to the traditional operating procedures. Technical and managerial weaknesses of many Sub Saharan African bureaucracies indicate that reforms should be implemented in gradual steps with modest expectations (Goldsmith, 1999). In addition, emphasis should be placed on proper wage incentives to retain human capital, so that civil service employees can not only carry out improved policies in a reformed system but also participate fully in the design of these reforms (Ul Haque, 1988, Olowu, 2001).

Rule of Law

"At a minimum, rule of law may be conceptualized as the expectation of equality of treatment under objective, accessible rules," beginning with the constitution which represents the shared values of citizens, defines and structures the state, and establishes the citizens' relationship to the state (Levy, 1997).

After decolonization, in many African countries the constitution was "simply a facade which political regimes unconcerned with constitutional law hid behind, as a technique to limit power" (Gonidec, 1996). During and following the recent wave of transitions to multiparty democratic systems, a series of new constitutions have been established with varying degrees of participation from the public.

Rule of law requires, that the government be willing to abide by the constitution and cede independence to the judiciary entrusted to protect the rights and obligations established in the document. Although most African constitutions guarantee the principle of separation of power, nearly all magistrates are appointed by the executive branch, upon which they also depend for career advancement (UNSIA, 1998).

Improving the rule of law in Sub Saharan Africa depends on improvement in many areas including the administration of the justice system, the provision of high-quality and ongoing legal training and education, the physical condition of courts, the management of procedures, the existence of an organized bar to promote professional standards and regulate admission to practice law, and published legislation, administrative regulations, and judicial decisions (Levy, 1997). The growth of the private sector, both domestic and foreign, depends on the extent to which there is fair, transparent, predictable, and timely law enforcement especially in areas such as contract enforcement and property law. The attraction of foreign investors may, in fact, be more dependent on this than domestic investors, who have, to some extent, adapted to the poor quality and enforcement of business law.

For example, in certain countries there is considerable tacit flexibility in contract enforcement. This reaction is quite rational, given the unreliability of courts to intervene quickly and fairly in conflicts. Various mechanisms have been developed to deal with this type of business environment such as reciprocity between companies that conduct repeated business, doing business only with companies that have earned a good reputation, and collective punishment of egregious contract violators. Such informal methods may work well in a tight-knit community of entrepreneurs, as discussed earlier, but the increased complexity and greater number of unknown actors in a diverse, growing and globally-integrated economy requires contract enforcement to be predictable and equitable (Kahkonen, 1998).

CORRUPTION

As mentioned in the introduction, the end of the cold war allowed creditors and donors to widen the scope of their considerations when determining the eligibility of developing countries for programs and loans. At the same time, the worldwide phenomenon of corruption has gained greater media coverage. The World Bank shifted from a policy of essentially refusing to consider political or social aspects to studying the effect of corruption on economic growth and actively promoting national anti-corruption efforts (World Bank, 1999).

The emergence of non-governmental organizations like Transparency International and Global Witness has also contributed to awareness and capacity building in efforts to fight corruption. Actors like the Organization for Economic Development (OECD) and the International Chamber of Commerce (ICC) have tried to tackle the issue with the OECD's 1999 Convention on Combating Bribery of Foreign Public Officials in International Business Transactions and the ICC's voluntary Code of Conduct.

There is, for the most part, consensus on the positive relationship between long-term growth and reduction of corruption. Some analysts have tried to explain that the connection is not so clear by citing examples of rapidly developing countries in Asia that also have a cultural tradition of "gift-giving" (Szeftel, 2000). However, one can also argue that a large part of the late 1990s financial crisis in that region was due precisely to corruption and lack of transparency.

Critics of anti-corruption efforts and conditionalities declare it unrealistic to expect to stamp out corruption in bureaucracies while at the same time retrenching and reducing the wage bill. They argue that poor-performing economies do not have enough private sector alternatives to wealth accumulation to absorb the unemployed and underemployed (Szeftel, 2000). Admittedly, a phased and multi-pronged approach is needed. Consensus is growing on the need for integrated "holistic" approaches of prevention and punishment of corruption with local/civil society participation including the following interdependent elements: political will of leaders, rule of law, policy change, civil service reform, and public/media oversight (Transparency International, 1996).

CASE STUDIES

The two country case studies in this chapter, Uganda and Ghana, were chosen because they are considered to have made significant progress in implementing stabilization and structural adjustment reforms. While growth rates have risen, they have not been high enough to pull the countries out of poverty and debt. In addition, investment and private sector growth have been greater than most non–oil producing African countries, although still limited. We chose to consider one governance issue in each country in order to examine the difficulties of improving governance and growth in a context of *relative* macroeconomic stability. Finally, the experience of Coca-Cola (Sub Saharan Africa's largest non–oil private sector employer) is also discussed briefly to show how a foreign investor's experience can differ widely in a number of African countries, due in part to governance issues.

GHANA: Governance and Privatization

Ghana's experience with privatization has in some ways been quite successful, yet it also illustrates how issues of governance can interfere with the growth of the private sector. Relative to the rest of Africa, Ghana is considered an early privatizer. By 1996, the government of Ghana had recorded the highest total amount of income from privatization in Sub Saharan Africa, a total of $417.3 million, with a large percentage coming from the Ashanti Goldfields transaction (White, 1998). Fortunately, attempts at privatization have been aided by the fact that they have taken place in the context of overall economic reform, starting with the Economic Recovery Program beginning in 1983. However, the weakness of government bureaucracies charged with this task, the uncertainty surrounding the leadership's commitment to withdrawing from the economy, and the lack of transparency during the process have all constrained further progress.

Since mid-1999, the macroeconomic situation has declined rapidly due to a sharp decline in the price of the gold and the second largest export, cocoa, which fell to a 20-year low in 2000. In addition, the price of imported oil increased by a factor of three. In the run-up to the 2000 elections, the government of President Jerry Rawlings made some extraordinary though ineffective expenditures. Since winning the December 2000 elections, the government of John Kufour has been making efforts to reverse the cycle of budget deficits and rising interest rates. Kufour has clearly declared his support for the private sector and commitment to combating corruption in press conferences as well as in the 2001 budget (Oxford, 2001, Ghana Budget, 2001).

The Divestiture Implementation Committee: Bureaucratic Weakness and Lack of Transparency

Ghana's Divestiture Implementation Committee (DIC) is charged with the privatization and divestiture of state-owned enterprises. Here, we distinguish privatization from divestiture by stating that the former involves the transfer of management authority from the state to a private enterprise and the latter does not (White, 1998). The DIC began operations in 1988 but was not formally established until 1993. It was around 1988 that the Rawlings government began more sincere efforts to promote the private sector, although some ambiguity about market-based economics was clearly discernable (IMF, 2000).

During the first few years, progress was quite slow. From 1989 to 1992, the government divested from only 59 enterprises out of more than 300. Of those 59, 26 were liquidated and produced no revenue (IMF, 2000). In 1995, there were attempts to re-energize the privatization efforts, with support from the World Bank and the UK Department for International Development. The DIC began to hire consultants, a divestiture procedures manual was introduced, and a specific target of 149 enterprises was set for 1997, which included four large strategic enterprises—Ghana Telecom, State Insurance Corporation, State Housing Corporation, and Mim Timber (IMF, 2000). The pace did pick up from 1994 to 1997 when 79 enterprises worth 756.6 billion cedis were privatized. However, of the strategic enterprises originally targeted in 1995, only Ghana Telecom was privatized four years later (World Bank, 2001). By the end of September 1999, 192 state-owned enterprises (SOEs) were divested (IMF, 2000).

There are additional reasons behind the slow progress that have little to do with the DIC. The public and some Members of Parliament representing the public strongly oppose privatization due to the perceived loss of employment it entails. Government employment and ownership in the economy is still seen as legitimate and desirable among different sections of Ghanaian society. In a survey of randomly selected citizens, almost 70 percent of the over 2000 respondents answered positively to the statement that "the government should retain ownership of its factories, businesses and farms" (CDD, 1999). There is also a deep-seated feeling of loss of sovereignty that accompanies the sale of "strategic" enterprises (i.e., large and in a sector traditionally held by the state, such as energy or transportation).

The thinness of capital markets continues to be a problem inhibiting progress in privatization. Although public flotation of privatization shares has been carried out in Ghana, it is usually not associated with the entry of new investors but with the retention of government shares (White, 1998). One study states that capital market deepening is hampered by divestiture programs that emphasize privatization through strategic investor financing rather than the Ghana Stock Exchange (USAID, 2001).

Also, government responsibility for end-of-service and severance payments has been an intractable problem. However, in order to examine fully Ghana's experience with privatization one must consider the strength of the institution responsible for its success. Some of the DIC weaknesses are undoubtedly due to insufficient resources. Studies point out that the small staff is commonly inexperienced in the operations of private investment markets. World Bank efforts to promote the use of local consultants has had mixed reviews. The initial assessment of a World Bank study claimed that consultants were able to speed up privatizations as well as build up domestic expertise. A more recent IMF review states that the local consultants were also inexperienced in divestiture, did not place enough emphasis on preparation, and did not proceed with any more transparency that the DIC (IMF, 2000).

Some analysts explain the slow progress in part by pointing to the fact that every divestiture, regardless of size, must be authorized by the office of the president (White, 1998). Although granting the privatization agency with the authority to approve transactions may be an element of more successful programs such as in Zambia, it is most likely not an option for Ghana. The public, private sector and other parts of the government are consistently calling for more transparency in the DIC. In fact, the 2001 budget calls for a financial and managerial audit of the DIC as well as audits of various divestitures. This reaction may be partly inspired by political motives to distance the present administration from the Rawlings tenure. It is definitely an acknowledgement of "the public outcry on the manner in which properties of the state were divested" and of the possibility that some of the companies divestitures "may have been tainted with corruption and fraud" (Republic of Ghana, 2001).

The result of one of these presidential audits led to the arrest of the head of DIC for allegedly colluding with a Nigerian publisher. The DIC paid Goldcity Communications Group, of which the publisher is managing director, 18 billion cedis for various consulting services, allegedly out of divestiture proceeds. This payment was supposedly to be made from World Bank funds devoted to this purpose. According to Ghanaian newspaper reports, only 3 billion cedis were used to pay for the services, leaving 15 billion cedis unaccounted for. While this latest example of suspicious activity is only an allegation, if all divestiture transactions and the destination of all proceeds were clearly published, the public, media, and opposition politicians would be less likely to think of the government's privatization program as it was described by an opposition member of parliament, "the behaviour of irresponsible Ebusuapanyin who sells away bequeathed family assets, misuses the proceeds and therefore impoverishes the family and generations unborn" (*The Independent*, 2000).

Telecommunications Privatization: The Importance of Clear Regulation

Once a privatization transaction has taken place, the task of the state is hardly completed. The impact of privatizing large, strategic enterprises is extensive. We now examine one of the largest privatizations that have taken place in Ghana, with a view to evaluating regulatory control.

The privatization of telecommunications in Ghana, in part to foreign investors, was a huge achievement, given all of the obstacles inherent in this type of transaction. Adequate provision of telecommunications (as well as other infrastructure such as electricity, water, and transportation) either directly or through properly regulated industries, is an extremely important Type 2 role for the state in fostering private sector growth. Infrastructure investments, however, require large volumes of equity and debt capital as well as long-term commitments.

Given the small capital markets in Sub Saharan Africa, this requirement generally means a reliance on foreign financing. This requirement is particularly problematic since revenue from these types of services is typically in local currency. Foreign infrastructure investors are therefore vulnerable to exchange rate fluctuations and convertibility regulations (Kerf, 1996). In addition, foreign investors are concerned about small market size, non-payment risks, inadequate regulatory frameworks, limited capacity and experience, and non-commercial risks, such as the politically sensitive nature of infrastructure prices, war, and expropriation (Kerf, 1996). Despite these constraints, this was the first time that privatization in Ghana was performed in a sector outside of parastatals.

The process had some admirable aspects in terms of equal treatment and competition. The bidding process was delegated to an internationally respected banker. The privatization aimed at maximum competitiveness in the sector, with the sale of shares in the dominant operation, Ghana Telecom (GT), as well as shares in a second national operator (SNO), which was given the right to compete with GT. The reform also encouraged competition in wireless and Internet services. Thirty percent of GT was sold to a consortium led by Telkom Malaysia. The 1997 results were quite positive, with an increase in fixed line subscribers of 33 percent, wireless connections 60 percent, and Internet connections 60 percent (Levy, 1998).

However, Ghana Telecom and the second operator position *only received one qualifying bid each*, preventing actual competition (other bids were disqualified for failing to post the required bid bonds).

Perhaps more important, the privatization took place before the industry regulations were fully in place. The telecommunications reform did include the establishment of a National Communications Authority (NCA) but did not specify the regulations that this agency was intended to enforce, or how it was to do so. For a time, only GT and the second operator had licenses to operate and all other companies were operating under an unclear legal basis. By the time the second operator was granted the bandwidth it was promised, some of it had been allocated to other operators.

Ghana Telecom, with its monopoly over international connections, was also supposed to interconnect other providers, but prices and level of services of these connections were not specified. In fact, there was a drawn-out struggle before GT finally did interconnect Westel, the company that was awarded the SNO (For-Mukwai, 2000). These problems and others that arose were resolved through informal political influence, rather than rule-bound governance.

Where rule-bound governance is not firmly established, the privatization process is built on informal political influence. Companies that do not have an interest in open, transparent rules of the game will try to evade regulation where possible (Levy, 1998). This was a case in which a Type 1 reform (decreasing state interference in the market) was severely hindered by the lack of Type 2 reforms (improving the government's provision of an environment conducive to market activity). Let us now turn to Uganda for a very different example of private sector-government interaction.

UGANDA: Private Sector Growth and the Uganda Manufacturer's Association

During the years following independence from Britain in 1962, Uganda experienced rapid agricultural growth, with a developing industrial sector and growing political and cultural leadership. By the end of Idi Amin's rule, which lasted from 1971 to 1979, Uganda had degenerated into one of the world's poorest countries. By 1986, real GDP per capita was 70 percent lower than in 1970 (World Bank, 2000). That year marked the takeover of Yoweri Museveni and the National Resistance Movement (NRM).

President Museveni's new government established a National Resistance Council (NRC) as its legislature. The NRC was dominated by Museveni supporters and was chosen from a range of political factions and ethnic and regional groups. Despite this diversity, room for discussion of policy alternatives was severely restricted (Scribner, 1997). Although there was a state-centered flavor to early economic proposals (the NRM's pre-1986 Ten Point Programme called for the building of an independent, integrated, self-sustaining economy), the government embarked on an Economic Recovery Program supported by the International Monetary Fund (IMF), World Bank, and bilateral donors. The government's firm commitment to the program ensured that many stabilization and structural adjustment measures were rapidly introduced. Inflation rates have been single digit since 1993-94, the exchange rate has been market-determined since 1993, real exchange volatility has been relatively limited and trade liberalization has been extensive (Reinikka, 1997).

The growth rate of GDP has jumped dramatically from less than 1 percent in 1986 to 4 percent in 1987, and continues to be significant. The economy grew at an average of 6 percent until the end of the 1980s and an average of almost 7 percent throughout the 1990s (IMF, 2001). Also during the 1990s, according to national accounts, private investment increased annually by an average 13 percent (Reinikka, 1997). However, as a percentage of GDP, total fixed investment remained low, between 15 and 20 percent.

Uganda still has relatively high investment barriers in place. In a 1998 Uganda Enterprise Survey carried out by the Uganda Manufacturers Association on behalf of the Uganda Private Sector Foundation and the World Bank, firms identified and ranked the constraints on their growth. While this type of research is quite subjective and vulnerable to multiple biases, it can still be indicative of where to place priorities. The major constraints of the firms questioned were:

1) High price of utilities; 2) High taxes; 3) Quality of utilities; and 4) High interest rates. Firms listed as secondary barriers: corruption, access to finance, tax administration, and cost of raw materials.

Investment is also constrained by the bureaucratic hurdles facing the foreign investor, presenting a good example of how reforms at the top have not reached the lower levels of bureaucratic operations. Uganda's negative list (the list of sectors in which foreign investment is banned) is rather small and the investment code provides for "equal treatment" of foreigners, giving the impression of openness to foreign investment. However, on a practical level, when a foreign firm attempts the first step of the arduous process of setting up a business, it is faced with separate registration forms for foreign investors (in addition to the seven required for all businesses). These time-consuming applications call for everything from police records to translations of parent company resolutions authorizing the subsidiary in question. There are even cases of foreigners being required to register their company prior to getting a residence permit, meanwhile another law requires a residence permit as part of the registration application (Emery, 1999).

However, it can hardly be said that all of the progress in policy reform that has been achieved in Uganda to date has been in vain. Investors are confidant that the changes made will not be reversed and that the business environment will continue to improve. One study found that investment rates in Uganda do not differ much from the Sub Saharan African average, yet interestingly the profit rates are lower. The lower profits are compensated for by the country's long record of macroeconomic stability, which lends an amount of certainty absent in other countries (Reinikka, 1997).

The Uganda Manufacturers Association (UMA) has played a crucial role in improving investment, reducing barriers, and generating private sector growth. The UMA was established in the 1960s but was largely inactive until 1988, a year after the Economic Recovery Program was started. The UMA is one of the largest organizations representing the broad industrial and commercial sectors of the Ugandan economy. The membership is comprised of close to 700 enterprises of all sizes (UMA website).

The UMA operates in an environment relatively open to the activities of civil society. Some analysts consider Uganda to have some of the best relations between non-governmental organizations and government in Africa (Tripp, 2001). Uganda operates under a "no-party" system, meaning that although opposition parties are suspended, they are not banned outright. Their members cannot open offices or hold rallies but can make statements to the press and run in elections as individuals. The media and publishing industries are relatively free and able to criticize the government as well. Civil society took advantage of the opportunities afforded it in the drafting of the 1995 Constitution, ultimately approved by an elected constituent assembly. In June 2000, there was a referendum to decide whether or not to switch to a multi-party system. Opposition parties called for a boycott, but it was not clear if voters listened to their appeal, as 50 percent of registered voters showed up to the polls. A continuation of the "no-party" or "movement" system was chosen in a process that international observers declared free and fair, but which fell short of providing a "level playing field" (IRIN, 2000). This relatively open atmosphere has in part allowed the UMA to operate and to some extent influence policy.

Also significant is the fact that since the early 1990s, Museveni has shown particular interest in nurturing the private sector. The President's Economic Council, chaired by President Museveni, in a collaborative effort with the UMA, initiated the Uganda National Forum in 1992. The purpose of the forum is to refine reform policies and assist in their implementation, (Scribner, 1997). The Uganda National Forum sponsored two conferences, in 1992 and 1994, to discuss various policies of concern to the four on-going working groups composed of outside individuals and academics: Investment and Export Promotion, Financial Sector Development, Tax Policy, and Capacity Building. At these forums the working groups report on progress made, analyze successes and failures, and highlight new areas for priority. Although direct linkage of advocacy and policy outcome is difficult to prove, one example of success commonly attributed to National Forum activities is that their recommendations led to the liberalization of interest rates, reduction of bank reserve requirements, and payment of interest on commercial bank deposits with the Central Bank (USAID, 1997).

The UMA uses several means to influence policy outside of participation in the Uganda National Forum, including publishing articles and conducting personal meetings with government counterparts on key issues. In 2000, UMA officials met with members of parliament to discuss among other items, budget concerns, tax reductions, interest rate reductions, and exchange rate fluctuations (East African, 2000).

Policy decisions are still taken by a small number of senior level government officials but the association provides some measure of influence on the process. The UMA members are some of the more prominent businessmen with good connections in the government. Government representatives involved with the UMA are senior level and have close contact with the President. The collaborative effort may not seem as potentially effective as an outright independent advocacy approach but that is not a likely alternative in the Ugandan context (Scribner, 1997).

Some of the areas of priority for the UMA are similar to those outlined in past surveys and studies of private sector obstacles (high taxes and interest rates). Other barriers may not be addressed with such determination by the UMA because of skepticism about the government's receptivity and/or ability to change (for example, increasing expenditure on infrastructure or eliminating corruption). In addition, the UMA's capacity and scope of work are limited by lack of adequate resources. The organization does not collect enough revenue from members to conduct projects independent of the government. The group does have some funds from other sources, including the United States Agency for International Development but only for short-term technical assistance. However, the UMA has proven itself very capable of adapting to changing circumstances and adept at finding funding sources.

The emerging business-government dialogue in Uganda demonstrates the constraints of domestic sources of pressure for governance reforms even while operating in a relatively open environment. It should also be noted that not all reforms pushed by industry associations should automatically be considered the best option for the economy or the country (e.g. the private sector will always prefer lower taxes regardless of the optimum level) but should be balanced by government against the interests of other sectors of society. Increased business-government dialogue is nevertheless an important element in improving good governance in a way that will enhance the growth of the private sector.

The two case studies discussed so far have dealt largely with domestic attempts to improve governance (privatization in Ghana and business-government dialogue in Uganda). The next section examines how a foreign investor's experience can differ widely in a number of African countries, due in part to governance issues. Coca-Cola, Africa's largest source of non-oil private sector employment, has had widely variable market growth in several countries on the continent. Coca-Cola is the exception rather than the rule in its belief that a loss in one country will necessarily mean a loss in all countries on the continent.

In most categories of investment, Sub Saharan African countries lag behind the rest of the developing world, despite the fact that Southern Africa in particular is richly endowed with both natural and human resources and is among the richest regions in the world in terms of minerals, agriculture, fisheries, water, energy, and tourism. The perceived risk of doing business in Africa, for both domestic and foreign investors, continues to be significant. Governance issues play a leading role in defining foreign investor perceptions.

COCA-COLA: A CASE STUDY OF FOREIGN OWNERSHIP IN AFRICA

To better understand the costs and benefits of investing in the private sector in Africa and how they relate to governance, it is useful to examine the franchise operations of one very active company in Sub Saharan Africa—Coca-Cola. Coca-Cola is the largest employer in the nonextractive industrial sector in Sub Saharan Africa, employing more than 100,000 people in production and distribution across the continent. It also generates an additional eight to ten jobs in the local economy for every job it creates, thereby accounting for more than a million jobs in Africa. Coca Cola has invested more than $600 million in Africa in the past five years and has over 130 production plants around the continent. Coca-Cola aims to double the size of its business in Southern Africa between 1998 and 2003 through investment in its operations. Together with its bottlers, Coke is a major player in the African private sector. The Coca-Cola system is Africa's biggest consumer products operation, serving 50 countries and 600 million consumers. Its brands include Coca-Cola, other groups' brands, and some local brands of soft drinks.

Coke's experiences in Africa are useful in terms of understanding the workings of the private sector in Africa. In Uganda, Coke has made great headway in terms of market share. The bottling company that owns the national franchise in Uganda is competing head to head with Pepsi, which has been in Uganda far longer than Coke. Coke's share of the country's market has risen from 30 percent in 1996 to 60 percent currently; the volume of sales has doubled in the same time period to approximately 72 million cases in 1998. Part of the reason is that Century Bottling, the holder of Coca-Cola's national franchise in Uganda, has distributed over 3,500 cooler boxes to drink vendors and opened four ice-making plants. Ice is delivered to vendors each morning, rather than relying on the power system for refrigeration, which is dilapidated and does not serve the entire country. The South African Bottling Company, which has owned the license to manufacture Coke in Uganda since 1996, employs a workforce of almost 1,000 people. New investment has included a $16 million bottling plant in Mbarara and a new plant to replace the old factory in Kampala.

A recent study showed that the Coca-Cola system had a significant multiplier effect on the South African economy (USC/WEFA, 1999). The study concluded that this system supported 178,205 employees in South Africa and that the employment multiplier is approximately 11 (i.e., an additional 10 jobs are created for every job generated by Coke). About 63 percent of the employment base is black South African and the value of production was 5.6 billion Rand in 1998. In addition to employment generation, Coca-Cola is a major source of tax revenues to the government, accounting for about 2 percent of its revenues. The study also shows that through downstream linkages, Coca-Cola provides South Africa's small vendors with a highly marketable product, thereby making a significant contribution to microenterprise development.

The story in Zambia, however, is entirely different, largely due to problems with the government. Coke has had to face a sharp decline in sales and a somewhat hostile bureaucracy determined to keep the price of Coke artificially high. The main problem has been a very high rate of taxation (25 percent of the wholesale price) that resulted in a 75 percent decline in sales in 1998. Although the commerce minister tried to reduce this tax rate to 5 percent, the finance minister argued that Zambia needed the additional revenues and rejected the offer. The result was a sharp decline of production, illegal imports of Coke from Zimbabwe and Malawi, and huge losses for Zambia Bottlers, owners of the Coke franchise in Zambia. Coke became more costly than beer in Zambia, and four times as expensive as Coke in Zimbabwe. This brought Coke's investment plan to a halt and hurt many of the street hawkers and vendors who sold Coke from sidewalk kiosks. In addition, the Zambian government has also been critical of Coca-Cola's merger with Cadbury Schweppes (Zambia) Limited, arguing that appropriate government authorization had not been obtained. This experience created added uncertainty in an already unstable economy.

The Coca-Cola story in Sub Saharan Africa is indicative of both the advantages and disadvantages of operating in the African private sector. On the one hand, Coke's successes reveal the tremendous opportunities in the private sector and the amount of employment that can be generated through foreign investment. On the other hand, some of its experiences reflect the frustrations of private sector investors, the ambiguity of government regulation, and the problem of over-regulation and taxation by the government.

CONCLUSIONS

Generating investment is central to the expansion and profitability of the private sector. Making governance reforms and making them more visible is a crucial part of this strategy. The following steps may be needed to achieve a significant increase in private sector activity.

Various countries, including Mozambique, South Africa, and Uganda have undertaken wide-ranging reforms over the past few years. Several more have been steadily reforming the economic and political systems. These efforts must be made more visible, both by donors and by African governments. There is no question that Africa suffers from a lack of visibility in the industrialized countries. The media are focused largely on humanitarian crises and conflict. Although these are issues that must be addressed immediately, we must also seek to raise the visibility of success stories. Much has been sacrificed (particularly in terms of consumption) to achieve macroeconomic stability and a positive rate of growth. These sacrifices must not go unnoticed. Efforts must be made by national governments, bilateral aid agencies, and multilateral development banks to identify investment opportunities in Africa.

Both the World Bank and the International Finance Corporation have repeatedly documented the cumbersome procedures that new investors must go through to set up a business in Sub Saharan Africa. As discussed earlier, some countries have over one hundred different procedures to open a business; others have bureaucratic systems that result in delays and frustration. No matter how much macroeconomic reform is undertaken, private investors will continue to be deterred by the massive amounts of red tape they confront in Africa. As countries in other parts of the world simplify their investment procedures and prepare to do business in an increasingly free-trade environment, Sub Saharan Africa runs a real risk of being left behind.

Despite all the attention paid to small businesses and indigenous firms, there is no doubt that foreign investment remains one of the most significant drivers of growth in the private sector. There is simply not enough capital in the domestic economy in most countries in Africa to generate the 5 to 7 percent annual growth rate necessary to make a significant reduction in poverty and unemployment. Foreign investment brings with it new skills, new management techniques, new technology, and access to new markets. It also provides a much-needed source of employment and growth. Promotion of foreign investment does not mean that the government must let foreign firms run amok, nor does it mean a race to the bottom in order to compete with neighbors. An appropriate policy environment and the strengthening of legal and other institutions will greatly enhance the impact of foreign direct investment.

Achieving and maintaining credibility is difficult; many governments have failed to do this because of political pressures, external shocks, and so on. But ultimately it is very important to attract a steady stream of investment and a broad-based private sector. Governments can also make commitments toward maintaining an attractive environment for investors by signing multilateral treaties. Other important steps toward increasing investment include strengthening the rule of law, making property rights more transparent, and enforcing marketplace transactions and contractual arrangements in a fair manner. Donors and other external parties can play a role in helping governments to build credibility and strengthen markets.

Several non-economic issues are critical to increasing investment in Sub Saharan Africa. In particular, researchers point to the need for conflict resolution and crime reduction. Recently, an increasing amount of attention has been focused on the relationship between good governance and the need for conflict resolution. It is beyond the scope of this essay to delve into each of these areas. But it is clear that further research must be done to investigate these issues.

The Ghana case study illustrated that the rule of law needs to be strengthened to increase the confidence of the private sector that the rules of the game will not change after they have made essentially irreversible commitments such as investing in infrastructure. The less than desirable business environment described in this case was due to the inability of senior level decision-makers to establish a strong institution provided with detailed regulations in a realistic timeframe. Political liberalization has to some extent provided an opening for the improvement of the business environment through public-private dialogue in the Uganda case study. The experiences of countries like Botswana and Mauritius with such dialogue provide encouraging examples of continual improvement of the business environment and private sector growth. Agencies of restraint can take the form of institutional change to make the new policy reforms more credible. These can leave less room for discretion by removing or reducing decision-making authority from government officials and other actors who are influenced by political power. Penalty-based agencies of restraint may also prove to be effective. Governments would need to make changes in formal or informal political institutions in order to create mechanisms of restraint that impose penalties for policy reversals. Governments could also act to lower the coordination of costs for exporters so that this group could organize itself and act as a lobbying power to promote policies favorable to increasing exports. Finally, external agencies of restraint include supranational authorities. Enforcement of rules can be carried out by reciprocal threats of members. Donor conditionality and rules advocated by the Multilateral Investment Guarantee Agency (MIGA) also fall into this category.

All of the elements of "good governance" discussed in this chapter are interdependent and focus should not be placed on one at the expense of another. Establishing appropriate policies and regulations depends on the commitment of the government to create them, with private sector input. Turning policy objectives into reality requires a streamlined, rationalized and properly remunerated civil service. Creating a business environment conducive to growth requires these two elements as well as the rule of law to handle conflict, clarify legal boundaries, and reduce risk. Finally, the elimination of corruption requires all of the above as well as considerable leadership from senior-level politicians and pressure from the media. Reduction in corruption and rent dissipation will greatly improve the efficiency and competitiveness of the private sector.

The theory behind "good governance" is that accountability demanded from the public and civil society groups will give all of the actors in the system (politicians, civil servants, private sector) incentives to act toward the improvement of the system. To put it a bit more bluntly, if (1) elected posts are actually threatened in regular free and fair elections, therefore, (2) performance is demanded of the civil service by politicians and individual positions or even entire institutions could be put in jeopardy, and (3) the rule of law routes the majority of actions into lawful channels (i.e. bribery is not generally an option) then ideally, the system is a self-correcting or, at least, self-improving one.

We know that the problems of governance described in this paper occur in countries the world over. Industrialized countries undoubtedly have their share of corruption (Szeftel, 2000). However, for each country a minimum level in a number of, if not all, elements of governance has to be reached in order to stimulate enough economic growth to increase employment and reduce poverty. Democratic consolidation inherently requires the passage of time, and change comes slowly to large institutions. It remains to be seen to what extent Sub Saharan African countries will react further to domestic and international pressure for the types of governance reform crucial to private sector growth.

REFERENCES

Bennell, P. (1997) "Foreign Direct Investment in Africa: Rhetoric and Reality," *SAIS Review* (Summer-Fall), pp. 127–139.

Bigsten, Arne, Paul Collier, Stefan Dercon, Marcel Fafchamps, Bernard Gauthier, Jan Willem Gunning, Abena Oduro, Remco Oostendorp, Cathy Patillo, Mans Soderbom, Francis Teal, and Albert Zeufack (1999). "Contract Flexibility and Dispute Resolution in African Manufacturing, Working Papers Series No. 99–20." Centre for the Study of African Economies, University of Oxford (August).

Brautigam, Deborah (2000) "Interest Groups, Economic Policy and Growth in Sub-Saharan Africa," African Economic Policy, Discussion Paper no. 40, U.S. Washington, D.C.: Agency for International Development (July).

Cameron, R. and C. Tapscott (2000) "The Challenge of State Transformation," *Public Administration and Development* 20(2): 81–86.

CDD Research Paper (1999) "Popular Attitudes to Democracy and Markets in Ghana," Center for Democracy and Development, Accra, Ghana (November).

Collier, Paul and Catherine Pattillo, eds (2000), *Investment and Risk in Africa* (London: St. Martin's Press).

Crook, Richard C. and Manor, James (1995) "Democratic Decentralization and Institutional Performance: Four Asian and African Experiences Compared," *Journal of Commonwealth & Comparative Politics*, 33, 3 (November).

The East African (2000) "Investors Seek Ugandan Government's help" (August 11).

Easterly, William (2001) "The Lost Decades: Developing Countries' Stagnation in Spite of Policy Reform, 1980–1998," The World Bank (February).

Emery, James J., Melvin T. Spence, Timothy S. Buehrer, and Louis T. Wells. (1999) "Administrative Barriers to Foreign Investment in Africa. Reducing Red Tape Washington, D.C.: The World Bank.

Evans, Peter (1995) *Embedded Autonomy: States and Industrial Transformation* (Princeton, NJ: Princeton University Press).

For-Mukwai, Gideon, F. (2000) "Liberalization Spurs Ghana Telecom Growth," *IDG News Service* (July 21). Available from www.idg.net/ldgns/2000/07/21/LiberalizationSpursGhanaTelecomGrowth.shtml.

Ghana Budget (2001) Available at www.ghanareview.com/Budget 2001. htm.

Goldsmith, Arthur A. (1998) "Institutions and Economic Growth in Africa," African Economic Policy Paper, Discussion Paper Number 7, USAID Bureau for Africa, Office of Sustainable Development (July).

Gonidec, Pierre-Francois (1996) "Constitutionalisms Africains," *Revue Juridique et Politique*, vol. 50, no. 1 (January-April).

Himbara, David (1994) *Kenyan Capitalists, the State and Development* (Nairobi: Lynne Rienner Publishers Inc.).

The Independent (2000) "Divestiture Programme Condemned," Accra (May 11).

International Monetary Fund (2000) *Ghana: Selected Issues*, IMF Staff Country Report, no. 2 (January).

International Monetary Fund (2001) *World Economic Outlook Database* (May). Available from www.imf.org/external/pubs/ft/weo/2001/01/data/index.htm.

Integral Regional Information Network (2000) "Uganda, Kagame, Museveni Meet to Repair Bilateral Relations," UN Office for the Coordination of Humanitarian Affairs (July 3). Available from www.reliefweb.int/IRIN/cea/countrystories/uganda/20000703.phtml.

Kahkonen, Satu and Patrick Meagher (1998) "Contract Enforcement and Economic Performance," EAGER African Economic Policy Discussion Paper No. 1, U.S. Agency for International Development, Washington, D.C. (July).

Kerf, Michael and Warrick Smith (1996) "Privatizing Africa's Infrastructure: Promise and Challenge," *World Bank Technical Paper* no. 337, The World Bank, Washington, D.C.

Kilby, Peter (1983), "The Role of Alien Entrepreneurs in Economic Development," *American Economic Review Papers and Proceedings*, vol. 73, pp. 107–111.

Levy, Brian (1998) "Between Law and Politics—Private Infrastructure in Africa," The World Bank, Washington, D.C. unpublished document (November).

Levy, David A. (1997) "Strengthening the Legislature and Judiciary for Improving Governance in Africa: A Case for the Rule of Law and Economic Development." *Online Journal of International Law and Development*, International Law Institute (August). Available from www.ili.org/pubjournal.html.

Lienert, Ian and Jitendra Modi (1997) "A Decade of Civil Service Reform in Sub-Saharan Africa," International Monetary Fund Working Paper, 97/179, Washington, D.C.: International Monetary Fund.

Lyons, Terrence (1997) "Ghana's Encouraging Elections—A Major Step Forward," *Journal of Democracy*, vol. 8, no. 2 (April).

McMillan, Margaret, Lynn Salinger, and Selina Pandolfi (1999) "Promoting Foreign Direct Investment in Labor-Intensive, Manufacturing Exports in Developing Countries," Consulting Assistance on Economic Reform II (CAER II), Discussion Paper no. 42, Harvard Institute for International Development (July).

Ottaway, Marina (1999) "Uganda and the Politics of Process," *Africa's New Leaders: Democracy or State Reconstruction?* (Washington, D.C.: Carnegie Endowment for International Peace).

Oxford Analytica Brief (2001) "Ghana: Conciliatory Kufour" (June 1).

Pigato, Maria (2000) "Foreign Direct Investment in Africa: Old Tales and New Evidence," World Bank, Africa Region (February), unpublished document.

Ramachandran, Vijaya (2000) *Investing in Africa*, Overseas Development Council Policy Essay no. 29 (Washington, D.C.: Johns Hopkins University Press).

Reinikka, Ritva and Jakob Svensson (1997) "Confronting Competition: Investment Response and Constraints in Uganda," World Bank Working Paper (November).

Republic of Ghana, (2001) The Budget Statement and Economic Policy of the Government of Ghana for the 2001 Financial Year (March 9). Available from http://ghanareview.com/Budget2001.htm.

Sachs, Jeffrey and Sara Sievers (1998) "Foreign Direct Investment in Africa," in the *Africa Competitiveness Report*, Geneva: World Economic Forum.

Scribner, Susan and Benjamin L. Crosby (1997) "Increasing the Influence of the Private Sector in Policy Reforms in Africa," *Monographs*, Implementing Policy Change Project, USAID (December).

Szeftel, Morris (2000) "Between Governance & Under-Development: Accumulation & Africa's 'Catastrophic Corruption,'" *Review of African Political Economy*, no. 84, pp. 287–306.

Transparency International (1996) *National Integrity Sourcebook*. Available from http://www.transparency.org/documents/source-book/index.html.

Ugandan Manufacturers Association, Available from www.uma.co.ug.

Ul Haque, Nadeem and Jahangir Aziz (1998) "The Quality of Governance: 'Second-Generation' Civil Service Reform in Africa," International Monetary Fund Working Paper, WP/98/164, Washington, D.C.

United Nations Conference on Trade and Development (UNCTAD) (1995) *Foreign Direct Investment in Africa*, New York: United Nations.

UNCTAD (2000) *World Investment Report 2000: Cross-Border Mergers and Acquisitions and Development*, New York: United Nations.

University of South Carolina and WEFA Southern Africa, "Multinational Enterprise, Employment, and Local Entrepreneurial Development: Coca-Cola in South Africa," unpublished manuscript (February 1999).

USAID (1997) "Government-Private Sector Collaboration in Uganda," *Democracy Dialogue*, United States Agency for International Development, Center for Democracy and Governance (Spring).

USAID (2001) "Constraints to Capital Market Development and Growth in Sub-Saharan Africa: The Case of Ghana," Policy Brief Number 57, EAGER, U.S. Agency for International Development, Washington, D.C. (February).

United Nations Special Initiative on Africa (UNSIA) (1998) "Accountability and Transparency in Africa: A Concept Paper," United Nations Special Initiative on Africa, Africa Governance Forum (II), Accra, Ghana, (June 25–26).

White, Oliver Campbell and Anita Bhatia (1998) *Privatization in Africa*, Directions in Development Series, Washington, D.C.: World Bank.

World Bank (1999) "Towards Collective Action to Improve Governance and Control Corruption in Seven African Countries," prepared as background for the 9th Annual Conference against Corruption, Durban, South Africa (October 10–15).

World Bank (2000) *Can Africa Claim the 21st Century?* Washington, D.C.: World Bank, (April).

World Bank (2000) *Country Brief: Uganda.* Available from http://www. worldbank.org/afr/ug/ctry_brief.htm. (September).

World Bank (2001) *1988–1999 Privatization Transaction Data*, Development Economics Prospects Group, Washington (April, 9). Available from http://www.ipanet.net/documents/WorldBank/databases/plink/ soceco/2ghana.htm.

CHAPTER 9

GOVERNANCE AND PRIVATE INVESTMENT IN AFRICA

JAMES J. EMERY

INTRODUCTION

The quality of governance directly affects the level and nature of private investment in a country. Private investment in turn is a major determinant of economic growth, and the ability of a country to reduce or alleviate poverty and improve the lives of its citizens. The relationship of governance to private investment is complex and is subject to many influences; this paper will examine a relatively narrow aspect of that relationship—complex administrative regulation of business as an enabler of corruption and poor governance—to draw implications on the relation between governance in Africa and the inability of most African countries to create a positive investment climate, attract significant flows of investment, and maintain consistently high growth rates.

The impact of poor governance on the private sector is not as severe nor as repressive for the general population as it is with respect to direct diversion of public funds, use of repressive force, and corruption of basic public services such as health and education. The amounts of money involved in securing bribes from the private sector are in most cases much less than can be gained from direct diversion of public funds, especially in resource-rich countries. The repression emanating from poor governance is one over economic activity, not personal freedoms, and so is not as severe in its impact on citizens. And the loss of business opportunities is probably not as directly important to most citizens, particularly the poor, as the failure of the state to deliver adequate basic services in health care and education.

Nevertheless, the impact of poor governance on private sector activity is crucially important in determining overall levels of private investment and the nature of that investment. A number of studies have validated the importance of corruption as a disincentive to private investment. A global survey of private businesses, which focused on obstacles to doing business, indicated that corruption was the leading constraint on business activity in developing countries overall; further, the study indicated that the Africa as a region ranked as being among the more corrupt (Batra et al., 2001). Several major rankings of competitiveness or the business climate incorporate directly measures of corruption or governance, such as Transparency International's Corruptions Perceptions Index (World Economic Forum, 2001; Transparency International, 2002). One service to businesses and countries focuses explicitly on a series of factors linked to the transparency of the legal/regulatory environment, and generates an "opacity index" that explicitly incorporates poor governance and corruption (Price WaterhouseCoopers, 2002). In general, the results of these surveys or empirical rankings based on surveys cites the effects of poor governance as increasing the uncertainty for business, raising costs—often far beyond the direct cost of bribery, and distorting the types of activity pursued by the private sector, all of which depress private economic activity, and hence incomes, employment, and growth.

The specific aspects of governance that affect private sector activity and private investment in particular, cover a range of interactions between the public and private sector, and include the following:

- Maintenance of policy distortions that create exceptional opportunities for rent seeking, patronage and pilferage;
- Use of direct government ownership for political and patronage objectives, and the corresponding exclusion of private activity in these sectors;
- Corruption and dysfunction of the judiciary system;
- Corruption in the granting of licenses, permits, and so on.
- Corruption or favoritism in the collection of tax revenues from business, including general taxation revenues normally collected by Revenue agencies and trade taxes collected by Customs Authorities;
- Corruption or arbitrary enforcement of business regulations such as labor, environmental, and other standards.

All of these factors are important determinants of the business climate, and feature prominently in assessments of competitiveness or the attractiveness of a country as an investment location. The first factor, policies that create substantial opportunities for corruption and diversion of funds, has been typical of the worst governance environments, often cryptically named "kleptocracies" or more politely as "state capture" by corrupt interests, of which Africa has claimed a number of examples. There are examples of exceptionally bad governance where natural resource revenues controlled by the state have raised the stakes in terms of potential opportunities, and led governments to deliberately maintain otherwise dysfunctional policies, such as in Nigeria under Abacha and Zaire under Mobutu. Yet these types of policies have also been commonly found in countries with much better governance practices as well. In general, they have been the subject of reform programs supported by external aid institutions, and except for extreme cases, have increasingly been addressed over the decade or more of economic reform programs in most African countries.

The use of state-owned companies as patronage vehicles has been widely documented, with the resulting inefficiencies and inadequacies in service provision and infrastructure that have resulted (World Bank, 1995). The successive privatization programs that many countries have adopted have steadily eroded the size of the parastatal sector in most African economies, but substantial pockets remain, particularly among those firms viewed as "strategic" during earlier rounds of privatization. The privatization process itself, often pursued via non-transparent means, also offered opportunities for patronage and rent-seeking. Although still an issue, the various issues around privatization are well acknowledged, even though the momentum for privatization in Africa may be slowing as the more difficult cases, strategic, and politically important firms remain in state hands. At the same time, the appetite by international firms for new investments in emerging markets in infrastructure sectors in particular has dried up, contributing to the loss of momentum on further privatization in Africa.

It is the remaining points concerning the judiciary, business licensing, tax administration, and the regulatory apparatus that have attracted somewhat less attention in the economic assessment of poor performance in Africa and investment climate analysis. Indeed, addressing these issues has been classed as "second-generation" reforms, indicating both a lower level of priority as well as a later place in logical sequencing of reform programs (IMF, 1999). The importance of these factors as determinants of the overall investment climate has, however, become paramount as the agenda for first generation reforms has proceeded, and there has been little in terms of investment flows in response. Indeed, it has been this lack of a "supply response" to reforms in Africa in terms of increased investment, which has characterized much of the experience of African countries in the 1990's.

This chapter focuses on one particular aspect of this set of factors—the administrative requirements for establishing a new company in Africa. Thus, we are looking at the mechanics of private investment, in particular all the bureaucratic requirements connected with new investment. The resulting assessment is also valid for many operational aspects of doing business that apply to existing firms as well as ones being newly established. The focus on new investment captures an important stated objective of most development strategies—that of attracting increased private investment and foreign investment in particular. The analysis of administrative requirements provides a specific look at the instruments of good or bad governance as it affects private investment, and thus helps to capture some of the essence of the resulting environment created by their structure and implementation. It allows more detailed and useful analysis of the impact of governance in practice than simply an analysis of the structure of policies and regulations, by focusing on their implementation as well.

Administrative Barriers to Investment

A significant volume of research and advisory assistance has been conducted for a number of African countries, following a comparable methodology, to identify the scope and nature of these second-tier administrative barriers to investment. This work has been undertaken by the Foreign Investment Advisory Service of The World Bank and International Finance Corporation, and the Services Group, acting as a contractor to the U.S. Agency for International Development. The analytical approach used in each case is quite simple conceptually. It consists of documenting, in precise detail, all the administrative requirements for establishing a firm and beginning operations. This includes all licenses, approvals, registrations, permits, or other formalities required to be in full compliance with existing laws and regulations. In addition, researchers also gathered data on the delays associated with each step, the costs, and the forms or information required. This research was typically done in full collaboration with government agencies, whose active participation in the process was solicited from the beginning, and with the support of the private sector, who provided confidential assessments of how various measures were actually implemented. (This work is presented in more detail in Emery and Spence, 2000. Much of the analysis presented in that report is summarized here, along with some updated information available since that publication. Morisset and Lumenageso, 2002, also provide a compilation and comparison of results of this work in West Africa). Later research has supplemented this analysis with more formal surveys of enterprises (FIAS, 2002, 2003).

The resulting information is typically divided into four areas, roughly corresponding to the chronological process of making an investment:

- General licenses, approvals, and other requirements for all firms, including general investment approval, approvals for incentives, tax registration, company formation, expatriate work permits, business licenses, and so on;
- Specialized approvals required for certain sectors or activities, such as are typically required for sectors involving resource utilization, tourism, financial services, transportation, and so on;
- Site development constraints, encompassing securing land, improving it, getting utilities services, and constructing buildings;
- Operational requirements, that firms encounter once they begin operations. These are the result of regulations governing labor, foreign exchange, international trade, standards, and so on (The Services Group methodology uses a slightly different characterization of requirements for establishing, locating, employing, and importing/exporting. Services Group, 2002).

The result is a comprehensive mapping of all of the bureaucratic and other routine requirements related to realizing a private investment project in the country. To date, such assessments have been undertaken for the following countries: Ghana, Uganda, Mozambique, Tanzania, Kenya, Senegal, Guinea-Bissau, Zambia, Zimbabwe, Mali, Madagascar, Lesotho, South Africa (including differentiation by province), Namibia, Nigeria, and Mauritania. The resulting assessment is specific to that country, and provides the basis for dialogue and design of reform or institutional change programs to address the resulting constraints. Nevertheless, there are a number of broad consistencies across countries that emerged. And, while there were significant institutional differences in individual countries and variances owing to their legal/administrative heritage that derived mostly from colonial administrations, there were also similarities.

Figure 9.1 shows a diagrammatic example of the process for a foreign manufacturing firm in Senegal. What is clear from this example is the complexity of the overall process and the potential for delays and rent-seeking behavior by officials. In Senegal, there were a total of 23 different "dossiers" or applications with supporting material required, with the need to pass before 31 different agencies of national and local

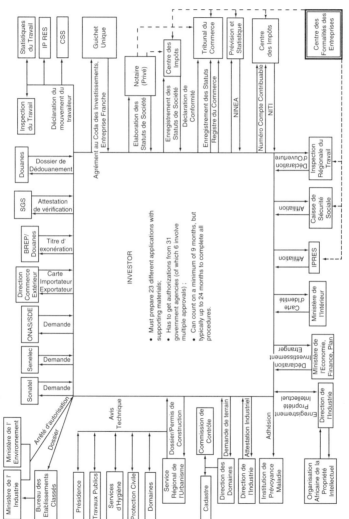

Figure 9.1   Senegal: Investment Procedures

government, of which six required multiple visits, adding up to a process that takes from nine months to two to three years to complete. This is by no means unique or uncharacteristic. Indeed, it is much better than in neighboring Guinea-Bissau or in Nigeria, for example, and probably on average rather typical for an African country. Some of the examples of this complexity are summarized for each type of administrative requirement as follows.

General Approvals

There are a number of steps typically required of all firms in the process of establishing a new business. In some countries, such as Mozambique, simply registering a company can be a long and expensive process; in others such as Kenya, it is theoretically easy, but outmoded legislation and a Registrar General's office with no resources made it unnecessarily cumbersome. These business registration requirements are necessary services for private investors: establishing a company, registering a trade name or copyrighting a logo are important protections. The needed reforms are not to do away with these requirements but to provide the services effectively. The greatest obstacles and delays have occurred with countries that require special approval and award fiscal incentives, for qualifying investments, typically those in sectors viewed as development priorities. Here the need to prepare detailed feasibility studies and demonstrate project compliance with (often vague) eligibility criteria pose additional burden on firms and delays long exceeding the legal time are common. Business licenses at a local level are another source of delays and duplicative submission of company and project data, but are usually an important revenue source for local authorities with limited taxation options. For foreign firms, special registration requirements for foreign investors are common, and significant delays are encountered in securing work permits for investors and expatriate managers. Duplicative tax registration procedures are common as well. As a result, these initial hurdles can often take many months, or even a year in some countries for complex projects.

Sectoral Licensing

An additional layer of scrutiny and evaluation of projects by governments is applied for certain sectors. These include, importantly, natural resource exploitation rights, or allocation of other limited resources for business use. Here, concession procedures are particularly non-transparent, yet award of concessions is the primary policy tool for resource management. Licenses may be granted for political reasons with little regard for performance or appropriate resource allocation. Governments have often been particularly weak in enforcement in these areas as well. As a result, effective resource management policies are often undermined, and optimum levels of investment and exploitation are usually not achieved (with divergence in both directions). Governments also extend sectoral regulation into detailed aspects of business operations, for example prescribing management structures and qualifications requirements for tourism companies, and limiting foreign investment, often in contradiction with stated policy in other laws.

SITE DEVELOPMENT

It is in buying or leasing land, constructing facilities, and securing utilities services that the greatest delays are encountered. While most land in Africa is government or communally owned, poor policy formulation, cumbersome and non-transparent procedures for making land available for commercial use, and tenure rights of informal occupants often make for a long and uncertain process for investors. Undeveloped markets in private real estate mean that reliance on public sector land is virtually a necessity. To develop the land and construct commercial or industrial facilities requires a series of approvals and licenses. Here again, significant delays can be encountered, and the responsible authorities are often poorly equipped to evaluate proposed plans. Securing connections to utilities services—power, water and sewer, and telephone—is also fraught with delays and frustrations for investors. While telecommunications and power privatization have proceeded in a few countries, leading to improved service, securing utilities services still constitutes a major problem in many countries. New connections may be impossible in some areas, or the cost of extension must be borne entirely by the investor. A general lack of industrial estates or other comparable developed industrial facilities means finding an existing building or even a fully serviced site in a desirable location can be quite difficult, so investors must typically be directly responsible for construction and all the related requirements.

OPERATIONAL REQUIREMENTS

Once operational, companies face a different series of interactions with government agencies. These are typically regulations and controls on foreign trade, foreign exchange, and labor and social security. While foreign exchange controls have in the past been one of the greatest sources of abuse and rent-seeking, due to the pricing distortions involved in managed exchange rates, these administrative allocation systems have largely been abandoned in favor of market-determined systems. Nevertheless, much of the red tape associated with exchange controls persists, often with little policy justification and duplication over controls and reporting required for trade transactions. The persistence of partially liberalized foreign exchange markets still provides ample opportunities for arbitrage among different markets, and encourages otherwise illegal cross-trading, leading to periodic and sometimes arbitrary enforcement actions by Central Banks, as happened in early 2002 in Nigeria. Labor regulations are often very loosely enforced in Africa, even though there may be extensive legislation on the books. This reflects perhaps a pragmatic stance of many governments, where conditions in the informal sector pose much greater social issues than the enforcement of regulations on a much smaller formal sector labor force. They are, however, often applied arbitrarily and can involve strong penalties for offending firms. It is the trade area, however, that corruption and poor governance are most widespread, with important implications for private firms' operations. Corruption in Customs Authorities is widespread in Africa, where a tacit acceptance of the nature of "porous" borders characterizes most regions. Firms who comply and pay duties are often saddled with delays and unfair competition from smuggled imports, and overall trade policy is undermined by the lack of enforcement. While tariff reform in many countries has reduced the potential gains from duty evasion, the results of the various studies point to the continuing corruption of most customs authorities.

THE IMPACT ON PRIVATE INVESTMENT

The overall picture of the investment climate in the African countries covered is thus, to varying degrees, hostile and bureaucratic. This is true even in those countries where serious reform programs have removed many of the major policies that acted both to foster poor governance on a grand scale and to deter private investment. Although clearly those countries are ahead of some of the reform laggards, such as Nigeria and Guinea Bissau, they still have not succeeded in creating an environment that is investor-friendly, but rather perpetuate one that fuels and enables poor governance and corruption. The relation between this administrative environment and governance is complex and has several dimensions.

First of all is the overall complexity of the process. Simply adding up the various requirements and the estimated time it all may take presents a dismal picture, as outlined above in Senegal. The overall complexity places a premium on means of circumventing, or speeding up the process, which creates a flourishing environment for corruption. Second, there were many cases of overly complex or poorly designed procedures. These included a number of cases of "Catch-22-like" vicious circles, where an investor could only qualify for the permit required if you already had another, which was in turn dependent on it. This type of situation was found in several countries, such as in Senegal for the requirement to disburse the capital to establish a company into a local bank account, where the bank required an investor's *carte d'identité* to open the account, which was only issued after the company was duly formed. While some countries, such as Uganda, openly acknowledged these problems and consistently defined an appropriate sequence, others did not, leaving investors pursuing an impossible chain of events until they could convince one party or another to make an exception.

Third, there were many cases where duplicative information was required at successive steps, and a large volume of supporting information is also demanded. There was little exchange of information among different agencies, nor was there much trust among them. Thus, for example, to secure a building permit one often would have to submit copies of the company statutes, not simply the record that the company was duly registered and the statutes submitted to the authorities who were actually concerned with them. A few countries had attempted to overcome this problem of simple registration with "one-stop-shops" for investor registrations, but essentially none were that effective. In many francophone countries another model of the Centre des Formalités des Entreprises was being implemented, whereby a computerized system of submitting standard information for various registrations was handled centrally and then distributed to the various agencies requesting it. This had been done with some success in Mali and Senegal, for example, where the program was administered by the Chambers of Commerce.

Fourth, in many specific areas the enabling legislation or the nature of the administrative requirement may not be unsound or overly complex, but the institution administering it is either lacking resources, poorly managed, or overly subject to political pressures. Many of the institutions concerned with business licensing and regulation are obscure agencies with limited visibility and perceived importance. They may operate outside of major ministries with indirect reporting lines and little in the way of strong oversight. Corporate registries, municipal business licensing agencies, immigration authorities, factories inspectorates, and sectoral licensing agencies are often examples of these. They are typically lacking in resources and capacity, and so are unable to do a proper job, even where their staff may be otherwise motivated to do so. Corporate records, whether kept by a registrar's office or a commercial court, often consisted of handwritten index cards filed in shoeboxes scattered around dimly lit storerooms. Searching for such records could take days or weeks. Factory inspectors typically could visit only a small portion of the industrial sites they were responsible for monitoring, and lacked money for fuel even if they had vehicles. In these cases the nature of the problem was often inadequate services being provided, so that firms were subjected to delays, and even bribes wouldn't necessarily bring better results.

Fifth, one finds an astonishing prevalence of petty obstructionist behavior by officials. They may be in a position to impose a requirement on a firm, and then act in classic rent-seeking fashion to leverage their position. Many of these offences may be petty; for example, the official who insists on a form, but the office has none available except for his own "private" copy. However, when presented with this behavior at every turn the result can be frustrating for investors.

Sixth, there are substantial areas of business regulation and taxation in African countries where corruption is the norm, or is not exceptional. This is certainly true of Customs authorities the countries reviewed in these studies, where the ability to bribe a few officers to avoid paying duties or reclassify goods into more favorable categories, is widespread. Officers also use their ability to stop commerce by obstructing export or exempt import shipments to extract bribes, where the urgency of the shipment gives them leverage, even though no duties may be charged. With many countries, tax administration is also arbitrary and subject to extensive negotiations. A typical procedure may involve a company submitting a return, the tax authorities responding with their own higher estimate of the taxes due, and then a negotiation. Most countries have non-existent or non-functional appeals mechanisms for tax disputes with the authorities. When revenue demands are high, tax inspectors may often proactively visit companies looking for various areas of non-compliance. These corrupt practices typically have a pervasive negative influence on business operations. Unlike predatory behavior directed at extracting rents from specific activities, this form of corruption is not tied to specific value being created, is spread throughout the economy and raises factor costs in general. Thus, it is much more likely to kill off economic activity, than if it were directed at simply extracting rents. (Shliefer and Vishny, 1993)

As a result of these factors, in all the countries assessed, which includes a broad spectrum of African countries, the environment for private investment remains negative or outright hostile. And this was true in many countries that had placed a priority on economic reforms and attracting private investment, particularly foreign investment. Thus, one can say that virtually no African country, with the exception of several not assessed in this manner, such as Botswana, Mauritius, and South Africa, has an investment climate that is reasonably attractive, transparent, and mediated by strong public institutions. While most have some form of fiscal incentives for new investment, devote resources to some kind of investment promotion organization, and send officials overseas on missions to promote the country to investors, the reality on the ground is shockingly divergent with the image that the countries may be portraying. While this is clearly a generalization, the inability of most African countries (again with the exceptions of those noted above plus some small countries with high rates of growth driven by natural resource exports) to generate and sustain high rates of private investment and economic growth is currently one of the continent's great economic problems.

One of the major factors underlining this poor economic performance is the low rates of investment in Africa. Sub Saharan Africa accounts for about five percent of GDP of all developing countries, yet for only four percent of FDI of all developing countries. Furthermore, this foreign investment is overwhelmingly in resource extraction sectors, primarily petroleum and mining. The picture for total private investment is even worse, with Africa generating only three percent of total private investment in all developing countries.

The low rates of aggregate private investment in Africa mask a particularly difficult challenge, that of the high rates of capital flight. Attracting foreign investment requires overcoming negative images, information barriers, language and cultural differences, and so on, in addition to demonstrating the fundamental returns from business activity. Domestic investors don't face these hurdles, and should be better equipped to cope with the nature of most uncertainties. However, in the most telling condemnation of the insecurity of African investment climates is the extent of capital flight. Some estimates have placed capital flight from Africa as the highest in the world, on a par with the Middle East, in terms of the percentage of private assets held abroad (Collier and Patillo, 1999). Other recent estimates place the volume of capital flight exceeding that of inward foreign investment and foreign aid, making Africa a net capital exporter (Boyce and Ndikumana, 2001). This is to a great degree a function of political instability and the historical weakness of most African currencies, but is also in part a reflection of the lack of security of property rights in Africa and the insecurity of the business climate due to cumbersome red tape and arbitrary enforcement (Ibi Ajayi and Khan, 2000). For successful African businessmen, the first and most important hedge against an uncertain future at home has been to move money into safe investments in hard currencies overseas. This has occurred despite the extensive capital controls in virtually all African countries that have limited outright transfers and investments.

The degree of regulatory and bureaucratic complexity these systems have generated are a clear deterrent to investors, which result from the delays, added costs, and uncertainty of trying to establish a business. Some surveys of the private sector have shown that regulatory compliance and other aspects of dealing with the government assume as much as 20 percent of managerial time and effort, and bribes are the primary means of reducing this burden, affecting over 80 percent of firms in Uganda, for example (Svensson, 2000). While these factors are an important deterrent to investment arising from poor governance, the impact also goes further than these relatively predictable impacts, to affect the basic property rights of private investors.

Due to the complex nature of most business regulation in Africa, virtually all firms are operating illegally in some respect. Thus, they are vulnerable at any time to reprisals for what may be otherwise minor and indeed routine noncompliance. This vulnerability, combined with the arbitrary nature of enforcement arising from poor governance means that firms can be closed down or worse for operating in exactly the same way as their neighbors, their competitors, or their clients and suppliers. This, indeed, is the quintessential nature of the business climate in most African countries—the fact that you can and most likely will be at some time singled out for what is on the surface simple enforcement of arcane or otherwise unclear and obscure regulations (Box 9.1).

The severity of this threat places a premium on political influence in the survival of a business, and makes such influence virtually essential for a business to thrive. A personal relation with a Minister or other high government official is a key element to business success in Africa. If not a personal relation, then via access to key officials firms can insulate themselves by furthering either the personal or political agenda of those officials by payments, or other means of accommodation. The nature of these relations is difficult to document or assess empirically. Some experts have simply noted that they play a strong role in business success in the broader context of anticipating and positioning a firm to respond to policy changes emanating in an unpredictable manner from government (Utomi, 1998).

The importance of political influence on business success and the ability of private business to influence political leaders in their policy determinations is perhaps universal; in the U.S., lobbying is elevated to a high degree of respectability, and political contributions by business groups to campaign funds are the currency of influence. However, what

---

Box 9.1:   Enforcement of Environmental Regulations in Ghana

In late 1998 a new hotel was being constructed in Accra, Ghana. This was a routine project, not unlike many other new facilities being constructed in the country. As it was nearing completion, an inspection for compliance with recently established environmental review procedures turned up a number of violations and instances of non-compliance. As a result, the government had the structure razed to the ground.

Was this strict enforcement of environmental laws impartial and in concert with the violations? Other projects had not been similarly treated, and Ghana's relatively recent environmental review procedures were still being established and were not well understood in the business community. The real reason, picked up and noted by the local press, was that the hotel's owner was a member of the political opposition. As this news was then getting widespread attention, the government responded by proceeding to raze indiscriminately a number of other structures under construction, all of which were also found to have some aspect of environmental non-compliance, in an attempt to counter the charges the actions were politically motivated.

These instances are not unique to Ghana, and are not restricted to environmental regulations—there are many other options that can serve just as well for the political aims. The case does illustrate well where the potential severity of arbitrary enforcement within a system of poor governance and its threat to fundamental property rights. The hotel owner, now that a new government is in power following the 2001 elections, is pursuing his claim in the courts, an action that would have been futile under the same government that had taken the action against his property.

Source: Accra Mail, various issues, 1998–2000

---

is unique in Africa is the need for such influence to insulate the firm from the ever-present threat of politically motivated actions based entirely on enforcement of existing laws and regulations. The key role of political influence is not necessarily on policy formulation, although this is also a concern, but on securing fundamental property rights that are otherwise at risk. The judiciary offers little in terms of protection in most African countries, and in any case the problem is that firms are actually in non-compliance and thus even in a responsive and independent judiciary wouldn't necessarily benefit from protection of rights by the courts.

These administrative barriers to investment have proven remarkably resistant to reform efforts. In each case in which an assessment was done, there were a number of actions that governments took to either remove obsolete regulations, eliminate the sort of double-jeopardy situations and anomalies that some regulations created, or otherwise use administrative changes to streamline or eliminate some of the procedures found to be without substantive merit. However, the kind of systematic action to address these constraints as part of an overall reform effort to improve the investment climate has not been implemented.

In some cases, attempts to improve enforcement of business regulation and eliminate corrupt practices have backfired. In Nigeria, for example, where corruption in Customs and the Port of Lagos makes it one of the most expensive and least efficient ports in the world, Customs attempted to attack corruption increasing resources for Customs inspectors, and imposing mandatory pre-shipment inspection as well as on-site inspection of all goods. In effect, this action merely added a layer of red tape to an otherwise unchanged and unreformed process, and hence made it worse. The business community complains bitterly that import clearance procedures are more complex, and clearance times longer without any improvement in enforcement (Marchat et al., 2001).

The result has been that while there have been some improvements, and the methodology and approach has proven a useful tool in the dialogue between government, the private sector, and donor institutions, fundamental change has been lacking. This has been explicitly confirmed in Mozambique, Senegal, and Ghana where the original analysis was updated several years later, specifically to identify where changes had been made (FIAS, 2001, 2002, and 2003). The difficulty in reforming these administrative barriers has been witnessed in a number of countries that otherwise were engaged in serious efforts to improve their investment climate and attract new foreign investment flows in particular.

THE POLITICAL ECONOMY OF INVESTMENT BARRIERS: FROM ROADBLOCKS TO RED TAPE

To understand the perpetuation of these types of administrative barriers to investment in Africa, one needs to look beyond their economic impact. While this is significant, it is probably less so for the government leaders than political imperatives. These systems, stifling as they are for private investment, serve the important purpose of extending control over private business by political entities. This control is important for what is perceived to be the effective exercise of political power in most African states. These systems are not perpetuated just to enable corruption and bribes, and hence the personal gain of government officials, although that is certainly a common by product. Only in that small group of resolutely "kleptocratic" states is the motivation of extracting as much financial gain as possible from private firms, the basis for maintenance of a complex and unproductive business regulation system.

African countries did not invent the complex systems of business regulation they now operate. In most cases these represent the legacy from earlier, more fundamentally flawed economic policy orientations. The starting point is the colonial administration systems operating in the British, French, and Portuguese colonies. Here economic activity was strictly controlled and regulated, with all attractive opportunities reserved for settlers and trading companies from the colonial parent, trade restricted in various ways to maximize the interest of those parties, property ownership and business operation reserved for colonial nationals, and in some cases job classes or professions also allocated on ethnic grounds.

Upon independence, the priority of the new governments was to seize control of this apparatus, and if not dismantle it, turn it around so that it no longer acted to constrain the interests of Africans. Nationalization was a key element of most economic strategies, to directly control the companies that previously functioned as the agents of the colonial system. Where this was not done, a myriad of controls over private business operations substituted for direct ownership and allowed the new nation states to assert their control over economic activity. The extension of political control over the economy was supplemented by new investments, often in industry, by governments, in many cases temporarily enriched by the increase in commodity prices that prevailed in the 1970's.

As African governments have subsequently liberalized, privatized, and sought to attract private investment, they have done so without the benefit of experience in managing open market economies. They have also done so without much confidence in the business community to produce positive economic results on its own, mediated mostly by competition rather than regulation and administrative control. And while they may be well guided by the institutions assisting them in these processes, and have proceeded slowly and incrementally to do so, most African leaders are attempting to establish something that has never existed in their countries, at least in large scale formal economic activity. (In subsistence activities and in the small scale informal sector one does find atomistic competition and an essentially unregulated environment). As they now grapple with the "second generation" reforms, reforming and/or creating the institutions that are required for a modern economy to function well, they themselves as well as their development partners are recognizing the difficulties and complexities of these complex institutional, behavioral, and microeconomic issues (World Bank 2002).

The maintenance of these complex administrative and regulatory systems and institutions that perform poorly by objective standards can create its own political constituency. The interests of those who benefit directly can be a strong barrier to reforming these institutions and the regulations they administer. Thus, for example, it has been exceptionally difficult to reform Customs administrations and privatize Port operations in most African countries. The direct beneficiaries, as well as the businesses that have learned to benefit from their ability to pay bribes rather than tariffs, have proven to be too important a political force to challenge.

More fundamentally, however, the needs of a modern market economy, and the institutions to support it, appear to be at odds with the political structure of most African economies. Insights from African political studies give us much better understanding of why, in spite of reform programs and governments seemingly interested in attracting private investment, they have yet to create a truly supportive environment. In fact, a dynamic private sector that thrives independent of government, other than some modest regulation and payment of taxes, is anathema for most African political leaders. The political systems they have inherited, created, and shaped from traditional and colonial political structures are founded on patronage, and require maintaining alliances with disparate groups in a hierarchical system. They are expected to deliver economic benefits directly, not through the independent operation of the private sector, and ensure these are used to cultivate bases of support (Lewis, 1996). These "neopatrimonial" states need not be kleptocratic or driven by predatory bureaucracies, although that result has not been uncommon in Africa. Indeed, many function reasonably well delivering stability and enough of opportunity and inclusion to keep themselves intact without recurrent crises. This fundamental priority—of maintaining themselves in power—has meant that control of the state apparatus and its use as a patronage mechanism to appease political allies and potential challengers is the most important exercise of power.

In recent decades, most African states have become more open than earlier in the post-independence period, when they were actively consolidating statehood and expanding the instruments of power. During this period roadblocks by government troops were a common projection of power as well as poor governance, as troops used their monopoly of force to interrupt the daily commerce and travel of ordinary citizens, both as an expression of political control and for immediate personal enrichment. In stable states roadblocks are no longer a staple of African life, and now appear mostly in conflict-affected states or those with persistent poor governance, where their political role is secondary.

However, the more complex and subtle form of roadblocks still exists for the private sector in the form of the red tape and administrative barriers discussed above. Businessmen are still subjected to a seemingly meaningless maze of requirements, many of which are duplicative or dysfunctional. Yet these have been difficult to dismantle, even by governments otherwise committed to opening the economy and encouraging private investment. This degree of administrative control serves an important political function, albeit indirectly. This function is to subject any business to arbitrary and punitive enforcement through entirely legal means at virtually any time, so that even a successful business in an unregulated sector is always exposed to political action, by subtle and indirect means, for which the courts or other forms of redress offer little counterweight. While no administration would set out to design such a system of business regulation for this purpose, having inherited it, governments have been slow to reform and improve those systems, at least in part because they have proven politically useful or expedient.

A successful businessman who is not somehow beholden to the political establishment for his success is a potential political threat. If he is an active member of the opposition or developing his own power base by virtue of his economic clout, then he is perhaps a real political threat. The patrimonial nature of much African politics makes this type of situation undesirable or intolerable. In weak states, the perceived threat from an emergent business sector is relatively greater, and hence the political utility of keeping private activity in check is even greater.

Such a threat is not posed by foreign investors. Their economic clout, often cited as overwhelming that of the state in which they may be operating, can be substantial without posing a political threat. Indeed, foreign investors can be a willing or unwitting source of patronage benefits, with an explicit political sanction required for their continuing operation.

Attempts by African governments to reform these systems, often with the encouragement of their development partners, have so far failed to overcome the problem. Certainly, tremendous improvements have been made, and many of the explicit barriers to business, such as restrictive investment codes, import and foreign exchange licensing, and so on, have been eliminated. Yet few have made much headway on the second tier reforms, particularly those highlighted here as administrative barriers. As a result, African investment climates, in general terms, still are unattractive to investors, and as a result, these countries have failed to attract significant foreign investment and to stem capital flight. To move forward to achieve this will require addressing the issue on a political level, for those governments who may be more willing to relinquish these types of control over private business with the promise of generating some form of political payoff in the not so distant future. Yet almost no African government has yet achieved political success and longevity by delivering economic growth and rising standards of living. The political sense of doing so, when it involves giving up traditional instruments of patronage and controls that have been so central to the maintenance and expression of political power, is not in any way clear. The African countries that have demonstrated economic success, such as Botswana and Mauritius, are viewed as exceptions and the subject of special circumstances.

Until this political equation is changed, there is unlikely to be truly positive change in African countries' investment climates. Even though governments may pursue reforms, and these will create improvements, the experience to date suggests they will not go far enough to relinquishing the structure and subtle mechanisms of control over business activity to assure a true measure of independence and establish true private property rights. Even more important, beyond reducing administrative controls and other regulatory barriers to investment, the task of assuring effective enforcement of appropriate business regulation and taxation also requires a fundamental shift in governance. In this sense, better governance needs to translate into administering business regulation and taxation to assure that level playing field, not the preferential and discretionary systems that have so far evolved. As more African political leaders are drawn from the private sector, they increasingly have the understanding of the impact of poor governance on business and confidence to relax many types of restrictive regulation in order to attract additional investment. Also, as the political experience of most leaders is based increasingly in the recent decades of declining governance, poor economic performance, and deteriorating social conditions, these imperatives become more important than those of Africa's first generation of political leaders in independence, whose goals were asserting the rights of statehood, securing political control, and maintaining fragile political structures. There is some promise of improvement in this critical area of creating a positive investment climate in Africa, but it will depend on changes in political structures needed to accept and facilitate the economic reforms needed.

REFERENCES

Batra, Geeta, Daniel Kaufmann, and Andrew H. W. Stone (2001) *Voices Of The Firms 2000: Investment Climate And Governance Findings Of The World Business Environment Survey*. Washington, D.C.: The World Bank.

Boyce, James K. and Léonce Ndikumana (2001) "Is Africa a Net Creditor: New Estimates of Capital Flight from Severely Indebted Countries," *Journal of Development Studies* 38:2.

Collier, P. and C. Patillo, eds. (2000) *Investment and Risk in Africa*. New York: St. Martin's Press, in association with the Centre for the Study of African Economics, University of Oxford.

Emery, James, Melvin T. Spence, Timothy S. Buchrer, and Louis T. Wells (2000) *Administrative Barriers to Foreign Investment: Reducing Red Tape in Africa*. Washington, D.C.: The World Bank.

Foreign Investment Advisory Service (2001) *Administrative Barriers to Investment in Mozambique: An Update*. Unpublished paper. Washington, D.C.: The World Bank.

Foreign Investment Advisory Service (2002) *Senegal: Le parcours de l'investisseur— Une Reevaluation* Unpublished paper. Washington, D.C.: The World Bank.

Foreign Investment Advisory Service (forthcoming 2003) *Ghana: Administrative Barriers to Investment: An Update*. Unpublished paper. Washington, D.C.: The World Bank.

Ibi Ajayi, S. and Mohsin S. Khan (2000) *External Debt and Capital Flight in Sub-Saharan Africa*. Washington, D.C.: International Monetary Fund.

International Monetary Fund (1999) "Conference on Second Generation Reforms, November 8–9, 1999." Available at www.imf.org/external/pubs/ft/seminar/1999/ reforms/index.htm.

Lewis, Peter (1996) "Economic Reform and Political Transition in Africa: The Quest for a Politics of Development." *World Politics*, 49:1.

Marchat, Jean-Michel, John Nasir, Vijaya Ramachandran, Manju Kedia Shah, Gerald Tyler, and Lan Zhao (2001) *Structure and Performance of Manufacturing Enterprises in Nigeria*. Regional Program on Enterprise Development. Washington, D.C.: The World Bank.

Morisset, J. and O. Lumenageso (2002) "Administrative Barriers to Foreign Direct Investment in Developing Countries." World Bank Policy Research Paper, no. 2848. Washington, D.C.: The World Bank.

PriceWaterhouseCoopers (2002) "Opacity Index." Available at www.opacityindex.com.

Shliefer, A., and R. W. Vishny (1993) "Corruption." *Quarterly Journal of Economics* 107.

The Services Group (2002) Available at www.tsginc.com/Governance.htm.

Svensson, Jakob (2000) "The Cost of Doing Business: Firms' Experience with Corruption in Uganda." World Bank, Africa Region Working Paper Number 6.

Transparency International, "Corruption Perceptions Index" at http://www.transparency.de.

Utomi, Pat (1998) *Managing Uncertainty: Competition and Strategy in Emerging Economies*, Spectrum Books.

World Bank (1995) *Bureaucrats in Business: the Economics and Politics of Government Ownership.*

World Bank (2002) *World Development Report 2002: Building Institutions for Markets.*

World Economic Forum, "African Competitiveness Index", in *African Competitiveness Report 2001.*

Chapter 10

Governance in the Security Sector

Nicole Ball, J. 'Kayode Fayemi, 'Funmi Olonisakin, Rocklyn Williams, with Martin Rupiya

Introduction

This chapter begins from the premise that people and states must be secure from the fear of violence at the local, national, regional, and international levels if an enabling environment for sustainable political and economic development is to be created. This means both that states must be adequately protected against external aggression and internal subversion, and that the lives of ordinary citizens must not be crippled by state repression, violent conflict, or rampant criminality.

Since the beginning of the colonial period, African security organizations—armed forces, police, gendarmerie, intelligence services, among others—have frequently been a cause of insecurity for both the state and its citizens, rather than a means of guaranteeing individual and collective security. African governments have often failed to abide by the rule of law in their relations with their neighbors or their citizens, and have frequently turned to the security organizations in order to maintain their grip on power or to pursue regional political objectives. Domestically, this has resulted in many coups d'états, and even where civilians remain in power, the security organizations have enjoyed considerable autonomy.[1] Externally, many of Sub Saharan Africa's recent wars have their roots in élite attempts to protect their privileged position domestically or to undermine other African governments whose foreign policies are viewed as injurious to the ability of these élites to remain in power.

African historical experience demonstrates that if internal and external security are not viewed as two sides of the same coin, it will be difficult to create societies that function on the basis of the rule of law and protect individual security. All too often, the armed forces have been given—or have assumed—the responsibility for guaranteeing law and order. This is not, however, a task for which they are well-suited and can hamper their ability to fulfill their primary function of protecting the state. The problem has been compounded by the failure to provide police forces and other portions of the criminal justice system with the resources they require to guarantee law and order. This chapter is accordingly addresses issues affecting the capacity of security forces to protect both the state and its citizens.

The inability of African security forces to provide a safe and secure environment for economic and political development arises to a large degree out of poor governance—both of the state in general and of the security sector in particular.[2] This chapter is concerned with democratic governance. While public-sector institutions will be a major focus of the discussion below, democratic governance implies more than the effective and efficient management of the public sector. It requires a legitimate, transparent, and trusted state that is accountable to its citizens.

Legitimacy and trust are fostered by a state whose government is democratically elected and operates on the basis of a constitution that is an expression of the general will of the nation. Accountability involves the capacity, or the power, to require an individual or an organization to justify behavior and/or the capacity to impose a sanction. Accountability depends crucially on the degree of transparency in society. Participation requires due attention to the role of the legislature as the representatives of the citizenry. Citizens must also be able to express their concerns more directly to their elected representatives and to government as a whole. Participation is one of the hallmarks of democratic governance, but non-state actors can have both positive and negative effects on the quality of governance. It is therefore important that non-state actors are also accountable for their actions.

Specifically with regard to the security sector, the security forces must be accountable to democratic, civilian governments, but these governments must also fulfill their responsibilities toward the security forces. Thus, it is important that the government respect the professional autonomy of the security forces at the same time as they expect the security forces to refrain from playing a direct political role in government and to be subordinate to elected civilian officials and the civil authorities in terms of policy making.

Section I identifies the major actors involved in security-sector governance. Section II argues that security sector reform is more appropriately viewed as a process of transformation than one of reform. Section III outlines some of the key issues relating to governance in the security sector. Section IV explores a series of crosscutting issues that affect the quality of democratic governance in order to identify the specific challenges and opportunities presented by the security sector: 1) constitutionalism; 2) leadership; 3) ownership, including the role of external actors; 4) human and institutional capacity, including the ability of civil society to fulfill three key functions: act as watchdogs, press for change, and provide technical input; and 5) incentives for change. Section V provides recommendations aimed at strengthening democratic, civilian-led governance in the security sector.

THE SECURITY COMMUNITY

A country's security community is composed of the totality of the actors that affect the security of the state and its citizens. Not all of these actors have as their primary objective enhancing state and individual security. Rather, as in the case of warlords, criminal gangs, and repressive or predatory governments, their existence and activities are a major cause of insecurity. Additionally, the same type of actor can play different roles, even within the same country. For example, there is a tendency to view civil society organizations as an unalloyed "good" while private security firms are generally viewed in a negative light. In fact, both can enhance the security of states and their citizens, and both can undermine it.

The following four groups of actors constitute the core of the security community and are frequently defined as "the security sector:"

- *Defense and intelligence bodies*: armed forces; paramilitary forces; coast guards; official militias; and intelligence services
- *Public security bodies*: police, judiciary, and correctional services
- *Security-sector management and oversight bodies*: legislatures and legislative committees; ministries of defense, internal affairs, justice, foreign affairs; office of the president; and financial management bodies (ministries of finance, budget offices, auditor's general's offices); other oversight bodies such as human rights ombudsmen, police commissions.
- *Non-core security institutions*: customs and other uniformed bodies

The security sector is not, however, solely responsible for the state of security in a country. It is also important to take into account the attitudes and actions of two other groups:

- *Non-statutory security force bodies:* liberation armies, guerrilla armies, traditional militias, political party militias, private security companies
- *Civil society:* professional organizations, research organizations, advocacy organizations, religious organizations, non-governmental organizations.

Together, these six groups comprise what is often called the "security community."[3]

Historical experience plays an important role in determining how the security sector and the broader security community are constituted in each country. Countries that lived under French colonial rule generally have gendarmerie, for example, while most former British colonies do not. In some countries, especially where ruling parties have emerged out of liberation movements, political parties have security cells; in others, they do not. Private security firms are not active in all countries. Nor are warlords, militias and other informal security groupings. Thus, a first step in assessing the quality of security-sector governance in any country is to identify the members of the security community in that country and to develop as full a picture of each actor as possible by analyzing factors such as its organizational culture and structure, its roles and strategies, and its management systems, practices and styles.

SECURITY-SECTOR REFORM OR SECURITY-SECTOR TRANSFORMATION?

In both the literature and official discourse on improving security-sector governance, the process of changing the security sector is described as "security-sector reform."[4] However, reform processes tend to be incremental and relatively ineffective in dealing with significant institutional weaknesses. Reforms may change the superficial appearance of an organization without fundamentally altering its character, culture, or the de facto balance of power within the organization, as the many attempts at restructuring post-coup armed forces in Africa and Latin America have repeatedly shown.

What is more, the term "reform" has many pejorative political connotations in democratically-inclined communities in the developing world, especially in Africa. Politically it is often associated with the implementation of policy decisions from above without any attempt to secure the broader participation of and consultation with non-state or legislative actors. Many of the reform strategies adopted in Africa have been undertaken to legitimize unpopular regimes and have failed to alter the existing balance of power within the state or between the state and society to any meaningful extent. Transformation, in contrast, entails a more profound intent on behalf of elected governments to ensure that the practices of the security forces are consistent with the democracies that they serve.

In consequence, countries with serious governance deficits may require a fundamental transformation of relations between the civil authorities and civil society on the one hand and the security forces on the other hand.[5] Such transformations should occur within a framework of democratic oversight and control. Equally important, they should be supportive of the roles and tasks that the different security organizations are mandated to execute. Transformation processes need to address four institutional aspects of each of the security bodies: its organizational character, its cultural make-up, its human resource practices and, critically, its political relationships with both the elected authorities and with the civil power. Failure to address all four of these areas will, invariably, result in a failure to address the fundamental character and purpose of the institution in question and thus reduce the likelihood that the transformation process will succeed.

Wide-ranging transformation processes are immensely difficult to accomplish in their entirety as efforts to transform the security sector in countries as diverse as Lesotho, Sierra Leone, and South Africa have demonstrated. The restructuring of the security sectors of many African countries, particularly those that are attempting to emerge from either an authoritarian or a violent past, demands a visionary and integrated transformational strategy capable of ensuring that the country's security institutions do not regress into previous patterns of behavior. In practice, shifting priorities, resource limitations, skills deficits, weak leadership, and the sheer novelty of the transformational terrain may bedevil such initiatives. Additionally, the very prospect of a thoroughgoing transformation may prove daunting to the political leadership. This may be particularly true in countries where the security organizations have played an important political role in recent years and their commitment to democratic governance is uncertain.

However, since the security forces have contributed in no small measure to the decline of economic and political governance in much of Africa, it will not be possible to strengthen African states without adequate attention to the security sector. Moreover, the security-sector transformation agenda is very much a human and institutional capacity-building agenda and, by definition, recognizes that states seeking to implement the agenda do not have strong institutions. The challenge is to identify priority activities and then to develop a step-by-step approach to the transformation process that is consistent with local capabilities.

Democratic Governance
and the Security Sector

That a significant transformation of the security sector is integral to democratic transitions in Africa was underscored during the 1990s with the simultaneous rise of people-driven challenges to militarization and authoritarianism of African politics and a sharp deterioration in the security environment in a large number of African countries. As Eboe Hutchful has observed,

> Democratic consolidation requires that both . . . "security" and . . . "accountability" . . . be addressed in a comprehensive manner. For this reason, security sector reform is a deeply political issue, not a technical one. Equally, for the transformation of the security sector to work, it must not be pursued in isolation, but rather form part of a more comprehensive restructuring agenda aimed at improving governance and promoting democratization.[6]

Hence, the crux of the security-sector governance challenge is the need to develop both effective civil oversight mechanisms and viable security institutions capable of providing security for the state and its citizens within the context of democratic development. The current constitutional reform taking place in many African countries is the latest episode in a lengthy effort to construct stable polities and civil-military relations (see section below).

The constraints on achieving a form of security-sector governance that consolidates democracy in Africa are, to a large extent, the same constraints on improving governance in other sectors. Existing constitutional frameworks have often been used to justify the status quo, or even worse, repression, rather than promote change. This problem has been compounded by weak rule of law and inadequate accountability. The political leadership and the security forces have frequently seen few, if any, benefits to change and therefore have not been committed to a process of transformation. The human and institutional capacity among both public and non-state actors that is necessary for a successful transformation process has been notoriously weak. Insufficient attention has been given to private enterprise as a change agent. External actors, particularly the development aid donors, have sometimes pressured governments to engage in reform in the absence of commitment to reform objectives on the part of the leadership. Even where there has been a degree of local political will to effect change, transformation processes have been severely hampered by a failure of the external actors to promote ownership on the part of the national stakeholders. Finally, regionalization and globalization are changing the environment in which all national stakeholders operate.

The following section will examine these constraints in more detail. In order to overcome these constraints, however, it is important to have a sense of the desired outcome—in this case, the characteristics that a democratically governed security sector should possess. A document published in 2000 by the UK Department for International Development has attempted to define principles of good governance in the security sector:

The key principles of good governance in the security sector can be summarized as follows:

- Security-sector organizations, particularly in the security forces, are accountable both to elected civil authorities and to civil society;
- Security-sector organizations operate in accordance with the international law and domestic constitutional law;
- Information about security-sector planning and budgeting are widely available, both within government and to the public, and a comprehensive and disciplined approach to the management of defense resources is adopted;
- Civil-military relations are based on a well-articulated hierarchy of authority between civil authorities and the defense forces, and on a relationship with civil society that is based on the respect for human rights;
- Civil authorities have the capacity to exercise political control over the operations and expenditure of the security forces and civil society has the capacity to monitor the security forces and provide constructive input to the political debate;
- An environment exists in which civil society can actively monitor the security sector and be consulted on a regular basis on security policies, resource allocation, and other relevant issues;
- Security-force personnel are adequately trained to discharge their duties in a professional manner consistent with the requirements of democratic societies;
- Fostering an environment supportive of regional and sub-regional peace and security has a high priority for policy-makers.[7]

It is widely agreed that these principles define objectives that are desirable for all governments and that no government anywhere in the world currently meets these objectives in their entirety. As a group, OECD governments come closest to meeting these objectives, although they too have room for improvement.

It is also clear that there are different paths to achieving these objectives. There is a growing recognition that the principles, policies, laws, and structures developed during a transformation process must be rooted in the reforming country's history, culture, legal framework and institutions. Countries can borrow from each other and have successfully done so in the area of security-sector governance. The solutions must, however, be developed locally and be appropriate to the context in which they are implemented.

While no transformation process is easy, African governments face particular constraints when seeking to implement these principles at the beginning of the twenty-first century. Governance structures and practices have traditionally been weakest and least defined in the security sector. Until very recently, the security sector has not been part of efforts to improve governance in Africa for reasons of domestic power relations, civilian capacity, and an unwillingness of external actors to address the problem constructively. This is now changing, as both internal and external stakeholders are coming to recognize the importance of strengthening security-sector governance in the context of peacebuilding and sustainable economic and social development.

Critical Issues of Governance as They Apply to the Security Sector in Africa

This section examines five crosscutting issues that affect the quality of democratic governance: 1) constitutionalism; 2) leadership; 3) ownership, including the role of external actors; 4) human and institutional capacity, including that of civil society; and 5) incentives for change. It identifies specific challenges and opportunities facing those seeking to strengthen security-sector governance. The recommendations in the later section follow from this discussion.

Constitutionalism

The task of creating and maintaining a viable and legitimate state that is accessible, efficient, accountable, transparent, and equitable has been one of the most critical and complicated challenges of the political transformation processes that African countries are currently undergoing. Governance has been the major vehicle for attaining this legitimacy and viability. Fundamental to the notion of governance is the ability of the state to provide efficient and well-functioning institutions and infrastructures of government—legally backed and socially coherent—that together establish and maintain an enabling environment in which human security is guaranteed and human development takes place.[8]

The meaning of good governance has been the subject of debate between promoters of the shrinking state and the champions of the inclusive state in which the establishment of a wide range of governmental and non-governmental institutions enable people to participate in society. One area in which there has been a great deal of unanimity, however, is the need to arrest the withdrawal of citizens from a state that fails to meet their basic needs. In such countries, there has been a widespread questioning of the legitimacy of the state among its citizens in the quest for a transparent, trusted, and accountable state.

Constitutionality versus constitutionalism

A major cause of this crisis of legitimacy has been the use of the constitution as the defining instrument for organizing unaccountable governments—constitutionality. Many African constitutions have been viewed as a set of rules and administrative arrangements meant not to regulate or limit excessive state power, but rather to validate newly independent states. Post-colonial governments used the letter of the law as the instrument for control and repression, and the military regimes that overthrew them perfected the art of manipulating the law to justify their hold on power. Helped by cold war-era superpower politics that facilitated monopolies on power by coercive rulers, the manipulation, trivialization, and disregard of the constitution became the defining characteristic of governance in much of post-colonial Africa.[9] Constitutions that sanctioned one-party states and racial segregation and provided cover for authoritarian civilian and military rule have been not only seen as legal but also legitimate documents regulating the conduct of state affairs, often to the detriment of the population.[10]

Yet a constitution by its very nature should be more than a mere set of rules and laws regulating society and government. It is more than a social contract or even the grundnorm. A constitution is rather an expression of the general will of a nation and a reflection of its history, fears, concerns, aspirations, and vision. It is, indeed, the soul of that nation. The constitution is that single document under which diverse and even ideologically opposed groups unite and rally in defense of democracy. However, for this to happen, the citizenry must claim ownership of the document.

The hostility to the post-colonial state that developed during the cold war years has encouraged the notion of a new constitutionalism that is people-driven and process-led. The objective is to reconstitute the African state along equitable, transparent, socially responsible, and just lines. The idea that the African state must be refashioned to reflect the realities of multifaceted societies has taken root at every level on the continent. This has been reflected in the constitutional conferences in Benin, Mali, Niger, the Democratic Republic of the Congo, and Cameroon in the early 1990s; in the successful constitutional arrangement of South Africa; and in the process-based constitutional commissions in Uganda, Ghana and Eritrea. From the experience of these countries, the last decade in Africa has witnessed an upsurge in the demand for constitution-based governance that broadly reflects, in terms of process and outcome, the will of the people. Today, there is a struggle for constitutional reform in at least 20 African countries. These struggles demonstrate to ordinary citizens why rule-based and consensus-driven governance matters.

The change in focus from constitutionality—where these documents are merely legal instruments with no standing with the people- to constitutionalism—where constitutions are now seen as a tool for bridge-building among members of civil society—represents the first and perhaps most critical step in shifting state ownership from the leaders to the people. To date, attention has been focused mainly on government. There has been less consideration given to consensus-building within civil society and between the ordinary citizen and the state. Yet in order to formulate African political cultures grounded in human rights and good governance, an organic link is needed between the constitution as a rule of law instrument primarily concerned with restraining government excesses, and the constitution as a legitimation of power structures and relations based on a broad social consensus in diverse societies.

Constitutionalism and the security sector

The interest in constitutionalism in Africa provides an opening for a reconsideration of the relationship among the security forces, the civil authorities, and society at large. The armed forces have played a central role in governing in a large number of African countries since the 1960s. Even where the armed forces have not directly ruled, the various state security forces have been actively involved in both the political life and the economies of their countries. The objective has been to ensure corporate and personal power, prestige and economic gain for selected members of the security forces and their civilian allies.[11] Creating well-governed, developmental states that operate according to the rule of law has not been on the agenda.

There is now widespread agreement that the achievement of human development and human security requires that the security forces leave the political and economic arenas. To ensure this outcome, constitutional principles based on key tenets of international law must provide the basis on which the security forces are composed and managed. Such principles should outline the political chain of command (including the role of the legislature), the chains of command within the various state security forces, the roles and tasks envisioned for those security forces, and the broad democratic principles to which the security forces will be expected to adhere in their conduct as professionals. Prior to their adoption, the application of these principles to the security forces should be discussed widely in order to achieve consensus on the general purposes, composition, and oversight of the security forces.

There are two steps to this process. First, the objectives of the security forces and the legal framework within which they are to operate, must be stated clearly in the constitution and other national legislation. Then, those provisions of the constitution and other relevant laws must be implemented. Many African constitutions contain the requisite provisions for democratic control of the security forces, and the constraint is implementation.

The South African constitution of 1996 declares that national security must be pursued in a manner consistent with domestic and international law, and that authority in the area of national security rests with the national executive and parliament, that is, the civil authorities. Additionally, the South African security services are forbidden from partisan involvement in politics. The 1995 Ugandan constitution envisions armed forces that are "non-partisan. . . professional, disciplined. . . and subordinate to the civilian authority established under this Constitution" (Art. 208 [2]). The 1991 Sierra Leone Constitution lists protecting the constitution as one of the principle functions of the Armed Forces of Sierra Leone and forbids any serving member of the armed forces from serving as president, vice-president, minister, deputy minister or member of Parliament.[12] Even where constitutional and other legal provisions are badly trampled, as was the case in Sierra Leone during the 1990s, the existence of a legal framework to guide the governance of the security sector offers a starting point for transformation processes.

Other countries lack all or part of the required legal framework. The constitution of Kenya, for example, appears to be entirely silent on the armed forces and only contains a short article concerning appointments to the Kenyan Police Force.[13] The constitution of Zimbabwe contains brief sections on the defense forces and the police and a somewhat longer section on the judiciary. Neither the chapter on the police nor the chapter on the defense forces refers to the requirement to uphold the constitution or other national or international laws. Nor does the Zimbabwean constitution forbid partisan political activity on the part of serving members of the security forces.

While there is widespread agreement in Zimbabwe that the entire constitution requires revision, there is significant disagreement on the objectives of such constitutional change. Nonetheless, it was clear that the role played by the security forces—army, police, air force, and intelligence services—in the efforts of President Robert Mugabe and the ruling Zanu-PF party to remain in power in 2001–2002 clearly contravened the tenets of democratic practice, if not those of the current Zimbabwean constitution. In May 2001, the army leadership—apparently concerned that the opposition party was attracting the support of many soldiers—began a campaign against the democratic opposition among the rank and file.[14] By early January 2002, just two months before the presidential election, the security forces issued a statement that placed them squarely in the Mugabe/Zanu-PF camp: "We would not accept, let alone support or salute, anyone with a different agenda" [than those who fought in the war against white rule].[15] The security forces also trained young people to disrupt the Movement for Democratic Change's electoral campaign, promising them jobs in the army and the police if Zanu-PF won the election.[16] A security bill that gave police sweeping powers to search and arrest opponents of President Mugabe and control political activities was adopted by the Zimbabwe Parliament in early January 2002.[17] All of these were important factors in the re-election of Robert Mugabe in March 2002.

Leadership

It is clear that the need for a new social contract between the state and its citizens that transfers the ownership of the state from the leaders to the citizens also requires greater attention to effective means of increasing the voice of the people in the governance of the state. To achieve this objective, greater attention needs to be given to the quality of leadership in Africa, in both the public and non-governmental sectors. Without a vision of a transparent, accountable, and just state that is widely accepted throughout society, it will be impossible to generate the political will to effect a significant transformation of governance in the security sector. Without this transformation of the security sector, efforts to strengthen governance in other state sectors and in society as a whole will ultimately fail.

Speaking to the OAU Summit in July 2001 on the causes of violent conflict in Africa, UN Secretary-General Kofi Annan argued strongly for improved leadership.

> . . . from Burundi to Sierra Leone to Angola to the Sudan and Western Sahara, we are confronted with persistent conflicts and crises of gover-

nance and security that threaten to derail our hopes for an African Union of peace and prosperity.

Bringing these conflicts to an end requires that we acknowledge two central truths: that they imperil the peace of all of Africa, and that they are to a great measure the result of misguided leadership which is unwilling or unable to put the people's interests first.

These crises are the responsibility of each and every African leader. . . . Individual leadership is decisive here—whether it points towards war or peace, reconciliation or division, the enrichment of the few or the development of an entire society.[18]

This argument applies equally well to the importance of leadership for democratic governance.

Leadership is important among a range of actors: senior political figures; lower-ranking politicians and bureaucrats; legislators; civil society; and senior officers of the security forces. It is important that each of these groups accepts the challenges of leadership. Often, the focus is exclusively on the executive branch of government and, within that, on the most senior levels, which produces a distorted view of governance.

Senior political figures

The heads of state and government unquestionably set the tone and ethical standards for those who work in government and the public service. If the head of state chooses, for example, to undermine the judiciary, subvert the electoral process, or engage the armed forces in partisan political activities in order to remain in power, it indicates to less senior leaders that similar deviations from democratic practice may be acceptable.[19] If, on the other hand, the head of state tolerates responsible political discourse even when it is at variance with his/her policies, accepts constitutional limits on terms in office, and refrains from politicizing the armed forces, police and other security services, the norms and practices of democracy are reinforced.

Lower-ranking politicians and bureaucrats

Important as the leadership of the senior political actors is, leadership of lower-ranking politicians and bureaucrats is also crucial to the achievement of sound democratic governance. As explained earlier, constitutional reforms that promise democratic, civil control of the security sector will fail to produce the desired outcome if a country's political and administrative leadership is not committed to taking the steps necessary to create effective institutions and ensuring that they function adequately.

Simply creating a ministry of defense separate from the armed forces, for example, does not guarantee that relations among the various stakeholders will enable it to function as it should in a democratic environment. Simply providing training to the police will not improve law and order if the political leadership thwarts the efforts of the police force to bring criminals to justice, prevents the police force from being adequately resourced, or fails to ensure that the other components of accessible justice—the judiciary, the correction system, the legal system—function in accordance with democratic norms and practices.[20]

In African countries, where power has tended to be highly concentrated in the executive, particularly the office of the president, interest in reform has frequently extended only to changes that do not threaten the executive's grip on power. However, the executive branch is by no means a homogenous unit. It is not unusual to find variations in positions and approaches among the various actors that comprise the executive. The office of the president or prime minister, the ministry of defense, the ministry of interior, the ministry of justice, and the ministry of finance may have different relationships with the security sector and different views of how that sector should be governed. Finance ministries, for example, are frequently interested in gaining greater control over the resources allocated to the security sector. Ministries of justice may have concerns about the quality of the police force or its use for political purposes. Differences such as these can open opportunities for reformers to try to set in motion a transformation process.

Differences among executive branch officials can also complicate transformation processes once they are under way, as ministers and senior officials exert negative leadership by seeking to retain their power and privileges. It is particularly important to guard against alliances of disgruntled civilians and security-force personnel. Few, if any, of the coups in Sub Saharan Africa have occurred without civilian involvement or encouragement. The weakness of democratic institutions and the absence of strong, democratically oriented leadership, facilitate the emergence of anti-democratic civilian-military alliances.[21]

Legislators

Even democratically elected civilian-led governments have not always sought to control the military and security institutions via a democratic process. True democratic control requires legislative oversight. Legislative oversight in turn requires access to information, an acceptance of the need for compromise between the executive branch and the legislature, and legislators capable of exercising their oversight responsibilities. The notion that the people should participate in deciding governance strategies has been anathema to many African leaders and has more often than not been discouraged, both by the domestic leadership and, at least until the end of the cold war, by many external actors. When participation is undervalued, information is not shared adequately, either within the executive branch or between the executive branch and the legislature and other oversight bodies.

The Tanzanian government's 2001 decision to purchase a military air traffic control system from the UK company BAE is atypical only in the publicity it received prior to final approval and the explicit involvement of the World Bank. The export license issued by the UK government in December 2001 stipulated that the World Bank would have to be satisfied that the system could be used for civil air traffic control as well. The World Bank expressed concern about the debt implications of the project when its technical evaluation concluded that additional expensive equipment would be required to make the system functional for civil purposes. This led the Bank to comment in December 2001: ". . . a civilian system more suited to a country with only eight military aircraft would cost a quarter of the price" of the proposed BAE purchase.

More typical was the lack of information provided to parliament and civil society on the proposed purchase. According to the *Financial Times*, the leader of Tanzania's main opposition party opposed the purchase on cost grounds and because the deal was negotiated without parliamentary consultation. Civil society groups expressed similar reservations. "Only reports in the UK press have informed Tanzanians as to what is happening," said Ibrahim Lipumba, head of the Civic United Front. "The issue was not presented in parliament in a way that delegates knew what was going on and the issue never came up in the public expenditure review, which was meant to take in the views of all civil society."[22]

As a result of decades of marginalization in the policy process, many African legislators are in no position to assume their appropriate role in a security-sector transformation process, much less spearhead such a process. In addition to a general weakness *vis-à-vis* the executive, African legislators generally have minimal capacity to exercise genuine oversight of the security sector, even where the appropriate oversight committees actually exist.[23] Many legislators are caught between pursuing an agenda that serves the interest of the people and one that protects their own position or that of the executive, on whom their continued stay in power also depends. Many legislators are ignorant of the role that the legislative branch *should* play in ensuring oversight of the security sector and are not well versed in the details of security policy. This is an environment that calls for responsible leadership on the part of legislators, particularly the chairs of committees that oversee the activities and expenditures of the security forces. In particular, they should seek to acquire the expertise necessary to make well-informed decisions and to enable them to carry out their oversight functions. They should also avoid seeking political advantage over the executive branch and concentrate on the substance of the issues under consideration.

Civil society

Civil society also needs strong leadership if its voice is to be heard by those in government. Civil society in Africa has been hampered to some extent by limited knowledge of the security sector. Its circumscribed expertise in security matters derives in large measure from the secrecy with which security matters have been shrouded and from the prevailing view that security is appropriately the domain of the security forces and therefore off-limits to civilians, particularly those outside government. A few individuals challenged this orthodoxy during the 1990s by establishing non-governmental organizations designed to create a public policy debate on security issues. The Military Research Group in South Africa, the Institute for Security Studies (ISS) in South Africa, the African Security and Dialogue Research (ASDR) in Ghana, and the Centre for Democracy and Development (CDD) in Nigeria are examples of such path-breaking efforts.

These organizations are the result of the vision and efforts of a very small number of concerned individuals with a high level of experience in or knowledge of security matters. However, it is not always necessary to have such detailed knowledge and experience to demand accountability of the government. In Sierra Leone following the restoration of the elected government that had been overthrown by the armed forces in May 1997, civil society began to question the need for armed forces. The government's announcement of its intention to reform the armed forces brought not only expressions of concern from civil society; it also engendered a number of practical suggestion for vetting future members of the armed forces for past human rights violations. Additionally, supported by resources from aid donors, government and civil society organized a consultation on the issue of new armed forces in October 1998. Participants included former members of the armed forces who had surrendered at the time of the May 1997 *coup d'état* and members of civil society from all areas of the country controlled by the government. Most members of civil society present initially took the position that Sierra Leone did not need a new armed forces. Some proposed that resources be directed toward the paramilitary Civilian Defence Forces (CDF) that were composed of traditional hunting societies such as the Kamajors that had stood by the government following the May 1997 coup. After three days of serious dialogue, members of civil society concluded that the country did indeed require armed forces. Unlike the old armed forces, however, any new army would have to be subordinated to democratic, civilian control, and oversight.[24]

Senior security-force officers

Finally, the senior officers of the security forces need to demonstrate their commitment to democratic principles and practices. As explained at the beginning of this chapter, African security forces—particularly the armed forces—have been a major source of insecurity and instability in the continent over the last 40 years. As such, they have contributed in no small measure to the continued state of maldevelopment in Sub Saharan Africa. For this process to be reversed, senior officers need to demonstrate their leadership.

Rather than overthrowing the elected government as in *Côte* d'Ivoire in December 1999, they need to make clear that the security forces are subordinate to the democratically elected government. Rather than taking partisan political stands as in Zimbabwe in 2001 and 2002, they need to promise to uphold constitutional principles and accept the rule of law.[25] They also need to support greater transparency in security sector planning and budgeting. As part of this process, they need to take a firm stand against the corruption that is often rife in resourcing the security sector as well as the diversion of state resources by the security forces in other ways, for example, by using military and police vehicles and manpower for private purposes.

OWNERSHIP

It is now well understood that reform processes will not succeed in the absence of commitment on the part of those undertaking the reforms, and that ownership is an important source of commitment.[26] A major problem in the area of security sector reform and transformation in Africa has been precisely the lack of African input to and ownership of the emerging reform agenda. Donors of both security assistance and development assistance aimed at supporting changes in the security sector, have tended to dominate the process of defining the reform agenda and, as during the cold war, have generally sought to use aid to advance their own interests.

Security assistance

During the cold war, African recipients of security assistance, particularly military assistance, often had to alter their military doctrine, training and arms procurement to suit the funders without any consideration of the traditional policy patterns or the reality on the ground. The situation is much the same at the beginning of the twenty-first century.

The US's African Crisis Response Initiative (ACRI) exhibits many of these problems. It was established in order to reduce demand for U.S. peacekeeping assistance in Africa. The training provided under ACRI by US troops has tended to focus on conventional peacekeeping doctrine and techniques rather than on doctrine and techniques relevant to the difficult conflict environment in which African armed forces now find themselves, including operations against guerrilla forces in difficult terrain.[27] Similarly, the French program *Renforcement des capacités africaines de maintien de la paix* (ReCAMP)[28] has focused on building the capacity of Africans to conduct peacekeeping operations in the region. The ReCAMP concept seeks to build this capacity through training schools for officers and other ranks, sub-regional peacekeeping training exercises, and pre-positioning of equipment in designated places in the region. While this approach complements ACRI in some respects, for example in its sub-regional approach, the issue of relevant doctrine remains to be addressed and African participation in the thinking and planning has been minimal.[29] What is more, the development of both ACRI and ReCAMP at about the same time has contributed to perceptions of a Francophone Anglophone divide in the region.

Since ReCAMP and ACRI are focused on peacekeeping, they do not address the broader issues of security sector governance. There are, however, other externally financed programs that do that, to varying degrees. At the beginning of 2001, for example, the UK had British advisers in Nigeria and Sierra Leone engaged in assisting the governments of those countries develop the capacity of their ministries of defense. The United States has also provided support to Nigeria to strengthen civil-military relations and reprofessionalize the Nigerian armed forces. In this case, however, assistance is being delivered by a private security company, MPRI.[30]

Within Nigeria, the US program has been widely seen as an effort— albeit one sanctioned by the Nigerian president—to transfer "models of civil-military relations from a different social-cultural context . . . into another context wholesale. . . . "[31] MPRI's failure to develop Nigerian ownership of its programs also created problems. Although MPRI staff consulted with their Nigerian counterparts when developing the assistance program, that program was actually written solely by US personnel at MPRI's Virginia headquarters. In consequence, MPRI has experienced considerable difficulty in developing strong working relationships with Nigerian military officers. Differences between the Nigerian presidency and the Nigerian armed forces concerning the MPRI program led to the dismissal of the Army chief-of-staff, General Victor Malu, in mid-2001. Malu's dismissal did not, however, improve relations between MPRI and the Nigerians, as the critical issue of ownership has yet to be resolved.

Objections from the armed forces, parliament, and civil society are not based on the belief that Nigeria requires no technical assistance to transform its defense sector. Rather, they arise out of the concern that insufficient attention has been given to building on what already exists in Nigeria by undertaking a domestically-driven process of assessing Nigeria's security needs and capacities and engaging external assistance only once that assessment has been carried out.

In 1998, the United States Department of Defense created the African Center for Strategic Studies (ACSS) to enhance "democratic governance in Africa by offering senior African civilian and military leaders rigorous academic and practical programs in civil-military relations, national security strategy, and defense economics."[32] The success of the ACSS in influencing security sector governance in Africa rests on its ability to engage local actors in the development and implementation of its programs. Only in this way will the norms that the ACSS seeks to embed be indigenized and a sense of ownership be developed. While ACSS has from its inception encouraged Africans to participate in its teaching program, it began to work more closely with Africans in shaping that program only in 2001. It also began to work at the sub-regional level in 2001, having chosen to conduct a number of high-profile regional seminars during its first two years of operation.

If the ACSS continues to engage Africans in developing its program and to work at the sub-regional level, its capacity to attract civilian and military leaders who are able to influence the process of reform in their various countries will be enhanced, as will its ability to influence sub-regional initiatives that can support national reform processes. Even so, African participation in the development and implementation of ACSS seminars and workshops is only part of what is needed. If there are no mechanisms for sustaining and consolidating its achievements (for example, beginning a dialogue between key civilian and military actors), ACSS will have only very limited influence. ACSS needs to work in genuine, sustained partnership with local organizations already involved in the reform process or with an ability to influence such a process positively. It is by ceding ownership to local institutions that the practical effects of programs such as the ACSS can be felt deeply within Africa.

Development Assistance

There are a variety of ways in which appropriately designed and delivered development assistance can significantly benefit security sector reform processes. Development assistance agencies can raise the profile of developing democratic control of military and security. They can help legitimate and empower pro-reform forces in the executive branch, the legislature, the security forces, and civil society. The donors can also provide critical technical assistance and supplement national financial resources.

It does not automatically follow, however, that because donors can provide useful assistance to countries seeking to improve the governance of their security sectors, they will do so. In fact, to date, very little of such assistance has been offered. There are many reasons why appropriate assistance has failed to materialize. Several of the most common reasons are related, either directly or indirectly, to the question of ownership.

Most development assistance agencies have been simply unwilling to provide assistance they logically should be offering to support the evolution of a democratically oriented security sector. The international development community has come to realize that when security sectors operate autonomously with scant regard for the rule of law, democratic principles, or sound public-sector management practices, critical development objectives—such as poverty reduction, strengthening the state to carry out key developmental tasks, and fostering a vibrant civil society sector—are extremely difficult, if not impossible, to achieve.[33] Nonetheless, this knowledge has yet to be fully incorporated into their policies or reflected in their operations.

Citing legal restrictions and past practice, donor agencies have been especially wary of providing assistance that might be construed as strengthening a country's defense forces. Since the early 1990s, a growing number of donors have begun to provide assistance to police and related judicial sector reforms, but, as argued in the "Democratic Governance and Security Sector" section of this chapter, unless internal and external security are viewed as two sides of the same coin, insecurity will continue to plague African countries.[34] What is more, the legal restrictions are in at least some cases overstated. World Bank officials, for example, frequently take the position that their articles of agreement forbid assistance "to the military." In fact, the Bank's articles state: "The Bank and its officers shall not interfere in the political affairs of any member; nor shall they be influenced in their decisions by the political character of the member or members concerned. Only economic considerations shall be relevant to their decisions, and these considerations shall be weighed impartially in order to achieve the purposes stated in Article I."[35] It is becoming increasingly difficult to argue, however, that a governance approach to the health or education sectors is acceptable, while a governance approach to the security sector, focusing on public-sector and public-expenditure management, constitutes political interference.

Often, it is the donors' development agenda that dominates the decision of what sort of assistance should be provided, and not the expressed needs of a reforming country.[36] Because the external actors are providing the funds, they often argue, with some justification, that they should be able to determine how their funds are used. African countries often allow external actors to shape national priorities because of the attraction of the financial resources being provided. There have, however, been rare cases in which such assistance has been refused. Both South Africa and Tanzania declined the invitation to participate in ACRI.[37] In the development sphere, aid recipients frequently have even less leverage. Thus, even when a country such as Ghana, which has shown a clear interest in strengthening civil oversight of the security sector requests assistance in this area, its major donors have declined to provide assistance because they have not seen improving security-sector governance as a priority for the country.

However, even where donors do provide African countries with assistance for transforming the security sector according to democratic principles, it has proven all too easy to provide the wrong kind of assistance. This occurs in part because donors do not take local conditions into account when offering assistance and allow their own interests to take precedence over those of the reforming country. When the Office of Transition Initiatives in the US Agency for International Development decided to help the government of Sierra Leone think through its requirements in the security sector in 1998, for example, it attempted to employ a computer-based methodology more appropriate for making decisions about military hardware acquisition than resolving serious political differences. It decided to use this methodology because the AID official responsible thought it would be the best way to introduce "more rigor" into the Sierra Leonean decision-making process. AID simultaneously ignored an African consultant's report outlining in some detail a locally-driven process for decision-making that was more suited to conditions in Sierra Leone.

Motivations for accepting inappropriate assistance

Why are the international donors of security and development assistance able to dictate the agenda in Africa? To a large extent, or course, it is because aid recipient governments require the financial support that the donors provide. But there are also domestic reasons. Local stakeholders can also have priorities that lead to the wrong kind of assistance being offered and accepted. Too often, for example, security sector reform is equated with professionalization of the security forces, especially the armed forces. An eagerness to receive this assistance makes governments willing to accept assistance that is less than optimal. Additionally, newly democratizing governments may not trust their security forces, particularly the armed forces, and are unwilling to allow them to play a major role in shaping a reform process. This was a major reason for President Obasanjo's decision to accept the US offer of assistance to reprofessionalize the Nigerian armed forces and for the Sierra Leone government to appoint a serving Nigerian general as head of the armed forces and a retired British police officer as inspector general of police.

Additionally, some African leaders have no interest in a significant reform of the security sector that has at its heart more transparent, accountable, democratically governed security forces. They may rely on the security forces to remain in power and therefore be unwilling to antagonize them and risk removal through a *coup d'état* or to otherwise undermine their power base. The *apartheid* regime in South Africa, for example, was highly dependent on the repressive power of the state security apparatus, as was the Mobutu regime in Zaire, and now the Democratic Republic of the Congo. African leaders, their families and close associates may also stand to gain personally from the lack of transparency and accountability in the security sector. Under these circumstances, international actors need to identify domestic change agents and consider how best to support them.

Human and Institutional Capacity

The problems identified in the preceding section are frequently compounded by a significant lack of capacity among African political leaders, bureaucrats and civil society to analyze security problems and manage and monitor the security sector that often leads to a feeling that they are incapable of specifying their own needs and reinforces the tendency to accept whatever assistance is offered. In common with many other developing and transition countries, most African states lack the ability to provide public goods for their people, including a safe and secure environment. Many African central governments possess a nominal administrative presence throughout their entire territory and are often severely constrained in their ability to formulate policy, plan appropriate strategies, prioritize their interventions, and execute those plans. Additionally, civil society is often limited in its knowledge of policy making and implementation in the security sector and is also constrained in its ability to fulfill three key roles—demand change, act as watchdogs, and provide technical input to the executive and legislative branches of government.

In part this lack of human and institutional capacity derives from historical factors. Africans had little experience of governing any aspect of the states they inherited at the end of colonial rule, and many African countries had no security forces to speak of at independence. What is more, in many parts of Africa, there was little opportunity to consolidate early post-colonial institutional development in the area of civil-military relations as authoritarian and military-led governments proliferated. Even in more open societies, the responsibility for formulating and executing security policy has been allocated primarily to the security forces themselves, especially the armed forces. Only a few civilians in the executive branch have been part of the policy process. Most members of government, the legislature, the civil service, and civil society have been discouraged from engaging in discussions of security policy or implementing security policies. It should come as no surprise that in countries with powerful militaries or with a history of military rule, such as Ghana and Nigeria, civilians have been particularly reluctant to engage in security debates in view of the sanctions suffered by those who sought to express opinions on the subject.

Addressing capacity gaps

The problems arising from inadequate human resource capacity have taken different forms. Perhaps the most profound are those arising from the lack of expertise in the area of policy formulation. Policy is a critical ingredient of sound governance in any sector. The act of policy formulation holds both governments and their institutions accountable for what it is they profess they will be doing. As such, policy constitutes a critical interface between the citizenry and those institutions that claim to be representing their interests. Policy should also reflect the core values and principles towards which people should aspire and, as such, provide an element of continuity within the governance framework. Finally, from a management perspective, good policy confers predictability on the actions of government and provides a rational framework within which resources can be allocated and options investigated.

Some of the capacity weaknesses relating to the security sector within the executive branch, the legislature, and civil society have been summarized in the section on "Leadership" above. There are several general points to be made here.

Government-wide versus sector-specific gaps.   First, it is important to distinguish between capacity gaps that exist in the security sector alone and those that are found throughout the public sector. For example, many of the basic skills involved in policy development, implementation and oversight in the security sector are essentially those that are required in other government sectors. Thus, for example, an auditor examining the accounts of the defense sector needs essentially the same skills as an auditor examining the accounts of the education sector. He or she will require some additional knowledge of defense equipment and will need to work under higher degrees of confidentiality; but a competent auditor can make substantial headway without a large amount of specialized security-related knowledge. The main problem is finding qualified auditors. In contrast, in order for a legislator or a staff member in the ministry of defense to make an appropriate decision on defense policy, resourcing, or procurement, he or she needs defense-specific, technical knowledge, just as he or she requires education- or health-specific, technical knowledge in order to make decisions on social policy, resourcing, or investments in the social sectors. In the early days of its transition, South Africa was able to draw on civil society to obtain much of the security sector expertise it lacked. This option is not available to most other African countries.

Inadequate processes.   A second general point pertains to the politics of policy development and implementation in many African countries. When *processes* are seriously inadequate, even the most effective human resources will not be able to overcome the deficiencies. When, for example, the executive branch refuses to act on legislative reports demonstrating that resources in the defense sector are not used as planned, significantly undermining the armed forces' capacity to function effectively, the problem is not one of human capacity. When the office of the auditor general and the legislature are legally forbidden to examine the choice of weapons procured or whether value for money has been obtained in arms procurement, the problem is not one of human capacity. Nor is human capacity the problem when the executive branch fails to abide by the decisions of the judiciary and removes, demotes, or otherwise intimidates judges.

Inadequate understanding of processes.   Third, the processes themselves may not be deficient, but civilians' knowledge of these processes, rather than security issues *per se*, may be inadequate. Many African legislators do not know what kinds of questions they can ask or do not understand the feasibility of undertaking certain types of studies in order to influence executive branch decisions. Many of them also do not understand how to draft legislation on security matters and do not understand how to use the committee system. In countries where the executive has tended to dominate relations with the security forces, legislators may also not be inclined to employ fully the powers vested in them by the constitution, even when the balance of power between the legislature and the executive begins to shift. Furthermore, in most African countries legislators do not have the resources to acquire support staff and consultants for technical advice.

Gender imbalance.   Added to this is the problem of gender imbalance. Women are very poorly represented in African legislatures in general, and the situation is more extreme for committees dealing with security issues. Only one woman serves on the parliamentary committees on defense in Nigeria, for example; none in police affairs or security and intelligence. There are no women on these committees in Ghana, Sierra Leone or Côte d'Ivoire. Some countries such as South Africa and, to a lesser extent, Ghana, are taking steps to rectify these problems as an integral part of the transition to democratic rule.

Mistrust of "the other."   Finally, levels of mistrust between civilians—in the executive branch, in the legislature, and in civil society—and security officials are often very high. Particularly, but not exclusively, in countries making a transition from military or authoritarian rule, many civilians find it difficult to interact with anyone in uniform. Even in countries with more open political systems, professional contact between civilians and security personnel has tended to be limited. The civilians' lack of technical knowledge of security matters often creates a sense of inferiority that can make it difficult to interact on an equal basis with security personnel. Security personnel often exploit this situation, claiming that the civilians' lack of technical knowledge makes them incapable of managing or overseeing the security sector. For their part, members of the security forces fear that they will lose their prerogatives and privileges, if the civil authorities gain more control over security policy and resourcing. In countries where the security forces have committed serious human-rights abuses, they are also concerned about being called to account. This creates strong disincentives to accepting greater transparency and accountability to the civil authorities among members of the security forces.

Building capacity

Cracks began to appear in the wall of secrecy surrounding the security sector in Africa in early 1990s as efforts were made to increase contacts and facilitate dialogue between security officials and their civilian counterparts. Some of these dialogues have been sponsored by non-African groups such as the ACSS and the Global Coalition for Africa. Increasingly, however, African civil society groups have been responsible for the growth in dialogue. The Security Sector Transformation Project (SSTP) at the Institute for Security Studies in Pretoria, South Africa, was established in the late 1990s to contribute to the development of an indigenous African intellectual and practical capability in the spheres of defense and civil-military management.

African institutions have also begun to support training for both civilians and security personnel. Members of the Military Research Group established the first non-governmental training program on defense and security in Africa at the University of Witwatersrand in 1993 with grants from the Danish Government. The Defence Management Programme was transformed into the Centre for Defence and Security Management and is now the coordinating partner in the Southern African Defence and Security Management Network, which links five SADC countries in defense and security research and training. Both security force personnel and civilians in government and civil society benefit from the CDSM courses. In West Africa, the ASDR and CDD/Lagos are hoping to establish training seminars for parliamentarians in Nigeria, Sierra Leone, Côte d'Ivoire and Ghana. The objectives of these seminars are to strengthen the capacity of the parliaments to carry out their oversight responsibilities in relation to the security sector. The SSTP in Pretoria has sought to develop policy analysis and policy synthesis skills among key executive, legislative and civil role players in many of the SADC countries.

INCENTIVES FOR CHANGE

The transformation of security policy is the product of a range of factors that, more frequently than not, are interdependent. In some countries, local actors drive the transformation process. In other countries, the process is strongly influenced by external actors. Even where external actors play a central role in pressing governments to engage in a transformation process and in determining the nature of that process, the reasons why change has become necessary are essentially the same as in countries where external actors play a smaller role. There are four major categories of factors that create the incentive for change, within Africa and elsewhere: 1) major shifts in the political environment; 2) major shifts in the strategic environment; 3) major shifts in the economic environment; and 4) cultural crisis within one or more of the security institutions.

Shifts in the Political Environment

Major shifts in the political environment within which security sector institutions operate can be either internally or externally driven. Most often, they are a combination of both. The vast majority of post-1990 transformation processes within both the developed and developing world owe their genesis to the end of the cold war to one degree or another. The ending of East-West global rivalry created an opportunity for domestic actors to reassess their relations with each other. In some cases, the loss of external support meant that domestic actors were faced with the necessity of addressing the political problems confronting their country, rather than using those problems as a means of leveraging political and financial support from their major power patrons.

The end of the cold war also enabled norms such as human rights protection, democracy, good governance, human development and human security to expand internationally. While there is good reason to question the sincerity and effectiveness of some of the groups and individuals calling for adherence to these norms, all of these appeals can by no means be dismissed as mere rhetoric. As the discussion about the new constitutionalism earlier in this chapter demonstrates, Africans will not support states that they do not believe are legitimate and that cannot provide them with the safe and secure environment necessary for human development. The new political space created by the end of the cold war that has enabled reformists in the state and the non-state sectors to express their views on a range of issues, including security policy, has been an important contributing factor to the spread of these norms.[38]

Other reform processes have come into being primarily as a result of major political developments within the country concerned. The end of apartheid ushered in a process of significant transformation throughout South African society that has led to major changes in the structure and functioning of the country's security forces. In Nigeria, the end of the Abacha era also opened the way for economic and political significant reforms. In Sierra Leone, the war against the Revolutionary United Front made it impossible to continue ignoring the failure of the political system to provide an environment conducive to either human development or human security. In consequence, the government has set out to reverse almost 40 years of security sector unaccountability to the civil authorities.

Shifts in the Strategic Environment

Major shifts in the strategic environment within which the security institutions operate may be a result of a fundamental shift in the regional balance of power (the end of the cold war) or a shift in the sub-regional balance of power (the demise of apartheid within South Africa). They may be long-term or short-term in nature. Shifts that appear likely to endure require a reassessment of a country's strategic environment and the roles that the security forces will play in protecting the state and its citizens against threats of violence.

In the current African strategic context, most countries do not require armed forces for "traditional" roles and tasks associated with defending the country against external threats. In the future, very few African countries will have the luxury of maintaining armed forces for traditional roles alone. Already many African armed forces are used for a variety of non-traditional purposes such as participation in regional security arrangements and peace missions, aid to the civil authorities during natural disasters, delivery of humanitarian assistance, support to domestic police services, protection against poaching activities, and provision of maritime security. The role of the police is increasingly shifting and expanding to include, for example, transnational crime. Changes in defense and police missions necessitate a review of a country's security environment and afford an opportunity to examine the governance of the entire security sector.

Shifts in the Economic Environment

Transformation of a country's security functions can, and often does, emerge as a result of a significant change in the economic climate within which the security institutions operate. Economic collapse and ongoing conflict in Sierra Leone have contributed to the initiation of a major transformation of both the armed forces and the police services. Finances, in this case, are simply not available to sustain the institution in the manner to which it was accustomed in the past.

The reprioritization of national needs by governments can also produce a decline in the share of the budget allocated to the security sector. The reordering of policy priorities in South Africa after 1994 was reflected first in the Reconstruction and Development Programme of 1997 and from 1998 in the Growth, Employment, and Redistribution (GEAR) strategy. Together, these contributed to a 60 percent drop in the defense budget in real terms during the 1990s. Throughout francophone West Africa, all security forces—especially the armed forces, police, and gendarmerie—are confronting serious financial constraints at the beginning of the twenty-first century, leading some security-sector officials to propose that security policies need to be reviewed and brought into line with available resources.

In yet other cases, economic constraints are created by the need to shift financial resources within the security sector. There is a growing sense within much of Sub Saharan Africa that the current crisis of public security has created an urgent need to transfer resources from defense to the police, while the rise in transnational threats to peace and security may require a shift from traditional defense forces to paramilitary-type forces and greater regional collaboration among police services.

Shifts Arising Out of Cultural Crises in Security Institutions

A fourth factor affecting the propensity of a country to engage in security-sector transformation is a cultural crisis within one or more of the security-sector institutions. Wide-ranging transformation processes are often initiated by a cultural crisis within a specific institution (which may, or may not, be a product of changes in the external environment). The behavior of both Canadian and Belgian soldiers in Somalia in 1991 led to a profound reexamination of the very essence of the armed forces in both countries. In Canada, this reexamination led to major changes within the armed forces. More recently, armed forces in South Africa, Nigeria, and Rwanda have been forced to transform in light of their previous history and their lack of representativeness at all levels of the organization.

Exploiting Change Factors

An important question facing reformers is how to use these various change factors to begin a process of transformation. Within Africa at the beginning of the twenty-first century, there are a number of opportunities that seem worth pursuing in this regard.

Regional initiatives. Many of the security problems confronting Africa are regional in nature. The wars in Sierra Leone and the Congo, to name just two long-running conflicts, will not be resolved without regional approaches. The land crisis in Zimbabwe has potentially explosive implications for other countries in Southern Africa such as Malawi and South Africa. Cross-border criminal activities—such as smuggling vehicles, narcotics and firearms, and illegal immigration—have grown in magnitude through Sub Saharan Africa.

These growing regional problems have begun to produce regional responses. Twelve Southern African countries created the Southern African Regional Police Chiefs Co-operation Organisation (SARPCCO) in the mid-1990s to combat cross-border crime.[39] In West Africa, a concern about the illegal transfer of small arms and light weapons led the sixteen members of the Economic Community of West Africa (ECOWAS) to endorse a moratorium on the import, export, and manufacture of light weapons in the region at the end of 1998. Not all initiatives to address regional problems are appropriate vehicles for strengthening governance in the security sector. Efforts should be made, however, to identify those regional initiatives and activities that lend themselves to strengthening security-sector governance.

The program established to implement the West African Small Arms Moratorium, the Programme for Coordination and Assistance for Security and Development or PCASED, envisions training for military, security and police forces of member states. Such training could in principle offer an opportunity to reinforce the importance of professionalization, human-rights protection, transparency and accountability.[40] Similarly, SARPCCO could be used as a vehicle for strengthening aspects of sound governance in the police sector. Regional and sub-regional political organizations such as the African Union, Southern African Development Community (SADC), ECOWAS, and the Manu River Union (Guinea, Liberia and Sierra Leone) are also organizations that can be encouraged to promote security sector transformation among member states. At present, however, these organizations do not have the capacity to undertake the necessary activities.

Civil society initiatives. A second avenue worth pursuing involves civil society. Although there are relatively few African civil society organizations with the capacity to influence the process of transforming security sector governance, it was argued in the section on "Leadership" that some of those that do exist have shown considerable potential for helping to change the terms of the debate in their countries as well as to provide technical support to reform processes. In addition to the activities described earlier, civil society organizations are undertaking a range of programs designed to inform policy and strengthen human and institutional capacity.

The Africa Leadership Forum, based in Nigeria, undertook a best practices study on demilitarization and security sector reform in 2001, which drew on research being undertaken in Southern and West Africa. A major objective is to feed this work into policy-making processes and political decisions at the national, regional, and international levels, including dialogues in civil and political society that seek to influence policy. A consortium of civil society organizations composed of SaferAfrica, CDD, ASDR and the African Strategic Peace Research Group (AFSTRAG) is working with SADC, ECOWAS and the Mano River Union to enhance the capacity of these organizations to support security-sector transformation. The consortium also seeks to work with the West African Parliament to develop a common constitutional code and principles on security-sector transformation and civil-military relations. The Southern African Defence and Security Management Network has, as one of its major objectives, the improvement of democratic management of defense and security functions in Southern Africa. Clearly, well-informed, professional civil society organizations can make a difference to the development and implementation of security policy, and opportunities to incorporate them into these activities should be pursued by all stakeholders.

Building security force commitment to change. One of the challenges of effecting change in the security sector is to convince the security forces that it is in their interest to engage in a transformation process. By its very nature such a process may seem threatening to the security forces. The argument can be made, however, that the security forces will benefit from a change in the status quo. There are two avenues that seem particularly fruitful to pursue in this regard. The first is professionalization of the security forces. The second is to enhance the effectiveness and efficiency with which resources are used by the security sector. Although both activities imply strengthening the technical capacity of the security forces and the ministries that oversee their activities, both have linkages to broader policy issues. In each case, it is important to have an adequate policy framework that will define the nature of the changes that need to take place to create more professional and improve resource use.

African states are already highly resource constrained, and the security forces in many countries have felt the effects of budgetary limitations. As the security sector becomes subject to effective, democratic civil management and oversight, resource constraints are likely to be felt with increasing intensity within the security sector. More transparency in the management of state resources, a more level playing field between the security sector and other government sectors, and greater expectations of accountability for all state institutions without exception will produce an environment in which the effective and efficient use of resources has a high priority. Indeed, in the absence of significant political and strategic changes, the effective and efficient use of resources is likely to be a potent stimulus for change in African security sectors. This is the area in which the development assistance donors have focused attention since the early 1990s, but, as explained above, not in a very constructive manner. While there is considerable internal support within Africa for fiscal responsibility in the security sector, the reform cause is not served by external demands for reductions in outlays on the security forces without a concomitant capacity for developing an affordable security sector strategy against which resources can be allocated and managed.

Building political commitment to change.   Finally, African societies are increasingly prepared to address the problems created by "the big man syndrome." One of the major impediments to security sector reform and transformation in Africa has been the unwillingness of heads of state and government to accept the need for improvements in security-sector governance. A major reason for that unwillingness has been the dependency of these leaders on the security forces for their positions of power, and hence their economic well-being. For a long time, it was impossible to discuss the need for an orderly, democratic transition in countries with strong presidential systems. With the end of the cold war and the political transitions that have occurred in countries such as Ghana, Mali, Nigeria, and South Africa, the need to promote democratic transitions throughout Sub Saharan Africa is discussed increasingly openly. While there is reason to believe that the days of aging leaders clinging to power are numbered, the path to that end is by no means straight, as the situation in Zimbabwe in 2002 demonstrated.

KEY CHALLENGES IN ACHIEVING DEMOCRATIC GOVERNANCE OF THE SECURITY SECTOR

The key challenges of achieving democratic governance of the security sector center around the creation of appropriate, accountable, and affordable security services and capacity among the civil authorities and civil society to oversee, monitor, and control the security services. This chapter has argued that in most African countries, achieving democratic governance of the security sector requires a transformation of that sector. Previous reform experiences in Africa and elsewhere around the world indicate that three factors are especially important to the success of such transform efforts:

1 the national leadership must be committed to a significant transformation process;
2 the principles, policies, laws, and structures developed during the transformation process must be rooted in the reforming country's history, culture, legal framework, and institutions;
3 the transformation process should be consultative both within government and between government and civil society;

As suggested in the previous sections, the existence of these conditions depends to a very large degree on domestic vision and political commitment to a transformation process. Translating vision and political commitment into concrete action requires attention to 1) the legal framework, 2) the policy framework, 3) human and institutional capacity, 4) prioritization, and 5) government responsibilities to the security forces.

Legal Framework

One of the initial steps that any democratizing government needs to undertake is the clear and unambiguous elucidation of the key constitutional principles that will govern the country's different security forces. At a minimum, the constitution should specify the lines of authority between all major stakeholders in the security sector (both civil and security force), the basic responsibilities of each of these actors, and the broad democratic principles to which the members of the security sector should, in their conduct as professionals, adhere. Subsidiary legislation defining the structure, roles and missions, and other aspects of the security services should also be developed.

The legal framework must, however, become more than a formal structure. It must be also implemented. Implementation depends in large part on that much-abused but still vital concept—political will. It also requires due attention to a policy framework for implementation, human and institutional capacity to implement, and the creation of an environment conducive to democratic governance of the security sector.

Policy Framework

It is essential to provide a clear policy framework to guide a process of strengthening security-sector governance. This generally tends to include strategic reviews for defence, public security, and intelligence leading to policy documents, concept documents, and transformation strategies for the different components of the security sector.

The advantage of providing such a policy framework for all members of the security community is threefold. First, it provides each stakeholder with a clear understanding of the activities on which resource allocation to the individual security forces will be based and provides benchmarks against which resource use can be measured. Second, such processes can provide the opportunity for governments to ensure that as wide a range of actors—security and non-security—are included in the policy formulation process as possible. A more participatory process removes security sector decision-making from the hands of a small group of technocratically-inclined individuals. Third, if correctly managed, such processes can bestow considerable levels of legitimacy on the members of the security community in the management of the nation's civil-security force relations and can significantly defuse the often-adversarial relationship that exists between the civil authorities and the security forces.

Where governments are reluctant to support the development of policy frameworks, external stakeholders should explore the possibility of supporting reform-minded individuals and groups in both the public sector and civil society. Such support might be verbal (aimed at legitimizing local reformers), financial, or technical. External actors should also make use of every opportunity to discuss the desirability of such policy frameworks with counterparts. External actors should take care not to undermine local efforts by pushing governments too rapidly. At the same time, they should not be excessively cautious in their approach, thereby missing opportunities to support nascent processes.

Human and Institutional Capacity

It is vital to undertake a realistic appraisal of the degree to which all members of the security community conform to the principles of democratic governance in the security sector. It is also important to assess their capacity to manage and implement ambitious security-sector transformation initiatives. Well-intentioned policy that has not taken into account the resource constraints, institutional limitations, human resource limitations, and political priorities of the country concerned will act as no more than a vision with little long-term, "on the ground" utility. Therefore, it is critically important to conduct a comprehensive analysis of the capabilities of each institution comprising the security community and an appraisal of the human resources available to those institutions. Civil society organizations should undertake similar assessments.

It is particularly important to ensure that civilians and the civil institutions of state are capable of carrying out their management and oversight responsibilities. Activities such as legislative training, creating security units within the ministry finance and the auditor general's office, creating a civilian-led ministry of defense, and strengthening the judicial system should have high priority. It is also very important to increase the skills and knowledge of civilians working in both the public sector and civil society in areas such as security studies; defense budgeting, planning, management and procurement; conflict management; judicial reform; and community policing.

Important as strengthening the knowledge and skills of the civil authorities and civil society and strengthening critical civil management and oversight bodies may be, it is also essential to strength the capacity of the security forces themselves to adhere to sound practice in terms of policy development and implementation; human and financial resource management; procurement, and the like.

PRIORITIZATION

Given the breadth of the security sector and the governance shortfalls in many African countries, prioritization is essential, both among the different components of the security sector and within each component. Given the immensity of many major transformation initiatives, the range of issues that need to be addressed, and the limited institutional capacity, realistic, and sustainable, interventions need to be identified. As demonstrated by efforts to improve the governance of all or part of the security sectors in countries such as Namibia, Zimbabwe, Uganda, South Africa, Mozambique, Nigeria, Sierra Leone, and Lesotho, a generic set of issues present themselves for immediate consideration in the management of such processes. These include:

1 building capacity among parliamentary oversight committees, the ministry of finance, auditor-general's office, the ministry of defense, ministry of interior, office of the president/prime minister, and other key oversight and management bodies;
2 developing a clear policy framework within which the country's civil-security sector relations can be articulated and managed;
3 managing the human resource issues confronting the security forces (demobilization, institution of equity programs in the recruitment and promotional policies of the various security forces and transformation of their leadership, command and management culture);
4 separating the armed forces and the police as necessary and reprofessionalization of the security forces;
5 addressing the problems of the entire public security system, not just those of the police force;
6 and preparing the security forces for new roles and tasks (peace missions, combating transnational crime, and military aid to the civil community for example).

Clearly all of these priority issues cannot be addressed simultaneously, and decisions must be made about which should be tackled first. Additionally, each of these priority areas consists of numerous sub-objectives and tasks. These also need to be prioritized.

Assigning a high priority to the issues listed above does not mean that other transformation issues such as involvement of the security forces in truth and reconciliation processes or the transformation of the education and training institutions are unimportant. Rather, the priority tasks should be undertaken in such a way as to create an enabling environment within which the longer-term transformation of the security institutions can proceed.

GOVERNMENT RESPONSIBILITIES TOWARD SECURITY FORCES

The government needs to elucidate clearly and unambiguously the responsibilities that the civil authorities have to the security forces of the country. These principles should be outlined in the constitution but can also be further clarified in subordinate legislation. Such principles should include: a) the provision of adequate resources for the security forces to accomplish their constitutionally-designated missions, b) the provision of clear political leadership to the security forces, and c) the prevention of political interference in the chain of command of the various security forces by the political leadership.

Balance of power within the security forces

Any transformation process that ignores the balance of power within the security forces, particularly the armed forces, will fail to transform the security forces of a democratizing country in any depth. It is imperative that the political leadership of the country understands both the de facto and the *de jure* balance of power within the security forces before initiating a process of transformation.

Special attention should be given to the armed forces because so many African armed forces have become notoriously factonalized since independence. The innumerable coups and counter-coups that pervade praetorian societies such as Ghana, Lesotho, Nigeria, Sierra Leone, and Zaire/DRC attest to this phenomenon. Many of these factions are, however, not necessarily anti-democratic. Even those countries that have emerged from decades of praetorian rule possess officers within the command echelons who are constitutionally inclined and supportive of the non-partisan and professional role of the modern military. Ghana, Lesotho, Nigeria, and South Africa provide excellent examples of this fact.

The fact that the armed forces frequently require special attention should not, however, blind the civil authorities to situations where the police, paramilitary forces and the intelligence service also require special attention. Where the police force has been militarized, for example, the transformation challenges are different from situations where the police have been marginalized and starved of resources.

The transformation of the security forces needs to ensure that progressive and constitutionally-inclined officers are deployed in those key nodal points within the command and staff hierarchy that are essential for long-term transformation of the institution. Typically these positions will include, particularly in the short-term, such posts as: the chief of the defense force, the chief of the most influential arm of service within the country concerned (in most African countries this tends to be the Army), the chief of the military intelligence function, the chief of the police; the key operational commanders (particularly at divisional and brigade level within the armed forces) and the defense strategy and planning staff.

In the medium to long-term, it is important to ensure that the key socializing institutions within the security forces are placed in the hands of constitutional and professional officers. Such institutions will include the planning, personnel, education and training components of the various security bodies. In strengthening the governance of the armed forces, it is also essential to ensure that the institutional capacity of the civilian component of the head office is strengthened and that supportive military personnel are seconded to the ministry of defense to assist civilian managers with the formulation of realistic policy, planning and budgetary forecasts.

NOTES

1 The autonomy of the security forces is a subject of considerable discussion. There are analysts who believe that the security forces rarely, if ever, intervene politically without the overt or tacit acquiescence or encouragement of civilians. Clearly, there are considerable convergences of interest between security and civilian Ñlites that influence the political role played by security forces.

2 K. Y. Amoako, Executive Secretary of the Economic Commission for Africa, has observed: "The capable state is the prerequisite for development. . . . Above all, good governance demands peace and security. We are not proud that Sub Saharan Africa, compared with other regions, has the largest share of its people affected by conflict. Until these conflicts are resolved, and the conflict-stricken societies rebuild, we cannot set Africa on the path to development. . . . [W]e must promote good governance in both the political and economic spheres. This includes strengthening financial management, building the capacities of parliaments and judiciaries, and rooting out corruption." K. Y. Amoako, "Fulfilling Africa's Promise: Millennium Lecture," London, December 17, 2001, http://www.uneca.org/eca_resources/ Meetings_Events/ Millennium_Lecture_Series/index.htm.

3 Additional formulations of this concept are found in Dylan Hendrickson and Andrezj Karkoszka, "The Challenges of Security Sector Reform," pp. 175–201, in *SIPRI Yearbook 2002: Armaments, Disarmament and*

International Security, Oxford [UK]: Oxford University Press, 2002, and Nicole Ball, "Democratic Governance in the Security Sector," paper prepared for UNDP Workshop on "Learning from Experience for Afghanistan", February 5, 2002, www.undp.org/eo/Publications/ afghanistan.htm.

4 For example, see Nicole Ball, *Spreading Good Practices in Security Sector Reform: Policy Options for the British Government*, London: Saferworld, December 1998; Malcolm Chalmers, *Security Sector Reform in Developing Countries: An EU Perspective*, London: Saferworld, January 2000; UK Department for International Development, *Security Sector Reform and the Management of Military Expenditure: High Risks for Donors, High Returns for Development*, report on an International Symposium, London: DFID, June 2000; Bonn International Center for Conversion, *Security Sector Reform*, brief 15, Bonn, June 2000; and Dylan Hendrickson et al., *Security Sector Reform and Development Co-operation: A Conceptual Framework for Enhancing Policy Coherence*, Report to the OECD/DAC, Paris, 2000.

5 According to *The Oxford Encyclopedic English Dictionary*, ed. Joyce M. Hawkins and Robert Allen, Oxford, UK: Clarendon Press, 1991, to transform something involves making "a thorough, dramatic change in the form, outward appearance, character."

6 Eboe Hutchful, "Toward Democratic Control of Armed Forces and Security Agencies in Africa," Discussion Paper prepared for the ACSS Leadership Seminar, Libreville, Gabon, January 31, 2000. (Revised for publication in Robin Luckham, J. 'Kayode Fayemi, and Gavin Cawthra, eds., *Governing Insecurity: Democratic Control of Military & Security Establishments in Nigeria and South Africa*, London: Pluto Press, forthcoming.

7 UK Department for International Development, *Security Sector Reform and the Management of Military Expenditure*, p. 46.

8 For a recent discussion on human security, see Human Security Network, "Human Security and Human Development: Linkages and Opportunities," Conference Report, 2001, www.humansecuritynetwork.org/report_may 2001_3–e.asp.

9 Julius Ihonvbere, *Towards a New Constitutionalism in Africa*, Occasional Paper, London: Centre for Democracy and Development, 2000.

10 Even in the twenty-first century, some of the technical and administrative concessions granted in the post-independence constitutions of Kenya and Zimbabwe continue to hamper efforts for constitutional change in these countries.

11 On Nigeria, see J. 'Kayode Fayemi, 'Soldiers in Business: Entrenched Military Interests and Nigeria's Political Economy,' Presented at the IPCOS/BICC International Conference on Soldier in Business, Military as an Economic Actor, Jakarta, October 17–19, 2000.

12 "Constitution of the Republic of South Africa, Act 108 of 1996," Chapter 11 "Security Services," www.concourt.gov.za/constitution/printer/ index.html; "The Constitution of the Republic of Uganda, 1995," Chapter 12, "Defence & National Security," www.parliament.go.ug/Constitute.htm, and "The Constitution of Sierra Leone, 1991 (Act No. 6 of 1991)," Chapter X—The Public Service, www.sierra-leone.org/constitution.html.

13 "The Constitution of Kenya," Revised Edition 2000, Chapter VIII, Art.
    108, http:// www.lawafrica.com/constitution/index.asp. The constitution
    does contain an entire chapter on the judiciary.

14 Basildon Peta, "Army Chief Decampaigns MDC," *The Financial Gazette*
    [Harare], May 24, 2001, www.fingaz.co.za/fingaz/2001/May/May24/
    1747.shtml.

15 President Mugabe had already characterized the leader of the main
    opposition party, the Movement for Democratic Change, as a traitor
    because he did not fight in the wars against white rule. Tony Hawkins,
    "Zimbabwe's Security Forces Back Mugabe," FT.com/*The Financial
    Times*, January 9, 2002, news.ft.com, and "Army Deals Blow to Mugabe
    Rival," BBC, January 9, 2002, news.bbc.co.uk/hi/English/world/Africa/
    newsid_1749000/ 174933.stm

16 Sydney Masamvu, "Terror Plot Exposed," *The Financial Gazette* [Harare],
    January 10, 2002, www.fingaz.co.zq/fingaz/2002/January/January10/
    220.shtml

    The ZANU-PF Youth Militia, known as the "Green Bombers," have been
    trained under the cover of a national service program which ostensibly
    teaches young people discipline and skills such as carpentry and metal fabri-
    cation. In reality, graduates have been used to harass opposition supporters.
    The national service program was first proposed in 1989 but established
    only in 2000, when ZANU-PF's popularity dropped precipitously. The
    budget allocation for the program rose from ZW$ 418 million in 2001 to
    more than ZW$ 2 billion in 2002. See Integrated Regional Information
    Network, United Nations, "Zimbabwe: Backlash against ZANU-PF Youth
    Militia," December 18, 2002, www.irinnews.org, search under "Southern
    Africa," then "Zimbabwe."

17 "SA Government Denounced Zimbabwe Army Remarks," Africa Online,
    January 11, 2002, http://www.africaonline.com/site/Articles/ 1,3,44589.jsp.

18 United Nations, "Secretary-General Evokes Promise Inherent in Launch of
    African Union," SG/SM/7884, AFR/331, July 9, 2001, www.un.org/
    News/Press/docs/2001/sgsm7884.doc.htm.

19 A 2001 International Crisis Group report on the political crisis in
    Zimbabwe noted that: "The first decade of Zimbabwe's independence was
    characterized by deliberate efforts to create a one-party state. The Lancaster
    House Constitution was amended several times to increase the powers of
    both the president and his cabinet ministers. The most barefaced amend-
    ment was Number 7 (1987), which abolished Mugabe's initial position as
    prime minister and created the all-powerful office of executive president.
    Mugabe has abused the powers in this constitutional amendment for his
    personal advantage and that of his party. Under them, he appoints virtually
    all senior officials in the civil service, the army, the police force, the dip-
    lomatic corps and other significant national institutions." International
    Crisis Group, *Zimbabwe in Crisis: Finding a Way Forward*, Africa Report
    No. 32, Harare/Brusssels, July 13, 2001, p.14, www.intl-crisis-group.
    org/projects/showreport.cfm?reportid=356.

20 The effect of military rule on the Nigerian judiciary has been described as follows: "The course and cause of justice has been perverted by the executive under the military, through such brazen assaults as refusal to obey its orders, removal, demotion or non-promotion of judicial officers and the cost of justice has become unbearable for the average Nigerian both in time and money." International IDEA, *Democracy in Nigeria: Continuing Dialogue(s) for Nation-Building*, Capacity-Building Series 10, Stockholm, 2000, p. 139, www.idea.int/publications/pub_country_main.htm. Massive subversion of the judiciary has occurred in Zimbabwe, particularly during 2001. See news reports from Irinnews.org (www.irinnews.org, search under "Zimbabwe") and the *Financial Gazette* (www.fingaz.co.zw).

21 Massive corruption on the part of civilian leaders has at times produced significant popular support for military rule in countries such as Nigeria. See, for example, International IDEA, *Democracy in Nigeria*, pp. 45–52.

22 World Bank, Development News, "World Bank Could Bar $40 Million Tanzania Air Traffic Deal," December 21, 2001, www.worldbank.org/developmentnews. Search Development News Archives under December 21, 2001.

23 National Democratic Institute, *The Role of the Legislature in Defense and National Security Issues*, Seminar Report, April 19–22, 1999, Dakar, Senegal, www.ndi.org/ globalp/civmil/civmil.asp.

24 See also, Centre for Democracy and Development, *Engaging Sierra Leone*, CDD Strategy Planning Series 4, London, 2000, especially pp. 37–43.

25 See, for example, International Crisis Group, *Zimbabwe in Crisis*, pp. 8–9.

26 A report on the role of development assistance in promoting reform published in 2001 concluded, for example, that "These studies of aid and reform in Africa confirm that when aid supports a country-owned development strategy, it can lead to sustained growth and poverty alleviation. The case studies also show that when reform is imposed from abroad, even as a quid pro quo for aid, it is not sustainable." James Wolfensohn, "Foreword," p. xi, in Shantayanan Devarajan, David Dollar, and Torgny Holmgren, eds, *Aid and Reform in Africa: Lessons from Ten Case Studies*, Washington, D.C.: The World Bank, 2001, www.worldbank.org/research/aid/africa/intro.htm. Similar findings were published nearly a decade earlier in Joan M. Nelson with Stephanie J. Eglinton, *Encouraging Democracy: What Role for Conditioned Aid?*, Policy Essay no. 4, Washington, D.C.: Overseas Development Council, 1992.

27 For more on ACRI, see for example, Roger Gocking, "The African Crisis Response Initiative," *African Affairs*, Vol. 99 No. 394, January 2001, pp. 73–95, and Jeremy Levitt, "The African Crisis Response Initiative: A General Survey," *Africa Insight*, Vol. 28, No. 3 and 4, 1998, pp. 100–108. See also the ACRI website, http://www.eucom.mil/Directorates/ECPA/index.htm?http://www.eucom.mil/Directorates/ECPA/programs/acri/main.htm&2.

28 Reinforcement of African Peace-keeping Capacities.

29 For a detailed discussion of the ReCAMP concept, see Eric G. Berman and Katie E. Sams, *Peacekeeping in Africa: Capabilities and Culpabilities*,

(UNIDIR and ISS), 2000, pp. 291–315, and the ReCAMP website: http:// www.defense.gouv.fr/ema/actualites/ recampgb.htm

30   The MPRI website provides a limited amount of information on its work in Nigeria: www.mpri.com/subchannels/int_africa.html.

31   J. 'Kayode Fayemi, "Dilemma of Civilian Control in a Post-Military State: Interpreting Recent Developments in the Nigerian Armed Forces," 2001.

32   www.africacenter.org/english/ e1000_center.htm.

33   Source: OECD, *Helping Prevent Violent Conflict. Orientations for External Partners*, Supplement to the *DAC Guidelines on Conflict, Peace, and Development Co-operation on the Threshold of the 21st Century*, Paris, 2001, para 59, www.oecd.org/dac, search under "Good Governance, Conflict and Peace," then "Conflict and Peace."

34   Several donors either had or were in the process of developing policies on supporting security sector governance in mid-2001. The UK has policies on security-sector reform and police reform. The Netherlands and UNDP were in the process of developing policies on security-sector reform. By 2002, a number of other countries were beginning to contemplate a more structured approach to the security sector.

There has been a tendency within the donor community to focus on the level of defense spending in aid-recipient countries. The attention to levels of expenditure reflects the belief that development-promoting activities should be given priority in poor countries. The attention to the defense sector reflects the fact that of all the components of the security sector, the defense sector tends to absorb the lion's share of resources. While it is true that expenditure levels do indicate government priorities, the donors' fascination with levels underscores a disturbing lack of understanding of what is necessary for sustainable reductions in resources allocated to the security sector. A focus on levels can also erode domestic support for significant changes in security sector governance by allowing opponents of reform to characterize donor demands for lower military spending as undermining the sovereign right of countries to protect themselves. For a brief outline of a process that links security policy, planning and budgeting with particular reference to the defense sector, see UK Department for International Development, "Annex 3: Security Sector Reform and the Management of Defence Expenditure. A Conceptual Framework," *Security Sector Reform and the Management of Military Expenditure: High Risks for Donors, High Returns for Development*, Report on an International Symposium, London: June 2000, pp. 41–55.

35   International Bank for Reconstruction and Development, *Articles of Agreement*, Article 4, section 10,www.worldbank.org/html/extdr/ backgrd/ ibrd/art4.htm#I11.

On the role of the World Bank and the International Monetary Fund in security sector reform, see Nicole Ball, "Transforming Security Sectors: The IMF and the World Bank Approaches," *Conflict, Security, Development*, Issue 1:1 (2001), http://csdg.kcl.ac.uk/Publications/assets/ PDF%20files/Ball.pdf.

36   The question of ownership is not, of course, limited to the security sector. The tendency of donors to be directive affects all of their relations with the

recipients of their aid. Since the end of the cold war, donors have made serious efforts to enhance the participation of beneficiaries in program design and implementation with a view to increasing ownership. While progress has undeniably been made, as with all cultural changes of considerable magnitude, much remains to be done to put the governments and people of aid-recipient countries "in the driver's seat." (The concerns expressed here about the behavior of donors should in no way be construed as downplaying the lack of interest many governments have in reform).

37   While Nigeria also turned down the invitation to participate in ACRI, it accepted a US offer to train its troops for peacekeeping. This has been seen in some quarters as an attempt by Nigeria to save face. The peacekeeping training being provided for Nigerian troops resembles what is provided under ACRI even though it is not officially part of the project. However, Nigeria had earlier rejected a move initiated by the US to significantly reduce the overall strength of its armed forces.

38   While there is good reason to believe that a good number of the civil society organizations that have sprouted throughout Africa since the early 1990s are primarily a reflection of donor priorities and funding, many of these organizations are home-grown and respond to local concerns. *In Funding Virtue: Civil Society Aid and Democracy Promotion*, Washington, D.C.: Carnegie Endowment for International Peace, 2000, Marina Ottaway and Thomas Carothers (editors) and their collaborators both underscore the value of civil society organizations to the democratization process and raise questions about the limits of these organizations and, most particularly, about the effectiveness of donor (primarily USAID) assistance to democracy-promoting civil society organizations.

39   On SARPCCO, see for example "Combating Cross-border Crime—The Southern African Experience," Speech by Juan Kotze, Inspector, Interpol National Crime Bureau, Pretoria, South Africa, March 23, 2000, at the Microsoft "Combating Cross Border Crime 2000" Conference, Cape Town, South Africa, http:// www.microsoft.com/europe/public_sector/ Gov_Agencies/127.htm.

40   The fact that ECOWAS member governments need to apply for exemptions to import small arms, for example for peacekeeping and training purposes, theoretically reinforces the concept of transparency. Of course, despite the moratorium, weapons have continued to flow into West Africa in a very non-transparent manner to fuel the war in Sierra Leone, to arm both the government of Liberia and Liberian opposition groups, and to support the anti-government forces that emerged in 2002 in Côte d'Ivoire. On the sources of arms available to both the government of Sierra Leone and the RUF, see Eric G. Berman, *Re-Armament in Sierra Leone: One Year After the Lomé Agreement*, Occasional Papers 1, Geneva: Small Arms Survey, 2000, www.smallarmssurvey.org/OccasionalPapers.html.

NOTES ON CONTRIBUTORS

Linda Cotton is a graduate of the School of Advanced International Studies of Johns Hopkins University and has worked at a number of non-governmental and research institutions, including Save the Children/USA and the Overseas Development Council. Since 1998, she has conducted research on trade and investment issues in Africa for the United Nations, Harvard University Center for International Development, and the School of Foreign Service of Georgetown University. She has also researched the timber industry in Central Africa and forest certification issues for Global Forest Watch of the World Resources Institute. She is currently conducting Investment Climate Assessments for the Regional Program on Enterprise Development of the Africa Private Sector Unit of the World Bank.

Ibrahim Elbadawi holds a Ph.D. degree in economics and statistics from North Carolina State University and Northwestern University. He is a Lead Economist at the Development Economic Research Group of the World Bank, and Manager of the Regional Program for Enterprise Development at the Africa Region of the World Bank. His research interests range from broader socio-economic issues such as the determinants of the risk of civil wars and the linkages between poverty and civil wars, to more traditional macroeconomic topics, such as exchange rate economics, capital flows, exports and comparative advantage, and growth.

James J. Emery currently directs Africa regional strategy for investment and private sector development at the International Finance Corporation, the private investment affiliate of the World Bank Group. He has researched and advised African governments extensively on investment conditions and bureaucratic red tape.

J. 'Kayode Fayemi is Director, Centre for Democracy and Development in Lagos, Nigeria. A civil-military relations scholar, Dr. Fayemi has written on democratisation, regionalism, and security sector governance in Africa. Among his recent publications is *Mercenaries: An African Security Dilemma* (Pluto Press, 2000). He sits on the advisory committee of the Global Network for Security Sector Reform.

Alan Gelb is Chief Economist for Africa at the World Bank. He provides strategic policy advice on African development issues and directs the bank's economic research, analysis, and advice to African countries. Before assuming his current position, he was staff director of the World Development Report "1996: From Plan to Market," and was chief of the transition division in the bank's policy research department. Mr. Gelb is a specialist on commodity prices, cooperatives, financial systems policy, and systemic reform. He has published several books and scholarly articles on these and related subjects, and recently co-authored *Can Africa Claim the 21st Century,* one of the most authoritative studies on African development.

Arthur Goldsmith is Professor of Management at the University of Massachusetts Boston and Senior Fellow at the University's McCormack Institute of Public Affairs. A specialist in development administration, Dr. Goldsmith is the author or co-author of three books and has published over fifty scholarly papers and book chapters, including recent articles on bureaucratization and democratization in World Politics and International Organization. He is currently completing a study of clientelism and patronage in developing and transitional countries.

Siri Golpen is a postdoctoral fellow, Department of Comparative Politics, University of Bergen. She holds a Ph.D. in political science. Thematically her work has focused on the issues of democratisation and human rights, constitution-making, judicial reform, reconciliation processes, institutional change and electoral assistance, labour relations, and fiscal welfare. Dr. Gloppen is currently involved in two research collaborations with Chr. Michelsen Institute on "Political institutions in Africa" and "Courts in Transition".

'Funmi Olonisakin is a Senior Research Fellow at the African Security Unit of the International Policy Institute, King's College London. Prior to this, she worked in the Office of the UN Special Representative of the Secretary-General for Children and Armed Conflict. She has been a MacArthur Foundation Research Fellow at the Department of War Studies at King's College London and a Research Associate at the Institute for Strategic Studies, University of Pretoria, South Africa. She is the author of *Reinventing Peacekeeping in Africa* (Kluwer Law Publishers, 2000) and co-author of *Peacekeepers, Politicians and Warlords* (United Nations University Press, 2000).

Dele Olowu teaches at the Institute of Social Studies at The Hague, Netherlands. He has degrees from Nigerian Universities (Ibadan and Ile-Ife) and had his post-doctoral programme at Indiana University where he also edited *The Failure of the Centralized State: Institutions and Self-Governance in Africa* with J. S. Wunsch. Besides several articles in journals and edited books, his other published books/monographs include *Ethics and Accountability in African Public Services* (edited with Sadig Rasheed, 1993), *African Perspectives on Governance* (edited with Goran Hyden and Okoth Ogendo, 2000), *Better Governance and Public Policy: Capacity Building for African Democratic Renewal* (with S. Sako, Kumarian Press, 2002); and *Local Governance in Africa* (with J.Wunsch, Lynne Rienner, 2003).

Lise Rakner (1963) is a Senior Researcher at the Chr. Michelsen Institute in Bergen, Norway. She holds a Ph.D. in political science. Her work has focused on issues of democratization and human rights, economic reform, taxation, institutional change, and international aid. Currently, Rakner is involved in research collaboration with the Danish Centre for Development Research on Taxation,

Aid and Democracy in Uganda, Namibia, and Tanzania. She also collaborates with the Department of Comparative Politics, University of Bergen, in research on political institutions in Africa.

Jesse C. Ribot is a Senior Associate at the World Resources Institute, where he directs the Africa Decentralization and Environment Initiative. Ribot was a research associate at the Harvard Center for Population and Development, a fellow at the Yale Program in Agrarian Studies, and a lecturer in Urban Studies and Planning at MIT. His research is on environmental justice, social vulnerability, and the effects of resource markets on local livelihoods. His most recent publications include: *Democratic Decentralization of Natural Resources: Institutionalizing Popular Participation* Washington, D.C.: World Resources Institute; and "A Theory of Access: Putting Property and Tenure in Place." In *Rural Sociology*. Forthcoming, 2003 (with Nancy Lee Peluso).

Vijaya Ramachandran is a senior economist at the World Bank, working on issues related to firm growth, entrepreneurship, and foreign investment. She has written articles on foreign direct investment in Asia and Africa, manufacturing and export growth in India, and is now working the dynamics of the private sector in Africa.

Martin Rupiya, Lt. Col (Retd), is Executive Director Centre for Defence Studies and Senior Lecturer in War & Strategic Studies, University of Zimbabwe, and currently Visiting Senior Fellow at the Centre for Africa's International Relations, University of the Witwatersrand, Johannesburg, SA. His recent publications include "A Political & Military Review of Zimbabwe's Involvement in the Second Congo War" in John F. Clark, ed. *The African Stakes of the Congo War* (Palgrave Macmillan, 2002) and "A Comparative Study of Democratic Civilian Control and the Reform of the Security Sector since 1991 in Tanzania and Zimbabwe?" African Security Dialogue & Research Centre, Accra, Ghana.

Aili Mari Tripp is Associate Professor of Political Science & Women's Studies and Director of the Women's Studies Research Center at the University of Wisconsin-Madison. She is the author of the award winning *Women and Politics in Uganda* (2000), *Changing the Rules: The Politics of Liberalization and the Urban Informal Economy in Tanzania* (1997) and co-edited *What Went Right in Tanzania? People's Responses to Directed Development* (1996) as well as *The Women's Movement in Uganda: History, Challenges and Prospects* (2002). She has also published articles and book chapters on women and politics in Africa; women's responses to economic reform; and the political impact of transformations of associational life in Africa.

Nicolas van de Walle is Professor of Political Science at Michigan State University, and a Non-Resident Fellow of the Center for Global Development. He has published widely on issues of political economy and democratization in Sub Saharan Africa. His most recent book is *African Economies and the Politics of Permanent Crisis, 1979–1999* (Cambridge, 2001). He received his Ph.D. from Princeton University in 1990.

Dr. Rocky Williams is a former Commander in Umkhonto We Sizwe (the guerilla Army of the African National Congress which has, since 1994, been integrated with seven other South African armed formations to form the South African National Defence Force). He played a key role in the restructuring of the South African military, Director of Operations in the South African Ministry of Defense. Since then, he has advised a number of African governments on security issues. Dr. Williams has lectured widely at South African, Southern African, African and international military institutions on civil-military relations, defence policy, and demobilization issues. He holds a Ph.D. in Civil-Military Relations, which he obtained from the University of Essex in England in 1992.

Index